Displacement and the Somatics of Postcolonial Culture

DISPLACEMENT

AND THE
SOMATICS OF
POSTCOLONIAL CULTURE

DOUGLAS ROBINSON

 THE OHIO STATE UNIVERSITY PRESS | COLUMBUS

Library of Congress Cataloging-in-Publication Data
Robinson, Douglas, 1954–
   Displacement and the somatics of postcolonial culture / Douglas Robinson.
      p. cm.
   Includes bibliographical references and index.
   ISBN 978-0-8142-1239-4 (cloth : alk. paper) — ISBN 978-0-8142-9341-6 (cd)
   1. Postcolonialism in literature. 2. Displacement (Psychology) in literature. 3. Identity
(Psychology) in literature. 4. Identity (Philosophical concept) in literature. 5. Refugees in
literature. I. Title.
   PN56.P555R63 2013
   809'.93353—dc23
                              2013019158

Cover design by AuthorSupport.com
Text design by Juliet Williams
Type set in Adobe Minion Pro
Printed by Thomson-Shore, Inc.

9   8   7   6   5   4   3   2   1

CONTENTS

In this salutary sense, a range of contemporary critical theories suggest that it is from those who have suffered the sentence of history—subjugation, domination, diaspora, displacement—that we learn our most enduring lessons for living and thinking. There is even a growing conviction that the *affective* experience of social marginality—as it emerges in non-canonical cultural forms—transforms our cultural strategies.

—Homi K. Bhabha, "The Postcolonial and the Postmodern"
(172, emphasis added)

What is the economy of sentiment surrounding the nation form? [. . .] What do we know about propaganda? We know nothing . . . when it works we don't know why it works. So what are the practices which produce affect for the nation? [. . .] What are the practices through which this set of feelings about this entirely abstract form are produced, and more importantly, reproduced?

—Arjun Appadurai, in conversation with Vikki Bell and Paul Gilroy in
1997 (Bell, *Historical Memory* 37–38)

IN HIS 1993 book *Moving the Centre,* Ngũgĩ wa Thiong'o describes racism as "a conscious ideology of imperialism" (117) that "often wages its offensive in print between hardcovers, magazines and newspapers long before it is imprinted on the general consciousness as the basis of personal and institutional practices" (126). I want to bracket the question raised by that claim of whether there has *ever* been a time before racism was imprinted on the general consciousness,[1] and go straight to the question that will help me clear the ground for a somatic approach to postcolonial identity, namely: who exactly *is* conscious in a conscious ideology, and of what, and just how conscious is s/ he? Is a conscious ideology one that its holder affirms consciously, so that the definitive criterion for a conscious racist ideology, for example, would be that its holder would be willing or able to say "I am a racist"? Or, taking one step back from that extreme reading, would it be enough for the holder of a con- scious racist ideology to be able to say "I hate black people," or "I feel uneasy around black people," without consciously labeling those feelings as racist? The problem with this approach to racism, obviously, is that then a person who has so successfully repressed his or her racism as to be able to say "I am not a racist" and believe it sincerely may still feel subliminally *inclined* to racist actions, to let a general racist "consciousness" serve as "the basis of personal and institutional practices," so that we would still want to call him or her a racist. But if racism serves as such a basis *unconsciously,* as it often seems to, in what sense is it a racist *consciousness* that so serves?

Or does Ngũgĩ mean that *imperialists* are the conscious ones, that impe- rialists consciously wage a racist offensive in print in order to imprint rac- ism on a not-quite-conscious ideology or "general consciousness," so that that ideology will in turn become "the basis of personal and institutional prac- tices"? In other words, does he mean that imperialists consciously (and per- haps repeatedly) *reinvent* racism as part of their strategy of oppression, which the masses then internalize in less conscious ways? This would constitute a kind of conspiracy theory of the origins—or at least the widespread dissemi- nation—of racism. Ngũgĩ seems to be modeling that dissemination as a three- stage process: first, racism is consciously developed by imperialists as a useful idea (ideology as thought structure); second, it is inculcated textually, through books, magazines, and newspapers, in a mass "consciousness" that may or may not involve actual conscious awareness (ideology as belief structure); and third, that consciousness becomes the basis of social practices that support the imperialist project (ideology as behavioral structure). Just before that earlier passage, in fact, from "The Ideology of Racism," he describes "the weapon of mental and spiritual subjugation" as "the ideological weapon" which "comes wrapped up in many forms: as religion, the arts, the media, culture, values, beliefs, even as feelings" (117), suggesting that someone, some group, namely imperialists, is *wielding* that ideological weapon, presumably as part of the second stage; in the latter passage, from "Racism in Literature," he defines ideology as "the whole system of symbols, images, beliefs, feelings, thoughts, and attitudes by which we explain the world and our place in it" (126), which sounds more like the third stage.

A good deal rides, in fact, on the ontopsychological status we assign racism and other ideological orientations and identities. If we treat them as biology, as "human nature," or even as "mammalian nature," as "hard-wired" into the autonomic nervous system, so that "we are all racists" becomes a universalizing/biologizing truth-claim, then we are stuck with them, or else stuck trying to discover the "racist gene" or to invent an "antiracism vaccine." If we want to resist this notion of racism as indelible in us, as a form of primitive mammalian xenophobia that can only be tempered and controlled, never eradicated, it is going to be important for us to historicize it, to show that it came from somewhere, that it was *introduced* into human dispositions. And it does seem to me that Ngũgĩ has something like this binary in mind, something like this absolute choice between a radically unattractive universalizing mystification of racism and a far more attractive historicist unmasking of racism—more attractive specifically because if something can be historicized, it can be resisted.

But then how *are* orientations and inclinations introduced into human dispositions? I think Ngũgĩ is quite right to insist, for example, that racism works by "sapping the moral energies of the victims by moulding and remoulding their personalities and their perceptions to make them view the world in accordance with the needs and programmes of the exploiter and the oppressor" (126), but think it unlikely that this sort of project could ever function on a conscious level, as *thought*. Surely in order to get black Africans to accede to colonial or neocolonial oppression and exploitation, imperialists have had to sap their moral energies and mold and remold their personalities and perceptions *unconsciously,* below the radar of conscious awareness. Consciousness of what is being done to us is our first essential step in a program of resistance, and thus something to be assiduously *avoided* by those intent upon sapping black Africans' moral energies. And in fact this notion of racism as a conscious ideology strains credulity even if we opt for the conspiracy-theory reading of Ngũgĩ's model and imagine imperialists as the original and sole conscious wielders of racist ideology—imagine them sitting around a table agreeing, "let's convince everybody that white skin signifies intelligence and culture and black skin signifies subhumanity, so that it seems *natural* for their work to fill our pockets, but let's make sure that we're the only ones wielding this ideology consciously, that everybody else, black and white alike, takes it for 'universal human nature.'" Surely imperialists too are always already racist, and mostly unconsciously so—indeed mostly to be distinguished from the victims of their exploitation not in the degree to which their racism is conscious but rather in the degree to which they are sociopolitically positioned and economically and emotionally prepared to profit from it?

In fact, how conscious are people typically? How conscious is "the general consciousness"? How many of our personal and institutional practices are shaped by consciously held views, values, norms, beliefs, opinions? If ideology or "the general consciousness" includes "symbols, images, beliefs, feelings, thoughts, and attitudes," how conscious is our possession or use of those things? How conscious are we typically of our beliefs or attitudes? How conscious are we of our feelings? When a symbol or an image works on us, from within or without, to what extent are even intellectuals conscious of that working? We can, by a great intellectual effort, *make* any of those things conscious; but it seems relatively uncontroversial to assert that normally they function in us beneath the level of conscious awareness.

And yet it is equally problematic to insist that ideologies wield us as their mechanical toys—that we are automata unconsciously motivated and directed by our ideological orientations. Death-of-the-subject deconstructions of human agency as just another fictitious construct of liberal bourgeois ideology are as passivizing and mystifying as universalistic biologisms: both make resistance unthinkable. Whether we are made mindlessly and will-lessly racist by God, biology, or some vaguely mentalist ideology, we are equally trapped— and in fact "ideology" then becomes just another mystified term for "God," or "biology," or "destiny," or what have you. In order to imagine the possibility of resistance, we have to imagine a subject with agency—a fictitious subject with limited agency, perhaps, a socially constructed virtual "self" that has pragmatic rather than ontological value, but a subject nonetheless, with the ability to plan and take action—and we have to explain how this subject is able to function in the complex middle ground between absolute automatism and absolute autonomy.

P.1 SOMATICS

The "somatics" in my title signals my attempt in the book to chart out that middle ground. I will be covering the rudiments of somatic theory in §1.1, and complicating the model throughout the book; but let me anticipate briefly here. The fundamental assumption in somatic theory is that normative orientations or inclinations are circulated through a population as *social feelings,* especially approval and disapproval, and that this collective circulation of feelings is the channel through which any group regulates itself—something I call "ideosomatic regulation," the term "ideosomatic" indicating my belief that the regulatory "ideas" that circulate are grounded less in *words* or *thoughts* (ideologos: idea as stable word/mind), and more in *feelings* or *somatic responses* (ideo-soma: idea as emotional body). (Actually, somatic response is body-becoming-mind—a homeostatic middle excluded by Cartesian mind-body dualism. See the Glossary for somatic terminology.) These somatic responses signal to us whether the group(s) to which we belong would approve or disapprove of the action we're contemplating—and while they can be brought to conscious awareness, we are not usually aware of their operation. We typically call them "hunches" or "gut feelings," rather inchoately distinguishing them on the one hand from whims (*unorganized* inclinations) and on the other from reasons (*analytical* inclinations).

A preliminary formulation, then: insofar as ideology is conscious thoughts, ideas, images, and beliefs, it is carried on the backs of ideosomatic impulses channeling collective approval or disapproval. The only way to sap a dark-skinned population's moral energies and to mold and remold their personalities and perceptions, for example, is to circulate to and through the larger group containing that population (light- and dark-skinned alike) racist ideosomatic impulses channeling images and ideas of the dark-skinned group charged with collective disapproval: contented collaborationist natives as domestic pets, say, angry rebellious natives as vicious wild animals. I borrow these images from Ngũgĩ's reading of Karen Blixen's *Out of Africa*: "What she is really saying," he notes there, "is that her knowledge of wild animals gave her a clue to the African mind," and "So to Karen Blixen, Kamante [her cook] is comparable to a civilized dog that has lived long with human beings, Europeans of course" (*Moving* 133). What makes Ngũgĩ's demystification of Blixen's racism so powerful, of course, is that his words are fueled by *feeling*, by carefully harnessed fury—the same kind of fury directed at and against rebellious African blacks like him by white imperialists and colonialists and their black collaborators, a regulatory fury that puts normative somatic pressure on the reader not just to accept the writer's valuation but to conform his or her whole emotional orientation to the writer's guidance. A writer or a speaker who channels powerful enough ideosomatic approval and disapproval (group regulatory guidance) into his or her words can indeed bring about large-scale personality and behavioral changes in readers or listeners—can make them (more) racist, in the colonial context, or in a decolonizing context less racist, or at least more guilty about their racism.

Implicit in this somatic approach is the assumption that the images Ngũgĩ identifies in Blixen's memoirs are not intrinsically negative, in the abstract, in the null context; an image of a human being as a domestic pet or a wild animal will have a negative effect only if it is charged ideosomatically with negativity, through the bodily force of collective disapproval (or if it is constructed as so charged by its audience, which, as we'll see, comes to the same thing). It's not just the context in which the image is offered to the reader or listener that limits its meaning, in other words; rather, the words carrying the image are themselves charged with feeling, saturated (to use Bakhtin's formulation) with ideosomatic tonalizations and attitudinalizations, and transfer those emotional orientations to the reader or the listener. Just as it is possible to inflect "you're my pussy cat" or "he's my loyal dog" or "what a jackal he is" with approval or disapproval, with loving admiration or contemptuous disgust, so too is it possible for Ngũgĩ to resomatize Blixen's loving admiration for the Kĩkũyũ, Kawirondo, and Wakambo who worked for her as patronizing racism—to "revoice" her racism, as Bakhtin would say, to reinflect it with his own disapproving tonalization, and to infect us as well with the resulting resomatization.

Bakhtin would also insist that these images have iterative histories behind them, iterosomatic histories by which countless somatizations of the images in actual discourse have charged them with a "positive" or "negative" tonalization that feels so stable as (almost) to constitute an objective semantics. "Pussy cat" and "loyal dog" have both been iterosomatized as predominantly "positive," though with an undercurrent of loving condescension; "jackal" is predominantly negative. It is possible to resomatize "pussy cat" or "loyal dog" negatively and "jackal" positively, but in doing so we can feel ourselves estranging a familiar somatic current. It is also possible to displace (abstract) the iterative history of this ideosomatic regulation out of these images and reify the cat and dog images as objectively or intrinsically (semantically) positive, the jackal image as semantically negative; but this dehistoricization/desomatization vitiates the abstraction and mystifies the process by which images and words come to mean anything at all.

Somatic theory attributes to the ideosomatics of racism (or of any other group orientation) the power to mold and remold personality because it takes individuality to be in large part a collective construct anyway, the product of ideosomatic regulation—what Nietzsche calls the internalization of mastery, or what Foucault calls discipline. We are, by and large, what the group says we are. And what the group "says," mostly, according to somatic theory, it says with its (dis)approving body language, but also with punitive physical pain (Nietzsche) and various physical and socioideological regimens (Foucault). To the extent that any one individual's experience of the world slips out of the group's control (and there is always some slippage, because ideosomatic regulation is a kluge), that individual may become the targets of intensified group regulation, which may generate shame and a redoubled effort to conform; but this stepped-up pressure may also generate rebellious impulses, which may ultimately impel the individual out of one group and into another. Thus

Ngũgĩ, for example, was impelled out of the group of elite collaborationist Anglophile Africans at the Alliance High School to which he had won a scholarship, and into the ideological camp of Marxism, African nationalism, and the Mau Mau struggle against British rule, a move marked by his name change from James Ngũgĩ to Ngũgĩ wa Thiong'o, and later also by his controversial decision to write only in Gikũyũ, no longer in English.

In somatic theory, any impulse that is perceived as nonconformist by the group is "idiosomatic," any specifically rebellious impulse "counterideosomatic": counterideosomaticity is a subset of idiosomaticity, which includes both *failures* and *refusals* to conform. But ideosomatic regulation can and often does break down as well, as social groups are thwarted in their ongoing attempts to regulate themselves homeostatically. The three essays in this book chart three different disruptions of ideosomatic regulation, and thus of the individual identities shaped and maintained by the group:

- (First Essay) *ideosomatic dysregulation:* the breakdown of ideosomatic regulation in the refugee experience, which destroys or scatters or contaminates the group;
- (Second Essay) *ideosomatic counterregulation:* the introduction into a group of a new and more powerful "corrective" ideosomatic regulation in the colonial experience, and again, at least in idealized theory, in decolonization; and
- (Third Essay) *paleosomatic regulation:* the survival of an old ideosomatic regulation into a new social context, in intergenerational trauma.

P.2 HOMEOSTASIS/ALLOSTASIS

Somatic theory begins in the homeostatic regulation of the individual organism: an entire iterosomatic history of sociobiological evolution provides for the emergence of regulatory emotions as homeostatic mappings of appetites and other body states, of regulatory feelings as mental representations or mappings of emotions, appetites, and other body states, and of rational thoughts as mental representations of feelings, emotions, appetites, and other thoughts. This is the body-becoming-mind. An appetite like hunger is itself a homeostatic body map of specific shifting biological states in the stomach (muscle contraction), endocrine activity (lowered blood glucose, raised insulin levels), fatty acid metabolism (raised fatty acid levels), and heat management (lowered body temperature)—all, of course, designed to prompt the organism to eat and maintain homeostasis (stability) around a set-point conducive to the organism's survival. But the emergence of an appetitive state does not lead mechanically to the satisfaction of the appetite; higher self-regulatory levels are activated as well, so that physiological hunger signals may be accompanied by emotions, which are felt, experienced as feelings, which in turn are thought (experienced as mental images and ideas). Based on the use of feelings to regulate emotional states, we may begin to feel eager as we move toward dinner, or annoyed if dinner is delayed; based on the emergence of thought to regulate feelings, we may institute a daily regimen, breakfast at 7 A.M., lunch at noon, dinner at 5 P.M. Not only that: the higher levels can trigger the lower levels, as when a feeling of sadness or loneliness triggers a hunger for comfort food, or a steaming-hot commercial image of dinner makes us realize that it's long past dinnertime and we're famished.

The study of homeostatic self-regulation in the individual organism begins to shift over into social theory when, say, repeated patterns of undersatisfied hunger in a family or a community trigger collective feelings of depression, resentment, or rage: in the colonial context you see the colonizer, fat and gouty with overeating, and build a mental comparison with your own family's and community's hungry bellies. What happens next is part of ideosomatic group self-regulation: you suppress your anger (convert it back into depression), because you want to be a good citizen, because you know that no good can come of rising up against superior power (i.e., the reigning colonial ideosomatic regulation is still functioning more or less smoothly in your group and inside each of its members); or you begin to build a new ideosomatic counter-regulation, work together in the group of the oppressed to retheorize hunger as a goad to political and even military action.

This would be group homeostatic self-regulation; but note that, to the extent that it arises in response to perceived social change, to a significant alteration in external conditions, it is technically group *allostatic* self-regulation. In the example from the previous paragraph, the overlord's overeating is itself an allostatic adaptation to wealth: it raises the homeostatic set-point around which his body regulates his food intake, so that it comes to feel physiologically necessary for him to continue (over)eating at that raised level. Your undereating is an allostatic adaptation to poverty: it has been lowering the homeostatic set-point for you and your family and community, so that if food suddenly became abundant, it might even be difficult to eat enough of it at first. This makes allostasis a far more pressing concept in the sociopolitical study of postcolonial and other at-risk identities than the more "normal" homeostasis, which reflects ideosomatic self-regulation in contexts of relative social stability.

Bruce S. McEwen, one of the leading medical theorists of allostasis, has coined the term "allostatic load" to describe "the long-term effect of the physiologic response to stress": "Allostasis—the ability to achieve stability through change—is critical to survival. Through allostasis, the autonomic nervous system, the hypothalamic-pituitary-adrenal (HPA) axis, and the cardiovascular, metabolic, and immune systems protect the body by responding to internal and external stress. The price of this accommodation to stress can be allostatic load, which is the wear and tear that results from chronic overactivity or underactivity of allostatic systems" (171). In conditions of acute stress, the organism adapts briefly and reversibly, turning an allostatic response first on and then off: in activation, the nerves and the adrenal medulla release catecholamines and the pituitary gland releases corticotropin, which prompts the adrenal cortex to release cortisol; in inactivation, cortisol and catecholamine secretion returns to baseline levels. In chronic stress, however, such as we typically find in the postcolonial contexts that we'll be looking at here—long-term physical and cultural displacement—the entire organism adjusts homeostatically to a higher level of readiness, raising base-line set-points, which alone creates considerable allostatic load. That load is often further compounded by inefficient system response: after months or years or even generations of coping with chronic stress, the stress hormones may (a) never activate fully, leaving the organism overexposed to stress, or (b) never deactivate fully, leaving the organism overexposed to stress hormones, or (c) activate and deactivate repeatedly, abruptly, disjointedly, disrupting the homeostatic stabilizations that are essential for smooth functioning. When an entire population is subjected to this sort of allostatic overload, the ideosomatic regulation that maintains social order (stable identities, a shared reality) almost always breaks down, and various socioemotional and sociopolitical pathologies result.

But not invariably. The disruption of ideosomatic regulation is also an opportunity, one that is occasionally accompanied by stunning explosions of artistic and philosophical creativity—as it was in the first years of the Soviet Union, during and immediately after the lengthy, brutal, and socially disruptive Civil War, before the Stalinist Thermidor began to shut it down in the mid-1920s. Postcolonial theorists often theorize postcoloniality in terms of this utopian response to ideosomatic dysregulation and counterregulation—Deleuze and Guattari's nomad thought and deterritorialization, for example, or Homi Bhabha's hybrid cultures—and have been criticized for this sexy utopianism by other scholars more solidly grounded in the often disastrous economics, politics, and social psychology of postcoloniality; but I will be arguing in the book that we need utopian theories of postcolonial identities precisely so that we don't simply succumb to the disastrous somatics of despair, don't simply thematize postcolonial populations as inevitably the passive victims of war, genocide, domination, and exploitation. I will also be arguing that the abstract binarisms of Saussurean thought that inform much poststructuralist theory (signifier–signified, speech–writing, synchronic–diachronic) have led many postcolonial theorists into discursive traps from which it becomes impossible to imagine a lived phenomenology of postcolonial identity. In the First Essay (§1.3.1) we will see Deleuze and Guattari theorizing the social machine as a protosomatic body-without-organs in order to steer clear of pure Saussurean discursivity; in the Second Essay (§2.2) I will also be pushing hard on the work of Homi Bhabha and Gayatri Spivak to bring out their own somatic thinking on postcolonial intersubjective affect.

One postcolonial theory that has attracted no utopian or other poststructuralist spins is intergenerational trauma, the theory that traumatized populations pass some form of allostatic overload on to their descendants—that allostatic overload is sustained not only through a single lifetime but at least from one generation to the next, and, some argue, through the collective lifetime of an entire culture, even for hundreds of years. This theory was first adumbrated by Friedrich Nietzsche in *A Genealogy of Morals,* where traumatic slave *experiences* survive for centuries as an allostatic/paleosomatic slave *morality,* and was picked and developed explicitly by Sigmund Freud, in *Totem and Taboo* and *Moses and Monotheism,* where his theorization of the history of religion entailed the intergenerational repression of an originary guilt, the guilt felt by the primal brothers at the murder of their father. The theory resurfaced in the 1970s, under the term "transgenerational transmission of trauma," and has been gaining momentum under the term intergenerational trauma in the 1980s, 1990s, and the new millennium, first in the context of the symptomatologies experienced by the second- and third-generation descendants of Holocaust survivors, later in broader contexts as well, especially perhaps the American Holocaust, the genocide, resettlement, and reeducation of Native Americans and its effects on later generations, whose disproportionate rates of PTSD, cardiovascular disease, diabetes, obesity, alcoholism, and early death suggest some sort of lingering, buried response to trauma. What plagues most intergenerational trauma research to date, I will be suggesting, is the lack of an adequate explanation of *storage,* of how and where the allostatic overload is stored during whole lifetimes and across generational gaps; Ruth Leys, for example, suggests that it is stored as *memories,* "veridical memories or representations of the traumatic event," as "literal replicas or repetitions of the trauma . . . that as such . . . stand outside representation" (229). It is important for her to represent those memories as "outside representation" because, as many intergenerational trauma scholars have noted, one of the most telling features of traumatic memories is their *absence* (see Fine)—suggesting that trauma is transmitted from generation to generation submentally, in some lower stratum of allostatic self-regulation. My theory of paleosomatic regulation is an attempt to solve this conundrum.

P.3 DISPLACEMENT

Displacement is a term used in many scholarly fields to indicate some sort of key shift in space or time: in the physical sciences, the displacement of air in an engine, of water by a ship's hull, of the earth's crust in various theories of global rebalancing; in the social sciences, time spent on the computer displaces face-to-face sociability and time spent watching television displaces reading. Criminal displacement theory argues that attempts to prevent crime by enhancing security measures actually only moves crime around, to a different place (geographical displacement), time (temporal displacement), target (target displacement), or type or method of crime (crime type or tactical displacement) (Felson and Clarke 25).

Sigmund Freud first theorized displacement (*Verschiebung*) as part of the dream-work, the displacement of elements in the dream-thought by entirely other elements in the dream-content, so that the dream becomes "differently centred from the dream-thoughts" (*Interpretation* 340). The displacement principle at work in that theory, that we unconsciously channel affect from feared to safe objects, has come to inform our understanding of numerous other key psychological phenomena as well, including transference and countertransference (the displacement of affect from a parent onto the analyst or the analysand), scapegoating (the displacement of affect from powerful or inaccessible objects to powerless objects, such as members of minority groups), and sublimation (the displacement of libido into socially useful outlets like art and work).

In structuralist and poststructuralist language theory, displacement began as a topical movement or shift of meanings and then in the mid-1950s was picked up by Jacques Lacan, drawing both on Freudian displacement and on Roman Jakobson's theorization of metonymy, as the structural principle behind the Peircean "signifying chain" (*Écrits* 170), in which meaning is endlessly displaced along the syntagmatic chain of signifiers, and ultimately is to be found (or "insists") only in that endless displacement ("the meaning 'insists' but . . . none of its elements 'consists' in the signification of which it is at the moment capable" [170]). By the early 1980s, something like this Lacanian concept had arguably become the organizing idea or strategy in post-structuralist thought: as Robert Young wrote in his introduction to his 1981 "post-structuralist reader" *Untying the Text*, "The name 'post-structuralism' is useful in so far as it is an umbrella word, significantly defining itself only in terms of a temporal, spatial relationship to structuralism. This need not imply the organicist fiction of a development, for it involves, rather, a displacement. It is more a question of an interrogation of structuralism's concepts by turning one against another" (1). Two years later, in 1983, Mark Krupnik collected a group of disparate essays under the title *Displacement: Derrida and After*, noting in his introduction that "if displacement is always with us in post-structuralist theory, it has no official status within it. It is no sacred word, unlike 'tension' and 'paradox' in the New Criticism, or 'intertextuality' and 'repetition' nowadays" (4). Gayatri Spivak's article in that collection, "Displacement and the Discourse of Woman," is pure feminist critique of phallogocentrism—there is not a trace of subaltern studies in it yet (1983 was the year she delivered the lecture that eventually became "Can the Subaltern Speak?"—an argument I analyze at the end of the Second Essay [§2.2.2.3]). She reads Freud on displacement against the grain, identifying his use of the term *Entstellung* ("distortion") as a surreptitious morphological translation of displacement (*ent* "away, aside" + *stellen* "to set or place") in order to focus attention on his displacement not of dream-thoughts but of the female subject, "the moment when woman is displaced out of this primordial masculinity" (172).

Displacement entered the sociopolitical discourse that feeds postcolonial studies in the sense of the forced geographical removal of individuals from their home or home regions; the people thus removed become displaced persons, also known as forced migrants or refugees. This is the subject of the First Essay. The term was later extended metaphorically to cultural displacements without geographical removal, as when a foreign power invades, occupies, and colonizes one's country and imposes a new ideosomatic regulation on one's group, "displacing" the old cultural regime through education and other forms of social and institutional discipline—the subject of the Second Essay. In the Third Essay I will be expanding the term slightly to include the temporal displacement of a traumatic group allostasis past the era of its contextual relevance.

I will, in other words, be discussing displacement almost exclusively in its sociopolitical extension, as a sociopolitical phenomenon that disrupts people's lives and identities. It would, however, be irresponsible for me to ignore the limitations and complications that a poststructuralist perspective would discover in the Freudian "displacements" in my project—the accusation, for instance, that as a white middle-class American male English professor who has never been a refugee and has never been colonized I am arguably studying a displaced object, a "safe" (because distant, because politically correct, because not-me) object that disguises my own political complicity in the sociopolitical damage I study. I am thinking in particular of accusations like these that Terry Eagleton vents in his 1999 review of Spivak's book *A Critique of Postcolonial Reason:*

> This book takes a few well-deserved smacks at the wilder breed of post-colonialist critics, whose fascination for the Other is in part a demoralised yearning to be absolutely anyone but themselves. ("Gaudy Supermarket" 5)

> But there are discreditable as well as creditable reasons for the speedy surfacing of post-colonialism, and Spivak remains for the most part silent about them. Its birth, for example, followed in the wake of the defeat, at least for the present, of both class-struggle in Western societies and revolutionary nationalism in the previously colonialised world. American students who, through no fault of their own, would not recognise class-struggle if it perched on the tip of their skateboards, or who might not be so keen on the Third World if some of its inhabitants were killing their fathers and brothers in large numbers, can vicariously fulfil their generously radical impulses by displacing oppression elsewhere. This move leaves them plunged into fashionably Post-Modern gloom about the 'monolithic' benightedness of their own social orders. It is as if the depleted, disorientated subject of the consumerist West comes by an extraordinary historical irony to find an image of itself in the wretched of the earth. (5–6)

> Deconstruction can indeed be a politically destabilising manoeuvre, but devotees like Gayatri Spivak ought to acknowledge its displacing effect, too. Like much cultural theory, it can allow one to speak darkly of subversion while leaving one's actual politics only slightly to the left of Edward Kennedy's. (6)

"Demoralised yearning to be absolutely anyone but themselves," "vicariously fulfil their generously radical impulses by displacing oppression elsewhere," "can allow one to speak darkly of subversion while leaving one's actual politics only slightly to the left of Edward Kennedy's": these are displacements in Freud's original sense of the term, liberal American students and postcolonial critics displacing their own uncomfortable complicity in their (our) country's imperialist domination and exploitation of the rest of the world onto safely foreign topics. Eagleton might have added that we white American non-Marxists also in the process distort (in Freud's displaced sense of *Entstellung,* as theorized by Spivak a decade and a half before her *Critique*) the safe foreign topics we study—but then according to him the same is true of Spivak herself, who, though a Third World feminist Marxist, for Eagleton is not nearly Marxist enough.

I not only plead *nolo contendere* to Eagleton's charges but intend to compound them by admitting that I here displace oppression still further: not just from America to the Third World, and not just from the plight of the Third World to theory, but from postcolonial theory to somatic theory. In fact, I went around and around on whether to use "postcolonial" at all in my title; I considered "postnational culture," "postcollective culture," even "postculture," and only finally settled on "postcolonial culture" because it suggested not just the transformation of traditional sedentary cultures but also their disruption in and by and through hierarchizing regimes of sociopolitical power. Still, in that light I'm not sure that the refugee experience necessarily counts as postcolonial—masses of people are displaced (First Essay) not only by colonial wars and campaigns of ethnic cleansing but also by floods, earthquakes, hurricanes, and other such decidedly nonpostcolonial phenomena—and the allostatic overloads that are passed down to later generations (Third Essay) can be caused by any number of traumatic events, not all of them tied to coloniality.

Still, despite my misgivings, I do think somatic theory has an important contribution to make to postcolonial studies. One of the biggest debates in the field almost from its beginnings in the late 1970s has been between those who understand postcoloniality politically, in terms of actions undertaken in the public domain, and those who understand it discursively, in terms of the fractalized thought-structures of French poststructuralist theory. Everything the "traditionalists" hold most dear—in Bart Moore-Gilbert's list, "the centred subject, the aesthetic sphere, foundational identities, the nation and nationalism, 'master'-narratives of liberation and emancipation, and authorial intention" (21)—seems to the poststructuralists hopelessly mired in an epistemologically discredited essentialist agenda that is complicit with colonialist thought; for the traditionalists, poststructuralist postcolonial theory is propagated by deracinated Third World intellectuals ensconced in prestigious U.S. universities and out of touch with the cultures they theorize, and consists of highly abstract but faux-politicized versions of First World linguistic philosophies that are complicit with global-capitalist/neocolonialist thought.[2]

I suggest that these two approaches to the study of postcolonial realities and identities are so radically and even ferociously polarized (see, for example,

Ahmad's *In Theory*) because they lack a theoretical framework for the analysis of the *interactions* between thought and action—between the private and public spheres, between psychoanalysis and sociology, between linguistic philosophy and politics. The poststructuralists—notably Edward Said, Gayatri Chakravorty Spivak, and Homi K. Bhabha—have worked very hard to politicize the differential strategies of poststructuralist thought, following Foucault in arguing that "the relations of discourse are of the nature of warfare" (Bhabha's paraphrase, *Location* 145); but it is almost invariably difficult, reading Bhabha and Spivak and their many followers, to see how a politicized deconstruction of the discursive traces of postcolonial identities might meet the traditionalists halfway, or even one-tenth of the way, because they don't know, and don't seem at all inclined to wonder, how discursive structures are converted into the group orientations that condition action. Bhabha and Spivak are brilliant at recuperating verbal texts (literary, theological, administrative, and anthropological) for poststructuralist theory, but they have no theoretical shuttle that would ferry the "relations of discourse" they discover there back into the felt or lived phenomenologies of (post)colonial warfare and other realities and identities; and the "traditionalists" don't seem to be particularly interested in building that kind of bridge or shuttle either. Terry Eagleton, for that matter, for all his ranting and posturing about liberal radicalism and fake Marxism—the review of Spivak's book is notoriously vicious—doesn't have a clue himself about the conversion of proletarian ideology into revolutionary action or proletarian action into revolutionary ideology. It just sort of happens, as if by magic. Ideology is mental and action is physical, and somehow the one keeps making the quantum leap into the other, through a black-box theoretical vacuum.

Somatic theory does model a shuttle of the necessary sort. It opens the black box through which discursive "inscriptions" are marked somatically for behavior and people, places, actions, and things are mapped physically-becoming-mentally into knowing and saying and believing. It explains how evaluative affect is not only circulated collectively through thoughts, words, actions, and orientations to places and things but stored as learned and more or less stable "structures" in the proprioceptive body of the group,[3] and how normative and counternormative pressures, impulses, and orientations do battle in that regulatory affective economy. Raymond Williams has theorized something like this somatic economy for a Marxism that Terry Eagleton has dismissed contemptuously as more liberalism, under the rubric "structures of feeling"[4]; and as we'll see in the Second Essay, both Bhabha and Spivak find themselves groping in this direction as well, Spivak even using Williams's phrase in her discussion of Kant's analytic of the sublime in the book Eagleton vilified, *A Critique of Postcolonial Reason* (14). But neither theorist quite knows what to do with postcolonial affect—certainly neither knows how to use it to build a theoretical bridge between thought and action—because, I'll be arguing, they lack somatic theory.

Ultimately I am interested here less in anything so vague and abstract as "postcoloniality" than in the disruption of ideosomatic regulation, something that I have in fact experienced first-hand, in spending half my adult life in foreign countries (especially perhaps the two years I've spent to date in post-Soviet Russia and the two years I've most recently spent in the Hong Kong New Territories). While the sociopolitical default setting of somatic theory is successful ideosomatic regulation, my interest in this book is in the failure of that regulation, in the theory's problematic borderlands, which I suspect will shed more light on ideosomaticity than would an exhaustive mapping of its ideal functionality.

This is in fact the transformative effect that postcolonial studies has on somatic theory: studying the dysregulatory effects of the refugee experience, the reregulatory effects of (de)colonization, and the paleoregulatory effects of intergenerational trauma forces the somatic theorist to explore and explain the *failure* of the ideosomatic model of regulation that lies at the core of somatic theory. My efforts to apply somatic theory to postcolonial culture have had the salutary effect of expanding the scope of somatic theory: I have here developed the concepts of paleosomaticity and endo- and exosomaticity, of loco-, meta-, poly-, and xenonormativity (and panicked loconormativity), and allostatic overload precisely in order to increase the conceptual capacity of somatic theory to account for the myriad "postcolonial" breakdowns of the "normal" homeostatic functioning that lies at the core of somatic theory. How do we explain the traumata that result from such breakdowns, and the survival of individual and group adaptations to trauma for generations and even centuries after the initial traumatizing event or series of events? How do we explain the movement not just of peoples but of their cultural normativizations, and the clashes that result from the normativizing pressures placed on individuals and groups by different cultures sharing a geography? How do we explain the apparent stability of "home," of familiar places and objects, even after they've been destroyed or lost forever?

P.4 THE STRUCTURE OF THE BOOK

I focus here on three broad areas of cultural identity-(de)formation that you may or may not agree are roughly postcolonial in genesis, one in each essay:

forced migration, (de)colonization, and intergenerational trauma. These can be thought of as vaguely sequential, beginning with the traumata that scatter citizens out into the world as refugees, moving through the attempts (first by the colonial power, and then by the politicians and intellectuals of the newly independent former colony) to manage and banish the traumata of the recent past, and ending with the survival of migratory and colonial traumata unto the second and third and nth generations—beginning with ideosomatic dysregulation (breakdown), moving through ideosomatic counterregulation (new organization), and ending with paleosomatic regulation (persistence of the old breakdown in the midst of the new organization).

Within each of these three essays, then, I do three things: I read the data-driven ("empirical") sociological and psychological studies of the phenomenon under consideration and suggest some ways in which somatic theory can organize and explain the data more powerfully; I apply the somatic theory developed in those early sections to a literary or cinematic representation or series of such representations of the phenomenon; and, finally, I apply somatic theory to a series of poststructuralist/postcolonialist theoretical spins on the phenomenon, pushing on the broken binary abstractions of structuralist linguistics that power poststructuralist theory in search of the vestiges of corporeal phenomenology that they don't quite manage to suppress.

The First Essay, "Displacement of Persons/Forced Migration/Ideosomatic Dysregulation," begins in §1.1.1 by outlining what I take to be the "primal scene" of refugee studies, the encounter between the "loconormative" therapist or researcher or aid worker and the "xenonormative" refugee, and complicates this scene in §1.1.2 by exploring the ways in which each side of this encounter dysregulates the other. §1.1.3 taxonomizes the refugee experience in terms of the dysregulatory effects of the event(s) in the home region that trigger(s) flight, of flight itself (including refugee camps), of early contact with the new host community, and of traumatic memories that continue to plague later interaction with the host community, supposedly after assimilation. §1.2 reads two texts by the Haitian-American author Edwidge Danticat: "Children of the Sea" as a study of dysregulation at home and in flight, and *Breath, Eyes, Memory* as a study of dysregulation in initial and continuing contact. The First Essay concludes in §1.3 with a discussion of the metaphorical uses to which migrants and refugees have been put in postcolonial theory, with examples from Deleuze and Guattari on "nomad thought," and from Iain Chambers on migrancy.

The Second Essay, "Displacement of Cultures/Colonization and (De)Colonization/Ideosomatic Counterregulation," begins in §2.1 with a reading of classic studies of the (de)colonizing process—C. L. R. James's *The Black Jaco-*

bins, Albert Memmi's *The Colonizer and the Colonized* and *Decolonization and the Decolonized,* and Frantz Fanon's *Black Skins, White Masks*—as a series of attempts to impose a new "corrective" ideosomatic counterregulation on an already existing one. §2.1.3.3 reads a cinematic representation of (de/re)colonization in the 2004 Spanish short film *Binta and the Great Idea.* The Second Essay concludes in §2.2 with a close reading of several essays by Bhabha and Spivak that tease out of their poststructuralist and Marxist theoretical strategies an emerging concern with postcolonial affect, including (in §2.2.2.4) Spivak's reading of Mahasweta Devi's novella "Douloti the Bountiful."

The Third Essay, "Displacement of Time/Intergenerational Trauma/Paleosomatic Regulation," reads the growing body of work on the phenomenon that is variously called the intergenerational, multigenerational, and transgenerational transmission of trauma. Following a quick prehistory of this theoretical orientation in Nietzsche's *Genealogy of Morals* and Freud's *Moses and Monotheism,* I summarize the empirical research in §3.1 and then devote the bulk of the essay (§3.2) to readings of three literary texts, James Welch's *The Death of Jim Loney* (1979), Toni Morrison's *Beloved* (1987), and Percival Everett's "The Appropriation of Cultures" (1996). Through these readings I also expand and develop the theoretical model broached in §3.1; and I conclude the essay and the book in §3.2.4 with a reading of Dominic LaCapra's application of the Freudian acting-out/working-through binary to trauma studies.

ACKNOWLEDGMENTS

I **BEGAN** writing this book while teaching a graduate seminar on its predecessor, *Estrangement and the Somatics of Literature* (Robinson 2008), specifically my concluding reading of Brecht's postcolonial play *Mann ist Mann,* and as they emerged I discussed my ideas for it with my students, Phillip Gordon and Katie Burnett. Phillip and Katie also read early drafts of the book and gave me many useful comments. Sandy Crooms at The Ohio State University Press was an early believer in the book and sensitively shepherded it through what proved to be a long and difficult acquisition process.

Displacement of Persons/ Forced Migration/ Ideosomatic Dysregulation

1.1 EMPIRICAL STUDIES

1.1.1 The Dysregulation and Reregulation of Refugee Reality and Identity

The German-born Norwegian psychotherapist Stefi Pedersen (1908–80), herself twice a refugee from Nazi Germany (she fled Berlin to Oslo in 1933 and took Norwegian citizenship, and then fled Nazi-occupied Norway to Sweden in 1943), writes in her 1949 article "Psychopathological Reactions to Extreme Social Displacements '(Refugee Neuroses)'" of World War II refugees displaced from various European countries to Sweden:

> Psychopathological reactions among refugees, which one has been able to observe especially during the recent world war, assume a middle-position between war-neuroses on the one hand and on the other the mental-hygienic difficulties met by emigrants of earlier times in the new countries to which they came. In common with the war-neuroses are the psychic traumata and the extreme physical exhaustion connection to the flight from the mother country; and the forced adjustment to unknown social relationships and the consequent necessity of finding places in new social

1

groups of varying patterns of behavior associate the refugees with the emigrants.

In those cases in which the experience of the flight is especially traumatic, it seems as though acute dissociations of consciousness, hallucinations, depersonalization, and amnesia assume a central position among the
psycho-pathological reactions. The sudden severance from the mother-
country, the flight and the pursuit, appear to arouse so much strong anxiety
that the sense of reality is temporarily set out of function, and thus there
occur false evaluations and lack of orientation in the new surroundings.
(344)

This is where I want to start: the disruptive effects that traumatic displacement is seen to have on refugees' social construction of both identity, through
depersonalization and other dissociations, and reality, through hallucinations and amnesia. Their identity, according to these therapeutic constructions, is inwardly split (dissociated) or socially isolated (depersonalized); the
group constructions of reality that seemed so real, so solid, and so stable in
the bosom of the old community are scrambled (hallucinations) or forgotten
(amnesia) in the painful transition to the new.

But by way of getting us started with this material, note Pedersen's specific
phrasings: "*the* sense of reality," she writes, "is temporarily set out of function." There is only one sense of reality; and it is a mental mechanism of some
sort that either functions properly or goes on the fritz. In the refugee, apparently, at least for a while, it malfunctions, with the result that "there occur
false evaluations and lack of orientation in the new surroundings." When "the
sense of reality" functions properly, there occur true evaluations; when it malfunctions, there occur false ones. These are problematic formulations, not just
because we now come to these issues after nearly a half-century of postmod-
ernist and poststructuralist problematizations of "reality" and "truth" and the
stable unity implied by "*the* sense of reality," but because Pedersen's simple
mechanical model of "the sense" of reality cannot explain how anxiety might
disrupt it. What power can anxiety have over the mechanical functioning of
"the sense of reality"? And why is its effect specifically to corrupt and falsify
evaluations of reality? Above all, how exactly is "lack of orientation in the new
surroundings" another effect of anxiety, and of the malfunctioning of "the
sense of reality" it occasions? Surely, at the very simplest level, it's the other
way around: the refugee's new surroundings are so radically and disturbingly
unfamiliar that the old stable group constructions of reality become inoper-
able, and the resulting disorientations cause the anxiety?

Let's read on:

These conditions obviously become more difficult when the refugee, immediately after he has come to a foreign country, is forced to find new social contacts, new work, a new place to live, and last but not least, new friends. For most of the refugees, this readjustment meant that they were forced to give up a great deal of the expectations and social ambitions they had had in their mother-country. They had to arrange their affairs under pressing conditions, they were relegated to a lower social position, they had to relinquish much of their influence in social groups (in their professions, at their places of work, in their families), they were looked upon with less respect, and they lost much of their individuality by becoming a number in the grey, anonymous mass of refugees.

I am, therefore, inclined to believe that the situation in which refugees find themselves is severely injurious to their self-assurance and can easily provoke—together with the original traumatic experience—the disturbances of consciousness of personality which the Danish psychiatrist Strömgren (5) considers to be the basis for the development of paranoid reactions.

The most comprehensive definition of consciousness of personality is to be found, remarkably enough, not in the work of Strömgren himself, but in that of Färgeman (2), who describes it as:

> "a complex of ideas that a human being has about his own capabilities, powers, and potentialities in every respect; his relationship to other people and to society. Briefly: a set of ideas of a most highly private and intimate nature. All endeavor, all earlier failures and all expectations of social and sexual success and of intellectual and ethical development are permanent constituents of consciousness of personality; and it thus acquires such an intimate nature that it is hardly surprising that most human beings are themselves fully aware of it only at rare moments."

This theory of Strömgren has a great advantage in that it joins together a broad social element and a special individual element by taking into consideration the social situation that has released an actual neurosis—which, for its own part, is conditioned by the patient's constitution and his earlier experiences and conflicts. (344–45)

This "broad social element" amounts to a social conditioning of individuality, a sense in which the individual is constituted as such in and by the group. The apparent oxymoron that "consciousness of personality" is in Freudian terms preconscious—that "most human beings are themselves fully aware of it only at rare moments"—is another function of its social origins: the individual is only rarely aware of his or her individuality because it is a collective rather than an individual or a personal construct. The true oxymoron in that passage is "self-assurance": the assured "self" that is severely injured by traumatic displacements is a group construct. How the group constructs and "assures" the self, and how the destruction or disruption of the group destroys or disrupts that self-assurance as well, is one of my primary concerns in the First Essay. Pedersen continues:

> A long list of other writers have devoted their attention to this interchange of effect between personal conflict and social catastrophe. It appears in Allers, who describes several cases of psychogenic psychosis among prisoners-of-war in foreign-language environments during the first world war. After the recent war, Gillespie (3), in particular, has called attention to the fact that most cases of amnesia after air-raids did not depend upon the very capability of remembering being itself set out of function by trauma, but rather, in the greater number of cases, the loss of memory evolved about a "defensive amnesia," in which self-reproach, in regard to the patient's own behavior during the bombing, gave rise to a suppression of all the memory material.
>
> What is new in this theory of Strömgren is not simply that he points out what a central psychic function this consciousness of personality is and how inseparably it is bound to social surroundings, but above all the importance he gives to the intimate interplay between paranoid reactions and changes or conflicts within the realm of the ego.
>
> I believe, therefore, that it is no mere coincidence that in the treatment of refugees one is almost everywhere dealing with paranoid reactions, which apparently indicates that severe social trauma—in and of itself—has a tendency to release paranoid reactions, regardless of the character structure involved. (345)

Note there the social orientation of self-reproach: the "self" as a group construct is one of the way-stations through which group norms circulate, specifically the group's normative attitudinalizations of behavior, including reproach. What R. D. Gillespie is suggesting in the 1942 book Pedersen cites is that the amnesia he found after air-raids was not simply a mechanical malfunctioning of memory but a social disruption of memory, the individual preemptively foreclosing on memories that would cause the group distress.

But why "*release* paranoid reactions"? This makes it sound as if paranoid reactions were lying in wait, held in storage, but dammed up by normal social relations, which, breaking down, could no longer contain the flood—or, to metaphorize that differently, as if "civilization" based on "consciousness of personality" were a thin veneer stretched flimsily across a great surging abyss of psychopathological response. That Pedersen also thematizes "normal" constructions of reality as "true" and paranoid constructions as "false" suggests that truth is a weak force everywhere besieged by the overwhelming forces of falsehood, and therefore in constant need of reinforcements from normality, from civilized social order, under the leadership of the psychotherapist ("No one, in fact, can be more opposed to war and conditions of social displacement than the psychotherapist" [354]).

1.1.1.1 THE PRIMAL SCENE OF REFUGEE STUDIES

Now let us turn to Pedersen's first case study:

> A woman, 30 years old, who had been in Sweden for several months, complained that she never got the right change back when she made purchases. When she went into a store, all the other customers were waited on ahead of her. One day, she said, a clerk in a large department store had indignantly turned her back upon her when she had asked to buy something. When she looked more closely at her own way of conducting herself, she discovered by herself that it had actually been her own behavior that had resulted in her being treated in the way she was. She stood, uncertain and embarrassed, in the background and let other people go ahead of her. When she was to ask for what she wanted, her voice was so uncertain and indistinct that the very busy department-store clerk had quite simply not understood that she had said anything at all.
>
> This patient felt as though the general attitude toward refugees in Sweden was just as she herself had judged it to be: unjust, degrading, and ostracizing.
>
> The patient completely lacked insight into her difficulties. She first visited me to discuss problems her daughter had been having in school. It became obvious that the daughter had adopted her mother's paranoid attitude. The child felt that she had been treated badly and neglected by both the other pupils and the teachers. When the mother clearly understood her false evaluation of the real situation, not only her own paranoid attitude

disappeared, but the child's as well—without the need for any further treatment. (346)

Notice especially that "by herself": certainly no coercion is involved in the client's movement to her therapeutic revelation, probably not even pressure. Completely lacking insight into her difficulties, with no nudging from her therapist, the client somehow magically begins to look more closely at her behavior and discovers that she is herself to blame for her "unfair treatment." This *true* perception of her relationship with the social situation in Sweden banishes her *false paranoid* perception and cures both her and her daughter. Pedersen, the refugee psychotherapist become refugee theorist, is merely present at the self-healing.

Our typical lack of awareness of "consciousness of personality," however, is as socially circulated as the consciousness of personality itself—which is to say that we are as little aware of the shaping or guiding effect we have on others as we are on the shaping or guiding effect they have on us. Something like this socially circulated unawareness is at work in Pedersen's approach to her client, I suggest: her own successful assimilation to Swedish society works on her *sub limen* to repress awareness of the guidance she gives this client. Pedersen, the professional or institutional representative of Swedish mental health, the client's exemplar of (refugee adaptation to) Swedish calm, fair, tolerant rationality, is her ideal guide to "true" perception, which is to say, to *Swedish* perception, to the proprioception of the Swedish body politic, or the group norms governing ordinary life in Sweden; and Pedersen's inclination to report the normative therapeutic guidance she has been giving her client as the client's own self-discovery is itself part of this guidance. A tolerant, liberal Swede or fully assimilated foreigner in Sweden would never *pressure* an immigrant into adjusting to Swedish group norms. Swedish group norms require that everyone accept Swedish group norms as *natural,* not as group norms at all but as the natural rational *telos* of right living, as a default state to which all things return at rest, and therefore as something that requires no coercion or pressure, and in fact recoils with ideological disgust and horror from such hostile and alien forces. Swedish group norms, in other words, require that Pedersen be simply the benign *witness* to the woman's transformation—so she is.

I would argue that something like this "therapeutic" encounter between assimilated therapist and unassimilated refugee constitutes the primal scene of refugee studies—this mundane clash between two value systems, one local, the other foreign, one central, the other peripheral, one included, the other excluded, one empowered, the other disempowered, one explaining and healing, the other perceived or portrayed as in need of explanations and a healing transformation. The scene is at once one of dysregulation, in that collectively organized communication (the circulation of mutually accepted norms) has broken down, and of reregulation, in that the authoritative representative of resettlement, of the new host community, manages to "convert" the refugee to an assimilative ethos that facilitates her inclusion in the community.

What I propose to do in the rest of §1.1.1, then, is to explore the *somaticity* of this scene—or, to run that the other way, to exfoliate the interactive complexities of the scene by way of introducing the key concepts of somatic theory.

1.1.1.2 SOMATIC MIMESIS, THE SOMATIC TRANSFER, AND THE SOMATIC EXCHANGE

Were the Swedes truly kind and open to this woman, and to refugees in general, as Pedersen seems to assume and to want her client to assume, so that the woman's feeling that she was being treated unfairly and unjustly was "false" and a sign of a "paranoid reaction"? Or was she in fact being treated unfairly and unjustly, and in order to get over her anger and suspicion simply had to adjust to life in Sweden as a refugee, to accept the dual "truth" that Swedes are suspicious and impatient with refugees and yet determined to portray themselves as fair-minded and open? We don't know, because we never do know. This particular form of uncertainty is unavoidable. That we don't know the "truth" behind all these constructions may seem like a limitation on the kinds of claims we can make about refugeeism; but of course in a Kantian universe such truth-claims are by definition unavailable to proof or disproof, and therefore they must be made not to matter.

What can matter is the observation that virtually all the truth-claims in this case study, both before and after the woman's "conversion," are based on interpretations of body language: Pedersen tells us that the woman felt ignored and neglected in stores because the clerks turned their bodies *to* other customers before her and *away* from her; and once the woman begins to "look more closely at her own way of conducting herself," she realizes that it was the clerks' readings of *her* body language that had made them respond to her as they did. She hung back, "uncertain and embarrassed"; she "let other people go ahead of her"; her voice was "uncertain and indistinct." Whether Pedersen is guiding her to these latter realizations or not, it is clear that before the client's therapeutic conversion she reads only the clerks' body language and fails to recognize the ways in which she too is participating in the ideosomatic regulation of the events in question, and after her conversion she reads the clerks' readings of her body language, thus nudging her interpretations of the events in the direction of what I call the *somatic exchange.*

The somatic exchange, simply put, is the circulation of group norms, values, orientations, and inclinations through the somatic economy of those involved—whether they are physically present to each other or only narratively or otherwise imaginatively projected. It is the definitive channel of ideosomatic regulation, the channel by which regulatory norms are circulated through the group in the form of somatic approval and disapproval responses. More specifically, they are circulated through the group in the form of both *outward body language* and *inward body states,* linked serially by the Carpenter Effect—the fact observed by William B. Carpenter in 1874 that we unconsciously tend to mimic other people's body language in our own bodies, picked up by Howard Friedman's nonverbal communication team in the late 1970s and early 1980s as the channel for the interpersonal transmission of emotional states (see also Hatfield, Cacioppo, and Rapson). In the early 1990s these findings were incorporated by Antonio Damasio's neurological research team at the University of Iowa into somatic theory: Ralph Adolphs headed up a smaller group that began to investigate it, and, beginning in 1994, to publish papers that addressed subjects' ability to recognize somatic states in other people's faces. None of the group's publications in the late 1990s, however, addressed the question of an actual transfer or transmission of evaluative/regulatory social feelings from one person to another; it was not until a medical paper published in 2002 that the subgroup offered a very sketchy neurophysiological model for what I call the *somatic transfer,* suggesting in a scant eight lines that "knowledge of other people's emotions may rely on simulating the observed emotion" (Adolphs 171). But the very next year, in his 2003 book *Looking for Spinoza,* Damasio summarizes that study and expands significantly on Adolphs's team's hints; let me quote at some length:

> It also is apparent that the brain can simulate certain emotional body states internally, as happens in the process of turning the emotion sympathy into a feeling of empathy. Think, for example, of being told about a horrible accident in which someone was badly injured. For a moment you may feel a twinge of pain that mirrors in your mind the pain of the person in question. You feel as if you were the victim, and the feeling may be more or less intense depending on the dimension of the accident or on your knowledge of the person involved. The presumed mechanism for producing this sort of feeling is a variety of what I have called the "as-if-body-loop" mechanism. It involves an internal brain simulation that consists of a rapid modification of ongoing body maps. This is achieved when certain brain regions, such as the prefrontal/premotor cortices, directly signal the body-

sensing brain regions. The existence and location of comparable types of neurons has been established recently. Those neurons can represent, in an individual's brain, the movements that very brain sees in another individual, and produce signals toward sensorimotor structures so that the corresponding movements are either "previewed," in simulation mode, or actually executed. These neurons are present in the frontal cortex of monkeys and humans, and are known as "mirror neurons."

The result of direct simulation of body states in body-sensing regions is no different from that of filtering the signals hailing from the body. In both cases the brain momentarily creates a set of body maps that does *not* correspond exactly to the current reality of the body. The brain uses the incoming body signals like clay to sculpt a particular body state in the regions where such a pattern can be constructed, i.e., the body-sensing regions. What one feels then is based on that "false" construction, not on the "real" body state.

A recent study from Ralph Adolphs speaks directly to the issue of simulated body states. The study was aimed at investigating the underpinnings of empathy and involved more than 100 patients with neurological lesions located at varied sites of their cerebral cortex. They were asked to participate in a task that called for the sort of process needed for empathy responses. Each subject was shown photographs of an unknown person exhibiting some emotional expression and the task consisted of indicating what the unknown person was feeling. Researchers asked each subject to place himself or herself in the person's shoes to guess the person's state of mind. The hypothesis being tested was that patients with damage to body-sensing regions of the cerebral cortex would not be capable of performing the task normally.

Most patients performed this task easily, precisely as healthy subjects do, except for two specific groups of patients whose performance was impaired. The first group of impaired patients was quite predictable. It was made up of patients with damage to visual association cortices, especially the right visual cortices of the ventral occipito-temporal region. This sector of the brain is critical for the appreciation of visual configurations. Without its integrity, the facial expressions in the photographs cannot be perceived as a whole, even if the photos can be seen in the general sense of the term.

The other group of patients was the most telling: It consisted of subjects with damage located in the overall region of the *right* somatosensory cortices, namely, in the insula, SII and SI regions of the right cerebral hemisphere. This is the set of regions in which the brain accomplishes the highest level of integrated mapping of body state. In the absence of this region, it is not possible for the brain to simulate other body states effectively. The

brain lacks the playground where variations on the body-state theme can
be played. (115–17)

This is the neurophysiological explanation of the "contagion" or "infection"
of feelings or somatic states from one body to another, the fact that yawns and
moods are so powerfully contagious: through empathy, based on seeing, hearing (about), or reading about external evidence of other people's body states,
we simulate those states. Nor is this a voluntary process undergone by especially sensitive people who deliberately project themselves into other people's
feelings, because they *want* to; it happens to all of us, all the time, except to
people with those specific types of brain damage Damasio mentions. It is not
just "sensitive" people who yawn, or fight the overwhelming impulse to yawn,
when they see other people yawning; it is virtually everyone. I call this *somatic
mimesis:* the almost instantaneous mimicking of other people's body states in
our own, which serves to "infect" us with other people's feelings.[1]

For example, in Pedersen's reconstruction of the somatic exchange in her
client's department-store experience, the client walks in hesitant, holding
back, neither casually shopping nor stepping forward properly to attract a
clerk's attention. Her body language is picked up by the clerks, unconsciously
mimicked and experienced inwardly as reticence, and ultimately interpreted
by them as an unreadiness to shop; politely, not wanting to force themselves
on a hesitant customer, they turn their attention to other shoppers. From the
clerks' point of view, which Pedersen supports, their behavior is normal and
normative; they have done nothing wrong, and indeed would doubtless be
surprised and even shocked to learn that someone (but a *refugee,* of course
she would!) had accused them of deviating from standard behavioral norms.
This is, of course, not the "truth"; it is the clerks' ideosomatic point of view as
reconstructed by Pedersen, mimetically simulated and so first experienced
inwardly by her from the client's reports, and then built into a therapeutic
interpretation.

As I reconstruct the client's presenting construction of the somatic
exchange, based on my own somatomimetic simulation of her body state and
interpretations of that body state from Pedersen's report, she walks into the
department store hesitant, timid, her heart pounding, her adrenalin pump-
ing, in a mild form of acute trauma, absolutely convinced in advance that
she is not going to be able to handle the upcoming transaction, and hoping
desperately that someone will step forward to help her, save her, come more
than halfway to walk her through the purchase of a few items in a language of
which she does not speak more than a few words. The clerks, seeing that she
is not a Swede, that she is poorly dressed, perhaps that her skin and hair are

darker than theirs, perhaps hearing her stammer out some garbled request in words that they hardly even recognize as Swedish, recoil with disgust and indignation. From the woman's point of view, which Pedersen rejects and corrects, her hurt and anger at this rudeness are normal and normative; she has done nothing wrong, has broken no laws, and simply because she is a foreigner, a refugee, has been treated badly by these native Swedes. This is, again, not the "truth" but (my somatomimetic simulation and reinterpretation of) the woman's somatomimetic simulation of their body states in her own, based on her unconscious mimicking of their outward body language (bodily posture—the turning away—and facial expression).

1.1.1.3 SOMATIC MARKERS AND SOMATIC STORAGE

In Pedersen's essay, one of the key features of her client's "paranoid" response to her new life in Sweden is its *persistence*: not only can she not give up her paranoia, but she manages to transfer it to her daughter as well; it is only after she has begun to work consciously back through her own behavior and attitudes that she is able to let it go, and at that point her daughter's paranoia disappears as well. My question is this: where and how is that "paranoia," or what I would prefer to describe as her xenonormative (non-Swedish) ideosomatic regulation, stored? Why is her belief that a clerk turning away from a speaking customer is rude so persistent? Why does her ideosomatic regulation remain active in her behavioral response, even as it is increasingly cut off from group kinesic confirmation and thus depleted of the feel of reality? How is her "paranoid" anger at Swedish behavior transferred to and stored in her daughter?

The persistence of behavioral orientations is one of the phenomena least well explained by other models, and best explained by somatic theory. In *Mimesis and Alterity*, Michael Taussig asks this question insistently: "If life is constructed, how come it appears so immutable? How come culture appears so natural? If things coarse and subtle are constructed, then surely they can be reconstrued as well?" (xvi). If Pedersen's client's non-Swedish response to Swedish department-store clerks is so dysregulatory, and yet is a mere *construction*, why doesn't she simply reconstrue it? Why is it so difficult to change what we believe, and how we act on what we believe? Why do cultural constructs feel so solid, so natural, so biological, even, as to seem to reflect universal human nature? "Try to imagine," Taussig goes on, "what would happen if we didn't in daily practice thus conspire to actively forget what Saussure called 'the arbitrariness of the sign'? Or try the opposite experiment. Try to imagine living in a world whose signs were indeed 'natural'" (xviii). The sign is actually only arbitrary in an arbitrary universalizing perspective, in a violently abstract perspective that attempts to universalize individual cultural constructs and so forces them to appear in their relativistic guise; within a specific culture, by contrast, every sign feels perfectly natural, feels immutable. To the comparative linguist, the use of the phonetic sequence [kæt] to refer to a furry feline domestic pet is arbitrary, but the monolingual English-speaker is unable to imagine calling a cat anything else—certainly not [ræt] or [bæt]—and while the polyglot knows that the use of that phonetic sequence is globally arbitrary, s/he also feels the *necessity* of each language's word for cat within the structure of feeling of each language.

Taussig's answer to his own question involves what he calls the "mimetic faculty," which "carries out its honest labor suturing nature to artifice and bringing sensuousness to sense by means of what was once called sympathetic magic, granting the copy the character and power of the original, the representation the power of the represented" (xviii). The apparent convergence between this notion and somatic theory's "somatic mimeticism" is striking; but the model Taussig borrows from Walter Benjamin and Theodor Adorno can't explain how mimesis "bring[s] sensuousness to sense." It just sort of happens. Taussig cites Adorno's praise for Benjamin's writing "as that in which 'thought presses close to its object, as if through touching, smelling, tasting, it wanted to transform itself,' and Susan Buck-Morss indicates how this very sensuousness is indebted to and necessary for what is unforgettable in that writing, its unremitting attempt to create 'exact fantasies,' translating objects into words, maintaining the objectness of the object in language" (2). There is in this formulation some sort of powerful mediating experience that bridges the gap between thought and the object, an experience that Adorno specifically identifies as affective; but in Taussig, as in Benjamin and Adorno, that experience remains mysterious, and indeed in Taussig is explicitly associated with magic. Anyone can think a likeness, think a mimesis, mentally assign "the copy the character and power of the original, the representation the power of the represented," and then feel that power drain out of it. No one can simply *think* that power and make it stick; some deeper magic is required to convert an object into a fetish object. Taussig devotes much of his first chapter to a study of a group of representational wooden figurines carved by the Cuna in the San Blas islands off Panama, figurines with magical curative powers that Taussig associates with their representational nature, with the fact that they are carved to resemble prominent Europeans and Americans, including Douglas MacArthur. The question he neglects to ask, however, is this: why do the figurines not have those magical curative powers for *us*—only for the Cuna? Why can I (or anyone else) not carve a Douglas MacArthur doll and go around curing people with it? What *is* the social process that converts the doll into a powerful fetish object? The somatic theory on which I draw here suggests that it is a slow iterative process by which the object is gradually *invested* with power, affectively occupied, cathected, *besetzt wird,* through the projection of exosomatic feelings into it, typically by the group, who circulate amongst themselves the feelings they are projecting into the object so that the object seems to become a part of their somatic exchange. A lone individual can fetishize an object as well, or even an imaginary friend, a figment, a ghost, but slowly, and subrationally—and an object fetishized by a lone individual will possess that fetish power or exosoma only for that individual, not for others. Nor does this exosomatization of objects, mental images, places, and so on necessarily operate through mimesis: the collective granting of exosomatic power to a mountain or a tree or a body of water, to a house or a garden or a path, to a skin color, to a string of beads or an amulet, to an abstraction like "honor" or "diversity" or "family values" is not mimetic at all and yet still empowers the object or the idea or the place for the group.[2] We will return to the concept of the exosoma below, in connection with the dysregulatory impact of the destruction of exosomatized objects and places in the refugee experience (§1.1.3.1) and the use of exosomatized dolls in an attempt to reregulate and resomatize the dysregulated self (§1.2.2.2).

So how is a cultural construct or fetish object "empowered," exosomatized, given the force and the feel of permanence and efficacy? One of the mainstays of somatic theory is the *somatic-marker hypothesis* developed in the late 1980s and early 1990s by Damasio's team to explain the autonomic underpinnings of rational decision-making. Damasio's model suggests that the ventral-tegmental area of the autonomic nervous system "marks" certain behavioral options "positively" or "negatively," with tiny subliminal quanta of emotional pleasure or pain that are measurable with a skin-conductance test (like a polygraph), and that when we "feel" these markers—typically way below the level of conscious awareness—we are guided by them in our prerational orientations to the making of a decision:

> The key components [in the decision we need to make] unfold in our minds instantly, sketchily, and virtually simultaneously, too fast for the details to be clearly defined. But now, imagine that *before* you apply any kind of cost/benefit analysis to the premises, and before you reason toward the solution of the problem, something quite important happens: When the bad outcome connected with a given response option comes into mind, however fleetingly, you experience an unpleasant gut feeling. Because the feeling is about the body, I gave the phenomenon the technical term *somatic* state

("soma" is Greek for body); and because it "marks" an image, I called it a *marker*. Note again that I use somatic in the most general sense (that which pertains to the body) and I include both visceral and nonvisceral sensation when I refer to somatic markers.

What does the *somatic marker* achieve? It forces attention on the negative outcome to which a given action may lead, and functions as an automated alarm signal which says: Beware of danger ahead if you choose the option which leads to this outcome. The signal may lead you to reject, *immediately,* the negative course of action and thus make you *choose among other alternatives.* The automated signal protects you against future losses, without further ado, and then allows you to choose from among fewer alternatives. There is still room for using a cost/benefit analysis and proper deductive competence, but only *after* the automated step drastically reduces the number of options. Somatic markers may not be sufficient for normal human decision-making since a subsequent process of reasoning and final selection will still take place in many though not all instances. Somatic markers probably increase the accuracy and efficiency of the decision process. Their absence reduces them. This distinction is important and can easily be missed. The hypothesis does not concern the reasoning steps which follow the action of the somatic marker. In short, *somatic markers are a special instance of feelings generated from secondary emotions.* Those emotions and feelings *have been connected, by learning, to predicted future outcomes of certain scenarios.* When a somatic marker is juxtaposed to a particular future outcome the combination functions as an alarm bell. When a positive somatic marker is juxtaposed instead it becomes a beacon of incentive. (*Descartes' Error* 173–74, emphasis in original)

To test the learning and storage of these somatic markers in specific decision-making contexts, a postdoctoral student in Damasio's program named Antoine Bechara invented a gambling experiment. In the first version of the experiment, subjects were given $2,000 in play money, placed in front of four decks of cards, labeled A, B, C, and D, and told that the object of the "game" was to end it with the maximum amount of money—to lose as little of the bankroll s/he had been given, and preferably to earn more. The player then picked up a card from any one of the four decks and followed the instructions printed on it—invariably either to take a certain amount of money from the experimenter, to give a certain amount of money to the experimenter, or to both give and take money. The player was not told how many draws s/he would be allowed, or anything else about the future play, including the differentiation of the decks: decks A and B typically both paid out and collected back higher sums, so that the risks were very high in drawing from them, and decks C and D both paid out and demanded back lower sums, making the risks in drawing from them low. The most a player would ever have to pay in drawing from deck C or D was $100; the highest payment required on a card in deck A or B was $1,250. "There is no way for the Player to predict, at the outset," as Damasio describes this experiment in *Descartes' Error,* "what will happen, and no way to keep in mind a precise tally of gains and losses as the game proceeds. Just as in life, where much of the knowledge by which we live and by which we construct our adaptive future is doled out bit by bit, as experience accrues, uncertainty reigns" (213).

The "players" or research subjects asked to play this experimental game included both Damasio's patients with damage to their ventral-tegmental areas and normals. What the experimenters found was that the two different groups played very differently. Typically, the normals would draw randomly from all four decks at first, become briefly attracted by high payoffs from decks A and B, but gradually, "within the first thirty moves" (213), as they were hit by big penalties, begin to shy away from those two decks and to draw more conservatively from decks C and D. As Damasio reports, "self-professed high-risk players may resample decks A and B occasionally, only to return to the apparently more prudent course of action" (213) after a few big hits. The ventral-tegmental patients, on the other hand, would draw systematically from decks A and B, and go bankrupt halfway through the game. One such ventral-tegmental-damaged player, whom Damasio calls Elliott, played this recklessly despite describing himself as a "conservative, low-risk person" (214)—and in fact despite knowing intellectually, by the end of the game, that decks A and B were the "dangerous" ones. "When the experiment was repeated a few months later, with different cards and different labels for the decks, Elliott behaved no differently from how he did in real-life situations, where his errors have persisted" (214). He was, Damasio writes, "engaged in the task, fully attentive, cooperative, and interested in the outcome. In fact, he wanted to win. What made him choose so disastrously?" (215).

Early speculation within the team included the possibility that the frontally damaged subjects had been somehow desensitized to punishment, and could be motivated only by reward; a closer look at their actual play, however, showed that "after making a penalty payment, the patients avoided the deck from which the bad card had come, just as normal subjects did, but then, unlike normals, they returned to the bad deck" (217). Almost certainly the ventral-tegmental patients were still sensitive to punishment, but the *warning* aftereffect of punishment did not last long—it seemed to wear off.

To test this hypothesis, Hanna Damasio developed a follow-up experiment, in which the players' skin-conductance responses were monitored with a polygraph machine. A spike would show that the player was experiencing a somatic marker, either warning the player against a given draw or encouraging one—in other words, the polygraph could not distinguish between positive and negative somatic markers but could indicate the presence of some learned (stored) somatic orientation, and thus could tell the experimenters when the decision was not made randomly.

What they found was that in the seconds following the drawing of a card, both groups, the frontally damaged patients and the normals, generated skin-conductance responses, or somatic markers. Both a high payoff and a high penalty generated these somatic markers—presumably a positive marker for a high payoff and a negative marker for a high penalty. The striking difference between the two groups lay in the fact that, after ten or twenty draws, the normals began showing a skin-conductance spike *before* drawing from one of the two "dangerous" decks, A or B: their autonomic nervous system had learned not only to *respond* negatively to those two decks, but to *predict* negative consequences of drawing from them, and thus to *warn* the subject to avoid them. In the normals, in other words, learned and stored somatic markers served an important anticipatory and cautionary function. In the frontally damaged patients, on the other hand, no such anticipatory somatic markers were ever registered. They would continue responding somatically to big payoffs and big penalties, but they would never feel a somatic marker *warning* them against drawing from deck A or B. Their damaged ventral-tegmental area was either not storing learned patterns or not using stored patterns to warn them against disastrous courses of action—probably, in fact, both.

What this suggests is that the group-sponsored and -supported ideosomatic orientations that we've seen at work both loconormatively (based on Swedish regulation) in Stefi Pedersen and the department-store clerks and xenonormatively (based on non-Swedish regulation) in Pedersen's refugee client are autonomically stored (synapticized through axonal guidance and myelination) and contextually activated collections of somatic markers. So too would be the Cuna Indians' fetishization of representational figurines—their conviction that the figurines could magically cure the sick, a conviction that apparently did frequently cure people. By guiding each minute decision an individual makes along collectively organized lines, these markers allow groups to impose moment-to-moment coherence on its members' reality. Because the learned somatic orientations that generate contextual markers are *stored* in that area—at least in those of us without brain damage in the ventral-tegmental area—group guidance or ideosomatic regulation possesses sufficient stability to make that imposed moment-to-moment coherence seem like the fabric of reality itself, the "way things are." That stability is an extremely useful thing in our ordinary lives; without it, we would be overwhelmed by the complexity of life. We could not hold a job or maintain a relationship—Damasio's ventral-tegmental patients do typically get fired and dumped, because they are unable to organize their reality around job tasks or relationship continuity. Certainly we could not cure the sick with carved wooden figurines, or with placebos.[3] But when our ordinary realities collapse, through what I'm calling the ideosomatic dysregulation of forced migration, that stability can also become a liability. As it becomes xenonormative, the somatic markers it generates for us become increasingly "unrealistic"—cut off from the loconormative group construction of reality—and therefore maladaptive. Like Damasio's patient Elliott, who continued to draw from decks A and B because it *felt right* to do so, the isolated refugee continues to ideosomatize reality xenonormatively, continues to act as it *feels right* to act, even though the new group—all of them strangers speaking a strange language—fails to confirm those feelings, fails to provide the expected somatic support for "right action," indeed often seems to act in utterly irrational and even insane ways. To the locals, the refugee acts equally irrationally and insanely, and may well be sent to a psychotherapist like Stefi Pedersen for treatment. This perceived irrationality on both sides of the loco-/xenonormative divide is one definitive sign of ideosomatic dysregulation.

1.1.1.4 SOMATIC (DYS)REGULATION AND ALLOSTATIC LOAD

So what is ideosomatic dysregulation? The easy answer is that it is a breakdown in the circulation of regulatory/normative pressures through the somatic exchange; but what breaks it down, and what, behaviorally, attitudinally, and cognitively, is the result? In terms of the questions I asked of Pedersen earlier in the essay, is it really true that anxiety can dysregulate a somatic exchange? Is there a certain allostatic load of anxiety that becomes ideosomatically dysregulatory, or is even a very low level of anxiety minimally dysregulatory? Or is anxiety not dysregulatory at all, but simply one of the byproducts and therefore signs of dysregulation? Or both? If anxiety is both a dysregulatory input and a dysregulated output of the allostatically adjusted somatic exchange, how does that work? And finally, if intense ideosomatic dysregulation entails the kinds of extreme breakdowns in the collective construction of identity and reality that Pedersen found—depersonalization and dissociation, hallucination and amnesia—how are those breakdowns triggered, or, in Pedersen's term, "released"?

The great integrator of psychological, psychoanalytical, and psychobiological research on affect regulation in our time is Allan N. Schore, in a series of books entitled *Affect Regulation and the Origin of the Self, Affect Regulation and the Repair of the Self,* and *Affect Dysregulation and Disorders of the Self.* In the emerging research model now being developed out of Bowlby's attachment theory, Kohut's self-psychology, and Damasio's somatic-marker hypothesis, affect regulation and dysregulation are products of nonverbal and largely unconscious/preconscious right-brain-to-right-brain communication, and specifically the communicative synchronization of affect through the mirroring of body language. Initially this regulatory communication occurs between the primary caregiver (Schore says simply the mother) and the newborn infant, and then in communicative dyads throughout the rest of the individual's life, especially the therapist–patient dyad. One of the weaknesses of Schore's integrative approach from the perspective of somatic theory is that he completely ignores the synchronization of affect in larger groups, despite the attention paid to the mother-father-infant triad by Freud and his most radical followers, including Jacques Lacan and Julia Kristeva, who associate what Schore calls affective right-brain body-based communication with the mother and verbal left-brain symbolic communication with the father; and certainly Freud was increasingly fascinated, toward the end of his life, especially in *Civilization and its Discontents,* with societal regulation of affect (the *Unbehagen* or dysregulation caused by misattuned societal regulation of *Behagen* or pleasure).

Schore writes in *Affect Regulation and the Repair of the Self*:

> Mutual gaze interactions increase over the second and third quarters of the first year, and because they occur within the "split second world of the mother and infant" (Stern 1977) are therefore not easily visible. This dialogue is best studied by a frame-by-frame analysis of film, and in such work Beebe and Lachmann (1988a) observed synchronous rapid movements and fast changes in affective expressions within the dyad. . . . This affective mirroring is accomplished by a moment-by-moment matching of affective direction in which both partners increase together their degree of engagement and facially expressed positive affect. The fact that the coordination of responses is so rapid suggests the existence of a bond of unconscious communication. . . .
>
> These mirroring exchanges generate much more than overt facial changes in the dyad; they represent a transformation of inner events. Beebe

and Lachmann (1988a) asserted that as the mother and the infant match each other's temporal and affective patterns, each recreates an inner psychophysiological state similar to the partner's. In synchronized gaze the dyad creates a mutual regulatory system of arousal (Stern 1983) in which they both experience a state transition as they move together from a state of neutral affect and arousal to one of heightened positive emotion and high arousal. (8)

Here "the child is using the output of the mother's right cortex as a template for the imprinting—the hard wiring of circuits in his/her own right cortex that will come to mediate his/her expanding affective capacities. It has been said that in early infancy the mother is the child's 'auxiliary cortex'. . . . In these transactions she is 'downloading programs' from her brain into the infant's brain" (Schore, *Affect Regulation* 13), so that "in dyadic, 'symbiotic states' the infant's 'open,' immature, and developing internal homeostatic systems are interactively regulated by the caregiver's more mature and differentiated nervous system. Self-objects are thus external psychobiological regulators (Taylor 1987) that facilitate the regulation of affective experience (Palombo 1992), and they act at nonverbal levels beneath conscious awareness to cocreate states of maximal cohesion and vitalization (Wolf 1988)" (14).

This would be the ideal model of good parenting, based on the regulatory attunement of affective right-brain communication through facial mirroring; but of course it doesn't always work, even in the best parents. "We know that the caregiver is not always attuned," Schore notes; "indeed, developmental research shows frequent moments of misattunement in the dyad, ruptures of the attachment bond. . . . Reciprocal gaze, in addition to transmitting attunement, can also act to transmit misattunement, as in shame experiences. The misattunement in shame, as in other negative affects, represents a regulatory failure and is phenomenologically experienced as a discontinuity in what Winnicott (1958) called the child's need for 'going-on-being'" (10–11). Unsurprisingly, then, dyadic attunement regulates, in the sense of modeling for the child a successful and pleasurable affect regulation, and misattunement dysregulates, causing interactive stress and, ultimately, if the stress state continues for too long without reattunement, the building of what Freud called "defense mechanisms" or allostatic reregulations that *block* attunement. "A body of clinical and experimental evidence indicates," Schore writes, "that all forms of psychopathology have concomitant symptoms of emotional dysregulation, and that defense mechanisms are, in essence, forms of emotional regulation strategies for avoiding, minimizing, or converting affects that are too difficult to tolerate" (Cole, Michel, and O'Donnell 1994 [27–28]). "If attachment is interactive synchrony," Schore notes later, "stress is defined as an *asynchrony* in an interactional sequence, and, following this, a period of reestablished *synchrony* allows for stress recovery" (39, emphasis in original).

Schore's interests lie almost exclusively in the mother–child dyad and its later reparative replications in the therapist–patient dyad; he does not discuss the effects on affect regulation of later severely traumatizing stress, such as we are concerned with here. It should be obvious, however, that brutal violence is not only an extreme form of asynchrony but also a dysregulatory transmission of radical misattunement, so that the victim of violence not only experiences a destructive breach of his or her defenses but also internalizes (somatizes) an affect-image of the victimizer's brutality, of the brutal disregard for his or her affective regulation. Allostasis makes this violently dysregulatory introject extremely difficult to dislodge—a fact that explains the long persistence of PTSD symptomatologies. Refugees propelled into flight by the experience of this sort of violence—especially of course by suffering it in their own bodies, but even by simply viewing or hearing about violence inflicted on neighbors and relatives and friends—will be dealing with ideosomatic dysregulation for years, even decades to come, most, perhaps, for the rest of their lives. As Schore describes these dysregulated states:

> Due to the impaired development of the right-cortical preconscious system that decodes emotional stimuli by actual felt emotional responses to stimuli, individuals with poor attachment histories display empathy disorders, the limited capacity to perceive the emotional states of others. An inability to read facial expressions leads to a misattribution of emotional states and a misinterpretation of the intentions of others. Thus, there are impairments in the processing of socioemotional information.
>
> In addition to this deficit in social cognition, the deficit in self-regulation is manifest in a limited capacity to modulate the intensity and duration of affects, especially biologically primitive affects like shame, rage, excitement, elation, disgust, panic-terror, and hopelessness-despair. Under stress such individuals experience not discrete and differentiated affects, but diffuse, undifferentiated, chaotic states accompanied by overwhelming somatic and visceral sensations. The poor capacity for what Fonagy and Target (1997) called "mentalization" leads to a restricted ability to reflect upon one's emotional states. Right-cortical dysfunction is specifically associated with alterations in body perception and disintegration of self-representation (Weinberg, 2000). Solms also described a mechanism by which disorganization of a damaged or developmentally deficient right hemisphere is associated with a "collapse of internalized representations

of the external world" in which "the patient regresses from whole to part object relationships" (1996, p. 347), a hallmark of early forming personality disorders. (*Affect Regulation* 47)

I would add only two things: first, that the collapse of internalized representations of the external world—what I call the ideosomatic dysregulation of collective reality constructs—is a hallmark of PTSD as well, or *late*-forming personality disorders; and second, because the victim of violence allostatically somatizes the dysregulatory effects of violence, this sort of collapse of empathy, affect regulation, and a stable self tends to be viral, to be transmitted from individual to individual and from group to group, so that the individual disorganized or dysregulated by violence tends to become a perpetrator of violence, and mobs beget mobs. The kinds of chaotic mob violence that in many cases propel whole populations into flight are themselves the viral products of earlier mob violence, and will tend to ensure that a tendency to mob violence is perpetuated.

But what about the ideosomatic dysregulation that ensues not from actual physical violence but simply from the disruption or destruction of the social and/or physical environment? What about the refugees who are traumatized by the scattering of their friends and family and the loss of their homes and other familiar places? Schore's dyadic approach can easily explain the dysregulatory effects of one-on-one violence, but it is more at a loss with the interactive stress caused by group disintegration and loss of familiar places. Somatic theory's focus on the group rather than the dyad as the primary channel of affect regulation helps to explain both phenomena by insisting that affect-regulation is transferred to the individual not once, in infancy, by a good enough mother, but constantly, throughout each individual's life, by the group—rendering the scattering of the group, obviously, profoundly dysregulatory. (The dysregulatory effects of the loss or destruction of familiar things and places are related to this, but in complex ways that I want to return to in a few pages, in the context of Maria Pfister-Ammende's study of Swiss refugee camps.)

Stefi Pedersen's first case study of the woman in the department store reminds us also that the dysregulatory effects of refugee trauma are generated not just by the destruction of the old group, at home, but also by the fraught transition to the formation of a new group, in the new host community. The divergence between Pedersen's client's early construction of the somatic exchange as signaling the unfair treatment of refugees in Sweden and Pedersen's "therapeutic" construction of it as signaling her client's maladaptation to Swedish group norms, for example, is a clear sign of ideosomatic dysregulation: because the client and the therapist do not share the same culture, have not been socialized into the same ideosomatic norms, their normative constructions of the somatic exchange in the same situation are centrifugal. Pedersen's normatology, successfully adapted to local Swedish ideosomatic regulation, is loconormative; her client's, still largely shaped by the foreign culture from which she came, is xenonormative. A radical unconscious clash between loco- and xenonormative regulation renders the group organization of behavior difficult or impossible and social interaction—and thus both identity and reality as socially regulated—potentially chaotic, which is to say, ideosomatically dysregulatory. The fact that Pedersen's client manages to impose *some* sort of regulatory interpretation on the department-store interaction—takes it to signal Swedes' unfair treatment of refugees—suggests that ideosomatic regulation has not broken down for her entirely, that she is not truly plunged into dysregulatory identity- and reality-threatening chaos and trauma; but the chronic stress that her repeated feeling of being treated unfairly generates in her constitutes an allostatic overload that dysregulates both her own life and her daughter's.[4]

A large part of the woman's problem stems from the fact that the normative tendency of ideosomatic regulation to normativize itself not as normative at all but simply as *natural,* as human nature, remains functional only so long as it is loconormative. As it is separated in space or time from the group that maintains it—as it becomes nonhegemonically xenonormative, or what we may call "subaltern xenonormativity"—it becomes an ideosomatic orphan, still active in the individual's behavioral response but no longer collectively supported, and therefore increasingly depleted of the (collectivized) feel of reality. For the isolated refugee, cut off from the home ethnos ("own" people, places, and things), subaltern xenonormativity is an internalized civilization parked over the abyss. It is a neurotechnology for making sense of things, for organizing sense-impressions, for imposing a coherent reality on the random bits and pieces flung at us by the world, that now labors on without those constant confirmatory pressures of the ideosomatic exchange—group body language, circulated iteronormatively through each individual—that made it seem truly functional, truly able to create a meaningful world.

The other part of the problem is that the normal functioning of ideosomatic regulation normatively suppresses this sort of analysis—this *awareness* that the group exists to organize reality and identity for us, to create and stabilize and naturalize a world for us, and that any extended absence from group pressures will therefore tend to decrease, destabilize, and denaturalize our world. The "background" functioning of homeostatic self-regulation, the fact that we do not need to be aware every moment of collective guidance in order to be guided by it, has practical benefits—*Hamlet* is in some sense a play about the failure of that background functioning, the complex intellectual dithering that ensues when we must make ethical decisions consciously, rationally, analytically—but those benefits collapse with the group that supports them. The normative naturalization of ideosomatic normativity therefore tends to render the individual ill-prepared for any breakdown in the group-normative construction of world.

And indeed Pedersen's client is severely handicapped by her inability to analyze her refugee situation relativistically, as a move from one normative organization of the world to another. Because she unconsciously (ideosomatically) universalizes her subaltern xenonormative orientation to social relations, she doesn't even realize that it has broken down, become inoperative, become an orphan technology; she believes that there is only one right way to behave, and she is conforming to that norm and the Swedes are not. She is conscious neither of the somatic exchange (bodily interactivity) nor of its divergent and therefore dysregulatory effects in her interactions with Swedes (loco-/xenonormative centrifugality). Pedersen's therapeutic intervention involves making her aware of both: teaching her both that she is sending somatic signals to Swedes too, not just passively receiving signals from them, and that she must now begin to reorganize her identity and reality around loconormative ideosomatic regulation.

But Pedersen would almost certainly regard my description of her "therapeutic intervention" as tendentious, given that she herself presents it as something that her client did for herself, with Pedersen as neutral observer. My description, as I say, emerges out of my somatomimetic simulation of Pedersen's body states, based on her report: I *feel* that she is not telling the whole truth about how she interacted with this refugee woman, that she is idealizing her somatic contribution to her client's cure. In my reconstruction, Pedersen thematizes her client's discovery of the somatic exchange so as to exculpate the Swedish clerks and blame the refugee woman not just for the clerks' behavior but for the misinterpretation of that behavior, suggesting that Pedersen is not the disinterested outside observer she would like us to think she is but a member of the local group, an ideosomatically invested participant in the normative circulation of Swedish social values. And in fact my reconstructive mimesis of Pedersen's body language and simulation of her body states suggest that she is guiding her client to her therapeutic discovery at least as powerfully with her body language as with her verbal guidance: a smile, a friendly but almost imperceptible inclination of the head, a slight relaxation of posture whenever the client "discovers" some further evidence of her paranoid misconstructions of the Swedish clerks' benevolence; a thoughtful frown, a raised eyebrow, a twisting of her upper body to quarter view whenever the client insists on her blamelessness, her helpless victimization by these Swedish xenophobes.

What, though, is the hermeneutical status of my claim to be able to reconstruct Pedersen's participation in the somatic exchange with her client, based only on Pedersen's written words? Does this mean I'm guessing? In somatic theory, somatomimetic simulation of body states is possible through both sensory *and* verbal channels—both when we see, hear, and sense someone feeling something and when we read or are told a story about someone feeling something. This is, in fact, intuitively correct: we are as powerfully moved by a scene in a movie or a novel as we are by a scene in real life, indeed often more moved by the artistic effect than by its real-life model, because in the artwork extraneous real-world elements that distract us from the simulation have been radically pared back. We have plenty of ordinary experiences of such comparisons as well: when we either see someone fall off a bicycle in shorts and a t-shirt, and watch bare skin slide along the asphalt, or hear or read the story of that happening, we cringe and shudder in sympathetic somatic response. Because the brain does not primarily distinguish between "real" and "narrated" events, between "current" and "remembered" events, between things that happen to others and things that happen to us—those distinctions are secondary analytical constructs that we impose on somatic response after the fact—it doesn't really matter whether I am Pedersen, or am present at her sessions with this refugee woman, or simply read her report more than half a century later: I am still going to respond somatomimetically to it, am still going to simulate her body states in my own.

This does not mean, of course, that my simulations of her body states are necessarily *accurate*—any more than her simulations of the clerks' and her client's body states were necessarily accurate, or the clerks' and refugee woman's simulations of each other's body states were necessarily accurate. Somatic theory is not about objectivity; it's about competing constructions, and the ideosomatic pressure brought to bear by the group on its members to unify those constructions artificially, to impose a political conformity on them. All I am claiming about my reconstructions of Pedersen's body language and body states in the somatic exchange with this refugee client is that they feel persuasive to me—or, rather, I am using my claim that they feel persuasive to *me* as part of my attempt to make them persuasive to *you,* to set up my somatic exchange with you in such a way as to make you agree that I'm right about Pedersen.

1.1.1.5 SUMMARY

We might encapsulate this reading of what I'm calling the primal scene of refugee studies, then, by suggesting that refugeeism channels two distinct kinds
of ideosomatic dysregulation, two distinct ruptures in the fabric of collective
normativity: one for the refugees themselves (displacement as the breakdown
of the group), the other for us as sedentary observers (displacement as the
contamination of the group). For the displaced, refugeeness is a subtraction
of ideosomatic regulation, the traumatic destruction of regulatory contexts;
for us as observers, it is an addition to ideosomatic regulation, the unsettling
introduction of an excess that disrupts regulatory contexts—as Liisa Malkki
puts it, "in the national order of things, refugeeness is itself an aberration
of categories, a zone of pollution" (7). Refugees find themselves thrust into
situations that make no sense to them, because they have been expelled from
the group contexts that impose order (reality and identity) on the world; for
the sedentary, refugees are the senseless, the nonsensical, the unreal-because-
excluded somehow treacherously (re)included within reality, the "beyond
the pale" (outside the paling fence that demarcates "home," the familiar, the
defined, the meaningful) somehow disturbingly discovered inside the pale.
Refugeeism as a social phenomenon is the awkward encounter between these
two dysregulations: the displaced find their way into a new regulatory group
context, typically by adjusting their old ideosomatics to the regulatory norms
of the undisplaced with whom they are resettled, who must somehow find
room in their collective sense-making apparatuses for the inexplicable, the
inscrutable. It is not surprising, then, that sociological refugee studies are by
and large assimilation studies, since assimilation is the definitive contact zone
between the two groups—or that psychological refugee studies consist almost
exclusively of mental-health diagnoses designed to identify and fix what is
wrong with refugees, preparatory to their assimilation.

1.1.2 The Reregulation of the Dysregulatory Refugee

The advantage of an imagined primal scene, obviously, is focus: it constitutes a
kind of ideal model from which all real-life messiness has been removed. Now
it is time to introduce some messes. What I propose to do here in §1.1.2 is to
take three closer looks at the reregulatory response to the refugee as dysregulatory force, as marshaled by the "therapist" side of the assimilative encounter,
the first (§1.1.2.1) in a refugee camp, where the reregulators are the outsiders,

the xenonormative group; the second (§1.1.2.2) in the resettlement community, where the reregulators (like Pedersen) are the loconormative group; the third (§1.1.2.3) in a comparison of the two. Then, in §1.1.3, I will return to the refugee's experience of dysregulatory displacement.

1.1.2.1 XENONORMATIVE REREGULATION

In an important article from 1981, "Framing Refugees as Clients," Dorsh Marie de Voe writes of the 85,000 Tibetans who followed the Dalai Lama in 1959 in his flight out of the path of Chinese aggression into the neighboring countries of Nepal and India, from which some later moved on to Bhutan, Sikkim, Switzerland, Canada, the United States, and other countries. What makes the Tibetan refugees an interesting case study is that for the half-century after their uprooting they have continued consistently to refuse offers of citizenship and chosen to retain refugee status, and as a result continue to receive considerable refugee aid from Western organizations. What interests de Voe is the "structure of thought" or "psychotopology"—Magorah Maruyama's term, which de Voe borrows for what I would call "ideosomatic regulation"— governing the group construction of specific travelers as either refugees or non-refugees, and thereby also the group organization of not just their living conditions but also their eventual social practices and orientations as well. She notes, for example, the "effective arbitrariness of who 'becomes' refugees" (91n7), citing the Indian government's division of the Tibetan travelers into Buddhist "refugees" and Muslim "citizens":

> When the Indian Government was confronted with flood of Tibetans in 1959, the refugees who were Muslim were detained. There has been, historically, a rather small community of Tibetan Muslims in Lhasa, Tibet, called by Tibetans "Lhasa-kachi" or, Lhasa Muslims. India would not let the Muslims in under the same category as the Buddhists, even though they were both of the same experience necessitating, in their minds, flight. In 1960, the Indian Government agreed to allow the Lhasa-kachis exile. However, they were not allowed to enter as "refugees" but rather as Indian citizens. This group of about 1,000 people was sent to Strinagar, Kashmir, in northern India, and the center of Muslim activity. There, on the outskirts of the city, the Lhasa-kachi are nearly-forgotten people. Without refugee status, they were "unknown" to helping agencies—even in the initial resettlement, and they were excluded from any rehabilitation schemes which were organized for a host of other Tibetan refugees. The Partition was not

so far in the past, and anti-Muslim sentiments combined with an historical distaste for Asian-looking people made India's decision to accept Tibetan Muslims extremely difficult. (91n7)

This is part of a lengthy footnote to her general point about the large group of Buddhists who were quickly designated and remain today "Tibetan refugees," namely, that

> The professional initially frames the refugee as "client" through an agreed upon set of criteria. This initial prejudicial judgment establishes the need hierarchy which is then matched to the services and expectations offered by the agency. In this sense, experts take custody of the refugees by taking custody of what they, the experts, have identified as the refugee's "problem." Refugees cannot effect their own release from the situation; only others can.
>
> Like other people who are clients, refugees are categorized with an impersonal quality, like property. Then, institutions interested in absorbing or rehabilitating refugees impose an organization of relevant facts, needs and goals in a way that the institutional structures can handle them. Even the absorption of immigrants depends on the outcome of an interplay between their desires and expectations and the extent to which they can meet the demands of the organizations controlling them. (90–91)

What I find initially interesting here for a study of the ideosomatic regulation of refugeeism is that the Western aid organizations that define a group of people as refugees in terms of specific needs that can be met by their organizational structures and resources are *xenonormative,* but now *hegemonically* xenonormative: they bring to the refugee groups their own foreign norms and values and the ideosomatic pressures that can regiment refugee experience in accordance with them and, unlike Pedersen's timidly xenonormative client in the Swedish department store, are able to make their group construction of reality stick, make it *become* reality. The refugees are initially xenonormative too, but they do not assimilate to the local culture; instead as time goes on, they iterate their xenonormativity as new loconormative cultures (most notably in Dharamsala, India, where the Dalai Lama settled), in much larger numbers—the tens of thousands—than Pedersen's client and her daughter. But as de Voe's research shows, the numbers don't really matter; they are still not large enough or powerful enough a group to take charge of the ideosomatic regulation of the aid-giving encounter, unable to import *hegemonic* xenonormativity into the new context:

Dependence begins when the refugees try to develop behaviors they per-
ceive as expected of them as clients in order to continue the flow of rewards
or aid. This form of self-estrangement contributes to the refugee's sense of
powerlessness. There is the constant fear of being "summoned before a bar,"
found guilty or inadequate. Indeed, the victim gets blamed for having the
problem and not collaborating to solve it. So, the Tibetans, for instance,
have learned to ask for sponsorship, to "see" their problem in the same way
the helpers define it, and to seek the same solutions. After twenty years of
such a relationship, Tibetans who do not "adapt" to the way things work
in exile express a fear of personal failure in the new terms. Their young
continually compete for the attention of aid organizations. To be connected
with westerners has become a kind of status in itself, despite resentment of
the foreignness it brings to the heart of the community. (93)

Here again we have a loco-/xenonormative clash, and again one that is
more or less stably resolved in favor of the more powerful group, the group
with the superior financial and iterosomatic resources, the aid-givers. While
in the Pedersen case the aid-givers were loconormative and the refugee xenonormative, however, in this case the aid-givers are (hegemonically) xenonormative and the refugees are (nonhegemonically) loconormative. As in
the colonial situation, in fact—the topic properly of the Second Essay—the
hegemonic xenonormative regime comes from Europe and the United States,
and imposes an ideosomatic *counterregulation,* a new "corrective" ideosomatic exchange, on the Tibetan refugees from the outside, and so engenders
in them not just willing and even eager conformity but "resentment of the
foreignness it brings to the heart of the community." Still, all the signs of successful ideosomatic regulation are here: the attempt to conform behavior and
self-understanding to group expectations, the definition of high status in the
group in terms of successful conformity, the fear that failed conformity will
bring unwanted consequences, and above all the circulation of somatic markers of approval ("the attention of aid organizations," "a kind of status") and disapproval ("found guilty or inadequate," "get blamed," "fear of personal failure")
as channels of normative reality-construction.

1.1.2.2 XENONORMATIVE-BECOMING-LOCONORMATIVE REREGULATION

A more recent and explicitly Foucauldian study of this reregulatory construction of internees as "certified" refugees by Western aid organizations, immigration officials, and mental health care providers is offered by Aihwa Ong

in her 1995 article "Making the Biopolitical Subject," reprinted as chapter 4 of her 2003 book *Buddha is Hiding* (I will follow along with the argument of the article, but will mostly quote from the book). "From the beginning," she writes, "American service agencies, church groups, and immigration officials working with the refugees tended to view them as threats, both ideological and medical, to the American body politic where many were to be settled. The goals of refugee recruitment, processing, and resettlement programs were to socialize refugees to a category of newcomers defined as contagious to and dependent upon the civil society" (*Buddha* 93)—or, in my terms, to reregulate refugees perceived as ideosomatically dysregulatory.

> Although there was overwhelming evidence that only a tiny percentage of refugees at KID [the Khao-I-Dang camp in Thailand] were Khmer Rouge members, a "Khmer Rouge screening process" rejected thousands on unsubstantiated suspicion that they participated in Khmer Rouge brutality or were affiliated with them. Stephen Golub has reported that the most circumstantial evidence, such as working involuntarily under the Angkar authorities or recounting stories that did not fit an assumed pattern of life in Khmer Rouge collective farms, was used to reject applicants. Translation problems and social differences such as the refugees' body language—smiling even under stress, reporting the deaths of relatives with a dispassionate face—made them Khmer Rouge suspects in the eyes of INS officers. (*Buddha* 58)

Those chosen for resettlement in the US were then given "orientation" training designed to socialize them to life in America, much of it, Ong shows, aimed at sanitizing the foreignness of bodies and foods: washing themselves daily to prevent body odor, ventilating their kitchens to prevent cooking smells from bothering neighbors, not spitting or urinating in public,

> because "Americans prefer clean public places." (This statement does not take into account that most poor refugees were resettled in low-cost, garbage-strewn neighborhoods.) They are also warned about sexually transmitted diseases.
>
> The prominence of desensing and sanitary measures drove home the "cleanliness is next to godliness" message of cultural citizenship—good hygiene as a sign of democratic sensibility. Refugees have to erase the smells of their humanity, submitting to a civilizing process that can be measured out in daily mouthwashes and showers. I remember being greeted at a poor Cambodian home with a woman spraying scent from an aerosol can.

When I inquired why she was doing it, she said she had just been cooking Cambodian food, which, she had learned, "smelled bad to Americans." (*Buddha* 97)

Ong also deals at length with the reregulatory construction of refugee mental health by care providers:

Thus, although the health providers are well-meaning and sympathetic, the pressure to "do something" with patients often means in practice that "cultural sensitivity" is used in a limited, strategic fashion to win patients' cooperation, facilitate diagnosis and buttress the doctors' authority, rather than to give equal time or relativize biomedical knowledge [33]. Such health workers are often unable to take a critical view of their own professional role when clinic discourse defines them as ideal care providers for Asian immigrants. Indeed, stereotypical cultural concepts are deployed to construct an intersubjective reality that seeks to manipulate, incorporate and supplant Khmer notions of healing, body-care and knowledge. A main argument of this essay is that Khmer patients themselves learn to manipulate these expectations for their own ends. ("Making" 1248)

A main argument of this book is that both sides of assimilative encounter as analyzed by Ong here, both the care providers' blindness to their own ideosomatic manipulations and the patients' manipulative adaptations to the ideosomatics of the host community, are perfectly ordinary functions of the ideosomatic regulation of reality and identity. These are the normative somatic pressures humans use to create and maintain group conformity and cohesion. The tonal indignation that lurks just behind the surface of Ong's rhetoric (in the article; it is edited out of the book) is partly a function, I suggest, of her unmasking strategies, her somewhat impatient demystifications of the idealized faces that members of these groups put on what they are doing and why—demystificatory strategies that seem to me to take individuals' submission to the ideosomatic regulation of knowledge, especially the knowledge of how knowledge is ideosomatically regulated, to be some kind of failing or weakness.

Partly also, though, I think, there is a kind of vestigial identity essentialism at work in Ong's approach, a belief that people should be and remain who they are, and not become something they're not in response to a new regulatory ideosomatic. Thus "Khmer patients themselves learn to manipulate these expectations for their own ends" becomes an accusation, directed primarily, perhaps, against the mystified care providers who think they are encountering "real" people shaped by a "real" culture but are in fact only encountering phantoms of their own normative group pressures. From the standpoint of somatic theory, encountering such phantoms is at once a symptom of, and a regulatory response to, ideosomatic dysregulation: both a reflection of the frustration the mental health care providers feel at not being able to organize the normative circulation of biomedical authority through these recalcitrant foreign bodies (because the bodies do not respond properly, do not show somatic signs of responding conformatively to local group pressures), and a renewed attempt to effect that circulation.

1.1.2.3 PANICKED LOCONORMATIVITY AND COSMOPOLITAN METANORMATIVITY

In her book-length study of Hutu refugees in Tanzania, the Finnish anthropologist Liisa H. Malkki reads "refugeeness" as a subversion of "the categorical quality of the national order of things" (6), as a liminal phenomenon that is by definition "unclassified/unclassifiable" (7), so that refugees become an anthropological anomaly, "at once no longer classified and not yet classified. They are no longer unproblematically citizens or native informants. They can no longer satisfy as 'representatives' of a particular local culture. One might say they have lost a kind of imagined cultural authority to stand for 'their kind' or for the imagined 'whole' of which they are or were a part" (7). "At this level," she adds, "they represent an *attack* on the categorical order of nations which so often ends up being perceived as natural and, therefore, as inherently legitimate" (8, emphasis added). In response to this perceived threat to the naturalization of the nation-state as the primary political emblem of categorical order, and thus to the universalization of hegemonic loconormativity, refugee studies tend, she argues, both to *interiorize* the anomaly as a problem "within the bodies and minds of people classified as refugees" (8), as a psychopathology, and to *exteriorize* "the refugee from the national (and, one might say, cosmological) order of things" (9).

Similarly, Giorgio Agamben writes in *Homo Sacer:*

If refugees (whose number has continued to grow in our century, to the point of including a significant part of humanity today) represent such a disquieting element in the order of the modern nation-state, this is above all because by breaking the continuity between man and citizen, *nativity* and *nationality,* they put the originary fiction of modern sovereignty in crisis. Bringing to light the difference between birth and nation, the refugee causes the secret presupposition of the political domain—bare life—to appear for an instant within that domain. (131, emphasis in original)

This "crisis" might, I suggest, be thematized along lines mapped out by Judith Butler, as a form of "panicked loconormativity," a desperate attempt to protect and police the ideal naturalization of loconormative ideosomatics through the analytical containment of the refugee—or, to quote Butler out of context, as "an incessant and *panicked* imitation of its own naturalized idealization" ("Imitation" 23, emphasis in original). Reading Butler through somatic theory, I would emend that formulation slightly to read "an incessant and panicked *homeostatic circulation of somatic mimeses* of its own naturalized idealization"—a somatic clarification of imitation as not just the production of mimetic images but also the circulatory dissemination through the group of loconormativizing somatomimetic *pressures* intended to stabilize the collective construction of identity and reality homeostatically. To the extent that the figure of the refugee introduces panic into this homeostatic group regulation, then, it might be seen as *allostatic panic,* a stress response to (perceived) destabilizing change in the sociopolitical environment.

If panicked loconormativity is quintessentially a sedentary phenomenon, normally found among the therapists and researchers and other authorities of refugees' resettlement communities, it can also be found, as Malkki's fieldwork with Hutu refugees suggests, among the displaced. She cites Paul Gilroy's concept of "ethnic absolutism," "a reductive, essentialist understanding of ethnic and national difference which operates through *an absolute sense of culture so powerful* that it is capable of separating people off from each other and diverting them into social and historical locations that are understood to be mutually impermeable and incommensurable" (Gilroy 115, quoted in Malkki 14–15, emphasis in original). Gilroy is primarily concerned with the expulsive operation of ethnic absolutism in sedentary loconormative contexts, for example the "contemporary politics of racial exclusion" (Gilroy 114, quoted in Malkki 15) that drives the British to exclude dark-skinned citizens from "the national body"—this would be a theorization of the impulse to ethnic cleansing that drives populations into refugee flight. But Malkki notes that "not all displaced people are led to challenge ethnic absolutism—on the contrary, I will argue that *some* circumstances of exile may positively *produce* it" (15, emphasis in original):

The most unusual and prominent social fact about the camp [the Mishamo Refugee Settlement in western Tanzania] was that its inhabitants were continually engaged in an impassioned construction and reconstruction of their history as "a people." The narrative production of this history ranged from descriptions of the "autochthonous" origins of Burundi as a "nation" and of the primordial social harmony that prevailed among the originary inhabitants (the Twa and the Hutu), to the coming of the pastoral Tutsi "foreigners from the north," to the Tutsi theft of power from the "natives" (Hutu and Twa) by ruse and trickery, and, finally, to the culminating mass killings of Hutu by Tutsi in 1972. These narratives, ubiquitous in the camp, formed an overarching historical trajectory that was fundamentally also a national story about the "rightful natives" of Burundi. The camp refugees saw themselves as a nation in exile, and defined exile, in turn, as a moral trajectory of trials and tribulations that would ultimately empower them to reclaim (or create anew) the "homeland" in Burundi. (2)

Since the Hutu refugees in Tanzania have been driven out of that idealized homeland, their constructions of national unity constitute a kind of panicked *xenonormativity* that suppresses panic by reconstituting itself as loconormativity—"ironically," as Malkki notes, "people there deployed their very refugeeness in an effort to achieve this!" (4), which is to say, they deployed their panicked xenonormativity in an effort to achieve the ideosomatized effect of serene loconormativity.

Those Hutu refugees resettled in the small Kigoma township took a different approach:

In contrast, the town refugees had not constructed such a categorically distinct, collective identity. Rather than defining themselves collectively as "the Hutu refugees" (or even just as "the Hutu"), they tended to seek ways of assimilating and of inhabiting multiple, shifting identities—identities derived or "borrowed" from the social context of the township. Here, identities were like "porous sieves" (Tambiah 1986:6) to move in and out of, and assimilation was always intricately situational. In the course of the everyday, those in town were creating not a heroized national identity, but rather a lively cosmopolitanism—a worldliness that led the camp refugees to see them as an impure, problematic element in the "total community" of the Hutu refugees heroized as a people in exile. (2)

This is roughly the assimilative encounter that I have identified as the primal scene of refugee studies, but Malkki here insists that what the Hutu in town assimilate to is not local Tanzanian ideosomatic regulation but a situ-

ationally disaggregated identity, a kind of identity versatility that ideosomatizes not panicked loconormativity but what we might call *metanormativity*,
the ability to perform multiple shifting normativities. Metanormativity might
be seen as the equivalent in the refugee encounter of Judith Butler's "camp"
identities, another kind of camp, the "parodic or imitative effect of gay identities" ("Imitation" 21)—for while the Hutu in the township do not exactly
parody the Tanzanians, their metanormative assimilation to Tanzanian identities some of the time serves the same mimetic function of undermining
the panicked loconormativity that would naturalize and universalize itself as
"pure national identity." Because it is a performative act, a kind of "lively"
cosmopolitan playacting, it undermines essentialist constructions of identity;
but because that performativity is also ideosomatized, circulated somatically
through the group as an approved construction of identity, it produces a collective calm that stands in significant contrast to panicked loconormativity.
(At least this is how Malkki presents it, perhaps romanticizingly: as "a sweeping refusal to be categorized, a refusal to be fixed within one and only one
national or categorical identity, and one and only one historical trajectory"
[4], which sounds to me like it might be a heroized postmodern/postcolonial
construct, one that deliberately obscures the dysregulatory pain and resulting
panic of assimilation. But then, I wasn't there.)

1.1.3 Types of Refugee Dysregulation

In refugee studies, Malkki notes, refugees "are constituted . . . as an anomaly
requiring specialized correctives and therapeutic interventions. It is striking how often the abundant literature claiming refugees as its object of study
locates 'the problem' not first in the political oppression or violence that produces massive territorial displacements of people, but within the bodies and
minds of people classified as refugees" (8). This therapeutic orientation, which
we've seen Malkki calling "interiorization," is a product of what I have been
identifying as the assimilative primal scene of refugee studies. What I want
to do here in §1.1.3 is to problematize that broad generalization with two
examples of refugee studies that partly do and partly do not fit Malkki's characterization—Maria Pfister-Ammende's taxonomy of refugee pathologies in
"The Problem of Uprooting" and Mia Flores-Borquez's tracing of her own
trajectory through the four stages of refugee dysregulation in "A Journey to
Regain My Identity"—followed by some reflections on the implications of
these empirical findings for postcolonial studies.

1.1.3.1 Types of Refugee Rootedness and Uprootedness in a Swiss Refugee Camp, 1944

Maria Pfister-Ammende was a Swiss Freudian psychoanalyst; her study of refugee dysregulation should be read as part of the collective "therapeutic" effort by the Swiss government to reregulate the refugee hordes that had fled Nazi Germany into the safety of neutral Switzerland, via a massive research project (of which she was the director) funded by the Swiss Academy of Medical Sciences in 1944 to study "the psychological aspects of the refugee *problem* in Switzerland" (7, emphasis added). Her analysis, she tells us, is "based on the records of psychological interviews of 300 'normal' refugees, 700 case histories of refugees and Swiss repatriates suffering from mental disturbances as well as on socio-psychological observations among about 2000 Soviet-Russian refugees" (7).

And yet, surprisingly, perhaps, given the general therapeutic tendency to pathologize the refugee, according to Pfister-Ammende "the overwhelming majority of the persons interviewed retained a sense of inner security and appeared to be rooted. They were held by: Natural, tangible *ties to their real, still existing country of origin* and to the relatives that remained there. These people regarded themselves as being away from home only temporarily. Their country was still a living reality, a social area of activity and spiritual shelter. Although the ties to their world had been cut outwardly, they were unimpaired within" (9, emphasis in original). I assume what she means there by "natural" is "unforced, organic," what I would describe with Derrida's term "iterative," so that what she calls "natural" ties would be ones formed slowly over time through group interaction; by "tangible" I assume she means "felt," which is to say somatic, so that tangible ties would be indices of the somatic exchange. The ties these refugees seem to feel to their home country and relatives, then—their "roots"—are iterosomatic impulses that they continue to circulate with remaining members of those original groups, or, if they are now completely cut off from those groups, circulate imaginatively, based on memory-images of the regulatory somatic exchange. Although that somatic exchange has now become xenonormative, they are—at least as viewed from without—still sustained by it, and "unimpaired within."

In other interviewees, these ties are more problematic. She describes the Zionists as sustained inwardly by ties to Israel, which they have never visited, to which they are simply hoping to emigrate—imaginary ties, in a way, in some sense just as imaginary as the remembered xenonormativity of those still rooted in a lost home, but somatically speaking the iterosomatic impulses that both groups circulate, whether of a lost past home or of a desired future one, are equally tangible and equally sustaining. And she describes the nostalgic, whose continued rootedness in the lost home country tends to overwhelm all their present experiences and future plans with melancholy and bitterness, and thus to destabilize their group identities. For them, the felt chasm between past rooted loconormativity and present uprooted xenonormativity, between the living feel of the circulation of iterosomatized values and norms through people, places, and things in an organic community and the waning regulatory efficacy of memory images of that somatic circulation in a refugee camp, is too painful to be ignored. Religious faith, too, seems to be easy for some refugees to sustain, despite the scattering of the faithful from the iterosomatized ritual practices and spaces, from the organic community that makes gods and spirits and other imagined supernatural forces and processes feel real and present by circulating the body language and body states of belief in them, while for others their uprooting from that community and those spaces has the effect of rendering the iterosomatic basis of religion empty and inefficacious, and the religion itself therefore a sham.

Significantly, Pfister-Ammende notes that "an *intimate relationship with others present,* whether friends or relatives, did not constitute as firm a hold as one would expect because the free flow of affection and the feeling of security in such ties suffered from the mental and emotional strain due to circumstances and the uncertain future" (10, emphasis in original). Even when some significant segment of the organic community survives intact, in other words—especially a couple, or a family, nuclear or extended—the regulatory circulation of ideosomatic cohesiveness and security is disrupted by the loss of iterosomatized group associations with persons, places, and things in the past and the inability of the remaining group to impose reassuring ideosomatic regulation on an "uncertain future."

And here let us return to the question of the exosomatization of places and things that I raised in my discussion of the application of Allan Schore's affect regulation theory to the refugee experience—the equally dysregulatory and traumatizing effects of scattering either familiar *people* (the regulatory group) or familiar *places and things,* suggesting a counterintuitive parallel between people (who can feel) and places and things (which cannot). I began to address this parallel in §1.1.1.3, in connection with Michael Taussig's discussion of the magical curative powers of carved wooden fetish objects; but Pfister-Ammende's vague references to "rootedness" seem to require a more thorough theorization of the group somatization of "home," of familiar spaces and objects. Since somatic response is a function of the mammalian nervous system, the somatic exchange is primarily a circulation of regulatory body language and body states through human groups—though it is also possible for humans to enter into a somatic exchange with other mammals, and people often do with their pets. It is also possible, however, for humans to exosomatize (put somatic roots down into) objects and spaces by circulating regulatory somatic responses to them through the human group: the way an object is touched or held or looked at, the way a space is walked through or paused in, the postural and gestural and other kinesic orientations to a thing or a place that a group circulates in the sense of picking them up from others mimetically and modeling them in turn for others' mimetic appropriation, all make it seem to the group as if somatic response (the "exosoma") were actually *growing out* of the objects and spaces in question. In the process, sense impressions—sights, sounds, smells, feels, tastes—are somatized as well, indeed often fetishized as the media through which exosomatic response is channeled between humans and objects and spaces (see Appadurai).

When Pfister-Ammende talks about "roots," therefore, and refers vaguely to "home" and the "existing country of origin," or, more specifically, to "familiar surroundings" or the "given environment" or a "maternal soil," she is, I think, getting at something like this exosomatization of places and things: the sense of being at home in a specific dwelling and a specific neighborhood because you and the other members of your group live in them and work in them and walk through them and stop to talk in them, and have been doing so for years; the sense of being at home with certain objects, cooking utensils, books, photos, pieces of furniture, because you and other members of your group handle them, use them. We know that it feels difficult to move from one house or apartment to another, even when we take our things with us, because at first everything feels different, feels alien, and it takes months, sometimes years, to exosomatize the new spaces so that they come to feel like our own, and to resomatize our old things in spatial realignment with the new spaces. The refugee is typically bereft of the old exosomatized places *and* the old exosomatized things, as well as the human group that originally helped exosomatize those places and things as familiar, as "own," as real.[5] And while some, especially the children, do begin quickly to exosomatize the new places and things, and to feel the group of refugees in a camp or other resettlement as the new relevant exosomatizing group, others, especially the older ones, take much longer to shift their somatic allegiances and alliances to the new group and the new places and things, and some never adjust at all.[6]

Pfister-Ammende classifies the "uprooted" (or ideosomatically dysregulated) individuals she found in the Swiss refugee camps into seven types: "[1] isolated individuals from groups needing, but lacking leadership; [2] persons with roots but suffering from severe trauma; [3] those identifying with a social or professional class" (12); [4] drifters and escapists, who "have been drifting all their lives and have never entered into a genuine relationship," and who "generally get along well in life, also as emigrants" (12); [5] neurotics, who may be temporarily liberated from their old fixationally somatized conflicts or may simply transfer "the object of their projections" (12) to the new surroundings; [6] egotists who take pleasure but "cannot give love or accept responsibility" (13); and [7] what she calls, in German, *Problematiker*, people who are "forever driven to deep and serious thinking about problematical questions" (13; bracketed numbering added). Pfister-Ammende says of types (4–7) that they are "rootless regardless of emigration," and indeed "some of them chose emigration unconsciously because they preferred this form of life to the demands and obligations of an organized society" (14)—so I propose to set them aside as not dysregulated by sociopolitical upheavals that might be described as (post)colonial.

The first group of ideosomatically dysregulated refugees are those whose at-homeness in ideosomatic regulation requires leadership—those for whom the kind of imperceptible somatic exchange that is typically found in a group of friends or other equals, where everyone acts unconsciously as both leader and led, where everyone circulates both authoritative and submissive somatic orientations, will not do. Pfister-Ammende finds this form of dysregulation "particularly in those individuals who had the chance to live in camps conducted by competent leaders. If the leadership failed, however, because a good leader was replaced by an incapable one, dramatic anxiety and flight psychoses of the entire group occurred" (10). She distinguishes between passive and active subtypes of this dysregulatory response:

> The passively reacting individual freezes: either he will become ill and wither away like a wounded animal, or he remains outwardly adjusted to his environment, hiding his total inner upset ("Innere Totalirritation") behind a perfect front. The inner chaos of such people is often masked by a semblance of indifference or amiability—their dreams or a Rorschach-test will reveal their true mental and emotional state. The actively reacting person may show frank antisocial tendencies. Withdrawn from his social environment through lack of libidinous ties, he lives in a state of irritation, disarray and alienation. It is difficult to establish real contact with these people and to restore their inner calm. (10–11)

The second group is so deeply traumatized as to be unable to marshal either xenonormative orientations ("people who have roots, but whose suffering has been so great that they cannot go on despite good will and great effort"

[11]) or new group membership ("the isolated individual who is unable to live outside his group" [11]—"his" group meaning the old group, now lost) as a regulatory foundation for a new life. "Such people frequently do not react at all and continue to exist in a state of living death . . . they were not in a state of inner upset but rather in one of silent hopeless surrender" (11).

Perhaps the most interesting of Pfister-Ammende's three dysregulated refugee types is the third, in whom the group affiliation destroyed by flight and resettlement is what Benedict Anderson calls an "imagined community," or what Kurt Vonnegut in *Cat's Cradle* calls a "granfalloon," a group formed not "naturally" (in Pfister-Ammende's term) or iterosomatically (in mine), through repeated iterations of a formative somatic exchange, but mentally, based on an unsomatized *wish* for connection. The imagined community is to the ideosomatically organized group as the Douglas MacArthur doll for the isolated Western artist is to the wooden carved Douglas MacArthur fetish object for the San Blas Cuna: an unsomatized simulacrum. Vonnegut's examples of granfalloons include "the Communist Party, the Daughters of the American Revolution, the General Electric Company, the International Order of Odd Fellows—and any nation, anytime, anywhere" (82), reminding us that the nation is Anderson's exemplary case of the imagined community, formed, he argues, around "national print-languages," standardized and thus "universalized" (nationalized) dialects that artificially unite speakers of regional dialects, sociolects, genderlects, and so on. The fact that the loss of their nation can be profoundly dysregulative for these refugees suggests that they were previously regulated not so much by ideosomatic group pressures as by the unsomatized *idea* of such pressures.[7] Pfister-Ammende also gives examples of "those who *identified themselves with their social class or profession* which had come to mean everything to them" (11, emphasis in original), and of middle-aged women who drew all their emotional resources from a stereotyped idea or image of themselves as mothers and wives:

> Not infrequently this type is unable to change or adjust, not for lacking activity but rather the ability for individual development and the creation of a life of her own. I have seen such women inaudibly break down after loss of home and husband. However they did continue to keep up appearances and the front they presented to the outside world appeared intact. They adjusted and even clung to their given environment, the camp, for instance. Although possessing strong feelings they were passive by nature; the vitality deriving from their environment had vanished and they had succumbed to the forces sweeping away their social milieu; security and stability were gone along with their social environment. We are here deal-

ing with a pseudo-rootedness ("Pseudoverwurzelung") because identification with and adherence to a social level have nothing in common with real security springing from a maternal soil, or with the vitality of those sustained by a universal idea for the common good. (11–12)

I would emend two of Pfister-Ammende's formulations there: first, by noting that a woman's "ability for individual development and the creation of a life of her own" is not a purely individual phenomenon; in order to feel right, to feel real, to feel authenticated or ontologized or even sociobiologized, "individual development" and "a life of her own" must be circulated through the group, must receive group approval and support, must in the end be *defined* as those things via somatic exchange within the group. This suggests that "this type is unable to change or adjust" not so much for lack of "the ability for individual development and the creation of a life of her own" but rather for lack of an ideosomatized group life of her own, a sense that she is somatically valued as an individual by a group. Her unsomatized stereotypes are not enough to sustain her. And second, "a universal idea for the common good" can quite obviously be just another unsomatized mentation that generates a granfalloon or a "pseudo-rootedness": that sort of idea will sustain identity through upheavals only if it has been, and continues to be, in flight and resettlement, iterosomatized through significant interaction with a group.

1.1.3.2 THE FOUR STAGES OF REFUGEE DYSREGULATION

Refugee dysregulation can also be organized into chronological phases or stages (based loosely on Stein, and Vega, Kolody, and Valle):

1. dysregulation at home (invasion, ethnic cleansing, civil war, ruthless dictator, natural disaster);
2. dysregulation in flight (loss of home and community, hiding, marching, refugee camps);
3. dysregulation of initial contact with new host community (pre-assimilation);
4. dysregulation of continued contact with new host community, despite assimilation, due to traumatic memories.

We have already seen some of these in the essay so far: Pfister-Ammende's study of the Swiss refugee camps gives us part of (2), and her first section, "Flight," gives us the other part;[8] Stefi Pedersen's first case study, the woman in the department store, gives us a single example of (3); and Dorsh Marie de Voe's study of Tibetan refugees, Aihwa Ong's study of Cambodian refugees, and Liisa Malkki's study of Hutu refugees all situate us roughly in the time frame of (4). Very few refugee studies focus on dysregulation of the home situation or dysregulation during flight, not just because clinicians and researchers are typically found either in stable host communities (like Pedersen and Ong) or in refugee camps (like Pfister-Ammende and Malkki), not in the midst of civil wars or ethnic genocides or on long forced marches, but also because, as I suggested above, the assimilative encounter between refugees and their new hosts (including the researcher) is the organizing moment of refugee studies. Some researchers, like Ong in the first two chapters of *Buddha,* do provide accounts told them by the refugees they study of their traumatic experiences before, during, and after their departure from their homes; but these tend to be background material, early stages in the chronological sequences that lead up to their main focus, internment and (especially) assimilation.[9]

Rather than theorize each stage in turn, I propose to take a quick look at a single first-person scholarly account that covers all four, a self-analytical refugee "memoir" entitled "A Journey to Regain My Identity" by Mia Flores-Borquez, who as a teenager in 1976 fled from Pinochet's Chile with her mother. As the daughter of a prominent leftist activist (the mother), Flores-Borquez was actively involved at a very early age in the election of Salvador Allende to the presidency in 1970, and, after his election, in various political activities in the new regime: "During this time I became a student union leader and fought for the rights of indigenous Mapuche Indian students who were the subject of much discrimination. I also politicized the farmers close to the college where I lived, and in a highly right-wing community, I was forgiven for my political actions because I was also developing cultural activities that had not previously reached the locality" (96).

The CIA-backed military coup in September 1973, then, which assassinated Allende and installed Pinochet in his place, was for her the dysregulatory event in (1), the home situation. Mother and daughter were placed under surveillance, and their house was repeatedly searched; the mother was fired from her teaching job and became unemployable, and the daughter lost her scholarship and, in order to continue her schooling, was forced to move to Santiago and live with her father. Under cover of cultural activities, both mother and daughter continued to struggle clandestinely against the military government, until the mother was captured by the secret service and tortured, drugged, and brainwashed; finally she managed to escape her captors and, with the help of others in the underground, abducted Flores-Borquez and took her into hiding, where for six months—the dysregulation in (2), flight—

fearing every moment for her life, the daughter cared for her mother and four other escaped torture victims, all of whom were severely traumatized. After many maneuverings, involving visas to four separate countries, they finally arrived in Britain, where she "experienced ignorance, rejection, hostility, violence, prejudice, and discrimination" (102)—the dysregulation in (3), initial contact.

Still, Flores-Borquez's intelligence and political activism helped her assimilate—as Maria Pfister-Ammende noted in the Swiss refugee camps, political convictions and activities help refugees remain rooted. She also attributes some of her assimilation to opportunism: "I have observed that in order to gain access to scarce resources, refugees with a political background internalize (Rycroft 1968) the values of the host community. This means that they are absorbed into the cultural orientation of 'economic' refugees. In order to survive (physically, socially, and psychologically) it would appear that refugees have to conform to the normative expectations of the culture that provides refuge. This is something that puts them in conflict with their own identity" (103)—their old identities, obviously, the ones shaped ideosomatically in the cultures they have left behind. This notion that an identity is a stable thing that is threatened by assimilation to another culture seems like it must have been one of the individualistic notions she picked up in the course of assimilating to British culture. She seems to want to portray her submission to British ideosomatic regulation as a refugee dysregulation; it is actually only an allostatic reregulation. She was well enough assimilated to attend Oxford, where she studied counseling; later worked at Oxford as a lecturer and research associate; and then became a research consultant at Oxford Brookes University, where she has been involved in international projects on forced migration, trauma, and refugee resettlement. Flores-Borquez is also the founder and director of Justicia, a charity organization dedicated to providing support for victims of human rights violations.

And yet despite her assimilation and professional success, throughout the nineteen years from her flight to her writing of this article in 1995 Flores-Borquez was plagued by a PTSD symptomatology including "weepiness, crying for no apparent reason, sleep disturbance, nightmares, loss of appetite, uncontrolled weight gain, cognitive impairment, anxiety, fear, suicidal thoughts, and social withdrawal" (98), or what she calls, quoting Walter Benjamin, a "state of emergency" (104)—the dysregulation in (4), continued contact. She herself did not associate these symptoms with her refugee experience until 1994, when widespread media coverage of "the plight of detained asylum seekers in the United Kingdom who, failing in their attempts to obtain political asylum, were faced with deportation" (97), produced in her a series of flashbacks from her previous experience, charged with intense identificatory traumata. Television images of "resolute men and women inside a high security fenced compound" and of "video cameras, uniformed guards, and barbed wire . . . evoked my own feelings of helplessness, as well as of anger, at my own involuntary captivity with the group of escaped severely tortured political prisoners prior to leaving Chile" (98).

In working through the impact that the 1994 media images of the detained asylum seekers had on her, Flores-Borquez realized that the most severely traumatizing moment in her past was her abduction by her mother—the dysregulation of (2), flight—and in fact that the trauma was worse because her abductor was her mother than it would have been had it been the secret service: "Summerfield (1993) points out that individuals with a political background who have experienced the trauma of repression and persecution, can come to terms with their experience better when they view it as the consequence of their political activities. As I recall now, I realize the feelings that I experienced then were that I had been abducted not by the secret service because of my activities in the underground resistance movement, but by my mother because of her activities" (99). "Thus," she notes, "at that crucial moment my deep political sense of duty was denied and my own identity demolished" (100). (This same identity that at the moment of abduction is "demolished" later "comes into conflict" with British assimilative pressures, suggesting that perhaps "demolished" is too strong a descriptive term; that she is radically dysregulated, however, is clear.) Her mother's assurances that she (Flores-Borquez) would sooner or later have been abducted as well did not help, especially since (a) her mother was convinced that the daughter would have been abducted as a way of putting pressure on the mother, and "even if I was raped and tortured in front of her, she would not reveal any information in order to save me" (100); and (b) she never felt loved by her mother, who was always more of a comrade than a nurturing mother. What's more:

> From the moment that I went into hiding, I became the voice of my mother. Due to the severity of the torture inflicted upon her, she lost the ability to walk and, once she had told me the details of her story, lost her ability to speak. I experienced, through her, the horrific nightmares that she suffered as well as witnessing by day her terror at any sound or movement, fearing that the secret service were trying to reabduct her. My world for six months was one in which people—my mother and the other four escapees—spoke of torture, exhibited horrific physical evidence of torture, and at night relived in their dreams the atrocities that they had experienced and observed done to others. (100)

Through the somatic exchange, in other words, Flores-Borquez not only assumes the voice but simulates the body of her mother, not only talks but walks and feels for and with her, experiencing in her own body, through the circulatory power of somatic mimeticism, her mother's pain and trauma and terror. Living in a somatic simulacrum of her mother's tortured body, at the same time as she was living in the pain and powerlessness she felt at being abducted and spirited out of her life into hiding by her mother, created an extreme ideosomatic dysregulation (2) in her, a breakdown in the normal functioning of her physioemotional body; but what kept her weeping irrationally, sleeping badly, eating little but gaining weight, living with constant anxieties, fears, and thoughts of suicide, and pulling away from other people for nineteen years was not so much that ideosomatic dysregulation but her allostatic *adaptation* to it, the building of her allostasis into a new (re)regulatory regime, the sublimation of trauma as a (new) normal state (4). This form of allostatic overload normalizes the adaptation to ideosomatic dysregulation into a kind of idiosomatic regulation, a "normality" that no one else around her experiences; but it is also an example of paleosomatic regulation, the survival of an old regulatory allostasis long after the era of its adaptiveness is past—the topic of the Third Essay.

The fact that the dysregulations of home (1) and of initial contact (3) seem to have had very little traumatizing effect on Flores-Borquez does not, of course, mean that they are invariably minor factors in the dysregulatory refugee experience: this is just one story, and there are tens of millions. Empirical studies (like Jensen or Vega, Kolody, and Valle) of refugee allostatic overload that attempt to establish which group is the most stressed, those dysregulated by (1) and (4), those regulated by (2) and (4), or those regulated by (3) and (4), are by their very nature inescapably inconclusive because no one could possibly study every refugee in the world, and no random sample could ever accurately represent an entire population.

1.1.3.3 ON THE SOMATIC EXCHANGE IN ACADEMIC AND LITERARY DISCOURSE

The somatic exchange consists of the *viral* circulation of somatic response, not just through the members of a given group but also from group to group. In this case, Flores-Borquez's mother and her fellow escapees form a group that shares the traumatizing experience of torture and imprisonment at least through the body language of physical pain, and probably also through somatized spoken words. Their somatic exchange is communicated through body language and spoken words to Flores-Borquez, somatically exchanged with her, primarily through the mother's words ("once she had told me the details of her story"), but also through visual and perhaps tactile impressions of body language ("witnessing by day her terror at any sound or movement") and bodily signs ("exhibited horrific physical evidence of torture"), so that she becomes a kind of outside member of the group herself, but more important so that mother and daughter constitute a new group, "infected" virally by the old. Flores-Borquez then becomes the new "carrier" who communicates that mother-daughter exchange through the medium of the written word, somatically exchanging it with potentially thousands of readers, including me, so that now Flores-Borquez and (at least) I form a new somatic exchange virally infected with the somatic responses of the mother–daughter exchange. Finally I become the carrier that communicates it to you, again through the written word, creating a new somatic exchange and a new viral infection. Each new group, by simulating in their own individual bodies the circulated body states of the carrier, and circulating also those individual simulations, experiences (feels, senses) a somatomimetic construct of what the old group felt, and feels the anti-torture ideosomatic pressures brought to bear in and by each group in turn. (The viral circulation of somatic orientations is my model for intergenerational trauma, the topic of the Third Essay.)

To the extent that this somatomimetic virus is carried by words, the somatics of language comes into play—the ways in which verbal language arises out of body language and never entirely detaches from it, the ways in which words are saturated with bodily orientations, inclinations, tonalizations, and other performances. If, as Shoshana Felman suggests, a speech act is "an enigmatic and problematic production of the *speaking body,* [it] destroys from its inception the metaphysical dichotomy between the domain of the 'mental' and the domain of the 'physical,' breaks down the opposition between body and spirit, between matter and language" (65, emphasis in original). The "enigmatic and problematic production" of Flores-Borquez's mother's speaking body in hiding, just barely able to produce a verbalization of pain before losing the capacity for speech altogether, is a powerful example of the somatics of language; as Flores-Borquez makes clear, the fully embodied speech acts her battered mother performs before falling silent are the primary carrier of her pain into her daughter's body.[10] In §1.2, §2.1.3.3, §2.2.2.4, and §3.2, I offer readings of postcolonial literary texts in terms of precisely this infectious power, this viral contagion of somatic response.

But what of academic discourse? In the somatic exchange Flores-Borquez sets up with her academic readers, including me (and through me, you), the medium of somatomimetic response is the academic written word, which reduces sensory and emotional detail and so retards and obstructs the somatic transfer, in order to give the somatic impression of a desomatized mind at work purely intellectually on a problem. Because the events she is describing actually happened to her, however, and because—I'm guessing—she assumes that her reader's understanding of her intellectual argument will depend to a certain degree on a felt sympathetic response to political victimization, she refuses to abstract her account as far as, say, Pfister-Ammende, down to nameless numbered typologies. She not only tells her own story in the first person, a narrative strategy whose somatic power is familiar to us from both conversational and literary storytelling; she constructs emotionally charged scenes that might in some academic contexts be considered inflammatory, because they so flagrantly invite emotional identification ("even if I was raped and tortured in front of her, she would not reveal any information in order to save me"). At the same time, she works hard to minimize the sensory and emotional specificity of her descriptions, for the most part reducing experiences to events, events to event-types, event-types to lists, and wherever possible inserting parenthetical indices of the out-of-body distancing effects of scholarly authorities: "Thus, according to a psychoanalytic explanation, it is because of the relationship I had with my mother—lack of a sufficiently nurturing environment—that I sublimated (Rycroft 1968) my own needs and shaped my identity by attempting to help and do things for others" (100).

No matter how rigorously it reduces felt experience to mental abstraction, however, academic discourse cannot completely obstruct the somatic transfer, because that transfer is never initiated by the "sender" (s/he does not send anything) and so cannot be controlled by the "sender" either. The somatic transfer is a mimetic body response built in and by the body of the listener or viewer, based on that body's sympathetic *projection* of feeling into the other person's words—or, for that matter, into anything else in the world, including the swaying of trees or the staccato buzz of a jackhammer or the blinking of a cursor on a computer screen. Anything we see or hear may seem to us to have feelings that it wants to share with us, because we have been socialized to construct meaningful communication by entering into somatic exchanges with humans, with pets, with computers, with cars, with Douglas MacArthur figurines, with anything at all, even if that means doing all the work ourselves. (The thing is, in mimicking other people's body language and simulating their body states we typically don't feel ourselves doing any work at all: it's mostly unconscious. So it seems like no problem to us to construct a somatic exchange with a cloud or a tree. We scarcely notice ourselves doing that either.)

Still, it does make a difference how we as writers and speakers build verbal edifices as media for readers' and listeners' somatomimetic response. The writer or speaker of verbal discourse may not be able to control the somatic exchange that ensues from it, but s/he can shape it. The six women whose written words we have been reading in this essay thus far have all used more or less the same academic discourse, some (Pedersen, Flores-Borquez) more personally, others (de Voe, Ong, Malkki, Pfister-Ammende) more impersonally, but all offering their readers abstract images of refugees designed to bring those readers into the somatic vicinity of the refugee encounter but not too close—not as close as, say, Edwidge Danticat does in the literary accounts of Haitian refugees that we'll be reading next in §1.2.

1.2 LITERARY REPRESENTATIONS: EDWIDGE DANTICAT LEAVING HAITI

Edwidge Danticat was born in Haiti in 1969. When she was four, her parents Rose and André Danticat, fleeing Jean-Claude "Baby Doc" Duvalier's terror by immigrating to the United States, left her and her little brother Eliab André in the care of relatives in Port-au-Prince and could not bring them to America until Edwidge was twelve, by which time she had two new brothers, Karl and Kelly. Danticat incorporated the rough outlines of this childhood refugee story into her first novel, *Breath, Eyes, Memory,* which she submitted as her M.F.A. thesis at Brown and then, in 1994, published with Random House/ Vintage: in the novel, Sophie Caco is left with her mother's sister Tante Atie virtually at birth, because her sixteen-year-old mother Martine has been severely traumatized by the rape in which Sophie was conceived, and Martine flees to the U.S. when Sophie is four and brings Sophie to live with her in Brooklyn when she is twelve. Like the viral somaticity of the mother–daughter relation in Mia Flores-Borquez's story, Martine's rape trauma soon "infects" Sophie as well, and the novel tells the story of both women's painful and frightening attempts to deal with the dysregulatory aftermath of sexual violence.

This first novel of Danticat's, then, covers roughly the third and fourth stages of the schematized "refugee experience" that I outlined in §1.1.3.2: the dysregulatory impact of initial contact with the foreign (new host) culture, the twelve-year-old Sophie in America, and the continuing dysregulatory effects of earlier trauma, suffered in stage (1), at home in Haiti, on later assimilation.

Danticat's second book, *Krik? Krak!* (1995), is a story collection; the first story in it is "Children of the Sea," an alternating series of letters between two teenaged lovers in the early 1990s, a boy who is fleeing the terror of the "new president" (Raoul Cedras) in a boat to Miami and a girl who is left behind with her parents, trying to escape Port-au-Prince and the savagery of the Tonton Macoutes, the militia (named for the Haitian bogeyman) that Baby Doc's father Papa Doc (François Duvalier) created to terrorize the Haitian populace into submission.[11] This story covers stages (1) and (2) of the schema, dysregulation at home and in flight; what I propose to do in this section is to read first the story as a fictional exploration of the ideosomatic dysregulation at home (1) that drives people into flight (2), and then the novel as a fictional exploration of the ideosomatic dysregulation that awaits them at the end of their flight (3) and that they carry with them into their new homes (4).

Danticat is also the author of *The Farming of Bones* (1998), about the 1937 genocide of Haitians in the Dominican Republic, and of *The Dew Breaker* (2005), about a Tonton Macoute who has moved to the United States and tried to put his own criminal past behind him, but who finds himself driven to confess to his American-born daughter what he did—but I will be referring to those books only in passing.

1.2.1 Home (1) and Flight (2): "Children of the Sea"

Let me begin with three remarks that Danticat has made in interviews about how she writes, for whom, and with what models:

> My models were oral, were storytellers. Like my grandmothers and my aunts. It's true, a lot of people in my life were not literate in a formal sense, but they were storytellers. So I had this experience of just watching somebody spin a tale off the top of her head. I loved that. She would engage an audience, and she would read people's faces to see if what she was saying was captivating them. If it was boring, she would speed up, and if it was too fast, she would slow down. So that whole interaction between the storyteller and the listeners had a very powerful influence on me. (Barsamian 33)

> I have always been fascinated by history, but the kind of history that's told by ordinary people; that to me is the biggest story of history/herstory— the personal narrative. That's why I wanted to recreate an event through one voice [in *The Farming of Bones*]. For example, I remember in high school reading *The Diary of Anne Frank* and feeling that through that one young woman's voice, we grasp the horror and the fear of her experience so strongly because we're not only getting a report of what's happening, but individual reactions to it. I've always been fascinated by these individual

voices in history and the fact that one person's voice adds to another and that creates a chorus. (Anglesey 36)

I have this mental split because I wonder, am I the one to write this story [*The Farming of Bones*]? Maybe someone who went through it should write it. In some ways I feel presumptuous, as though I were taking their place, but in some ways to be able to write it, you have to feel as though someone is lending you their voice, their story, and you're the mediator. (Shea 50)

Storytelling is not a solo art; it is a group performance, grounded in the somatic interaction between teller and listeners ("engage," "captivating," "boring," "speed up," "slow down"). Stories are told by a succession of such group performances, a series of single voices telling personal stories to listeners, and the series of "reports" and "reactions" themselves form a kind of iterative group or "chorus." And stories are "lent" from one teller to another, retold, so that each successive teller mediates the story to a new audience, a new group.

If we take this collective conception of storytelling to be Danticat's utopian ideal, the narrative situation in "Children of the Sea" signals the dystopian disruption of that ideal: the boy in the boat and the girl in Port-au-Prince tell their stories to each other in the form of letters that their respective addressees will never see:

Your father will probably marry you off now, since I am gone. Whatever you do, please don't marry a soldier. They're almost not human. (4)

i don't sketch butterflies anymore because i don't even like seeing the sun. besides, manman says that butterflies can bring news. the bright ones bring happy news and the black ones warn us of deaths. we have our whole lives ahead of us. you used to say that, remember? but then again things were so very different then. (5)

In that sense, in fact, the story's narrative structure reperforms the refugee tale it tells: if group storytelling in Danticat's utopian model is both the ideal image and the verbal channel of ideosomatic regulation, the destruction of the storytelling group becomes not only a powerful poetic image of but the ideal narrative strategy for ideosomatic dysregulation. The book's title, *Krik? Krak!*, alludes to the utopian ideal, but in this very first story in the collection Danticat specifically contextualizes the traditional Haitian storytelling exchange in terms of its collapse, its inability to reregulate the refugees on the boat as a cohesive group: "We spent most of yesterday telling stories. Someone says,

Krik? You answer, Krak! And they say, I have many stories I could tell you, and then they go on and tell these stories to you, but mostly to themselves" (14). The boy's ideal addressee, the girl he loves and has had to leave behind in order to flee Duvalier's repression—he has been involved in a radio show that opposed the dictator—is physically absent, making it impossible for him to tell her his stories; the other people on the boat are physically present and therefore potential story-listeners, but their fear and despondency prevents even their stories from reaching the others, so that they end up telling them "mostly to themselves." Their fear and despondency are born not just from the very real danger that their boat will sink and they will all drown—this does in fact happen—but from their social and political isolation, their awareness that they have been banished from the human community:

> I feel like we are sailing for Africa. Maybe we will go to Guinin, to live with the spirits, to be with everyone who has come and has died before us. They would probably turn us away from there too. Someone has a transistor and sometimes we listen to radio from the Bahamas. They treat Haitians like dogs in the Bahamas, a woman says. To them, we are not human. Even though their music sounds like ours. Their people look like ours. Even though we had the same African fathers who probably crossed these same seas together. (14)

Social isolation breeds social isolation: because they know they are unlikely to be granted asylum anywhere they happen to land, they find it difficult to bond together in the boat. The dysregulatory somatic exchange of refugee flight is viral. Its virality is not unstoppable—as Pfister-Ammende's research showed, some refugee groups do manage to resist the dysregulatory impulse—but fighting it requires massive ideosomatic resources that traumatized groups typically cannot marshal.

But the virality of a dysregulatory somatic exchange does not stop at the peripheries of a refugee group, at the gunwales of a leaky boat, at the shifting boundaries of the "Third World." One of the reasons that we non-refugees typically put up defenses against refugee stories is that we are all too uncomfortably aware of their power to infect and dysregulate us as well. In this case, as Angelia Poon notes, "Since this exchange of letters cannot occur, only the reader is in a privileged position to read both sides of the correspondence" (par. 10). Each letter-writer writes to "you," the boy to the girl, the girl to the boy, but the only "you" who is actually "there" to receive the letters and hear the stories is the reader, who thus becomes the mediatory third party in their group, not only the mail carrier but the somatic go-between, the channel by which each one's love should make its way to the other. This places a heavy burden on the reader's shoulders: s/he is shaped somatically by the group (of three, the boy, the girl, and the reader, or of four, including Danticat herself) not simply to *desire* their happy reunion but to *effect* it. That becomes our job in the story: to bring the two lovers back together, to plug the leaks in the boat, to melt the hearts of the Bahamanian or Miamian authorities so the boy and his fellow boat people will be allowed into the country, to keep the Tonton Macoutes from killing or raping or otherwise traumatizing the girl, to help her escape Port-au-Prince and ultimately Haiti itself, across the Caribbean to the United States. But of course we can't do it. We aren't up to it.

they start to pound at her. you can hear it. you can hear the guns coming down on her head. it sounds like they are cracking all the bones in her body. manman whispers to papa, you can't just let them kill her. go and give them some money like you gave them for your daughter. papa says, the only money I have left is to get us out of here tomorrow. manman whispers, we cannot just stay here and let them kill her. manman starts moving like she is going out the door. papa grabs her neck and pins her in the latrine wall. tomorrow we are going to ville rose, he says. you will not spoil that for the family. you will not put us in that situation. you will not get us killed. going out there will be like trying to raise the dead. she is not dead yet, manman says, maybe we can help her. i will make you stay if i have to, he says to her. my mother buries her face in the latrine wall. she starts to cry. you can here madan roger screaming. they are beating her, pounding on her until you don't hear anything else. manman tells papa, you cannot let them kill somebody just because you are afraid. papa says, oh yes, you *can* let them kill somebody because you are afraid. they are the law. it is their right. we are just being good citizens, following the law of the land. it has happened before all over this country and tonight it will happen again and there is nothing we can do. (16–17)

Célianne is lying with her head against the side of the boat. The baby still will not cry. They both look very peaceful in all this chaos. Célianne is holding her baby tight against her chest. She just cannot seem to let herself throw it in the ocean. I asked her about the baby's father. She keeps repeating the story now with her eyes closed, her lips barely moving.

She was home one night with her mother and brother Lionel when some ten or twelve soldiers burst into the house. The soldiers held a gun to Lionel's head and ordered him to lie down and become intimate with his mother. Lionel refused. Their mother told him to go ahead and obey the soldiers because she was afraid that they would kill Lionel on the spot if he put up more of a fight. Lionel did as his mother told him, crying as the soldiers laughed at him, pressing the gun barrels farther and farther into his neck.

Afterwards, the soldiers tied up Lionel and their mother, then they each took turns raping Célianne. When they were done, they arrested Lionel, accusing him of moral crimes. After that night, Célianne never heard from Lionel again.

The same night, Célianne cut her face with a razor so that no one would know who she was. Then as facial scars were healing, she started throwing up and getting rashes. Next thing she knew, she was getting big. She found out about the boat and got on. She is fifteen. (23–24)

Want it as we might, we find ourselves powerless to save the two, to protect them from harm. As the story progresses, they get farther and farther apart, the reader's somatic mediation is stretched thinner and thinner as the boy's situation becomes more and more desperate and the girl's stories of Macoute brutality become more and more traumatizing, until the boy is dying and the girl is seeing black butterflies, and it's the reader's fault, the reader is the one who can't stop the violence of the Tonton Macoutes, can't keep the boat seaworthy, can't prevent the boy from throwing his notebook overboard, can't protect these two young lovers, can't make a safe haven for love. The characters exosomatize objects in a last-ditch effort to save something from destruction, but their exosomata too are destroyed, lost, the boy's notebook, Célianne's dead baby (and her own tormented fifteen-year-old body), and the butterflies:

> i am getting used to ville rose. there are butterflies here, tons of butterflies. so far none has landed on my hand, which means they have no news for me. i cannot always bathe in the stream near the house because the water is freezing cold. the only time it feels just right as at noon, and then there are a dozen eyes who might see me bathing. i solved that by getting a bucket of water in the morning and leaving it in the sun and then bathing myself once it is night under the banyan tree. the banyan tree is now my most trusted friend. they say banyans can last hundreds of years. even the branches that lean down from them become like trees themselves. a banyan could become a forest, manman says, if it were given a chance. from the spot where I stand under the banyan, i see the mountains, and behind those are more mountains still. so many mountains that are bare

like rocks. i feel like all those mountains are pushing me farther and farther away from you. (25–26)

She threw it overboard. I watched her face knot up like a thread, and then she let go. It fell in a splash, floated for a while, and then sank. And quickly after that she jumped in too. And just as the baby's head sank, so did hers. They went together like two bottles beneath a waterfall. The shock only lasts so long. There was no time to even try and save her. There was no question of it. The sea in that spot is like the sharks that live there. It has no mercy.

They say I have to throw my notebook out. The old man has to throw out his hat and his pipe. The water is rising again and they are scooping it out. I asked for a few seconds to write this last page and then promised that I would let it go. I know you will probably never see this, but it was nice imagining that I had you here to talk to. (26–27)

Both letter-writers speak of magic, the boy of the Protestants who "are hoping something will plunge down from the sky and part the sea for us" (7), the girl, a few lines later, "if I knew some good *wanga* magic, I could wipe them off the face of the earth" (7), meaning the Tonton Macoutes. The reader feels these as indirect speech acts, indirect requests to wield that kind of performative magic on behalf of these two young lovers, speak the words and the sea will be parted and the Tonton Macoutes will be killed and the two lovers will be reunited in Miami.[12] But it doesn't happen, because the reader isn't as powerful as s/he wants to be, doesn't have that performative magic. By this point in the story Danticat is circulating both impossible hopes and a crushing hopelessness through the group that includes the two storytellers and the reader, letting the boy and the girl put desperate somatic pressures on the reader to help that only underscore the reader's (like their own) helplessness. The notebook as the magic talisman or fetish object that, by storing story, will unite the lovers created by story; the butterflies exosomatized as messengers from him to her, wordless story-tellers who will tell her that he is all right, he has survived, he is in Miami waiting for her: these exosomata are offered the reader too as tools of redemption, but they don't work. Like the girl's mother in the latrine, prevented by her husband and by her own terrible knowledge that he is right, that nothing they could do would save Madan Roger, and they would die horrible deaths as well or be raped and brutalized, the reader too is caught up in collective emotional currents that cannot issue forth into action, that can only keep generating frustration and desperation and desolation, and can ultimately be released only in tears. As Bob Corbett reports in his online review of *Krik? Krak!,* when he read the story out loud to a group of university students, "there wasn't a dry eye in the room when I finished, including mine." Personally, I don't know how he finished. I can't even whisper the story to myself without choking up and becoming unable to go on.

> now there are always butterflies around me, black ones that i refuse to let find my hand. i throw big rocks at them, but they are always too fast. last night on the radio, i heard that another boat sank off the coast of the bahamas. i can't think about you being in there in the waves. my hair shivers. from here, i cannot even see the sea. behind these mountains are more mountains and more black butterflies and a sea that is endless like my love for you. (28–29)

1.2.2 Doubled Assimilation (3/4): *Breath, Eyes, Memory*

1.2.2.1 OUTWARD DISPLACEMENT

In *Breath, Eyes, Memory,* Danticat also creates a group identification that includes the reader, but a far more problematic one, one that tends first toward the exclusion of others and the suppression and outward displacement of shared feelings, and only gradually opens up as the novel proceeds. When Tante Atie tells Sophie that her mother has sent for her, has arranged for a plane ticket so Sophie can fly to New York and live with her in Brooklyn, she is desolate, as Tante Atie is the only mother she has ever known: "I only knew my mother from the picture on the night table by Tante Atie's pillow" (8). But Tante Atie convinces her not to cry:

> She squeezed my hand and whispered, "Remember that we are going to be like mountains and mountains don't cry."
> "Unless it rains," I said.
> "When it rains, it is the sky that is crying." (28)

The socially acceptable way to deal with painful emotions is simply not to feel them—to become as unfeeling as a mountain. Tante Atie gives Sophie another object lesson in how to feel when you feel bad about something: fake it.

> I picked up the spoon and began to eat. Tante Atie's lips spread into a little

grin as she watched me. Her laughter prefaced the start of what was going to be a funny story.

There were many stories that Tante Atie liked to tell. There were mostly sad stories, but every once in a while, there was a funny one. . . .

Whether something was funny or not depended on the way Tante Atie told it. That morning, she could not bring the laughter out of me like she had in the past. It was even hard for her to force it out of herself. (19)

Don't feel the bad things; only feel the good things. If you feel like crying, be a mountain, but a laughing mountain. At the airport, Tante Atie can't help herself—she cries—but Sophie has already learned her lesson, and is stoic, calm, because depersonalized. When she lands in New York and her mother is thrilled to see her, she is still a mountain, for many months. Her depersonalization is the allostatic overload with which she adapts to her radically transformed situation: new country, new language, new mother (see also Braziel, N'Zengou-Tayo).

What is interesting about Danticat's literary portrayal of Sophie's depersonalization, though, is that her allostatic response to geographical displacement is imaged through Freudian displacement. For example, Sophie is almost late for her plane because, as the cab takes her and Tante Atie through Port-au-Prince to the airport, riots break out all around them: the inner turmoil she is suppressing is displaced onto the social scene.

We stopped in front of the main entrance. The smoke had been coming from across the street. Army trucks surrounded a car in flames. A group of students were standing on top of a hill, throwing rocks at the burning car. They scurried to avoid the tear gas and the round of bullets that the soldiers shot back at them.

Some of the students fell and rolled down the hill. They screamed at the soldiers that they were once again betraying the people. One girl rushed down the hill and grabbed one of the soldiers by the arm. He raised his pistol and pounded it on top of her head. She fell to the ground, her face covered with her own blood.

Tante Atie grabbed my shoulder and shoved me quickly inside the airport gate.

"Do you see what you are leaving?" she said.

"I know I am leaving you." (34)

No hysterics: just the facts, just the bare knowledge of whom she is leaving. She doesn't need hysterics, because hysteria has exploded all around her.

On the plane, she remains calm as a woman brings a little boy in, "crying and stomping his feet, trying to wiggle out of her grasp. She cornered him against the seats and pressed him into the chair. She held him down with both her hands. He stopped fighting, slid upward in the seat, raised his head, and spat in her face" (36–37). Sophie reaches out a hand to him:

> He grabbed my hand and dug his teeth into my fingers. I hit his arm and tried to get him to release my fingers. He bit even harder. I smacked his shoulder. He let go of my fingers and began to scream.
>
> The woman rushed over. She pulled him from the seat, raised him up to her chest, and rocked him in her arms. He clung to her body for a moment then pulled away, digging his fingers into her neck. She stumbled backwards and nearly fell. He slipped out of her arms and ran out of her reach. She dashed down the aisle after him. (37)

It turns out that the boy's father, a corrupt government official, has just been killed in the rioting, and the boy is being flown to New York to live with relatives—into the unknown, just like Sophie. Sophie, who does not want to go either, could have resisted her displacement with the same kind of desperate emotional violence as the boy displays, but doesn't, perhaps because she doesn't need to: he expresses her suppressed feelings for her.

What am I suggesting, here—that Sophie has the *power* to displace her feelings onto other people? That *she* makes Port-au-Prince explode in riots, *she* inserts her suppressed resistance into the boy's unruly body? No. Danticat does it, of course. But Danticat does it not merely to "symbolize" Sophie's suppressed emotions, but rather to draw her readers into those emotions, to enable us to share Sophie's feelings, to circulate through us not only Sophie's dysregulatory trauma at being torn away from her home but also her expulsive reregulation of that trauma as well. She is able to displace Sophie's feelings onto other people because, of course, she is creating the group that feels those feelings, Sophie, Tante Atie, the boy, the rioters, and us as her own imaginary other, and can circulate whatever feelings she likes through that group, by whatever route—by obstructing or damming up feelings of angry resistance in Sophie, for example, and rerouting them through the rioters and the little boy to us. That way Sophie can detach herself, dissociate from her pain, and (as it were) bond with us as the witnesses and certifiers of her calm, create with us an everything's-fine-nothing-bad-is-happening-here somatic exchange, as if to say, "See? Over there's the problem; not in here."

I say "as it were" because Sophie is of course not a living, breathing subject but a somatomimetic projection that we generate in our own bodies; but such is the power of somatic mimeticism that we seem to feel her feelings as powerfully as we do the body states we simulate in somatic exchanges with flesh-and-blood friends, with "real people." Our friends' feelings too are a somatomimetic projection that we generate in our own bodies: there is no significant phenomenological difference for us between the imagined "reality" of a friend's feelings and the imagined "reality" of a literary character's feelings. Both are simulations that, because they are channeled through our limbic system and therefore map real emotions that our bodies are experiencing, *feel real.*

1.2.2.2 DOLLS

When Sophie arrives at her mother's apartment in Brooklyn she finds an odd thing: her mother has a doll that she cares for like a daughter.

> "If you don't like the room," my mother said, "we can always change it."
> She glanced at the picture as she picked up a small brush and combed the doll's hair into a ponytail.
> "I like the room fine," I stuttered.
> She tied a rubber band around the doll's ponytail, then reached under the bed for a small trunk.
> She unbuttoned the back of the doll's dress and changed her into a pajama set.
> "You won't resent sharing your room, will you?" She stroked the doll's back. "She is like a friend to me. She kept me company while we were apart. It seems crazy, I know. A grown woman like me with a doll. I am giving her to you now. You take good care of her." (45)

It does seem a bit crazy—it is the first somewhat disturbing discovery Sophie makes about her mother—but in an important sense the displacement of Sophie's feelings onto surrogates in her departure from Haiti has prepared us for it. The doll is (at least) Martine's Sophie-surrogate, just as the rioters and the angry little boy were Sophie's Sophie-surrogates. "She kept me company while we were apart," Martine says: we don't know yet why they were apart, but we now know that for eight years Martine has replaced her absent daughter with a doll, a thing, a fetish object, perhaps, a thing somatized as a real little girl who could keep her company. The significant point to note here is not simply that Martine's Sophie-surrogate is an inanimate object, a thing without subjectivity or agency, but that it is an inanimate object that feels to her like a living person, feels like a friend, someone who can keep her company. Martine now surrenders the doll to Sophie, and that is the last we hear of it: another interesting fact.

In *The Second Sex* Simone de Beauvoir famously theorizes that the doll to the little girl serves more or less the same identity-organizational function as the penis does to the little boy:

> But even if the young girl has no serious penis envy, the absence of the organ will certainly play an important role in her destiny. The major benefit obtained from it by the boy is that, having an organ that can be seen and grasped, he can at least partially identify himself with it. He projects the mystery of his body, its threats, outside of himself, which enables him to keep them at a distance. True enough, he does scent danger in connection with his penis, he fears its being cut off; but this is a fright easier to overcome than the diffuse apprehension felt by the little girl in regard to her 'insides,' an apprehension that will often be retained for life. She is extremely concerned about everything that happens inside her, she is from the start much more opaque to her own eyes, more profoundly immersed in the obscure mystery of life, than is the male. . . . [T]he little girl cannot incarnate herself in any part of herself. To compensate for this and to serve her as *alter ego*, she is given a foreign object: a doll. It should be noted that in French the word *poupée* (doll) is also applied to the bandage around a wounded finger: a dressed-up finger, distinguished from the others, is regarded with amusement and a kind of pride, the child shows signs of the process of identification by his talk to it. But it is a statuette with a human face—or, that lacking, an ear of corn, even a piece of wood—which will most satisfyingly serve the girl as substitute for that double, that natural plaything: the penis. (278)[13]

This analysis suggests that Martine's doll is not just a Sophie-surrogate but a Martine-surrogate as well: that what mother is handing to daughter is not just the objectified daughter but the objectified mother, not just inanimate other but inanimate self. Like the bandaged finger, like Célianne's self in "Children of the Sea," Martine's self is wounded, dysregulated; the doll is the reregulatory deanimation of that wounded self, a projection of the wounded self outwards onto a safely unfeeling thing, which is then imaginatively *reanimated* as safely unfeeling self/other. (This reregulation does not work for Célianne: having thrown her dead baby into the sea—having drowned her deanimated doll—she cannot but jump in after it and drown herself.)

A few pages later, in a Haitian store, Sophie sees "small statues of the beautiful *mulâtresse,* the goddess and loa Erzulie" (52), a powerful vodou figure based on an actual African slave named Erzulie Danto who, according to the folklore, was mutilated by her own people during the Haitian slave revolution in the late eighteenth or early nineteenth century: the other slaves cut out her tongue to prevent her from divulging dangerous secrets. As Donette A. Francis notes in her excellent reading of the novel's sexual violence, "Erzulie Danto is mute and must speak through body language" (87), which connects her implicitly with Sophie, who at this point in the novel is hardly communicating at all, verbally *or* kinesically, except through the mute written word with the reader (see also Braziel, Jurney). But Sophie tells us that Erzulie was her childhood image of her absent and silent mother:

> As a child, the mother I had imagined for myself was like Erzulie, the lavish Virgin Mother. She was the healer of all women and the desire of all men. She had gorgeous dresses in satin, silk, and lace, necklaces, pendants, earrings, bracelets, anklets, and lots and lots of French perfume. She never had to work for anything because the rainbow and the stars did her work for her. Even though she was far away, she was always with me. I could always count on her, like one counts on the sun coming out at dawn. (59)

The beautiful and glamorous but absent mother is depicted as virgin and healer, but above all as *imaginary,* a projection of desire as spirit. Sophie's grandmother will later give her a statue of Erzulie, as consolation "for the pain we have caused you" (157), and Sophie will let the mountain cry: "I held the statue against my chest as I cried in the night. I thought I heard my grandmother crying too, but it was the rain slowing down to a mere drizzle, tapping on the roof" (157). At the end, when Martine dies, Sophie dresses her for her funeral in a bright red dress, so "she would look like a Jezebel, hotblooded Erzulie who feared no men, but rather made them her slaves, raped *them,* and killed *them*" (227, emphasis in original). Like Martine dressing the Sophie-doll, Sophie here dresses the Martine-doll, an inanimate object that she somatizes as alive, as powerful, as a comfort, as healing. It is not, in other words, just that Erzulie is a strong spiritual *image* of woman that can be used analogically to attribute greater but still imaginary power to a weak (or in this case dead) woman, as Francis suggests in her reading of this scene: "In calling on Erzulie, a symbol of bodily survival and resistance and the protector of women who are suffering from abuse, Sophie conjures these defiant characteristics for her own mother" (87). It is also that Erzulie is a doll, a dead object, now the dead body of her mother, which the living can somatize or fetishize as superalive, magically alive, more living than the living. To put it in the terms I offered in §1.1.3.1, the living can circulate among themselves powerfully somatized images of the object-as-alive, of life-embedded-in-the-object, until the object seems to be circulating those somatomimetic impulses as well, seems to be a living member of the somatic exchange.

Shortly after Sophie tells us that she used to imagine her absent mother as Erzulie, back when she was twelve, Martine tells her a dissociated version of the story of her conception: at sixteen Martine was grabbed by a man, probably a Tonton Macoute, dragged into the cane field, and brutally beaten and raped. "She did not sound hurt or angry," Sophie tells us, "just like someone who was stating a fact. Like naming a color or calling a name. Something that already existed and could not be changed" (61). Flat affect, like a mountain or a doll: the ultimate somatic defense against (or allostatic response to) severe trauma. We later learn that Martine did not dissociate immediately: she lived in terror for months, "terrified that he [the faceless Macoute who raped her] would come and tear out the child growing inside her. At night, she tore her sheets and bit off pieces of her own flesh when she had nightmares" (139). Dissociation from the dysregulatory pain of that rape is for Martine a hard-won victory, an allostatic adaptation—but as allostasis it is also a surrender to the dysregulation, a surrender not only of control but of consciousness as well to the dysregulatory somatomimesis of the violence that "she" (or some inchoate mapping function in her nervous system) internalized in the rape. By dissociating from it, she lets it run and ruin not only her life but also her daughter's: "It took me twelve years to piece together my mother's entire story," Sophie tells us. "By then, it was already too late" (61). Like Mia Flores-Borquez, Sophie has already internalized her mother, the raped mother, the suffering mother, the dissociated mother: "Some nights I woke up in a cold sweat wondering if my mother's anxiety was somehow hereditary or if it was something that I had 'caught' from living with her. Her nightmares had somehow become my own, so much so that I would wake up some mornings wondering if we hadn't both spent the night dreaming about the same thing: a man with no face, pounding a life into a helpless young girl" (193). The displacement of unsafe feelings onto a safely external object, like a doll or a daughter's body, like a riot or an unruly child, like a religious object or a dead mother, brings relief from the trauma that dysregulates the dissociated body, but it also circulates that displacement to others, and so perpetuates the violence.

Sophie was once an internal part of Martine, a living simulacrum of the violent act, man, and penis that put her there and therefore a dysregulatory being, something that Martine had first to expel from her body and then distance from her life, leave behind in Haiti when she fled to America. Both childbirth and refugee flight were acts of dissociation, depersonalization, and desomatization for Martine. Having installed the newborn child with her sister in Haiti and her own body in America, Martine found a new object as a further repository for her dysregulatory feelings, the doll. As de Beauvoir writes, "The main difference [between the penis and the doll] is that, on the one hand, the doll represents the whole body, and, on the other, it is a passive object. On this account the little girl will be led to identify her whole person and to regard this as an inert given object" (306). De Beauvoir's analysis moves from here to the socialization of the (untraumatized) little girl as *like* a doll, pretty and passive; but her symbol of the process, the doll, works equally well as a symbol of Martine's dissociative response to rape. When Martine has finally projected enough of her inner dysregulation out onto the world, and so achieved a deadened simulacrum of inner regulation, she brings Sophie to New York and gives her the doll—and the circle is complete. The story is over. Or so Martine evidently hopes. As it turns out, of course, she's dead wrong.

1.2.2.3 DOUBLING

Six years later, at eighteen, Sophie tells Martine that she is in love with a man, and Martine begins "testing" her, inserting a finger into her vagina weekly to feel for her hymen. "Testing," which Sophie describes as part of a Haitian virginity cult (154), is passed on from mother to daughter: her grandmother did it to her mother and Tante Atie; her mother does it to her. All of them hate it; so far, all of them have passed the pain and the humiliation of the practice on to the next generation.

In her discussion of the practice, Francis writes: "Even after the death of Atie and Martine's father, the women of the Caco family still desired this patriarchal romance, which would confer legitimacy and respectability. Once this romance became unrealizable for Martine because of her rape, and unrealizable for Atie because she did not have the proper level of education, they transferred this desire onto Sophie" (82). But I wonder: what does Atie's level of education have to do with it? And why does Francis assume that "this romance" can only be vested in a single female offspring at a time? Viewed somatically, the quest for purity isn't a single "desire" that is "transferred" from one female family member to another; in this ideosomatic regime *all* unmarried women's bodies are fetishized by the group as pure or corrupt, virgin or whore, marriageable or unmarriageable. This is a process akin to the fetishization of dolls or statues or carved wooden figurines as possessing magical healing powers: the girl's intersubjective power to circulate group somatic response, feelings and thoughts, is collectively suppressed so that her body might be objectified as an inert thing, as a telltale collection of physical signs, the tightness or looseness of the vaginal opening ("She would put her finger in our very private parts and see if it would go inside" [60]) or the thinness or thickness of a stream of urine ("If you pee loud, it means you've got big spaces between your legs" [136–37]). This suppression and this objectification and the proper physical signs and the purity that they establish are circulated ideosomatically through the group as intensely positive feelings; any discovery of signs pointing either to pollution or to the girl's somaticity, her disturbing ability to feel and circulate pain, shame, humiliation (Tante Atie, for example, "used to scream like a pig in a slaughterhouse" [60]), is powerfully dysregulatory, and thus smothered under an overwhelming iterosomatics of disapproval.

To facilitate this objectification and thus to avoid disapproval—to escape both *feeling* the physical pain and the emotional humiliation of "testing" and *causing* the dysregulatory effects on her mother of her own somatic response—the girl dissociates, vacates her body, a psychic strategy that Danticat associates explicitly with the vodou act of "doubling," splitting the body into physical and spiritual doubles and leaving the physical body behind in order to travel in the spirit world[14]: "I had learned to *double* while being *tested*. I would close my eyes and imagine all the pleasant things that I had known. The lukewarm noon breeze blowing over a field of daffodils" (155, emphasis in original). "After my marriage," she adds, "whenever Joseph and I were together, I *doubled*" (156). Somatically speaking, what she is doing is depersonalizing the body, desomatizing it—withdrawing somatization from the body as iterosomatically identified and realized by the group, splitting somatic response off from the collectivized fetish object of the virginity cult, and thus from the ideosomatic exchange that is inflicting these wounds on her, so that the wounds are inflicted not on "her" but on a split-off thing, the doll of her own objectified body. As I say, the danger in this doubling is that it facilitates the objectification not only of the girl's and later the woman's own body, but in time of her daughter's as well: dissociation dynasticizes the violation. The traumatization inflicted on the physical body persists as a body memory, an ideosomatized muscle memory that continues to impel action not only despite but through desomatization, through the failure of idiosomatic response to identify and realize the circulatory power of the trauma, and block it, at least, perhaps even to rechannel it, so that it does not issue forth into traumatization of the next generation.

1.2.2.4 SELF-RAPE, SELF-ABORTION

The weekly vaginal tests that Martine inflicts on Sophie are intended, obviously, to identify the watershed moment at which Sophie moves from virginity to whoredom, from purity to impurity. As Sophie comes to understand the testing dynamic, however, the tests become a mere obstruction, a barrier to her future happiness with Joseph, her older boyfriend, a black Creole from Louisiana who loves her and wants to marry her and is willing to wait to have sex with her until Sophie is ready. More than that: they objectify the vagina as that obstruction. This introduces an important twist on de Beauvoir's theorization of penises and dolls: in her quasi-Freudian reading, girls identify with dolls because they lack an easily objectifiable sexual organ that might be somatized as a symbol of the self. For Sophie, Martine's testing performs something like this genital objectification, somatizes the vagina as a sexual synecdoche for her whole person, for the person who wants to marry and have sex with Joseph. After testing commences, Sophie no longer needs dolls, external projections of self: she has her own vagina, as a boy has his penis. But where boys are taught to somatize their penises as self-projections of "autonomy, of transcendence, of power" (de Beauvoir 306), Sophie is taught by virginity testing to somatize her vagina as blockage, as an obstruction to the flows of her power, as negation.

And so, when it becomes clear to her that she cannot simply marry Joseph and have "legal" sex with him—he is older, Martine's age, sixteen years older than Sophie, and not Haitian, and what Martine calls a "vagabond" (78), a musician, and therefore from Martine's traditional Haitian point of view not an appropriate husband for her daughter—she smashes the obstruction, the negative symbol of her whole person. She takes the pestle from the kitchen and breaks her own hymen with it. In this way she frees herself from the virginity cult, violates it, transgresses it, performs herself as "impure" and therefore beyond testing, beyond the reach of the ideosomatic regulation that controls virgin girls; but she also severely damages her vaginal opening and the part of her somatized self that was identified with her vagina. Her mother, hurt and angry at her "betrayal" ("You would leave me for an old man who you didn't know the year before" [85]), releases her: "You just go to him and see what he can do for you" (88). But as a result Martine cuts Sophie out of her life completely for several years, even after Sophie is married to Joseph and gives birth to a little girl, Brigitte: the first loss. The second is sexual pleasure: she tears her vagina badly, has to have stitches, and comes to think of sex as intrinsically not only painful but evil (123). "Joseph," Sophie tells us, "could never understand why I had done something so horrible to myself. I could

not explain to him that it was like breaking manacles, an act of freedom"
(130).

Joseph, who is not the daughter of a rape victim, presumably wonders
why she didn't just elope with him, or, if she felt she had to break her hymen
in order to be free of the virginity cult, let him do it with his penis. There is no
way he can understand that her self-rape with the pestle frees Sophie to be like
her mother, another rape victim, sexually brutalized by an inanimate object.
Just as Martine somatized the doll as both her child and her dissociated self,
just as Sophie somatized first the Erzulie statue as her mother and then her
mother's dead body as Erzulie, and just as Sophie, tested by Martine, somatized her vagina as her dissociated self, so too does Sophie here somatize the
pestle as alive, as "a man with no face, pounding a life into a helpless young
girl" (193). Four weeks later, Sophie and Joseph are married, and Sophie—
feeling "it was my duty as a wife" (130)—lets him have intercourse with her,
despite intense pain. "That first very painful time gave us the child" (130)—
just as "that first very painful time" with the Tonton Macoute gave Martine
Sophie.

After a couple of years of marriage, Sophie flees Joseph to Haiti—fleeing
not so much Joseph, who is a good man, but her own pain in the marriage,
in life—and Martine comes also, to bring her back. After they return to New
York, Martine tells her that she is pregnant—shamefacedly admitting that she
has been having sex out of wedlock with her Haitian lover Marc. Marc wants
to marry her, wants her to have the baby, but Martine can't stand the idea,
wants to abort it: "The nightmares. I thought they would fade with age, but
no, it's like getting raped every night. I can't keep this baby" (190). Sophie
tries to talk her into getting therapy, but Martine refuses: "I am afraid it will
become even more real if I see a psychiatrist and he starts telling me to face
it. God help me, what if they want to hypnotize me and take me back to that
day? I'll kill myself" (190). As Donette Francis writes, "Martine's relationship
to her sexuality is shaped during this violent scene of subjection [the rape]. In
addition to breaking her will to speak, this perpetrator engenders a traumatic
body memory so that Martine subsequently equates the sex act with pain and
violation. Paradoxically, while her silence probably saved her life, in the final
analysis, Martine's inability to speak this trauma results in her death. Martine
literally becomes subsumed by the traumatic after-effects of her rape because
she never confronts nor revises the trauma. Instead she attempts to live as if
the trauma has not irrevocably altered her subjectivity—her mind and body"
(81–82).

Sophie also tries to get her mother to compare this pregnancy, two decades
after the rape, the father a man she loves, with the one that brought her into

the world: "It must have been harder then but you kept me," but her mother is adamant: "When I was pregnant with you, *Manman* made me drink all kinds of herbs, vervain, quinine, and verbena, baby poisons. I tried beating my stomach with wooden spoons. I tried to destroy you, but you wouldn't go away" (190). Just as Sophie penetrates her vagina with a pestle, Martine pounds her pregnant belly with wooden spoons, inanimate cooking utensils as implements of rape and murder—not just to *free* the two women from their "manacles" but to *repeat* the traumatic effect of those manacles, to recirculate the internalized somatomimesis of the rapist's violence. Because this mimetic violence reenacts the initial violation desomatizingly, dissociatively, however, rather than resomatizingly, it just keeps circulating the old somatic response, and thus "frees" the women only to the minimal control over trauma that Freud identifies as the death drive, the desire to deanimate the traumatized body slowly, repetitively, on their own terms.[15]

Martine's self-directed violence becomes ever harsher when she begins to hear the fetus talking in the rapist's voice:

> "Yes, I am sure, it spoke to me. It has a man's voice, so now I know it's not a girl. I am going to get it out of me. I am going to get it out of me, as the stars are my witness."
>
> "Don't do anything rash."
>
> "Everywhere I go, I hear it. I hear him saying things to me. You *tintin, malpròp*. He calls me a filthy whore. I never want to see this child's face. Your child looks like *Manman*. This child, I will never look into its face."
>
> "But it's Marc's child."
>
> "What if there is something left in me and when the child comes out it has that other face?"
>
> "You mean what if it looks like me?"
>
> "No, that is not what I mean." (217)

Sophie has never looked like her mother; Martine believes that that is because "a child out of wedlock always looks like its father" (61). Since the rapist's face was covered, Martine does not know what he looked like, but takes Sophie's face to be a genetic representation of it. Now, though, she is afraid that the new baby (also conceived out of wedlock) will look not like its father but like the rapist—that "there is something left in me," some genetic material that will reproduce the rapist one more time. And in a sense she's right, though the material that keeps reproducing the rapist in her and for her and through her is not genetic but somatic: her somatomimetic reproduction of the rape, which her dissociation has left to its own devices. Here it reproduces the rapist's voice, which, coming from inside her body, must to Martine's mind be the voice of the fetus; surely it will reproduce the rapist's face as well, perhaps his whole body, like an evil clone, an avatar. Martine has spent her entire adult life trying to escape this man; now, she thinks, he has been reborn inside her.

So she stabs herself in the belly, seventeen times, with an "old rusty knife" (224), and dies of a massive hemorrhage. Her self-abortion kills the rapist-somatomimesis by killing the body that is its host: she aborts her self, the self that she could never quite dissociate from the body that could never stop remembering the rape.

The complete dysregulatory cycle experienced by Martine and Sophie, then, begins with the rape in the cane field, in Haiti, in the home situation (1), and continues in Martine's flight from that rape (2), first through wild, frantic attempts to abort the fetus while in hiding from the Tonton Macoutes, then, in migration to America (3), through dissociation, desomatization, the displacement of somatic response onto safe inanimate objects, like the Sophie doll. In a sense, America is another Sophie doll, another safely inanimate object or collection of objects and spaces onto which Martine can displace her Haitian somatic dysregulation. Bringing Sophie to America is the next step in this desomatizing process, as Martine is then able to displace her trauma onto Sophie as a living-but-desomatized doll, through "testing" (4). From Sophie's point of view, and thus for the novel's narrative, (1–3) here is backstory, prehistory, her attempt to understand what has happened to her own feelings by tracking their origins in her mother's life; her own (1–3) is a byproduct of Martine's (4). Sophie is uprooted from the only home and the only mother she has ever known (1–2) in order to live in America with a traumatized stranger who happens to be her birth mother. Like her mother, she responds to the traumatic effects of uprootal through dissociation, desomatization, displacement of somatic response onto external objects and events (3), which facilitates the internalization of Martine's dysregulatory somatomimeses of the rape, through the mimetic contagion of nightmares and "testing"; these somatomimeses continue to impel Sophie too into mimetic violence (4), especially the self-rape with the pestle. As Sophie begins to work back through the dysregulation therapeutically, attempting in a sexual phobia group and in one-on-one therapy to resomatize her trauma, Martine gets pregnant and finds herself unable to deal with the antidissociative resurgence of somatic mimeses of the rape, especially the apparent emanation of the rapist's voice from her fetus, so she brings the repetitive mimetic cycle to a close by violently deanimating both the fetus and her own body, finishing the job that the rapist started.

1.2.2.5 RESOMATIZATION

Sophie's narrative has a pugilistic, largely pessimistic feel to it, because for most of the novel both women's primary response to somatic dysregulation is desomatization, trying not to feel the pain, which only repeats the dysregulation thanatotically, in Freud's sense. Indeed it may not be too much to say that the novel mostly seems mired in hopelessness because it is steeped in Freud's death drive, the "Nirvana principle" whose "aim is to conduct the restlessness of life into the stability of the inorganic state" ("Masochism" 160)—and, perhaps, because it is steeped inchoately in Freudian psychoanalytical models in general, whose only alternatives to the repetition-compulsions of the death drive are the infantile pleasure principle and the jaded adaptations of pleasure to the reality principle.

Toward the end of the novel, however, Danticat begins to introduce new therapeutic pressures on Sophie, through her sexual phobia group in Chapter 31 and one-on-one therapy in Chapter 32. Both are explicitly somatic, based on therapeutic resomatization, the reliving or replaying of traumatic scenes from the past in a transformative group context that circulates new and life-affirming somatomimeses through the sufferer's body response. Sophie's sexual phobia group consists of just three women, herself and Buki, an Ethiopian woman dealing with the trauma of clitoridectomy, and Davina, a Chicana incest survivor; their group rituals seek to rechannel the negative thanatotic repetition-compulsions that have been blighting their lives in positive ways:

> "I am a beautiful woman with a strong body," Davina led the affirmations.
> "We are beautiful women with strong bodies." We echoed her uncertain voice.
> "Because of my distress, I am able to understand when others are in deep pain."
> "Because of our distress, we are able to understand when others are in deep pain."
> I heard my voice rise above the others.
> "Since I have survived this, I can survive anything." (202)

They write letters to their abusers and read them aloud. They write and burn the names of their abusers. Sophie tells us that "I felt broken at the end of the meeting, but a little closer to being free" (203)—but her optimism rings a bit hollow, as if the group's resomatization exercises were just another panacea that could not possibly transform how she actually felt. And indeed she earlier responds to her husband's encouraging noises about how much therapy is helping that it isn't, really (185). We cannot simply begin to feel differently about ourselves and others and things and places—cannot simply resomatize reality and identity—because the somatic markers our autonomic nervous systems create to remind us of what we've learned are actually "soft-wired" into our brains. They travel along whole networks of myelinated axons and dedicated synapses that have been generated specifically to send us these learned signals. They are designed *permanently* to protect us from harm, *persistently* to remind us not to do the things that have endangered us in the past. They are so firmly entrenched in our somatic orientations to word and deed that they typically seem to us to be not somatic constructs at all but "personality," even "human nature": they constantly tempt us to essentialize somatic phenomenology as ontology. Groups are powerful resomatizing forces in our lives, and in many ways Sophie is in the right place, circulating somatic affirmations with other sexually traumatized women; but the group that chants "We are beautiful women with strong bodies," much as they really want and need to believe it, is ultimately powerless against trauma.

Sophie's therapy session with Rena, the "initiated Santeria priestess" (206), in the next chapter explains why the group affirmations aren't working: she has to relive the original trauma, the rape. She has to resomatize not just her own body, but her father:

> "I would rather not call him my father."
>
> "We will have to address him soon. When we do address him, I'll have to ask you to confront your feelings about him in some way, give him a face."
>
> "It's hard enough to deal with, without giving him a face."
>
> "Your mother never gave him a face. That's why he's a shadow. That's why he can control her. I'm not surprised she's having nightmares. This pregnancy is bringing feelings to the surface that she had never completely dealt with. You will never be able to connect with your husband until you say good-bye to your father." (209)

The process of first saying hello to the father, to the father's face, and then goodbye to that face, is intended to resomatize the rape: to bring Sophie's violent origins to consciousness, not as an abstraction but as a physical face in a physical place, so that the traumatic feelings of pain and humiliation and loss can be refelt, somatically reprocessed.

"During your visit [to Haiti], did you go to the spot where your mother was raped?" Rena asked. "In the thick of the cane field. Did you go to the spot?"

"No, not really."

"What does that mean?"

"I ran past it."

"You and your mother should both go there again and see that you can walk away from it. Even if you can never face the man who is your father, there are things that you can say to the spot where it happened. I think you'll be free once you have your confrontation. There will be no more ghosts." (210–11)

And in a sense Sophie does do this with her mother; as the others are throwing dirt on her mother's coffin she tears herself away and runs down to the cane field:

> There were only a few men working in the cane fields. I ran through the field, attacking the cane. I took off my shoes and began to beat a cane stalk. I pounded it until it began to lean over. I pushed over the cane stalk. It snapped back, striking my shoulder. I pulled at it, yanking it from the ground. My palm was bleeding.
>
> The cane cutters stared at me as though I was possessed. The funeral crowd was now standing between the stalks, watching me beat and pound the cane. My grandmother held back the priest as he tried to come for me.
>
> From where she was standing, my grandmother shouted like the women from the market place, "*Ou libéré?*" Are you free?
>
> Tante Atie echoed her cry, her voice quivering with her sobs.
>
> "*Ou libéré!*" (233)

Sophie's attack on the cane field is again mimetic violence, but this time directed outward, not against her own body, and against an inanimate surrogate for her rapist-father, a thing, a phallic doll that, because it fights back, can be somatized as alive, superalive, as a magical avatar of the original perpetrator of the violence. "Importantly here, however," as Donette Francis writes, "the violence is enacted on the canefields rather than on her own physical body. In this way, she frees herself from the debilitating subjection implicit in the previous scenes. Sophie's actions here must be understood as her willful re-membering of devastations enacted upon the bodies of her family members" (87). But note that the cane stalk is not a *random* surrogate for the rapist-father, chosen just because it happens to spring back at her when she pushes it over: it is part of the scene of the original rape of Sophie's mother, the scene of Sophie's violent conception, part of a place in fact that for the Caco women was somatized with terror even before the rape. Sophie's grandfather died of heatstroke while working in that same field. Every time Sophie goes near it, she is given some reminder of death and mutilation: "The hammering echoed in my head until I reached the cane fields. The men were singing about a woman who flew without her skin at night, and when she came back home, she found her skin peppered and could not put it back on. Her husband had done it to teach her a lesson. He ended up killing her" (150). Flying without your skin is called doubling. Later, while Joseph is pounding away at her in sex, Sophie doubles and imagines herself flying in the spirit to her mother: "I would visit her every night in my doubling and, from my place as a shadow on the wall, I would look after her and wake her up as soon as the nightmares started, just like I did when I was home" (200). At the cane field it seems even that flight from pain is denied her. At the cane field, doubling would get her killed.

By fighting the cane stalk, therefore, Sophie not only does somatic battle with her rapist father: she reengages the dysregulatory ideosomatic regime that keeps her in thrall. By uprooting the cane stalk Sophie resomatizes her own traumatic uprooting—from Haiti, from her own body—and is free.

1.3 THEORETICAL SPINS: METAPHORICAL MIGRANTS

When Sophie is eighteen and first getting to know her next-door neighbor in Brooklyn, the older black Creole musician from New Orleans who becomes her husband, Joseph, she tells him that she is going to college in the fall, and he asks what she is going to study. She doesn't know, but says medicine, because her mother wants her to be a doctor; but she says it with a hesitant body language that Joseph understands immediately as signaling an unvoiced tension that she feels between the positivity of family plans and the negativity of her own dreams ("I had never really dared to dream on my own" [72]). He suggests cautiously that it's important to have a passion for what you do and to stay open to experience, but Sophie counters with the ideology of family loyalty, of doing what the family decides is best:

> "It is okay not to have your future on a map," he said. "That way you can flow wherever life takes you."
> "That is not Haitian," I said. "That's very American."

"What is?"
"Being a wanderer. The very idea." (72)

Sophie herself has "wandered" from Haiti to New York, but she is not a wanderer. Haitians in New York are called "boat people" by the Americans, but they are not wanderers. What prevents them from becoming wanderers is their attachment to the group, to the ideosomatic organization of lives, of selves, of individualities by families and communities. She here identifies the individualistic idealization of isolation from the group, the transformation of the inevitable disjunctures in ideosomatic identities into a new idiosomatic principle, a *freedom* from group determination, as a "very American" idea—one that is still alien to her.

In a sense what Sophie is doing here is refusing to metaphorize her experience of geographical displacement as a kind of anti-road-map road map of postcolonial identity, a blanket *carte blanche* to a romantically becoming-displaced future. This "very American" idea, though, is one that has caught the imaginations of postcolonialist and other radical theorists since the publication of *L'Anti-Oedipe* in 1972: metaphorical readings of migrancy, of nomadism, of the refugee, readings of people on the move as tropes for a fragmented postmodern postcoloniality, or for the counterhegemonic intellectual as a shadowy mystical hero hip-deep in pomo/poco fragments and fractals but supremely undaunted by them. Gilles Deleuze and Félix Guattari write of "nomad thought," Rosi Braidotti of "nomadic subjectivities"; Homi Bhabha writes of "migratory identities," Carole Boyce Davies of "migratory subjectivities"; Edward Said suggests somewhat more cautiously in *Culture and Imperialism* that, "while it would be the rankest Panglossian dishonesty to say that the bravura performances of the intellectual exile and the miseries of the displaced person or refugee are the same, it is possible, I think, to regard the intellectual as first distilling then articulating the predicaments that disfigure modernity—mass deportation, imprisonment, population transfer, collective dispossession, and forced immigrations" (333)—or, more accurately, as first distilling, then *idealizing*, then metaphorizing those predicaments. Not that postcolonial idealizations of the migrant or the refugee are conventionally idealized, which is to say, *patently* Panglossian; they are often quite dark. But a romanticizing impulse can nevertheless typically be found at work in them just beneath the surface, a determination to assign utopian value to any metaphor that infects sedentary order with disorder, stasis with movement, collective conventions with iconoclasm, ideosomatic regulation with idiosomatic deregulation.

1.3.1 Schizzes and Flows: Nomad Thought

The *Anti-Oedipus* of Deleuze and Guattari precedes Said's *Orientalism* (1978), considered by many to be the founding text of postcolonial theory, by six years; their third part there, "Savages, Barbarians, Civilized Men," begins with the notion that "to code desire—and the fear, the anguish of decoded flows—is the business of the socius" (139), and rings the changes in that model through a series of epochal "machines." The first is what they call the "primitive territorial machine," in which "the great nomad hunter follows the flows, exhausts them in place, and moves on with them to another place" (148):

> Such are the two characteristics of the hunter, the great paranoiac of the bush or the forest: real displacement with the flows and direct filiation with the god. It has to do with the nature of nomadic space, where the full body of the socius is as if adjacent to production; it has not yet brought production under its sway. The space of the encampment remains adjacent to that of the forest; it is constantly reproduced in the process of production, but has not yet appropriated this process. The apparent objective movement of inscription has not suppressed the real movement of nomadism. But a pure nomad does not exist; there is always and already an encampment where it is a matter of stocking—however little—and where it is a matter of inscribing and allocating, of marrying, and of feeding oneself. (148)

But the nomad is still a largely empirical figure for them here: not yet a metaphor. Three chapters later, they analyze colonization as oedipalization, or oedipalization as a kind of colonization, looking at a "cure among the Ndembu" (167) as reported by Victor Turner as only *seemingly* Oedipal, to *us*, who are "conditioned to say Oedipus every time someone speaks to us of father, mother, grandfather":

> In fact, the Ndembu analysis was never Oedipal: it was directly plugged into social organization and disorganization; sexuality itself, through the women and the marriages, was just such an investment of desire; the parents played the role of stimuli in it, and not the role of group organizers (or disorganizers)—the role held by the chief and his personages. Rather than everything being reduced to the name of the father, or that of the maternal grandfather, the latter opened onto all the names of history. Instead of everything being projected onto a grotesque hiatus of castration, everything was scattered in the thousand breaks-flows of the chieftanships, the

lineages, the relations of colonization. The whole interplay of races, clans, alliances, and filiations, this entire historical and collective drift: exactly the opposite of the Oedipal analysis, when it stubbornly crushes the content of a delirium, when it stuffs it with all its might into "the symbolic void of the father." Or rather, if it is true that the analysis doesn't even begin as Oedipal, except to our way of seeing, doesn't it become Oedipal nevertheless, in a certain way—and in what way? Yes, it becomes Oedipal in part, under the effect of colonization. . . . Both are true: the colonized resists oedipalization, and oedipalization tends to close around him again. (168–69)

"The thousand breaks-flows": there is no attempt here, as there will be in *A Thousand Plateaus* eight years later, to metaphorize these complex filiational turbulences as intrinsically *nomadic*. "It would seem," Deleuze and Guattari write in that latter book, "that a whole nomad science develops eccentrically, one that is very different from the royal or imperial sciences. Furthermore, this nomad science is continually 'barred,' inhibited, or banned by the demands and conditions of State science. . . . The fact is that the two kinds of science have different modes of formalization, and State science continually imposes its form of sovereignty on the inventions of nomad science" (362). "The great State mathematicians did their best to improve its status, but precisely on the condition that all the dynamic, nomadic notions—such as becoming, heterogeneity, infinitesimal, passage to the limit, continuous variation—be eliminated and civil, static, and ordinal rules be imposed upon it" (363). Nomad thought in *A Thousand Plateaus* is a hydraulic science of turbulence in flows, one that "produc[es] a movement that holds space and simultaneously affects all of its points, instead of being held by space in a local movement from one specified point to another" (363).

As Caren Kaplan notes about a parallel binary in *Thousand Plateaus*, however, major and minor language ("For the majority, insofar as it is analytically included in the abstract standard, is never anybody, is always Nobody—Ulysses—whereas the minority is the becoming of everybody, one's potential becoming to the extent that one deviates from the model" [*Thousand* 105]), becoming-minor, like becoming-nomad, is a *choice*. While it is by definition something that *happens* to minorities, foreigners, nomads, migrants, and refugees, for the First-World artist or intellectual, living in the colonial center—Deleuze and Guattari in Paris, Sophie's Joseph in New York—it is an alternative lifestyle. "For example," Kaplan writes, "I would have to pay attention to whether or not it is possible for me to *choose* deterritorialization or whether deterritorialization has chosen me":

> For if I choose deterritorialization, I go into literary/linguistic exile with all my cultural baggage intact. If deterritorialization has chosen me—that is, if I have been cast out of home or language without forethought or permission, then my point of view will be more complicated. Both positions are constructed by the world system but they are not equal. Of course, Deleuze and Guattari are suggesting that we are all deterritorialized on some level in the process of language itself and that this is a point of contact between "us all."[16] Yet we have different privileges and different compensations for our positions in the field of power relations. My caution is against a form of theoretical tourism on the part of the first world critic, where the margin becomes a linguistic or critical vacation, a new poetics of the exotic. One can also read Deleuze and Guattari's resistance to this romantic trope in their refusal to recognize a point of origin. Theirs is a poetics of travel where there is no return ticket and we all meet, therefore, en train. Reterritorialization without imperialism? Can language provide a model of this process? Who dares let go of their respective representations and systems of meaning, their identity politics and theoretical homes, when it is, as Kafka rightly noted, "a matter of life and death here?" ("Deterritorializations" 191)[17]

This is an important corrective to Deleuze and Guattari's mystique of the nomad. There is a significant difference between the traumatized refugee, involuntarily cast out of home and community, fleeing dysregulatory violence at home into the dysregulations of long marches (hunger, physical exhaustion, loss of familiar social and physical structures), internment (forced inactivity and helplessness, rape, theft, and other predations), and assimilation into a new culture (the waning power of xenonormativity), and the oppositional intellectual sitting in his or her study at home, surrounded by familiar books and other objects, the spouse and kids in the next room, imagining and idealizing the refugee's drift away from xenonormativity as a trope of oppositional thought.

But note that Kaplan's corrective is itself no less problematic, no less a form of "theoretical tourism on the part of the first world critic," no less a "poetics of the exotic." Kaplan imagines and idealizes the refugee too, simply in a dystopian rather than utopian direction. She too sits in her study (as I do in mine), surrounded by her familiar books and other objects, imagining herself having "been cast out of home or language without forethought or permission." She fails to note that the tidy binary she sets up between the sedentary First World intellectual (choice, stable home and language, power) and the refugee (no choice, destabilized living conditions, powerlessness) is a binary between the Me and the Not-Me, between self and other, between "what I have" and others defined in terms of a lack of "what I have," an abstract mathematical subtraction of my possessions (choice, stability, home, friends, work, books, power) that renders the refugee a kind of negative image of Me, an othered and peripheralized negation of sedentary intellectual life here in the center. (I too, for that matter, binarize ideosomatic regulation here at home and ideosomatic dysregulation in the refugee experience, so that refugeeness becomes a deviation from and thus theoretical limitation on my somatic norm.)

But, then, what is a scholar to do? It's not just that we're trapped in our own skins; we're also trapped in our own groups, in the limitations our iterosomatic histories with certain specific groups tend to place on our knowing and saying and doing. For humanities scholars, those limitations tend to include not only a sedentary lifestyle but a heavy reliance on the printed word—we are not anthropologists, ethnologists, or sociologists expected to do fieldwork (say, in a refugee camp, like Pfister-Ammende, or in an immigrant community, like Ong); we read books and articles. Deleuze and Guattari were never nomads, or Ndembu, or actually met any member of either group: they read about them. Kaplan has never been a refugee, and most likely has never met one either: she's read about them. We read, and construct ideosomatically regulated images of otherness, ideosomatically regulated relationships between self and other: we objectify (we do what Deleuze and Guattari call "State science," reduce the other to inert facts, numbers, structures, and categories taken to be ideally distant and different from ourselves); we identify, we project (we do what Deleuze and Guattari and Kaplan all do in imagining themselves mobile, organize thought around an imagined affinity between self and other).

But in fact Deleuze and Guattari push hard on this subject–object binary, this conventionally regulatory notion that we can either isolate subject and object or build bridges between them, in their articulation of a radically collectivist theory of human being-in-the-world: "The social machine, in contrast, has men for its parts, even if we view them *with* their machines, and integrate them, internalize them in an institutional model at every stage of action, transmission, and motricity. Hence the social machine fashions a memory without which there would be no synergy of man and his (technical) machines" (*Anti-Oedipus* 141). Motricity is motor operations; the motricity of the social machine would include such shared motor activities as dancing, singing, cheering, applauding, marching, parading, drumming, having sex, exercising, and playing team sports. What is transmitted through shared motricity is regulatory feeling or homeostatic synergy, which is circulated not just through humans but through the human-machine (or cyborg) interface as well, and, as I've been suggesting, through the group–place interface that exosomatizes places and things as "home," "holy," "powerful," and so on. The "memory" that Deleuze and Guattari describe as fashioned by the social machine—what I call iterosomatics—is borrowed from Nietzsche ("A thing is branded on the memory to make it stay there; only what goes on hurting will stick" [*Genealogy* II.3]), and thus from protosomatic theory: "Cruelty," they write, "has nothing to do with some ill-defined or natural violence that might be commissioned to explain the history of mankind; cruelty is the movement of culture that is realized in bodies and inscribed on them, belaboring them" (145). Cruelty as *the* movement of culture through bodies is a Nietzschean (anti)idealization, of course: it is really only *a* movement of culture through bodies. But it is a powerful one, one that transmits both regulatory and dys-regulatory synergies, the internalization of mastery both for conformity to group norms (as in Nietzsche's Germans) and for the viral spread of disruptive violence (as in Danticat's Haitian Tonton Macoutes).

Their incipient somatics of language is also implicitly Nietzschean: "And if one wants to call this inscription in naked flesh 'writing,' then it must be said that speech in fact presupposes writing, and that it is this cruel system of inscribed signs that renders man capable of language, and gives him a memory of the spoken word" (145)—a *somatic* memory, clearly: a felt memory, felt by the individual as a part of the social machine, which circulates the synergistic flows of desire (including cruelty) through "men or their organs" (145).[18]

In this somatic conception of "machinic" social regulation, any stray impulse that cannot be harnessed to normative group synergy will be felt as idiosomatic, divergent, deviant, individualizing in a collectivist regime and therefore, perhaps, "nomadic" in a sedentary regime. To theorize such stray idiosomatic impulses as "nomad thought" or "nomad science" is to imagine a counterregime, a deregulatory regime that intensively and extensively minoritizes the major, reassembles the systematic, sends turbulences through dammed and locked waters.

To the extent that deregulation becomes a group norm, of course, it too circulates *regulatory* pressures that organize the thoughts and words and beliefs and actions of, say, postmodern/postcolonial thinkers. In this new "deregulatory" group, it becomes possible to be perceived as "not nomadic enough," not deregulatory enough, too sedentary, too traditional, too regressively attached to the old ideosomatic paradigms, stable binary realities and identities, stable analytical categories and typologies. Idiosomatic deregulation is only idiosomatic and only deregulatory as a moment of perceived resistance to or deviation from ideosomatic regulation; as soon as a new group begins to form around a new normativity associated with that resistance, resistance becomes ideosomatically regulatory, and lingering traces of the *ancien régime* in each group member's somatic response come to be perceived as the new idiosomatic deregulation. The postmodern/postcolonial thinker then feels pressure to police his or her inner and outer life for stray idiosomatic impulses toward reactionary analytical order, and weed them out before they become visible to other members of the "nomadic" group. Only the fully regulated group member will be perceived as properly nomadic.

That the historical nomad, migrant, and refugee are only allegorical figures of this counterregime, exemplary cases chosen by the sedentary deregulatory theorist to focus and organize resistance metaphorically, may make this idiosomatic deregulation seem callous or opportunistic or even exploitative to members of other groups, especially, perhaps, First World intellectual groups whose (de)regulatory strategies involve the pious objectification or subjectification of the refugee as traumatized and suffering. But then the assumption that it is possible to avoid reducing others to constructs—that anyone ever apprehends anyone else as more than a somatized construct—is just more piety.

1.3.2 Migrancy and Identity

The somatic tensions that this postmodern/postcolonial normativization of metaphorical "nomadism" or "migrancy" generates in members of the group might be explored by reading along for a page or two with Iain Chambers in the opening pages of his 1994 book *Migrancy, Culture, Identity:* "For recent apertures in critical thought instigated by certain internal displacements in the hearth of the West (feminism, deconstructionism, psychoanalysis, post-metaphysical thought)," Chambers writes, "have been increasingly augmented by the persistent question of a presence that no longer lies elsewhere: the return of the repressed, the subordinate and the forgotten in 'Third World' musics, literatures, poverties and populations as they come to occupy the economies, cities, institutions, media and leisure time of the First World" (3). This is a nice image: the stable sedentary "hearth of the West" undergoes "internal displacements" and out of those displacements generates various differential discourses that bring about a return of the repressed, so that the "Third World," initially a ghost of our own Western repressions, turns out to be very real, and to occupy "subordinate and forgotten" spaces within the "First World." This is the transformation of various idiosomatic/deregulatory pressures within the old "hearth of the West" ideosomatic regulation into a new (re-/counter-) regulatory regime based on the metaphorical return of the refugee repressed, the normativization of the previously excluded periphery as the allegorical core, the symbolic center.

Note, though, that in Chambers's formulations this transformation is effected not by the group, somatically, but abstractly, discursively, by "differential discourses," and specifically by the act of discursive displacement, which increasingly becomes a kind of romantic hero in the passages that follow, a stand-in for the social machine that iterosomatizes (memorializes) utopian theorizations of migrancy: "The belief in the transparency of truth and the power of origins to define the finality of our passage," Chambers writes, "is dispersed by this perpetual movement of transmutation and transformation. History is harvested and collected, to be assembled, made to speak, re-membered, re-read and rewritten, and language comes alive in transit, in interpretation" (3)—harvested, collected, assembled, made to speak, and so on by differential discourse, by *discursive* transmutation and transformation. And: "For the nomadic experience of language, wandering without a fixed home, dwelling at the crossroads of the world, bearing our sense of being and difference, is no longer the expression of a unique tradition or history, even if it pretends to carry a single name. Thought wanders. It migrates, requires translation. Here reason runs the risk of opening out on to the world, of finding itself in a passage without a reassuring foundation or finality: a passage open to the changing skies of existence and terrestrial illumination" (4). Language, thought, and reason are the definitive nomads here, the wanderers, the migrants. "This inevitably means another sense of 'home,' of being in the world. It means to conceive of dwelling as a mobile habitat, as a mode of inhabiting time and space not as though they were fixed and closed structures, but as providing the critical provocation of an opening whose questioning presence reverberates in the movement of the languages that constitute our sense of identity, place and belonging. There is no one place, language or tradition that can claim this role" (4). This does not mean, I'm guessing, another material *way* of living in the world; it is just another subliminal *sense* of being in the world. It does not mean giving up our sedentary lifestyles and actually becoming displaced persons; "it means to *conceive* of dwelling as a mobile habitat," as a mode of inhabiting the *concepts* "time" and "space" as "providing the critical provocation of an opening whose questioning presence reverberates in the movement of the languages that constitute our sense of identity, place and belonging." As the keywords in that wonderfully pomo/poco clause suggest, it's all discursive: critical, provocation, opening, questioning, presence, reverberates, movement of languages, constitute, *sense* of identity, place, and belonging.

This is not (just) obfuscation on Chambers's part; in assigning agency to abstract differential discourse rather than the somatic synergy of the social machine he is conforming his own discursive behavior to felt collective (post-structuralist) norms that privilege thought and deprivilege feeling, privilege verbal language and deprivilege body language, and above all enforce these binaries as mystifications of group pressures to conform. He is obeying the rules. He is doing what he knows (*feels*) he must do not merely in order to get published but also to win group approval.

The telling regulatory/mystificatory moment in these early pages of Chambers's book is telling. He first warns us:

> The accumulated diasporas of modernity, set in train by "modernisation," the growing global economy, and the induced, often brutally enforced, migrations of individuals and whole populations from the "peripheries" towards Euro-American metropolises and "Third World" cities, are of a magnitude and intensity that dramatically dwarf any direct comparison with the secondary and largely metaphorical journeys of intellectual thought. Analogy is risky. There is always the obvious allure of the romantic domestication and intellectual homecoming that the poetic figures of travel and exile promise. (5–6)

This is the standard cautionary note, signaling the acute pomo/poco awareness that human beings are suffering out there, in contradistinction to our own comfortable lives. But then Chambers adds: "Still, it is a risk to be run. For the modern migrations of thought and people are phenomena that are deeply implicated in each other's trajectories and futures" (6). This seems to suggest that we have to go ahead and theorize migrancy anyway, whatever the risks, because refugees and other migrants are as deeply implicated in the trajectories of our theorizations of migrancy as we are in the refugee experience and other real-world forms of migrancy. Problematic as that notion is—implicated how, exactly?—the deeper problem I find in Chambers's formulation has to do with the elided agents behind his passive verbs. Even if we allow him the questionable notion that there is some sort of mutuality between migrants and theorists of migrancy, who exactly is implicating us in the refugee experience? Who exactly is implicating refugees in poco theory? That seems like an impertinent question, somehow—as if there isn't, and doesn't need to be, any individual or group desire fueling this implication; as if "implicated" is a simple impersonal ontological claim (don't think *de*personalized: think the static objectivism of impersonality), a participial passive whose absented agent is the universe, the omnipresent Ontos itself. But isn't that precisely the kind of question a theorist should be asking of his own formulations?

Something like this same mystifying grammar is at work in "it is a risk to be run" as well: it's not that *I* want to run this risk, or that I feel impelled to run it by pressures from my group; the risk is simply there to be run. The pressure to run the risk comes somehow impersonally from the risk itself, from its thereness. And what is the risk that is to be run? The risk of analogy, of comparing the migrancy of poststructuralist thought with the migratory plight of millions. But why is that risky? It just is. No specific risk: just risky. Chambers's explanation of that risk is another grammatical mystification: "There is always the obvious allure of the romantic domestication and intellectual homecoming that the poetic figures of travel and exile promise." Figurative language *promises* things, alluring things, the allure of home, the allure of the romantic *nostos*. But why is this a risk? Given that "the allure" has an impersonal promiser and no grammatical promisee at all, it can't be a risk to *people;* it's just a risk. Tellingly, in fact, the only people in that quotation are the millions of refugees to whose suffering Chambers is paying passing lip service: the "migrations of individuals and whole populations." Note that those migrations are "set in train" not by specific Western modernizers but by "modernisation"; that "induced" and "brutally enforced" are more participial passives with absent agents as well; and that it is the migrations themselves that "dwarf any direct comparison," not the migrants or the Western intellectuals invoking the migrations in order to facilitate their direct comparisons.

A cynical translation of Chambers's mystificatory rhetoric here into somatic terms would be that he is under ideosomatic pressure from Western poststructuralist intellectuals since Deleuze and Guattari simultaneously to romanticize language, thought, culture, and identity by analogy with forced migration—to find a way to feel "forced" by the sociopolitical and economic facts of the displacement of millions to cut his mental images of language, thought, culture, and identity loose from the sedentary habits of two millennia of stabilizing Western objectivism—*and* to avoid trivializing forced migration and the suffering of the refugee as mere fodder for postmodern/poststructuralist/postcolonial tropes. Because the new regulatory discourse figures the refugee as both the return of the *repressed* and the *return* of the repressed, as both something alien and distant and half-forgotten and as something present and unforgettably pressing, normative figurations of the refugee must (will inevitably) partake of both what Kaplan calls "theoretical tourism" and the stern condemnation of theoretical tourism, both the casual Western exploitation of the refugee experience as a trope for oppositional thought and pious expressions of sympathy and solidarity for refugee suffering. And if this pair of polarized pressures corresponds to the first two opposed commands of Gregory Bateson's theorization of the double-bind—(1) romanticize/trivialize the refugee,

(2) sympathize with the refugee—the third command traps the thinker in the bind by mystifying it as no bind at all, as no one's commands, as not really happening. Hence the depersonalizing rhetoric, which situates agency in some abstract parallax realm for which Chambers need not take responsibility.

This translation would recontextualize all of Chambers's null-context claims in terms of two group regulations, both virtual but with real consequences for Chambers's professional and perhaps even emotional life: the group of Western postcolonialist intellectuals who attend conferences and write and read books and articles on migrancy, culture, and identity, and the group of actual refugees whose cultures and identities are at risk of migratory dysregulation. Both groups are virtual in the context of Chambers's writing because they are not physically present as he writes: they have to be imagined, their ideosomatic pressures (approval, disapproval) imaginatively prefelt or transfelt. The former group is made up of a loose conglomeration of people he has met at conferences and guest lecturing gigs and people he has corresponded with (especially perhaps Stuart Hall's group at the University of Birmingham, where he did his doctoral work), as well as anonymous readers of his books and articles either for presses and journals or, like me, as part of the circulation of pomo/poco images and ideas and tonalizations and attitudinalizations through the group. It is essential to yield to this group's pressures in order to get published, invited to deliver guest lectures, and appointed to university posts (Chambers is Professor in the History of English Culture at the Istituto Universitario Orientale in Naples); professional success in that group also circulates respect, admiration, and self-esteem. The latter group, the migrants, is unlikely ever to read Chambers's work, but they have powerful proxies in and around the former group, who frown on (express ideosomatic disapproval of) the trivialization of Third World suffering in order to score points with Western intellectuals.

But of course the cynicism of this translation is manifestly unfair, especially insofar as I seem hypocritically to be exempting myself from my own critique. We are all ideosomatically regulated to conform to our own group's norms, and the relevant group for both Chambers and me is Western intellectuals of a certain stripe, nourished on poststructuralist and postmodern discourses, interested more in language, culture, and identity than in the brute material facts of geographical displacement, economic exploitation, political persecution, internment, the distribution of foodstuffs, and the like. Because our group has of late grown increasingly interested in those brute facts, we have had to find ways to shift our thematizations of our linguistic and cultural interests so as to seem to include "the refugee experience" in them—and this book is no more exempt from that analysis than Chambers's is. And while I do think that Chambers's depersonalizing rhetoric is mystificatory, and that he is conditioned ideosomatically to those rhetorical mystifications by the post-structuralist postcolonialists in the group, I also recognize that Chambers is struggling to problematize and personalize those mystifications, for example in passages like this one:

> Does this all mean I have nothing to say, that every gesture that begins in the West is inherently imperialist, merely the latest move in the extension of my power regarding the others? It is perhaps here that the political and ethical implications of the arguments advanced in this book can be most clearly grasped as an attempt to fracture the vicious circle between speakers and the spoken for. For, in breaking into my own body of speech, opening up the gaps and listening to the silences in my own inheritance, I perhaps learn to tread lightly along the limits of where I am speaking from. I begin to comprehend that where there are limits there also exist other voices, bodies, worlds, on the other side, beyond my particular boundaries. In the pursuit of my desires across such frontiers I am paradoxically forced to face my confines, together with that excess that seeks to sustain the dialogues across them. Transported some way into this border country, I look into a potentially further space: the possibility of another place, another world, another future. (5)

What Chambers is saying here is that his book is basically about Western discourses of otherness, Western discourses of "other voices, bodies, worlds," of "the possibility of another place, another world, another future." In other words, he is writing about *us,* about *our* interactions with non-Western others—which is, I suggest, the only honest way to write anything: to admit frankly that we cannot step outside of our own skins and the groups that give those skins socioemotional and political definition.

Still, let me note the Whitmanesque grandiosity of Chambers's "I"-rhetoric there: "in breaking into my own body of speech, opening up the gaps and listening to the silences in my own inheritance, I perhaps learn to tread lightly along the limits of where I am speaking from. I begin to comprehend that where there are limits there also exist other voices," and so on. Chambers stands alone, a *kosmos,* containing not only his "own body of speech" but his "own inheritance" as well, presumably the voices of those who have shaped him, but they aren't other voices to him, they're simply his inheritance, that which has accrued to *him* over the years of his life, his listening and speaking, his reading and writing. He has a place from which he speaks: it is his alone. And in interrogating it, "opening up the gaps and listening to the silences" in that place, that inheritance, he discovers its limits, and begins to "compre-hend"—read: to "imagine"—that "other voices, bodies, worlds" exist in the interstices of those limits, in the "excess that seeks to sustain the dialogues across them." Somewhere outside Chambers's song of himself there are other people, but his "I" is so large a *kosmos* that he can only imagine them as an "excess" to his own peripheries and a concomitant *potential* for dialogue, an abstract *seeking to sustain* dialogue.

What he is forgetting, then, is the group construction of the self: the extent to which his "I" has been shaped collectively by the many groups to which he has belonged in his life—the extent to which other people are not just a deper-sonalized (past) "inheritance" or (future) "excess" but the enabling condition of his social being. In this ideosomatic conception, Chambers does not have a "body of speech" all on his own; he is a part of, and is dynamically and shift-ingly shaped by, a dialogue within each of the groups to which he belongs, a dialogue charged with regulatory impulses that circulate normative pressures through him. The sum total of those dialogues and those pressures constitutes not only his "body of speech" but also his world, the world as seen and spoken through his eyes and lips, from within his skin; and it is that body, that col-lectivizing/individualizing body, that he needs to "break into," open up gaps in, in the sense of entering into dialogues with "other voices, bodies, worlds," not so much "on the other side" (since there is no one "this" side or "that" side but numerous fictitious sides constituted collectively as part of in-group/out-group policing) but instead from outside *all* the current dialogues that shape him.

Displacement of Cultures/ (De)Colonization/ Ideosomatic Counterregulation

TO THE EXTENT that postcolonial studies may be said to have a "center" or "core," this is it: the study of colonization and decolonization. By comparison, refugee studies is marginal, centrifugal, ancillary, supplementary, shunted out of the realm of the paradigmatic colonial encounter into the borderlands or hinterlands of postcoloniality, and therefore far more attractive to poststructuralist migrancy theorists: refugees, as I noted in the preface, can be driven out of their homes and homelands not only by colonial and postcolonial forces like wars of liberation and ethnic cleansing but also by natural disasters, which may only occasionally and only by a stretch of the imagination be blamed on the colonial encounter. And intergenerational trauma studies is more marginal still, which is why I defer it till the Third Essay. The center of the field, and the center of this book, is the cultural displacement—or what I call the ideosomatic counterregulation—of the native by the colonizer, followed by the dream, or the myth, conditioned by the original colonial counterregulation, of the cultural displacement of the colonized by the decolonizer.

By the same token, of course, I risk boring you by treading well-worn ground. If discussions of C. L. R. James, Albert Memmi, Frantz Fanon, Homi Bhabha, and Gayatri Spivak are virtually obligatory in a study of postcoloniality, that expectation alone might potentially make this entire essay stale goods, banal, trite. The fact that Bhabha and Spivak broke new ground in the field by theorizing postcolonial affect obviously makes them important focal points in a somatic study of postcoloniality; but their pioneering efforts along these lines were noticed back in 1998 by Elizabeth Jane Bellamy. And if those efforts have largely been forgotten and ignored in the decade and a half since, is that perhaps a sign that no one really wants to be bothered with such matters anymore?

My pressing concerns throughout this Second Essay, and thus the grounds for my insistence that these iconic thinkers are worth another look, lie somewhere in the excluded and vacated middle between postmodern/poststructuralist discursivism and Marxist/(inter)nationalist activism. Not only can a more theoretically complex new look at postcolonial affect turn Bhabha's and Spivak's early (and rather tentative) interventions into a methodological platform for mediations between the opposing camps that still divide the field; I believe that somatic readings of James on violence and Nietzschean slave morality, Memmi on the failures of decolonization, and Fanon on the social construction of race can help us radically rethink some key issues in postcolonial studies.

In §2.1.3 I will be reading Fanon's *Black Skin, White Masks,* which he describes as an empirical study, "a clinical study": "The attitudes that I propose to describe are real. I have encountered them innumerable times" (12). He also, at least at the outset, explicitly situates his empiricism in terms of his own experience: "Since I was born in the Antilles, my observations and my conclusions are valid only for the Antilles—at least concerning the black man *at home.* Another book could be dedicated to explaining the differences that separate the Negro of the Antilles from the Negro of Africa" (14, emphasis in original). Of course he can't help himself; once he gets going he begins generalizing freely about "the Negro," theorizing "the black man," and freely admitting that objections to such generalizations are valid and apply to him as well: "In the beginning I wanted to confine myself to the Antilles. But, regardless of consequences, dialectic took the upper hand and I was compelled to *see* that the Antillean is first of all a Negro" (172–73, emphasis in original). Here in the Second Essay I'm going to try to stretch myself, to mix a metaphor, across the horns of the same dialectic: to treat three exemplary early analyses of (de)colonization both as empirical case studies, limited to specific (post) colonial experiences—James on Haiti, Memmi on the Maghreb, and Fanon on the Antilles—and as exemplary theorizations of (de)colonizing ideosomatic counterregulation that are generally applicable to "postcolonial culture." What I gain from this double vision is economy: it allows me to use James, Memmi, and Fanon to set up a series of sample somatic theorizations of (de)colonization without having to (pretend to) cover the whole field.

I'll also be bringing other, more theoretical perspectives to bear on each exemplary postcolonial critic in the first three sections: Friedrich Nietzsche on James, Arif Dirlik on Memmi, Hélène Cixous and Robert Young on Fanon. In §2.1.3.3 I'll also be reading the 2004 UNICEF-sponsored Spanish short *Binta y la gran idea* as a neocolonizing representation of decolonizing counterregulation; and in §2.2.2.4, after my somatic exfoliations of Bhabha and Spivak on postcolonial affect, I conclude with a look at Spivak's reading of "Douloti the Bountiful" by Mahasweta Devi.

2.1 EMPIRICAL STUDIES

2.1.1 C. L. R. James

> The difficulty was that though one could trap them like animals, transport them in pens, work them alongside an ass or a horse and beat both with the same stick, stable them and starve them, they remained, despite their black skins and curly hair, quite invincibly human beings; with the intelligence and resentments of human beings. To cow them into the necessary docility and acceptance necessitated a régime of calculated brutality and terrorism, and it is this that explains the unusual spectacle of property-owners apparently careless of preserving their property: they had first to ensure their own safety.
>
> These slaves were being used for the opening up of new lands. There was no time to allow for the period of acclimatization, known as the seasoning, and they died like flies. From the earliest days of the colony towards the middle of the eighteenth century, there had been some improvement in the treatment of the slaves, but this enormous number of newcomers who had to be broken and terrorized into labour and submission caused an increase in fear and adversity.
>
> —C. L. R. James, *The Black Jacobins* (11, 56)

C. L. R. James was born in 1901 in the British Crown colony of Trinidad, attended the Queen's Royal College in Port of Spain, and upon graduation taught school for six years (one of his students was the young Eric Williams, Trinidad and Tobago's first prime minister and "Father of the Nation"), during which time he also wrote cricket journalism, short stories, and a novel (*Minty Alley,* not published until 1936). He also got involved with the *Beacon* anticolonialist group and began to write books (*The Life of Captain Cipriani: An Account of the British Government in the West Indies,* 1932) and pamphlets (*The Case for West-Indian Self Government,* 1933) against colonialism.

In 1932 he moved to England, where he expanded his involvement in the West Indian independence movement to pan-African agitation, becoming chair of the International African Friends of Abyssinia; along with his childhood friend George Padmore he also became an influential member of the International African Service Bureau, through which he met later Ghanaian president Kwame Nkrumah, of whom he would later write *Kwame Nkrumah and the Ghana Revolution* (1977). During these years in England he also spent time in France researching his history of the 1791 Haitian revolution, *The Black Jacobins* (1938), which remains his best-known book today; the research also inspired a play, *Toussaint L'Ouverture*, which was produced in the West End in 1936, starring Paul Robeson.

In England James also joined the Trotskyist movement and published three books of Marxist theory, and when he moved to the United States in 1938, he visited Lev Trotsky in exile in Mexico, went on a speaking tour to promote the movement, and engaged in a series of published dialogues with Trotsky himself. He also became very active in Marxist politics, first in the Socialist Workers' Party, then helping found the Workers' Party (WP), where he (cadre name "J. R. Johnson") and Trotsky's former secretary Raya Dunayevskaya (cadre name "Freddie Forrest") formed the Johnson-Forrest (JF) Tendency. Dunayevskaya, the founder of what was then called Marxist Humanism and later became known as the "New Left," was doing the first English translation of Marx's *Economic and Philosophical Manuscripts of 1844* (one of the foundations of Marxist Humanism), and she and James cotranslated the "Critique of the Hegelian Dialectic and Philosophy as a Whole." In 1939 James followed Dunayevskaya in splitting with Trotsky over the nature of the Soviet Union: where Trotsky saw it as a degenerated workers' state, and the WP saw it as bureaucratic-collectivist, the JF Tendency saw it as state-capitalist and disinclined to support the liberation movements of oppressed minorities. In 1952 James was detained by the U.S. government for overstaying his visa by ten years, and, while waiting on Ellis Island to be deported, wrote a study of Melville entitled *Mariners, Renegades and Castaways: The Story of Herman Melville and the World We Live In*, had it privately published, and sent a copy to every member of the U.S. Senate, hoping (in vain) to convince them to let him stay.

After a few years in England, he returned in 1958 to Trinidad, where his old student Dr. Eric Williams offered him the job of editing *The Nation* for the pro-independence People's National Movement; his advocacy of a West Indies Federation led to a falling-out with Williams and resignation of the editorship, however, and he spent the remaining years of his life in the U.S., where he taught at Federal City College (1968–80), and England, where he died in 1989. His best-known book from this period is *Beyond a Boundary* (1963), a kind of cricket memoir that is also a study of decolonization.

Most of my remarks, however, will be devoted to a reading of James's early history of the Haitian Revolution, *The Black Jacobins,* from which my epigraphs are taken. In an era of colonial discourse analysis, it is worth remembering that people were physically and culturally displaced in the colonial context not only with discourse, but also with brute physical force. Of course brute physical force too can be troped as discourse, especially, perhaps, coming out of Foucault's *Discipline and Punish* by way of Kafka's "In the Penal Colony," as the "inscription on bodies" of discipline and punishment. Since in Kafka's story the actual punitive speech acts of the judges are etched on the skins of the convicts,[1] it is possible to *think* of what James calls the "régime of calculated brutality and terrorism" that the French colonizers of Saint-Domingue (renamed Haiti in 1804[2]) launched against their slaves in order to "cow them into the necessary docility and acceptance" as essentially a discursive regime. And this is a useful trope: it helps us think about physical pain more complexly than simply as an overwhelming bodily experience that shuts down thought. But it is also important not to naturalize this trope as reality—not to let it iterosomatically shut down thought about the bodily experience that in turn shuts down thought.

It's ironic, in fact, that poststructuralist theorists, whose intellectual tradition was powerfully shaped by Friedrich Nietzsche, should be so eager to iterosomatize physical pain as a discursive formation. In *On the Genealogy of Morals,* after all, Foucault's direct model for *Discipline and Punish,* Nietzsche specifically theorized physical pain as the primary "mnemotechnic" channel of "civilizing" discipline:

> "How does one create a memory for the human animal? How does one go about to impress anything on that partly dull, partly flighty human intelligence—that incarnation of forgetfulness—so as to make it stick?" As we might well imagine, the means used in solving this age-old problem have been far from delicate: in fact, there is perhaps nothing more terrible in man's earliest history than his mnemotechnics. "A thing is branded on the memory to make it stay there; only what goes on hurting will stick"—this is one of the oldest and, unfortunately, one of the most enduring psychological axioms. In fact, one might say that wherever on earth one still finds solemnity, gravity, secrecy, somber hues in the life of an individual or a nation, one also senses a residuum of that terror with which men must formerly have promised, pledged, vouched. It is the past—the longest, deep-

est, hardest of pasts—that seems to surge up whenever we turn serious. Whenever man has thought it necessary to create a memory for himself, his effort has been attended with torture, blood sacrifice. The ghastliest sacrifices and pledges, including the sacrifice of the first-born; the most repulsive mutilations, such as castration; the cruelest rituals in every religious cult (and all religions are at bottom systems of cruelty)—all these have their origin in that instinct which divined pain to be the strongest aid to mnemonics. (II:3, 192–93)

This is not a discursive theory. Physical pain here is not "inscribed" on the body in signs or symbols—though of course it can be metaphorically retheorized along those lines. What Nietzsche offers us in the Second Essay of the *Genealogy* is a protoneurological[3] theory of the counterregulatory effect pain has on the human nervous system. He has just postulated in the human animal a "faculty of oblivion," "an active screening device, responsible for the fact that what we experience and digest psychologically does not, in the stage of digestion, emerge into consciousness any more than what we ingest physically does" (II:1, 189). This faculty of oblivion, precursor of Freud's unconscious, has for Nietzsche a specifically homeostatic neurophysiological function: "to shut temporarily the doors and windows of consciousness; to protect us from the noise and agitation with which our lower organs work for or against one another; to introduce a little quiet into our consciousness so as to make room for the nobler functions and functionaries of our organism which do the governing and planning" (II:1, 189). "There can," Nietzsche insists, "be no happiness, no serenity, no hope, no pride, no *present*, without oblivion. A man in whom this screen is damaged and inoperative is like a dyspeptic (and not merely *like* one): he can't be done with anything . . ." (II:1, 189). Nietzsche, himself a dyspeptic whose gastrointestinal disorders frequently shut down his ability to think,[4] positively *longs* for the homeostatic screen that would protect him from the "noise and agitation with which our lower organs work for or against one another."

And yet, he says, that faculty of oblivion also tends to block our ability to make and keep promises, and thus to retard the civilizing process—and pain, he says, especially brutal punitive pain, has been our regime for remembering, for imposing a memory on a "naturally forgetful" nervous system:

Now this naturally forgetful animal, for whom oblivion represents a power, a form of strong health, has created for himself an opposite power, that of remembering, by whose aid, in certain cases, oblivion may be suspended— specifically in cases where it is a question of promises. By this I do not mean a purely passive succumbing to past impressions, the indigestion of being unable to be done with a pledge once made, but rather an active not wishing to be done with it, a continuing to will what has once been willed, a veritable "memory of the will"; so that, between the original determination and the actual performance of the thing willed, a whole world of new things, conditions, even volitional acts, can be interposed without snapping the long chain of the will. But how much all this presupposes! A man who wishes to dispose of his future in this manner must first have learned to separate necessary from accidental acts; to think causally; to see distant things as though they were near at hand; to distinguish means from ends. In short, he must have become not only calculating but himself calculable [*berechenbar*], regular even to his own perception, if he is to stand pledge for his own future as a guarantor does. (II:1, 189–90)

This is as good an encapsulation of the European counterregulatory colonizing ideal as we have: to take the "naturally forgetful animal" of Africa or Asia or the Americas and force him or her through physical pain and other disciplinary regimes (education, religion, law) to remember, to "continue to will what has once been willed," to "become not only calculating but himself calculable." By creating a "muscle memory" or somatic marker, disciplinary pain goes on hurting after the whipping or the torture has physically ended, and so becomes the internalized agent of the colonizer's discipline ("only what goes on hurting will stick"), the exosomatized calculus or *Rechenstein* (lit. calculating stone) inside the colonized's organism that makes him or her calculable. In this sense disciplinary pain is simply an intense channel of social disapproval—or else the body language of disapproval is simply a milder channel of disciplinary pain. Pain is used to establish in the individual the authority of the group; once that authority has been established, the somatomimetic circulation of body language and body states through the somatic exchange will ideally suffice to stabilize social regulation. It may also not suffice, of course, leading to idiosomatic deregulation and either ostracism, if the idiosomatic deregulators are in a small enough minority or, if they become a strong enough power within the group, counterregulatory revolt.

Of course Nietzsche is specifically interested in how "we"—"Westerners" from the ancient Greeks and Hebrews to the Germans—have civilized "ourselves," but parallel quotations from his Second Essay and the opening pages of *The Black Jacobins* make it clear that colonization entailed the exportation of exosomatized European self-torture to the "primitives" that Europeans found abroad:

It needs only a glance at our ancient penal codes to impress on us what labor it takes to create a nation of thinkers. . . . Germans have resorted to ghastly means in order to triumph over their plebeian instincts and brutal coarseness. We need only recount some of our ancient forms of punishment: stoning (even in earliest legend millstones are dropped on the heads of culprits); breaking on the wheel (Germany's own contribution to the techniques of punishment); piercing with stakes, drawing and quartering, trampling to death with horses, boiling in oil or wine (these were still in use in the fourteenth and fifteenth centuries), the popular flaying alive, cutting out of flesh from the chest, smearing the victim with honey and leaving him in the sun, a prey to flies. By such methods the individual was finally taught to remember five or six "I won'ts" which entitled him to participate in the benefits of society; and indeed, with the aid of this sort of memory, people eventually "came to their senses." What an enormous price man had to pay for reason, seriousness, control over his emotions—those grand human prerogatives and cultural showpieces! How much blood and horror lies behind all "good things"! (Nietzsche II:3, 193–94)

But there was no ingenuity that fear or a depraved imagination could devise which was not employed to break their [the African slaves'] spirit and satisfy the lusts and resentment of their owners and guardians—irons on the hands and feet, blocks of wood that the slaves had to drag behind them wherever they went, the tin-plate mask designed to prevent the slaves eating the sugar-cane, the iron collar. Whipping was interrupted in order to pass a piece of hot wood on the buttocks of the victim; salt, pepper, citron, cinders, aloes, and hot ashes were poured on the bleeding wounds. Mutilations were common, limbs, ears, and sometimes the private parts, to deprive them of the pleasures which they could indulge in without expense. Their masters poured burning wax on their arms and hands and shoulders, emptied the boiling cane sugar over their heads, burned them alive, roasted them on slow fires, filled them with gunpowder and blew them up with a match; buried them up to the neck and smeared their heads with sugar that the flies might devour them; fastened them near to nests of ants or wasps; made them eat their excrement, drink their urine, and lick the saliva of other slaves. One colonist was known in moments of anger to throw himself on his slaves and stick his teeth into their flesh. (James, *Black Jacobins* 12–13)

The only real difference between these "ancient" German tortures, found in Germany as "recently" as the fifteenth century, and the more "modern" colonialist tortures found in Haiti and other slave-owning colonies in the eighteenth and nineteenth centuries, is that Nietzsche and James—both of them products of such "civilizing" regimes, centuries later—attribute different motivations to them. For Nietzsche, they are intended to teach the individual "to remember five or six 'I won'ts' which entitled him to participate in the benefits of society"; for James they are motivated by fear and "a depraved imagination," by "the lusts and resentment of [the slaves'] owners and guardians." Also, of course, the German victims of this regime "come to their senses": the result in the individual is "reason, seriousness, control over his emotions." James writes that "the majority of the slaves accommodated themselves to this unceasing brutality by a profound fatalism and a wooden stupidity before their masters" (15).

This difference is partly due to the different time scales in Nietzsche and James: Nietzsche is looking back on the millennia of Western civilization leading up to his own time, while James (at this point in his book) is looking at the early weeks and months of enslavement, perhaps at most years, the "seasoning" of slaves. At a deeper level, though, it is also conditioned by the difference that Nietzsche is interested in the Western civilization of other Westerners, the German civilization of other Germans, while James is studying the French "civilization"—the breaking, cowing, and terrorizing—of African slaves, who are not so much fellow humans to be civilized as they are dangerous chattel, animal enough to be chattel and human enough to be dangerous. But then Nietzsche does not entirely ignore the colonial applications of his genealogy:

> By way of comfort to the milksops, I would also venture the suggestion that in those days pain did not hurt as much as it does today; at all events, such is the opinion of a doctor who has treated Negroes for complicated internal inflammations which would have driven the most stoical European to distraction—the assumption being that the negro represents an earlier phase of human development. (It appears, in fact, that the curve of human susceptibility to pain drops abruptly the moment we go below the top layer of culture comprising ten thousand or ten million individuals. For my part, I am convinced that, compared with one night's pain endured by a hysterical bluestocking, all the suffering of all the animals that have been used for scientific experiments is as nothing.) (II:7, 199–200)

Nietzsche's genealogical argument seems essentializing here—with "animals" and "Negroes" not only culturally but also physiologically early and low and Europeans culturally and physiologically late and high, and with educated liberal European women even later and higher on the genealogical hierarchy of civilization than European men, indeed absurdly so—but his apparent essentialism is in fact a mapping of what he is theorizing as the counter-regulatory *transformation* of physiology over the last thousand years or so. It's not just that Europeans today (and especially "hysterical bluestockings") are more susceptible to pain than Europeans were seven or eight centuries ago, or than dark-skinned people are today; it's that people whose ancestors were brutalized for centuries are more susceptible to pain than people whose ancestry is relatively new to the brutality of the "civilizing" process. Pain has a kind of intergenerationally cumulative effect, Nietzsche is suggesting, so that the more "civilized" we become, the less pain is needed to regulate us: the tiniest twinge or threat of pain and we yield, we conform. "Perhaps," he writes, "it is even legitimate to allow the possibility that pleasure in cruelty is not really extinct today; only, given our greater delicacy, that pleasure has had to undergo a certain sublimation and subtilization, to be translated into imaginative and psychological terms in order to pass muster before even the tenderest hypocritical conscience" (II:7, 200). Racist and sexist as Nietzsche's genealogical hierarchy here unquestionably is, therefore, it is a constructivist rather than an essentialist form of racism and sexism: what would make "hysterical bluestockings" more susceptible to pain and "Negroes" less would not be any kind of innate physiological difference but the relative duration in the two groups of the intergenerational transmission of punitive pain-based ideosomatic counterregulation.

The two constructions of the motivations behind that counterregulation—Nietzsche's that it was designed, however horrifically, to civilize its targets, and James's that it was a repressive reaction-formation born out of the Haitian colonizers' fear, resentment, lust, and depravity—also represent two radically opposed constructions of the colonizing ideosomatic exchange. At one end, Nietzsche's internalization of mastery, it seems that the group imposes a painful counterregulatory regime on its members in order to discipline them to conformity, to make them iterosomatize punitive pain as introjected master(y), "self-mastery" as submission to group normativity. At the other end, James's description of the "seasoning" of slaves, it seems that the group is defined in terms of the circulation of potentially dysregulatory feelings—that everyone, slave-owner and slave alike, feels at least fear and resentment, that the slaves are afraid of the slave-owners' resentment and the slave-owners are afraid of the slaves' resentment—and that each side harbors and sooner or later expresses violent impulses as an outward *channel* for those feelings. In this latter construction the somatic exchange serves no "civilizing" function at all: it may be designed to terrorize the slaves into docility and submission, but it becomes instead a kind of ideosomatic pressure-cooker for fear, resentment, and brutal reaction. The "cultural" legacy of that pressure-cooker in Haiti, of course, can still be all too viscerally felt two centuries later in (§1.2) the work of Edwidge Danticat.

From Nietzsche's point of view, James's construction of the colonial somatic exchange would have to be seen as still circulating that same fear, that same resentment, and thus as a textbook case of what he calls "slave morality":

> The slave revolt in morals begins by rancor turning creative and giving birth to values—the rancor of beings who, deprived of the direct outlet of action, compensate by an imaginary vengeance. All truly noble morality grows out of triumphant self-affirmation. Slave ethics, on the other hand, begins by saying *no* to an "outside," an "other," a non-self, and that *no* is its creative act. This reversal of direction of the evaluating look, this invariable looking outward instead of inward, is a fundamental feature of rancor. Slave ethics requires for its inception a sphere different from and hostile to its own. Physiologically speaking, it requires an outside stimulus in order to act at all; all its action is reaction. The opposite is true of aristocratic valuations: such values grow and act spontaneously, seeking out their contraries only in order to affirm themselves even more gratefully and delightedly. . . .
>
> All this stands in utter contrast to what is called happiness among the impotent and oppressed, who are full of bottled-up aggressions. Their happiness is purely passive and takes the form of drugged tranquility, stretching and yawning, peace, "Sabbath," emotional slackness. Whereas the noble lives before his own conscience with confidence and frankness (*gennaios* "nobly bred" emphasizes the nuance "truth" and perhaps also "ingenuous"), the rancorous person is neither truthful nor ingenuous nor honest and forthright with himself. His soul squints; his mind loves hide-outs, secret paths, and back doors; everything that is hidden seems to him his own world, his security, his comfort; he is expert in silence, in long memory, in waiting, in provisional self-depreciation, and in self-humiliation. (I:10, 170–72)

One obvious question to ask Nietzsche here is where his own rancor at "slave morality" comes from—why he seems to be *accusing* slaves and their descendants of compensating by imaginary vengeance, saying *no* to an outside Other, or, "full of bottled-up aggressions," finding happiness in doing nothing, as if all that were somehow a base and shameful response to enslavement. The obvious answer is that the morality he is most interested in demystifying as slave morality is that of his own now powerful group, that of Western philosophers (Socrates, Mark Migotti argues, is for Nietzsche the first "Thersites of genius" (758) who shames the nobles with his slave morality), of Christians, of German Lutherans—and he is the son of a Lutheran pastor. His romanticized conception of "noble morality" as "grow[ing] out of triumphant self-affirmation," then, would be his projection of a utopian ideal into the past and present as a kind of hopeful prefiguration of his own future freedom from his own slave rancor against the old slaves become new masters, the ascetic priests among both the Jews and the Christians.

Despite his aggressive dysphemizing of slaves and euphemizing of their masters, however, Nietzsche's analysis of slave morality is acute, and anticipates much colonial discourse analysis of the decolonization process[5]—which in fact suggests, as I'll be arguing in §2.1.2.2, that decolonization is not the reversal but rather the next stage of colonization. The image of "rancor turning creative and giving birth to values" explains not only Christianity but also the politically volatile value systems of many former colonies today, always ready to "compensate by an imaginary vengeance" or, in ethnic cleansing and other forms of seemingly excessive violence, actual vengeance for imaginary (transferential) crimes. His notion that slave morality says "*no* to an 'outside,' an 'other,' a non-self, and that *no* is its creative act," that "slave ethics requires for its inception a sphere different from and hostile to its own," feeds Freud's conception of negation, which has been extraordinarily influential in the shaping of our understanding of colonial and postcolonial discourse. His suggestion that slave morality or decolonization is grounded at base in the "reversal of direction of the evaluating look" anticipates not only the contemporary understanding that decolonization involves the reversal of the energies of colonization but also the somatic notion that body language, or rather the transformative circulation of body states through somatic mimeses of body language, is the primary channel of social regulation. Nietzsche's notion that slave morality survives as body-becoming-mind (susceptibility to pain creatively mapped as a value system) in cultures that have not been enslaved for centuries also introduces, under the rubric of "genealogy," the concept of the intergenerational somatic transmission of trauma, to which we will be returning in the Third Essay. And the last lines in that quotation clearly adumbrate early analyses of the impact of colonization on the colonized by Albert Memmi in *The Colonizer and the Colonized* (§2.1.2) and Frantz Fanon in *Black Skin, White Masks* (§2.1.3): "the rancorous person is neither truthful nor ingenuous nor honest and forthright with himself. His soul squints; his mind loves hide-outs, secret paths, and back doors; everything that is hidden seems to him his own world, his security, his comfort; he is expert in silence, in long memory, in waiting, in provisional self-depreciation, and in self-humiliation."

Again, in *The Black Jacobins* James describes only the initial stages of this reversal:

The slaves destroyed tirelessly. Like the peasants in the Jacquerie or the Luddite wreckers, they were seeking their salvation in the most obvious way, the destruction of what they knew was the cause of their sufferings; and if they destroyed much it was because they had suffered much. They knew that as long as these plantations stood their lot would be to labour on them until they dropped. The only thing was to destroy them. From their masters they had known rape, torture, degradation, and, at the slightest provocation, death. They returned in kind. For two centuries the higher civilization [what Nietzsche would call "noble morality"] had shown them that power was used for wreaking your will on those whom you controlled. Now that they held power they did as they had been taught. In the frenzy of the first encounters they killed all, yet they spared the priests whom they feared and the surgeons who had been kind to them. They, whose women had undergone countless violations, violated all the women who fell into their hands, often on the bodies of their still bleeding husbands, fathers and brothers. "Vengeance! Vengeance!" was their war-cry, and one of them carried a white child on a pike as a standard. (88)

For James, clearly, this is "compensation," but not quite as "imaginary vengeance": they were returning violation for violation, torture for torture, death for death. In a sense, though, there was an imaginary component to their vengeance as well: no white woman they raped had ever raped a black woman, rendering vengeance-rapes the infliction of compensatory violence on symbolic or imaginary targets. Of course the white wives and daughters of plantation owners had enjoyed the fruits of their husbands' and fathers' exploitations of slaves, and were therefore complicit in the colonial system for the degradation of human beings; but this too is a symbolic or imaginary complicity.

In his next paragraph, however, James does begin to convert his justified rancor into a value system, into what Nietzsche calls slave morality:

And yet they were surprisingly moderate [he adds in a footnote: "This statement has been criticized. I stand by it"], then and afterwards, far more humane than their masters had been or would ever be to them. They did not maintain this revengeful spirit for long. The cruelties of property and privilege are always more ferocious than the revenges of poverty and oppression. For the one aims at perpetuating resented injustice, the other is merely a momentary passion soon appeased. As the revolution gained territory they spared many of the men, women, and children whom they surprised on plantations. To prisoners of war alone they remained merciless. They tore out their flesh with red-hot pincers, they roasted them on slow fires, they sawed a carpenter between two of his boards. Yet in all the records of that time there is no single instance of such fiendish tortures as burying white men up to the neck and smearing the holes in their faces to attract insects, or blowing them up with gun-powder, or any of the thousand and one bestialities to which they had been subjected. Compared with what their masters had done to them in cold blood, what they did was negligible, and they were spurred on by the ferocity with which the whites in Le Cap treated all slave prisoners who fell into their hands. (88–89)

The rebelling slaves were more "humane" than their "bestial" masters: this is the reversal of the evaluating look of which Nietzsche wrote, the transvaluation of value that seizes the moral high ground out of the ashes of the master's one-time vaunted superiority, now "revealed" (reconstructed) as criminal and subhuman. "The cruelties of property and privilege are always more ferocious than the revenges of poverty and oppression. For the one aims at perpetuating resented injustice, the other is merely a momentary passion soon appeased." This, it should be clear, is not simply journalistic reportage; it is a new morality, a decolonizing morality that justifies the excessive violence of rebelling slaves as "a momentary passion"—an understandable lapse from their true inner moral superiority—and condemns the excessive violence of the masters as systemic injustice.

Of course, this is not to join Nietzsche in condemning slave morality; it is rather to apply his analysis of slave morality without the condemnation. Indeed the classic analyses of the social psychology of the formerly colonized are quintessentially attempts to understand the dysregulatory impulses in decolonizing cultures in the specific explanatory context of the colonizations that conditioned those dysregulations, and thus in a very real sense to extend and consolidate Nietzsche's genealogical analysis of slave morality, to explain the persistence of slave morality in a decolonizing context genealogically, as something *produced*—and intergenerationally reproduced—rather than innate.

As a Marxist, in fact, James does not indulge much in this sort of psychoanalytical or other slave-moralizing of decolonization. His later discussions of decolonization, *Modern Politics* and *Party Politics in the West Indies*, as well as "Black Sansculottes," his 1964 updating of his history of postcolonial Haiti to Papa Doc Duvalier and the Tonton Macoutes, by and large focus on the political ramifications of economic issues like land reform and the nationalization of industry. He comes closer to an analysis of what Nietzsche calls slave morality in his 1963 memoir of cricket (and generally the culture of decolonization), *Beyond a Boundary,* or in his 1964 review of Orlando Patterson's Jamaican Rastafari novel *The Children of Sisyphus:*

> The Rastafari are one example of the contemporary rejection of the life to which we are all submitted. The Mau-Mau of Kenya do the same. The Black Muslims of the United States are of the same brand. . . .
>
> But Rastafari and Mr Patterson are West Indian. They are both new. Their world is just beginning. They do not suffer from any form of angst. They have no deep-seated consciousness of failure, no fear of defeat. That is not in their history. Mr Patterson does not, cannot, convince the reader that the life he is describing is absurd. Horrible, horrible, most horrible it is. But it is not absurd. The prostitute who tries to lift herself out of the squalor, the filth of the Jungle is consciously impelled by "ambition." The other prostitute whose pathetic destiny equals the horrors of her existence is impelled by her passionate wish to give her daughter a secondary education. The colossal stupidities, the insanities of the Rastafari are consciously motivated by their acute consciousness of the filth in which they live, their conscious refusal to accept the fictions that pour in upon them from every side. It is the determination to get out of it that leads them to their imaginative fantasies of escape to Africa. These passions and forces are the "classic human virtues." As long as they express themselves, the form may be absurd, but the life itself is not absurd. The fate of Rastafari and Mr Patterson himself are very closely linked. And this book is one proof of their common distress and common destiny. (164)

Here, clearly, the genealogical analysis of Nietzsche (and later of Freud and Foucault) is not very hard at work: "They are both new. Their world is just beginning. They do not suffer from any form of angst. They have no deep-seated consciousness of failure, no fear of defeat. That is not in their history." The Rastafari simply *reject* "the life to which we are all submitted," *refuse* "to accept the fictions that pour in upon them from every side." And, to James's mind, fictions are precisely what they are: not the iterosomatic traces of colonialism that are now circulated by their own group and so feel like realities, like human nature; just patent lies and propaganda pouring in upon them from the outside, and so easy to resist. "The colossal stupidities, the insanities of the Rastafari are consciously motivated by their acute consciousness of the filth in which they live," but that filth has no history, no genealogy, certainly no genealogy of the body-becoming-mind, no history of the evaluative look. I assume that James's denial of the impact of colonial history on Jamaican poverty is ironic, a kind of satirical double-voicing of Rastafari idealism; but the fact that James does not analyze that history, does not genealogize the emergence of "the colossal stupidities, the insanities of the Rastafari" out of the brutalizing experience of colonization and slavery, renders this too a very sketchy critique of decolonizing slave morality. In what ways is Rastafarian religion a counterregulatory *revision* of the "colossal stupidities" and "insanities" of colonial culture? Presumably for the Marxist James one thing that makes the Rastafari movement stupid and insane is that it is a religion; another, perhaps, that it is more a Judeo-Christian "heresy" than an African syncretic religion like vodou or candomblé. But James does not raise these questions; again, he is more interested in the political and economic issues:

> But neither the economic masters nor the political inheritors (the coloured middle classes) want to have in their midst anything or anybody disturbing their precarious peace. The freedom which would enable the Rastafari to build their new Jerusalem in Jamaica's green and pleasant land would enable the Pattersons to steel and temper their weapons upon some dark and satanic mills. Their walls may appear to be very solid. But they are no more than the walls of Jericho. They would tumble at the sound of trumpets. But the trumpets must sound in Kingston, in Port of Spain, in Bridgetown and in Georgetown. From London (and in London) they are horns from an elf-land, blowing only faintly. (165)

2.1.2 Albert Memmi

> So goes the drama of the man who is a product and victim of colonization. He almost never succeeds in corresponding with himself.
>
> —Albert Memmi, *The Colonizer and the Colonized* (140)

> The decolonized experiences a form of stationary dismemberment, torn and pulled from every side.
>
> —Albert Memmi, *Decolonization and the Decolonized* (57)

Albert Memmi was born to Arabic-speaking Jewish parents in the French colony of Tunisia in 1921, studied philosophy at the University of Algiers and the Sorbonne, and after university took a teaching job back at his old high school in Tunis. In 1953 he published his first novel, *La statue de sel* (*The Pillar of Salt*), a semiautobiographical tale about a young Jew from the Tunis ghetto who breaks with his family tradition to become an intellectual and a fiction-writer but is paralyzed throughout, like Lot's wife, by his solitude. He was an ardent supporter of the anticolonial liberation movement, but upon independence in 1956 he found himself ostracized from the new nationalistic Muslim society, and moved permanently to France, where he taught high school and eventually, in 1970, accepted a post at the University of Nanterre. His most famous book, *Portrait du colonisé, précédé du Portrait du colonisateur* (*The Colonizer and the Colonized*), was published in 1957, with a preface by Jean-Paul Sartre; its sequel, *Portrait du décolonisé* (*Decolonization and the Decolonized*), appeared nearly fifty years later, in 2004, when Memmi was in his early eighties. His other novels include *Agar* (*Strangers*), *Le Scorpion ou la confession imaginaire* (*The Scorpion*), and *Le Désert ou la vie et les aventures de Jubaïr Ouali el Mammi* (*The Desert*); his other nonfiction works include *L'Homme dominé* (*Dominated Man*), *La Dépendance* (*Dependence*), *Le Racisme* (*Racism*), *Le Nomade immobile* ("The Immobile Nomad," not yet translated), and several works on Judaism, *Portrait d'un juif* (*Portrait of a Jew*), *La libération du Juif* (*Liberation of the Jew*), and *Juifs et Arabes* (*Jews and Arabs*).

What I want to do in §2.1.2.1 is to read *The Colonizer and the Colonized* and *Decolonization and the Decolonized* intertextually, beginning with the latter, which blames the patent failure of decolonization almost entirely on the decolonized themselves, on the greed and corruption and violence of their leaders. This constitutes a radical rethinking of *Colonized*, perhaps even a rueful recantation in the light of subsequent history—but also, I want to argue, a forgetting. In §2.1.2.2, then, I will build on a few passing remarks in *Decolonized* and recent work by Arif Dirlik and others to show that what Memmi takes to be the *failure* of decolonization is in fact the *illusion* of decolonization, the hegemonic myth that decolonization as the counterregulatory "reversal" of colonization is a viable project—an illusion that, Dirlik argues persuasively, is actually a phantom projection of colonialism in its ongoing evolution from military and economic occupation into neocolonialist globalization, or what I propose to call the colonialist metanarrative of development. In §2.1.2.3, finally, I will take a look back at Memmi's discussion of "the colonizer who refuses" from *Colonized* as an autocritical perspective on my own project here.

2.1.2.1 THE FAILURE OF DECOLONIZATION

There is a certain cognitive slippage between Memmi's two books on colonization and decolonization that I find particularly telling, as it seems to reflect his confusion about the five-decade persistence of what I would call colonial ideosomatic regulation: because he lacks a model that would adequately explain that persistence, it seems to him as if there must be none, as if the belief that decolonization continues to be regulated by (slightly displaced) colonial ideosomatics must be sheer illusion, a flimsy excuse apologists invent to let the young nations off the hook.

For example, he describes the poor blacks' hostility toward the Italian and Korean business owners in their neighborhood in Spike Lee's *Do the Right Thing*, and comments:

> My friends asked me why they didn't do what the Asians or Italians did. My pained response was that these immigrant groups obviously help one another. As soon as they arrive in the country, they are taken in by their extended family, assisted by various civic associations. Why don't the blacks have their own associations? The explanation given is that this is contrary to their "mentality," that they dislike associations, and so on. When the questioner insists, the real reason is given: "Because they were slaves!" "But," he responds in astonishment, "that was a long time ago!"
>
> Black Americans are not a decolonized people [why not?⁶], although they have certain traits in common with them, just as they have certain traits in common with the colonized. But their evasive responses are the same. It is the fault of history, it is always the fault of the whites. Dolorism is a natural tendency to exaggerate one's pains and attribute them to another. Like the decolonized, as long as blacks have not freed themselves of dolorism, they will be unable to correctly analyze their condition and act accordingly. (*Decolonized* 18–19)

This is a complaint that he recurs to over and over in the book: "If the decolonized are still not free citizens in a free country, it is because they remain the powerless playthings of some ancient fate. If the economy fails, it's always the fault of the ex-colonizer, not the systematic bloodletting of the economy by the new masters, not the viscosity of their culture, which fails to address its present and the future" (20), and "Apologists go out of their way to learnedly explain that what can be criticized today in Islam are merely the remnants of an anti-Islamic period, overlooking the fact that we might have done away with such remnants since then" (33). Yes, we might have, but that isn't exactly a fact that might be overlooked; it's a potential that hasn't been realized. The interesting question that Memmi wants to address, and can't, is *why* it hasn't been realized. His only hesitant explanation is the greed and the corruption of the leaders of the new nations, but he himself recognizes that these are just more symptoms of the problem, not its cause.

Or again:

> Why such continued desperate violence? The embarrassed historians among the formerly colonized have not failed to look for explanations. They claim this is simply a bad habit inherited from the colonial period, an additional wound. They note that there was considerably less of an emotional outpouring when the colonized suffered at the hands of the colonizers. So be it. We try to relieve our sense of guilt any way we can. But now the violence occurs among the formerly colonized, against their own people. In spite of the passage of time, the situation has not only endured, it has gotten worse. (52–53)

It's easy enough to point out that he himself predicted something very like this enduring recourse to violence in his earlier book, a half century before:

> Uncertain of himself, he [the ex-colonized] gives in to the intoxication of fury and violence. In fact, he asserts himself vigorously. Uncertain of being able to convince others, he provokes them. Simultaneously provocative and sensitive, he now makes a display of his contrasts, refuses to let himself be forgotten as such, and becomes indignant when they are mentioned. Automatically distrustful, he assumes hostile intentions in those with whom he converses and reacts accordingly. He demands endless approval from his best friends, of even that which he doubts and himself condemns. (*Colonized* 135–36)

It's harder to recognize that Memmi has in both books the conceptual or at least imagistic tools with which to work through this problem to an explanation, but doesn't quite know what to do with them: "Obviously," he sighs in *Decolonized*, "nothing comes of nothing; the actual face of the world's young nations bears the imprint of their colonial past along with their own history" (21). After all his complaining about ex-colonized historians using the colonial legacy as a lame excuse for their country's lack of decolonizing progress, Memmi here (briefly) adopts the same position—but what I'm most interested in there is the facial trope for that lingering legacy. What kind of imprint is left by the colonizer on the colonized's face? If this were James's history of Haitian slavery, it might be a scar left by a whip; but Memmi's own argumentative history suggests that what he means here is the imprint left by somatic mimeticism, the assimilative effect empathetic mimicry has on body language, and through body language both outward appearance ("the actual face of the world's young nations") and inward body states. In *Colonized*, for example, he wrote extensively of the colonized's imperfect but powerfully transformative attempts to assimilate his or her behavior, posture, gestures, accent, and tone of voice to that of the colonizer: "At the height of his revolt, the colonized still bears the traces and lessons of prolonged cohabitation (just as the smile or movements of a wife, even during divorce proceedings, remind one strangely of those of her husband)" (129). Those traces of prolonged cohabitation are not just kinesic but somatic, which is to say, not just outwardly mimetic but inwardly evaluative and thus collectively regulatory, and not just a passing physiological tropism but persistent over time ("*still* bears the traces"), which is to say, stored as somatic markers.

By the time he comes to write *Decolonized*, however, Memmi has forgotten his earlier protosomatic insistence on this *lasting* mimetic transformation of the colonized: "Like buffalo that follow their leader," he writes, "even when he leads them into a ravine, human animals display a kind of gregarious mimicry" (19); "The presidents of the new republics generally mimic what is most arbitrary about the colonial power" (60). Mimicry is not purposeful, not transformed by or transformative of the (post)colonial encounter; it is "gregarious" and "arbitrary," sheer superficial mammalian behavior (which is not to suggest that mammalian behavior is actually this superficial). In the earlier book the accusation that "the colonized is an ape" is attributed to the colonizer: "The shrewder the ape, the better he imitates, and the more the colonizer becomes irritated" (124). Now, after long somatic training in colonial mimesis and even longer exile in France, Memmi has himself assimilated to the colonizer's irritation, and no longer remembers what he knew in *Colonized*, that somatic mimesis *is* assimilative, counterregulatory, and that the assimilation is extremely difficult to reverse.

His analysis of the colonial counterregulation in *Colonized* is, in fact, one of the most powerfully insightful sections of the book. I mean the "Mythical portrait of the colonized" and "Situations of the colonized" chapters of Part Two. He begins there by defining the colonizer's "mythical portrait of the colonized" as a "series of negations," a definition that seems to anticipate poststructuralist readings of postcolonial identities as the emptying-out of the plenitude of idealized colonizer identities: "The point is," he writes, "that the colonized means little to the colonizer. Far from wanting to understand him as he really is, the colonizer is preoccupied with making him undergo this urgent change. The mechanism of this remolding of the colonized is revealing in itself. It consists, in the first place, of a series of negations. The colonized is not this, is not that. He is never considered in a positive light; or if he is, the quality which is conceded is the result of a psychological or ethical failing" (83–84). He seems even more like a protopoststructuralist colonial discourse analyst a couple of pages later: "What is left of the colonized at the end of this stubborn effort to dehumanize him? He is surely no longer an alter ego of the colonizer. He is hardly a human being. He tends rapidly toward becoming an object. As an end, in the colonizer's supreme ambition, he should exist only as a function of the needs of the colonizer, i.e., be transformed into a pure colonized" (86).

But the abstract differentiality (subalternity) of this image-analysis, the sense in which the dehumanized object-ideal of the "pure colonized" is at once the infinitely deferred cancellation of subjectivity and the iterative negation of the colonizer's alter ego-ideal, is everywhere in these chapters resaturated with evaluative affect. Even in that first apparently protopoststructuralist formulation above, for example, Memmi tendentiously somatizes his abstract equations with pathos: "means little" and "far from wanting to understand him as he really is" both surge with the hurt anger of the child led to expect love from his or her neglectful parents. Memmi's depiction of the colonizer's objectification of the colonized is not so much an analytical proposition as it is a fully embodied speech act, less abstract or discursive than *inflammatory,* intended to incite rebellion against it: the colonizer's counterregulatory ideal resomatized as the colonized's revolutionary anti-ideal.

And indeed on the very next page he gives us a powerful account of what I call the somatic exchange, troping it this time not with sight (mimicry) but with hearing (echo), once again suggesting that colonial counterregulation works by being *circulated as evaluative affect* through the colonized:

> More surprising, more harmful perhaps, is the echo that it excites in the colonized himself. Constantly confronted with this image of himself, set forth and imposed on all institutions and in every human contact, how could the colonized help reacting to his portrait? It cannot leave him indifferent and remain a veneer which, like an insult, blows with the wind. He ends up recognizing it as one would a detested nickname which has become a familiar description. The accusation disturbs him and worries him even more because he admires and fears his powerful accuser. "Is he not partially right?" he mutters. "Are we not all a little guilty after all? Lazy, because we have so many idlers? Timid, because we let ourselves be oppressed." Willfully created and spread by the colonizer, this mythical and degrading portrait ends up by being accepted and lived with to a certain extent by the colonized. It thus acquires a certain amount of reality and contributes to the true portrait of the colonized. (*Colonized* 87–88)

This is an almost letter-perfect description of the iteronormative effects of ideosomatic regulation: the colonizer circulates a negative or accusatory image of the colonized through "all institutions and in every human contact," till it "excites" a harmful "echo" in the colonized's own somatization of the world. This is no mere superficial mimicry, no ephemeral echo, no "veneer which, like an insult, blows with the wind": it sticks. "The accusation disturbs him and worries him even more because he admires and fears his powerful accuser": the ideosomatic hierarchy in the colonial encounter circulates not just "mythical and degrading portraits" but the evaluative affects that accompany and confirm those portraits, admiration and fear for the colonizer, worry and disturbing self-loathing for the colonized. And so, gradually, the colonial ideosomatic counterregulates the colonized's group construction of reality and identity: "It thus acquires a certain amount of reality and contributes to the true portrait of the colonized." This counterregulated reality/identity, Memmi notes, anticipating Foucault, is institutionalized (note here again the image of facial mimesis):

> This conduct, which is common to colonizers as a group, thus becomes what can be called a social institution. In other words, it defines and establishes concrete situations which close in on the colonized, weigh on him until they bend his conduct and leave their marks on his face. Generally speaking, these are situations of inadequacy. The ideological aggression which tends to dehumanize and then deceive the colonized finally corresponds to concrete situations which lead to the same result. To be deceived to some extent already, to endorse the myth and then adapt to it, is to be acted upon by it. That myth is furthermore supported by a very solid organization; a government and a judicial system fed and renewed by the colonizer's historic, economic and cultural needs. Even if he were insensitive to calumny and scorn, even if he shrugged his shoulders at insults and jostling, how could the colonized escape the low wages, the agony of his culture, the law which rules him from birth until death? (91)

What begins as an apparently discursive formulation, the "series of negations," is expanded first to the intersubjectivity of the social economy of value, and then to economic, cultural, and legal institutions that govern every aspect of the colonized's life—and each stage of the expansion is saturated with affect: the indignation at neglect in the "series of negations"; the detestation, disturbance, worry, admiration, and fear in the "echo that it excites in the colonized himself"; the calumny and the scorn and the agony that run like a bass note through the low wages and other legal depredations.

The final stage in this process is the breaking point, at which revolution becomes possible:

> Now, into what kind of life and social dynamic do we emerge? The colony's life is frozen; its structure is both corseted and hardened. No new role is open to the young man, no invention is possible. The colonizer admits this with a new classical euphemism: He respects, he proclaims, the ways and customs of the colonized. And, to be sure, he cannot help respecting them, be it by force. Since any change would have to be made against colonization, the colonizer is led to favor the least progressive features. He is not solely responsible for this mummification of the colonized society; he demonstrates relatively good faith when he maintains that it is independent by its own will. It derives largely, however, from the colonial situation. Not being master of its destiny, not being its own legislator, not controlling its organization, colonized society can no longer adapt its institutions to its grievous needs. But it is those needs which practically shape the organizational face of every normal society. . . . However, if the discord becomes too sharp, and harmony becomes impossible to attain under existing legal forms, the result is either to revolt or to be calcified. (98)

Or, more commonly, both: to be calcified and then to revolt, and to carry the calcification over into the revolution and the decolonization. "Colonized society," Memmi writes, "is a diseased society in which internal dynamics no longer succeed in creating new structures. Its century-hardened face has become nothing more than a mask under which it slowly smothers and dies. Such a society cannot dissolve the conflicts of generations, for it is unable to be transformed" (98–99).

And then, nearly half a century later, we find him shaking his head at the fulfillment of his own predictions, *accusing* the former colonies of not dissolving those untransformable conflicts: "For lack of anything better, governments promote folklore, arts and crafts, and tourism. As for tourism, it's better to be a servant than to go hungry. Even in Tunisia, which is often cited as an example for its recent success against poverty, at least a third of its revenue comes from the tourist industry. But these are dead ends. For they perpetuate the artificial character of the economy of these nations and maintain their dependence on the developed world, whose obsequious or rebellious clients they have become, instead of moving toward relative independence, which demands the courage of breaking with established structures and moving resolutely toward the future" (*Decolonized* 11–12).

And we find him accusing the Arab-Muslim nations of the Maghreb of not pluralizing the (post)colonial somatic exchange: "To restore some sense of balance Arab-Muslim intellectuals would have to make use of a tradition other than the submission to dogma and power, of siding with opinion. However, there no longer exists, if there ever did in the Arab-Muslim world, that great public tribunal characteristic of democracy, where everyone can publicly give his opinion without unnecessary risk. True controversies are rare, except possibly for unimportant details, where disagreements occur against a background of underlying unity. As a result, any condemnation of wrongdoing and scandal always comes from the exterior, from those outside the community, leading to suspicions of bias or perversity" (33). "There no longer exists, if there ever did": what exactly is the charge here? That Muslim Arabs have *banished* democracy, or that they never had it? "[I]sn't it astonishing," he complains, "that there are no discordant voices, even if they are wrong?" (33). How could this possibly be astonishing to the man who at 36 so brilliantly theorized the ways in which the colonized were locked into that somatic exchange of aggressive insecurity, the institutionalized circulation of calcified/inflamed self-loathing? Is this the fifty-years-after hangover of revolutionary idealism, the rueful aftermath of the impossibly hopeful belief back then that the revolution would once and for all toss the colonizer's mythical portrait on the bonfire?

2.1.2.2 THE CAPITALIST METANARRATIVE OF DEVELOPMENT

Decolonization and the Decolonized may not be a particularly cogently argued book, but it is full of trenchant observations. Here is one: "The situation is not one in which, as has been repeated so complacently, several civilizations clash. There is now a single, global, civilization that affects everyone, including fundamentalists, who seem to have no qualms about using cell phones, the Internet, the banking system, automobiles, and planes, and may one day just as easily embrace rockets and sophisticated weapons—technologies they did not invent. It is far from clear that they are entirely sincere in claiming to defend values that have become increasingly unsustainable" (44). There is, in other words, no clash between Christian and Islamic civilizations, or between Western democracy and Muslim theocracy: there is only one global civilization. On the face of it, this is naïve: of course there is a civilizational clash between the Euro-American and Arab-Muslim worlds! What is naïve about Memmi's remark, though, is really only its absolutism, his radical binary insistence that "the situation is *not* one in which . . . several civilizations clash." Actually, it is *both* one in which several civilizations clash *and* one increasingly dominated by a single global civilization—which is to say that the clash between the Christians and the Muslims, or between democracy and theocracy, or between the "First World" and the "Third World," or whatever names we want to put on the two camps, is itself at least partly conditioned and regulated by the emerging global civilization. But what is globalization but the latest economic and cultural guise assumed by colonialism—or, more broadly, the latest colonialist guise assumed by capitalism? And if Memmi is right both that the Arab-Muslim world was conditioned by colonialism to its current jihadist fervor and that this new global phase of capitalist/colonialist culture (still) dominates it, then the lack of progress toward true independence that he laments in the "decolonization" of the Maghreb is in fact not a *failed counterregulation* of colonial ideosomatics but a displaced function of continuing (neo)colonial *regulation*.

In a 2002 article entitled "Rethinking Colonialism," Arif Dirlik argues persuasively that postcolonial criticism orients itself to the study of the legacies of the colonial past through "assumptions that derive their plausibility from its context in globalization," and that, viewed from this new context, "colonialism no longer appears as 'the highest stage of capitalism,' as Lenin wrote of imperialism (1969), but a stage on the way to globalization—the most recent phase in the spatialization of the world by a capitalism that has yet to live out its history" (429–30). The main burden of Dirlik's argument, following Partha Chatterjee in *Nationalist Thought and the Colonial World* and Ania Loomba in *Colonialism/Postcolonialism* (215–31) on the replication of colonial discourses and practices in decolonization, is that *both* colonization and decolonization were products of that earlier stage, which all three scholars associate with nation-building:

> For all the retroactive readings of the nation back into the past, nations in the colonial world were products of colonialism, if inadvertently. While colonial policy and its effects varied widely, it is arguable nevertheless that, in contrast to nation building in Europe, European colonizers had little interest in the political integration of colonial territories into national entities, or the homogenization of their cultures into national cultures—which for obvious reasons were contrary to their interests. We may recall here the violence with which movements for national liberation and sovereignty were met with across the colonial world and the ideological efforts to discredit national liberation movements by identifying them with a global Communist conspiracy. Nevertheless, to realize their own interests in the

colonies European colonizers had little choice but to establish administrative boundaries in accordance with their needs and abilities, to seek
to impose uniform rules on the colonies that took account, in varying
tdegrees in different places, of local practices, and to create functionaries
recruited from the local population to facilitate colonial rule. (Dirlik 436)

They also, of course, replicated in the colonies what Dirlik describes in earlier
European nation-building as "the erasure (at least in intention) of local cultures and the promotion of a homogeneous national culture that would endow
the nation with cultural identity" (436), as when the Spaniards chose the Taga-
logs as the principal ethnic group in the Philippines and made *la lengua tagala*
the indigenous *lingua franca* for the islands—a status it continues to enjoy
in an independent Filipino nation today—or when the Belgians organized
the cultural identity of colonial Ruanda-Urundi around the Tutsi, "promot-
ing the Tutsi within the colonial administration and economy" while "legal
and bureaucratic barriers preventing Hutu upward mobility were cemented"
(Johnson 160), leading to ongoing tension and violence between the two
groups, most horrifically of course the Hutu genocide of 800,000 Tutsi in the
spring of 1994. "Anticolonial nationalism," Dirlik notes, "would emerge in the
end out of the ranks of the native functionaries of colonial rule, who were both
of the new structure of power and shut out from its rewards, and who were
keenly aware by virtue of their colonial education of the fundamental differences that distinguished colonial rule from national politics in Europe" (436).

What I want to pick out of Dirlik's article for particular emphasis, however,
is his discussion of the Three Worlds model, which he identifies as the primary
casualty of postcolonial theory's rejection of metanarratives in favor of "'borderlands' conditions, where the domination of one by the other yields before
boundary crossings, hybridities, mutual appropriations, and, especially, the
everyday resistance of the colonized to the colonizer" (433):

> The "Third World," the location for neo- and postcolonialisms, was a
> product of a systemic understanding of the world in terms of capital-
> ism and socialism—the "First" and the "Second" Worlds understood in
> developmental terms—which showed the Third World alternative paths
> to its future. Politically, the idea of the Third World pointed to the neces-
> sity of a common politics that derived from a common positioning in the
> system (rather than some homogeneous essentialized common quality,
> as is erroneously assumed these days in much postcolonial criticism). As
> colonialism had preceded the emergence of a Second World, the world of
> socialism, the Third World had historical priority to the Second, which

points also to the priority of capitalism in the systematic shaping of the world, to which socialism was a response (which also made socialism into an attractive goal in the liberation from colonialism). (433)

In an era of globalization, Dirlik argues, this model, focused as it was on the developmental trajectories of nations, is no longer relevant:

> Nevertheless, the present world is a world that is radically different from the world of decolonization in the immediate aftermath of World War II. Capitalism has reinvented itself and opened up to the formerly colonized, who are now participants in its global operations. Former colonials are in the process of colonizing the "mother" countries, bringing the earlier "contact zones" of the colonies into the heart of formerly colonialist societies. These motions of people force a redefinition both of nations and national cultures. Postcolonial intellectuals, having arrived in the First World, call into question cherished ideals of Eurocentric notions of progress and knowledge, for which they are rewarded by widespread acknowledgment of the vanguard role they play in the production of knowledge. New entrants into the ranks of capitalism revive cultural legacies erased by Eurocentrism to claim alternative paths to the future. As the former three worlds are configured so that it is possible to find Third Worlds in the First and First Worlds in the Second, so are class relations globally, so that it is now possible to find in the global ruling class representatives from all the former three worlds. (439)[7]

But if that's the case—or rather, since clearly it's at least partly the case, if that's the *whole* case—what are we to make of chestnuts like this, taken from an earlier (1994) Dirlik essay but virtually ubiquitous as a nonce problem in postcolonial studies: "Taking the term literally as post*colonial*, some practitioners of postcolonial criticism describe former settler colonies—such as the United States and Australia—as postcolonial, regardless of their status as First World societies and colonizers themselves of their indigenous populations. (Though to be fair, the latter could also be said of many Third World societies)" ("Postcolonial Aura" 336)? Is this slippage further evidence of the hybridization of the Three Worlds in a globalized economy and culture? Or is it evidence that the old Three Worlds metanarrative continues to circulate ideosomatically in the midst of widespread hybridization? I suggest it's the latter, in fact: if some former colonies become Second World colonizers (the People's Republic of China colonizing Tibet) and others become First World neocolonizers of vast tracts of the Third World (the United States, which is also still involved in the old colonial project, in Afghanistan and Iraq), isn't that a prime example of the First and Second Worlds showing "the Third World alternative paths to its future"? I would argue, in fact, that Dirlik's "fairness" should be extended to a recognition that, in turning successful decolonization into supremely exploitative neocolonizing First World status, the United States is not at all an anomaly in the capitalist/colonialist Three Worlds model, but rather an exemplary case of it.

Still very much at work in our mythological thinking about development, in other words, even in the midst of the global hybridization celebrated by postcolonial theorists, is an idealized nation-centered movement "up" the Three Worlds, from the Third to the Second to the First, or even—the ideal case is again of course the United States—from the Third directly to the First. That's where all postcolonial nations are ideologically supposed to want to go. Some, barred from the First, take great oppositional pride in their rise to the Second: Cuba, North Korea, Venezuela, arguably even Iran, if we're willing to shift our definition of the Second World from socialist anticapitalism to *any* anticapitalist or anti-First World opposition. This vision of the Second World is Frantz Fanon's clarion call in *The Wretched of the Earth*: "Two centuries ago, a former European colony decided to catch up with Europe. It succeeded so well that the United States of America became a monster, in which the taints, the sickness, and the inhumanity of Europe have grown to appalling dimensions. Comrades, have we not other work to do than to create a third Europe?" (313). At least one Second World superpower, the People's Republic of China, is arguably positioning itself either to dominate the First World or to become a new First World of its own: Third to Second to First. The reports of the Second World's death, in fact, are greatly exaggerated.

I would go further. Since the late 1970s or early 1980s, some historians have been speaking of a Fourth World,[8] comprising the indigenous populations colonized by (among others) Third World former colonies: the Karen by Burma and Thailand; the Meo, Akha, Lahn, and others by Thailand; the Naga by India; the East Timorese by Indonesia; the Tamils by Sri Lanka; the Tibetans by the People's Republic of China; the Ainu by Japan; the Kurds by Iran, Iraq, Syria, and Turkey; the Maori by New Zealand; the Pitjantjatjara, Yirrkala, Gurindji, and Warlpiri by Australia; the Quinault, Hopi, Navajo, Lakota, Iroquois, Inuit Athapaskans, and Aleuts by the United States; the Maymara and Quechua-speaking peoples by Peru; the Miskito, Sumo, and Rama by Nicaragua; the Baruca, Cabecares, and Bribris by Costa Rica; the Zapotec, Mixe, and Mayans by Mexico; the Shaba, Luba, and Kasai by Zaire; and many others. This "fourth-worldization" of indigenous populations by Worlds One through Three is generally considered a tragic irony; I am suggesting it is endemic to the capitalist/colonialist metanarrative of development, which directs development up the worlds, *Fourth* to Third to Second to First, the counterregulatory displacement of groups (language groups, ethnic groups, settler groups, refugee groups), first as Fourth World colonies or other dominated entities, then through wars of national liberation as "decolonized" Third World nations, and finally as Second and First World powers ready to dominate and exploit others in a colonial and eventually globalizing neocolonial mode.

But Fourth World activists and theorists would dispute that last formulation: for them the indigenous peoples, tribes, language groups, and ethnic groups of the Fourth World are nations too, "imaginary communities," certainly, in Benedict Anderson's term, but in that no different from the nations of Worlds One through Three. What distinguishes First, Second, and Third World nations from Fourth World nations for them is simply international recognition:

> With but very few exceptions, authorities have shied away from describing the nation as a kinship group and have usually explicitly denied that the notion of shared blood is a factor. Such denials are supported by data illustrating that most groups claiming nationhood do in fact incorporate several genetic strains. But such an approach ignores the wisdom of the old saw that when analyzing sociopolitical situations, what ultimately matters is not *what is* but *what people believe is*. And a subconscious belief in the group's separate origin and evolution is an important ingredient of national psychology. . . . Since the nation is a self-defined rather than an other-defined grouping, the broadly held conviction concerning the group's singular origin need not and seldom will accord with factual data. (Connor 380)

Fourth World nations for these scholars are self-defined nations whose national status is (as yet) systematically denied by the self- *and* other-defined nations of Worlds One through Three. This suggests that in a (post)colonial context the nation is not just an imaginary community, but an imaginary community first ideosomatized as a directionality, as an impetus toward geopolitical upward mobility. The nation was the invention of the "First World" before it was called that, Europe during the era of the trizygotic birth of capitalism, the nation state, and the colonial project; it is the convergence of the latter two under the aegis of the first that iterosomatizes nation-thinking with the aspiration to improved collective status. The anticolonial wars of national liberation beginning with the United States in the 1770s and Haiti in the 1790s and continuing through the nineteenth and twentieth centuries to today have been essentially wars designed to "upgrade" colonized peoples to the status of nations, which is to say—anachronistically in some cases, since the Three Worlds model was not invented until the mid-twentieth century—to "raise" them on the capitalist or colonialist metanarrative of development from the Fourth to the Third World. For a Fourth World group to *call* itself a nation is thus to organize itself for the next step up, to iterosomatize images of its future as a nation-state. A newly liberated people is internationally recognized as a nation, which is to say that the group that circulates ideosomatized images of this people's nationhood grows exponentially; once it has thus "become" internationally what it has long felt it is locally, a nation, a Third World entity, it begins positioning itself for either the colonizing Second World or the neo-colonizing/globalizing First World. In this sense the significant difference between neocolonizing former colonies like the United States and tradition-ally colonizing former colonies like Ethiopia (which colonized Eritrea from 1961 to 1991) is that the neocolonizers are more "successful"—which is to say that they have advanced further along the capitalist/colonialist metanarrative of development.

But of course it's also important to remember that decolonization has not been the only historical path to the Third World:

> But, then, there have been other countries—such as Turkey which has *not* been colonised, or Iran and Egypt, whose occupation had not led to colonization of the kind that India suffered—where the onset of capitalist modernity and their incorporation in the world capitalist system brought about state apparatuses as well as social and cultural configurations that were, nevertheless, remarkably similar to the ones in India, which *was* fully colonized. In this context, we should speak not so much of colonialism or postcolonialism but of capitalist modernity, which takes the colonial form in particular places and at particular times. After all, the United States was also once a colony, or a cluster of colonies; so was Latin America to the south of the US, Canada in the north, not to speak of the Caribbean islands. But later history has taken in each case a very different turn. When applied too widely, powerful terms of this kind simply lose their analytic power, becoming mere jargon. (Ahmad, "Politics" 7)

Another nation with state apparatuses and social and cultural configura-tions that are remarkably similar to those in Turkey, Iran, Egypt, and India is the Russian Federation, which as the Soviet Union was until the last day of 1991 the definitive Second World anticapitalist empire. Never colonized, it has undergone considerable economic turmoil throughout the 1990s and into the new millennium that would not count as decolonization either, though its cronyist fire-sale privatization of national industries in the years after the collapse of the Soviet Union and the initial near-collapse of its political infrastructure, combined with continued high rates of poverty and unemployment two decades into the new regime, make post-Soviet Russia strikingly resemble Third World countries emerging from the oppression of Fourth World colonization; its weak struggles against the old Marxist-Leninist-Stalinist counterregulation also resemble the inertia of decolonization as Memmi describes it, and its gradual return to autocracy under Vladimir Putin signals the tenacity of the old ideosomatic regulation even in the midst of rapid capitalization and globalization; and the greatest cultural and ideological division in the country today is between the nationalistic Russophiles who envision a restoration of Russia's imperial might as the leader of the Second World and the global-minded Westernizers who envision the assimilation of the Russian Federation into the Euro-American First World. At the same time, having granted independence to many of its former colonies, both internal (Armenia, Azerbaijan, Belarus, Estonia, the Republic of Georgia, Kazakhstan, Kyrgyzstan, Latvia, Lithuania, Moldova, Tajikistan, Turkmenistan, Ukraine, Uzbekistan) and external (Bulgaria, Czechoslovakia, East Germany, Hungary, Poland, Romania), Russia continues to dominate 29 colonized "autonomous" (their autonomy has been severely reduced under Putin) republics, oblasts, and okrugs, each consisting of one or more Fourth World "titular nationalities" and several other Fourth World "indigenous nationalities" as well; and since 1999 it has been fighting a "separatist movement"—a war of national liberation—in the Autonomous Republic of Chechnya.

With the complexity of this history in mind, then, I have titled this subsection the *capitalist* (rather than colonialist) metanarrative of development— and take the various colonial and postcolonial histories organized by that metanarrative to be only one channel that capitalist modernity has taken. (By "metanarrative," of course, I mean not what actually happens, but a homeostatic mapping of group responses to cultural displacement, a story that is iterosomatized as the true meaning or pattern governing displacement. "Meta" in metanarrative signifies the additive quality of bodily-becoming-mental mapping, the building of an explanatory regime out of allostatic somatic response to displacement.) It would not be difficult, either, to trace the anticapitalist trajectories of the Second World as partial deregulations or counterregulations of capitalism—but that's another story.

2.1.2.3 THE COLONIZER WHO REFUSES

If decolonization is ideosomatically normativized (affectively narrativized) not as a deidealized reversal of the colonial ideosomatic counterregulation, then, but rather as an idealized displacement of that regulatory regime, the most successful forms of decolonization will involve the pursuit of radically transformed colonial ends. These days, of course, those ends entail globalization not only as transnational economic interests and free trade but also as the creation of prestigious university chairs and departments for the theorization of transnational postcoloniality. This book too would thus stand revealed as a decolonized and anticolonial but still neocolonizing study of the global "free trade" of shared evaluative affect—the work, to put it in Memmi's terms from *Colonized*, of a "colonizer who refuses," an anticolonial member of a group that continues to benefit from colonialism: "He may openly protest, or sign a petition, or join a group which is not automatically hostile to the colonized. This already suffices for him to recognize that he has simply changed difficulties and discomfort. It is not easy to escape mentally from a concrete situation, to refuse its ideology while continuing to live with its actual relationships. From now on, he lives his life under the sign of a contradiction which looms at every step, depriving him of all coherence and all tranquility" (20). Memmi is writing here in the mid-1950s, of course, of an anticolonial colonizer living in a colony—a proliferation Frenchman living in colonial Tunisia, say—hence his insistence on the "difficulties and discomfort" of this hypothetical person's situation, the living of his life "under the sign of a contradiction which looms at every step, depriving him of all coherence and all tranquility." The situation is rather different for an anticolonial American intellectual, descendant of white settlers, living two centuries after independence—but in fact not radically different. The difference rather involves what Nietzsche would call the *sublimation and subtilization* of "difficulties and discomfort": as an anticolonial intellectual I am aware that the relative material comfort in which I live is in large part generated by my country's neocolonial exploitation of the Third World; my greatest source of discomfort is my uneasy awareness of just how easy it is not to be discomforted by this fact. In order to feel the leftist colonizer's discomfort of which Memmi writes, I have to produce it not only intellectually but also idiosomatically, "rebelliously," refusing and in part deregulating the ideosomatics of United-Statesian triumphalism ("America is the greatest/richest/most powerful country on earth") through the collective exosomatization of images of Third World sweatshops, child labor, poverty, widespread unemployment, local economies run by remote control from the boardrooms of multinational corporations, and so on. Memmi writes that

"The intellectual or the progressive bourgeois might want the barriers between himself and the colonized to fade; those are class characteristics which he would gladly renounce. But no one seriously aspires toward changing language, customs, religious affiliation, etc., even to ease his conscience, nor even for his material security" (37)—and while I would disagree with him superficially, at a deeper level he is still quite right. People do "seriously aspire toward changing language, customs, religious affiliation": I did it myself when I was 16, moving to Finland; women marrying into foreign cultures have done it for millennia; translators, interpreters, and other intercultural subjects are typically the products of such serious aspirations; and, of course, Memmi neglects to mention here what is implicit in his argument, that it is fairly rare for people to want to assimilate to a culture *lower* on the developmental four-world metanarrative but quite common for people to aspire seriously to assimilate to a higher-status culture.[9] (What he means but does not spell out here is that the French do not seriously aspire to become Arabs. But that happens too.) The deeper question, though, is this: would I give up my middle-class income and lifestyle, my intellectual work, to show solidarity with the Third World on whose exploitation I indirectly live? "Thus," Memmi writes, "while refusing the sinister, the benevolent colonizer can never attain the good, for his only choice is not between good and evil, but between evil and uneasiness" (42–43).

His final conclusion on the colonizer who refuses is also mostly true: "He will slowly realize that the only thing for him to do is to remain silent. Is it necessary to say that this silence is probably not such a terrible anguish to him? That he was rather forcing himself to fight in the name of theoretical justice for interests which are not his own; often even incompatible with his own?" (43). Probably most antineocolonial Western intellectuals do feel more comfortable remaining silent about their own indirect complicity in the neocolonial exploitation of the Third World. And even those of us who do talk and write about that complicity find ways of silencing our own uneasy voices of self-accusation, typically by *raising* those voices just slightly, intensifying the unease into a careful public self-condemnation designed to impress others with our sincerity—as I've been doing in this subsection.

2.1.3 Frantz Fanon

The black is a black man; that is, as the result of a series of aberrations of affect, he is rooted at the core of a universe from which he must be extricated.

> The problem is important. I propose nothing short of the liberation of the man of color from himself.
>
> In other words, the black man should no longer be confronted by the dilemma, *turn white or disappear;* but he should be able to take cognizance of a possibility of existence. In still other words, if society makes difficulties for him because of his color, if in his dreams I [as his psychoanalyst] establish the expression of an unconscious desire to change color, my objective will not be that of dissuading him from it by advising him to "keep his place"; on the contrary, my objective, once his motivations have been brought into consciousness, will be to put him in a position to *choose* action (or passivity) with respect to the real source of the conflict—that is, toward the social structure.
>
> —Frantz Fanon, *Black Skin, White Masks* (8, 100)

Frantz Fanon was born in 1925 on the island of Martinique, then a French colony; his hatred for colonialism was sharpened early by the Vichy French naval troops who were blockaded on Martinique in 1940 and who vented their racism openly on the Martinican people. He joined the French Free Forces and fought the Germans in France, was wounded and received the Croix de Guerre. In 1945 he returned briefly to Martinique, long enough to work on the parliamentary campaign of his friend and former teacher Aimé Césaire (running on the communist ticket) and complete his bachelor's degree; he then went to France to study medicine and psychiatry as well as literature, drama, and philosophy (he sat in on Maurice Merleau-Ponty's lectures). Qualifying as a psychiatrist in 1951, he did a residency with François de Tosquelles, who insisted on the shaping power of culture in psychopathology, practiced psychiatry in France for a year and a half, and wrote *Peau noire, masques blancs* (1952, translated into English as *Black Skin, White Masks,* 1967). In 1953 he accepted the *chef de service* post at the Blida-Joinville Psychiatric Hospital in Algeria, where he introduced the radical methods of sociotherapy; after the outbreak of the Algerian revolution in 1954, he joined the Front de Libération Nationale and began to study Algerian culture closely, later applying his experiences to the writing of both ecstatic revolutionary books like *L'an cinq de la révolution algérienne* (1959, translated into English as *A Dying Colonialism,* 1965) and *Les damnés de la terre* (1961, translated into English as *The Wretched of the Earth,* 1965), and psychology-of-culture studies like "The Marabout of Si Slimane" (the manuscript of which was lost). In 1956 he publicly resigned his post at the hospital, in his letter of resignation forswearing his French assimilationist background; expelled from Algeria, he returned to France and secretly traveled to Tunis, where he wrote for *El Moudjahid,* his writings for which were collected posthumously in *Pour la révolution africaine* (1964, translated into English as *Toward the African Revolution,* 1967). Diagnosed with leukemia, he refused to rest, dictating *The Wretched of the Earth* in ten months; he received treatment in both the Soviet Union and, later, with the help of the CIA, the United States, where he died in 1961.

As the two sentences/paragraphs of the first epigraph above suggest, Fanon's decolonizing project was at least in part protosomatic: "the result of a series of aberrations of affect" would be the result of an iterosomatic counter-regulation, so that "the liberation of the man of color from himself" that he proposes would actually be not from the "self" but from that colonial iterosomatization of self that *seems* real, seems like a true self, but is in fact only "aberrant." Of course, "aberration" there implies a universalized or transcendentally stabilized normativity that is alien to somatic theory, which would rather posit in the colonized population's becoming-counterregulated a *poly*normativity generated by the clash of two or more regulatory groups; but something like this relativized conception of normativity is at least implicit in the functional identity Fanon posits between "universe" and "himself," his two tropes for the ideosomatic prison from which the "black man" must be extricated/liberated. If his self is *a* universe in which he has been *rooted* and must (and can) be *uprooted,* if there are many selves and many universes in which it is possible to root or radicate a black body, then there is no transcendental norm that might be used to thematize a single (colonial) radication as "aberrant." It is therefore only possible to label a colonizing radication or ideosomatic regulation as a "series of aberrations of affect" from a tendentious stance of decolonizing eradication, a postcolonial attempt to counterregulate the colonial "self" or "universe"—once again, as in Memmi, an inflammatory speech act.

There is, in fact, a radical sociogenic fuzzy logic to Fanon's psychoanalytical take on postcolonial identities, a sense that for him subjectivities are always in a state of becoming, becoming-white, becoming-black, becoming-rooted, becoming-unrooted—and that these becomings are the minute fractal byproducts of massive somatotectonic shifts, the affective grinding together of hugely complex social, political, economic, cultural, and ideological affect-circulatory regimes. There is also the sense, only passingly adumbrated in *Black Skin, White Masks* and fully developed in *A Dying Colonialism* and *The Wretched of the Earth,* that these grinding pressures are ultimately too much for "the black man," and issue finally into revolutionary violence: "The Negro is a toy in the white man's hands; so, in order to shatter the hellish cycle, he explodes" (*Black* 140).

My remarks in this section will focus mostly on *Black Skin, White Masks,* in terms first of the exosomatic imagination of becoming black or white, and then of the paralyzing power of the Hegelian dialectic as applied to black dis-alienation by Jean-Paul Sartre.

2.1.3.1 COLONIZATION AS BECOMING-WHITE/BECOMING-BLACK

As Fanon's title *Black Skin, White Masks* suggests, his analysis of coloniza-tion in the book is almost exclusively devoted to race, to counterregulatory somatizations of skin color. He does occasionally digress from his main theme, however, into more general postcolonial reflections on colonial counterregulations:

> To understand something new requires that we make ourselves ready for it, that we prepare ourselves for it; it entails the shaping of a new form. It is utopian to expect the Negro or the Arab to exert the effort of embedding abstract values into his outlook on the world when he has barely enough food to keep alive. To ask a Negro of the Upper Niger to wear shoes, to say of him that he will never be a Schubert, is no less ridiculous than to be surprised that a worker in the Berliet truck factory does not spend his evenings studying lyricism in Hindu literature or to say that he will never be an Einstein.
>
> Actually, in the absolute sense, nothing stands in the way of such things. Nothing—except that the people in question lack the opportuni-ties. (95–96)

Of course it's not just that the people *lack* the opportunities; nor is it just that they are denied the opportunities. It is that they are constructed in *terms* of the lack of opportunities. They are regulatorily somatized to that lack. Their lack of opportunities is circulated iterosomatically through the groups that deter-mine their realities and their identities. The "new form" that the colonized are expected first and foremost to shape is the counterregulatory form of colonial-ism, European "civilization" not as Schubert or Einstein but as submission to the colonizer's authority, submission to labor with little or no remuneration, submission to a racialized hierarchy of human worth, and submission to a prescribed lack of opportunities. Implicit in Fanon's polemic here, however, is also an answer to those who imagine the colonized as *incapable* of becom-ing a Schubert or an Einstein, of "embedding abstract values into his outlook on the world," and therefore as *in need* of the colonial regime that keeps them down, keeps them effectively enslaved to the life of the body by providing them "barely enough food to keep alive." If by "[the] embedding [of] abstract values" we take Fanon to be referring to the body-becoming-mind, that mental mapping of body states by which an organism or group of organisms homeostatically regulates its internal and external environment, then clearly the core problem is not just that the colonized don't have enough to eat but that they don't have (are constructed as lacking) the power to regulate their own internal *or* external environments—what happens to them, and even how they feel about what happens to them. Obviously, it is an extremely sophisticated form of colonial counterregulation that can extend its regulatory reach into the colonized's ability to feel, say, anger at oppression, or even a wistful disappointment at not being able to do what s/he wants—a sophistication that is specifically made possible by the somatic exchange, by the circulation of normative/evaluative affect through the bodies of a population. "When the Negro makes contact with the white world," Fanon writes, "a certain sensitizing action takes place. If his psychic structure is weak, one observes a collapse of the ego. The black man stops behaving as an *actional* person. The goal of his behavior will be The Other (in the guise of the white man), for The Other alone can give him worth. That is on the ethical level: self-esteem" (154). Here, clearly, "the Negro" and "the black man" are Antillean code for "the colonized" of any color and any gender, "the white man" for "the colonizer": despite his racialized terms, Fanon is not really addressing race here. The "sensitizing action" he describes is the conformation of the colonized's somatic response to the colonizer's counterregulatory regime, which is "The Other" in both the external (other person) and the (Hegelian/Lacanian) internal sense, the colonizer-introject that takes over the colonized's affective economy and manages its circulatory flows. "If his psychic structure is weak, one observes a collapse of the ego" is sheer Freudian individualism, focused on the individual's "psychic structure" and "ego" as autonomous fortresses that may be destroyed by the white invaders; the rest of that formulation, however, is more amenable to somatic paraphrase. The Other, after all, is the counterregulatory voice of the (colonizing) group inside the (colonized) individual's head, the actional orientation of the group in the individual's behavior, and, most tellingly, the constitutive force of external group approval reconstituted as self-esteem, the (white colonizing) ethnos reconfigured as the (black colonized) ethos.

By far the most interesting focus of Fanon's analysis of colonization, however, has to do with the iterosomatics of race, becoming-white and becoming-black: "Then I will quite simply try to make myself white: that is, I will compel the white man to acknowledge that I am human" (98). If the white colonizer defines "to be human" in terms of his or her own whiteness, then to be human the black colonized must *become* white. Or:

The black schoolboy in the Antilles, who in his lessons is forever talking about "our ancestors, the Gauls," identifies himself with the explorer, the bringer of civilization, the white man who carries truth to savages—an all-white truth. There is identification—that is, the young Negro subjectively adopts a white man's attitude. He invests the hero, who is white, with all his own aggression. . . . Little by little, one can observe in the young Antillean the formation and crystallization of an attitude and a way of thinking and seeing that are essentially white. When in school he has to read stories of savages told by white men, he always thinks of the Senegalese. . . . Subjectively, intellectually, the Antillean conducts himself like a white man. But he is a Negro. That he will learn once he goes to Europe; and when he hears Negroes mentioned he will recognize that the word includes himself as well as the Senegalese. (147–48)

The black schoolboy becomes white, "conducts himself like a white man," until he goes to Europe and becomes black. The mutability of skin color in this formulation suggests that "racial" skin pigmentation is not so much a physiological as it is an exosomatic phenomenon—that not just the white mask but the black skin "itself" as well are exosomata, ideosomatized images of skin that are circulated through the somatic exchange as naturalized realities. The "is" in "But he is a Negro" would thus be a descriptor not so much of an ontological fact as of an ontologizing process, the group iterosomatic stabilization of a becoming or a flux:

If there is an inferiority complex, it is the outcome of a double process:
    —primarily, economic;
    —subsequently, the internalization—or, better, the epidermalization—of this inferiority. (11)

The inferiority complex circulated iterosomatically by white colonizers through the black colonized population is simultaneously internalized as feeling and epidermalized as skin color, which is to say exosomatized as constitutive feeling about skin color.

Or, in one of the most telling formulations of this process:

Out of the blackest part of my soul, across the zebra striping of my mind, surges this desire to be suddenly *white*.

I wish to be acknowledged not as *black* but as *white*.

Now—and this is a form of recognition that Hegel had not envisaged—

who but a white woman can do this for me? By loving me she proves that I am worthy of white love. I am loved like a white man.

I am a white man. (63)

Here *her* white skin functions as *my* white mask: the desire to simulate somatomimetically, through the body language of her love, the exosoma of her skin color, to "borrow" or "share" her positively somatized pigmentation and overlay it on top of my negatively somatized pigmentation, an exosomatic upgrade, as it were, renormativization upwards of the exosomatic value collectively assigned the color of my skin. Henry Louis Gates Jr. says that race "pretends to be an objective term of classification, when in fact it is a dangerous trope" (5), so that saying "he's black" is like saying (to use Ngũgĩ's example) "he's a wild animal" (133), and Gates is right, of course, except that race-troping is not just a discursive phenomenon: the race-trope is exosomatized as reality, as identity, and therefore *becomes* reality, shapes identity. Exosomatically repigmentizing black skin as white is exactly like taking over the magical power of a fetish object, internalizing its healing force, possessing the exosomatic charge that has been iterosomatized into or onto it by the group—except that the exosoma of a fetish object can be transferred to any given member of the group only by a person vested by the group with the authority to make the transfer, a shaman or a priest. The object's taboo power is too strong for ordinary people; it would kill them; they would profane it. For the black man, in Fanon's formulation, the white woman is that shaman, that priest. Only she, by loving him, can transfer the exosomatic fetish power of white skin, indeed its taboo power: "desire for that white flesh that has been forbidden to us Negroes as long as white men have ruled the world" (René Maran, *Un homme pareil aux autres,* quoted in Fanon, *Black Skins* 70). To paraphrase Fanon, the black man wants to reexosomatize his skin color positively, to upgrade the negative exosoma projected onto dark skin, and fantasizes that this would involve the transfer not just of the exosoma attached to light skin but also of the actual skin color.

Interestingly, though, as a black man Fanon seems unable to resist inflecting his verbal critiques of this fantasy with the exosomata of his group: his deconstructions of black men desiring white women in Chapter 3 ("The Man of Color and the White Woman") are themselves saturated with that desire, with an almost ecstatic longing[10] for what he is seeking to banish from black men's somatic exchange, while his deconstructions of black women desiring white men in Chapter 2 ("The Woman of Color and the White Man") are overwhelmingly somatized with disgust, the typical revulsion toward the exosomata of an out-grouper:

For after all we have a right to be perturbed when we read, in [Mayotte Capécia's] *Je suis Martiniquaise:* "I should have liked to be married, but to a white man. But a woman of color is never altogether respectable in a white man's eyes. Even when he loves her. I knew that." This passage, which serves in a way as the conclusion of a vast delusion, prods one's brain. One day a woman named Mayotte Capécia, obeying a motivation whose elements are difficult to detect, sat down to write 202 pages—her life—in which the most ridiculous ideas proliferated at random. (42)

He presents the black man desiring white women in the first person with only implicit quotation marks, not quite identifying with the "I" of those opening lines ("I am a white man") but not entirely repelled by it, either; he presents the black woman desiring white men in the first person with explicit quotation marks, and recoils from identification with that "I" as from vermin ("perturbed," "vast delusion," "most ridiculous ideas proliferated at random"). The black man's fantasy of becoming white through sexual love for a white woman is presented as "a purely subjective conflict" (70); the black woman's fantasy of becoming white through sexual love for a white man is "a vast delusion." The black man's motivations in desiring white women are obvious to him, because they are circulated through his (male) group; the black woman's motivations in writing a book about her desire for white men are an utter mystery to him ("whose elements are difficult to detect"), because they are alien to his group. In his specific verbal formulations, Fanon expresses solidarity with blacks of either gender; in the somatic charge that powers those formulations, he expresses solidarity with black men desiring white women and scorning black women.[11]

Fanon offers a more nuanced discussion of what it means—what it has been made to mean in the colonial context—to be "black" in the long "Negro and Psychopathology" chapter:

To come back to psychopathology, let us say that the Negro lives an ambiguity that is extraordinarily neurotic. At the age of twenty . . . the Antillean recognizes that he is living an error. Why is that? Quite simply because— and this is very important—the Antillean has recognized himself as a Negro, but, by virtue of an ethical transit, he also feels (collective unconscious) that one is a Negro to the degree to which one is wicked, sloppy, malicious, instinctual. Everything that is the opposite of these Negro modes of behavior is white. This must be recognized as the source of Negrophobia in the Antillean. In the collective unconscious, black = ugliness, sin, darkness, immorality. In other words, he is Negro who is immoral. If I order my

life like that of a moral man, I simply am not a Negro. Whence the Martinican custom of saying of a worthless white man that he has a "nigger soul."
Color is nothing, I do not even notice it, I know only one thing, which is
the purity of my conscience and the whiteness of my soul. "Me white like
snow," the other said. (192–93)

I'm white, because moral, and immoral, because black; color is nothing and
color is everything; my soul is white and pure, and "unconsciously I distrust
what is black in me, that is, the whole of my being" (191): all this is the neurosis Fanon describes as sociogenically produced by the colonial "collective
unconscious," which he has just been arguing, contra Jung, "is cultural, which
means acquired" (188), "the result of what I shall call the unreflected imposition of a culture," so that "the Antillean has taken over all the archetypes
belonging to the European" (191).

   This "unreflected imposition of a culture" is of course Fanon's term for
what I call ideosomatic counterregulation, the circulation through a population of new "corrective" regulatory pressures, designed to displace and replace
the existing culture. It is unreflected in the sense that one does not notice it
happening, does not reflect on it consciously or analytically; it is indeed a "collective unconscious," or what Fredric Jameson calls a "political unconscious"—
a term that helps mitigate the universalizing connotations of Jung's archetypal
conception, but does little to help us understand the "ethical transit" by which
one unreflected culture or political unconscious is imposed on or in place of
another. For that we need not just the negativity of the *un*conscious but also
the positive action of the somatic exchange.

   For the individual born into a colonized condition, of course, like Fanon,
the "unreflected imposition of a culture" is simply socialization, ideosomatic
regulation, not counterregulation: the counterregulatory regime is already in
place when he is born and he simply must be iterosomatized to it. "When I
am at home," he writes, describing his early childhood in the present tense,
"my mother sings me French love songs in which there is never a word about
Negroes. When I disobey, when I make too much noise, I am told to 'stop acting like a nigger'" (191). These are the embodied speech acts by which a regulatory ideosomatic is passed from generation to generation: Fanon's mother
has so effectively conformed her thoughts and feelings and behavior to the
counterregulatory colonialist regime that she unreflectingly channels that
regime to her son through the powerfully somatized vehicles of romantic song
and parental anger. "Somewhat later," he adds, exosomatizing books by white
authors as themselves "white," "I read white books and little by little I take

into myself the prejudices, the myths, the folklore that have come to me from Europe" (191–92). This is, again, an "unreflected" internalization not just of conscious belief structures but of the ideosomatization of those structures, the felt evaluative orientations, the iterosomatic inclination to value "the prejudices, the myths, the folklore that have come to me from Europe" as truths, as realities, as the way things are. These ideosomatic orientations and inclinations cannot be easily identified as coming from any particular person or group, or even easily brought to consciousness; they are diffusely disseminated through the entire population as felt binary valuations, white good, black bad, white strong, black weak, white smart, black dumb, white cultured, black primitive, white moral, black immoral, white spiritual, black sexual, white yes, black no. These simple binaries are stored in each member of the colonized population as somatic markers unconsciously guiding all internal and external decision-making. And, as Fanon writes, "cultural imposition is easily accomplished in Martinique. The ethical transit encounters no obstacle. But the real white man is waiting for me. As soon as possible he will tell me that it is not enough to try to be white, but that a white totality must be achieved. It is only then that I shall recognize the betrayal" (193).

This betrayal places at the "ontological" core of each colonized individual a relational "flaw," an introject of the "Manichean"[12] colonizer–colonized relation that makes it impossible to describe that individual in purely individual terms:

> As long as the black man is among his own, he will have no occasion, except in minor internal conflicts, to experience his being through others. There is of course the moment of "being for others" of which Hegel speaks, but every ontology is made unattainable in a colonized and civilized society. It would seem that this fact has not been given sufficient attention by those who have discussed the question. In the *Weltanschauung* of a colonized people there is an impurity, a flaw that outlaws any ontological explanation. Someone may object that this is the case with every individual, but such an objection merely conceals a basic problem. Ontology—once it is finally admitted as leaving existence by the wayside—does not permit us to understand the being of the black man. For not only must the black man be black; he must be black in relation to the white man. (109–10)

I read that first sentence as Fanon's groping toward a formulation: obviously everyone experiences his or her being through others, as he recognizes immediately in the next sentence ("There is of course the moment of 'being for others' of which Hegel speaks"), but there is something *different* about the being-for-others of the colonized, which Fanon wants to thematize in terms of the distorting *presence* of the colonizer, so that the "black man . . . must be black in relation to the white man." But he recognizes that even among other blacks, "the black man" will have occasion to experience his being through others "in minor internal conflicts"—which is to say that any flare-up of idio-somaticity will make "the black man" *aware* of "his being through others." "Experience" in that first sentence thus comes to reflect the body-becoming-mind, the movement of social feeling toward a mental mapping, so that even if our being is always shaped by others through the circulation of social feel-ings, we *experience* that shaping only when ideosomatic regulation is dis-rupted, either through idiosomatic deregulation ("minor internal conflicts") or ideosomatic counterregulation ("black in relation to the white man").

Note that Fanon's discussion here might be taken as a ground-zero for-mulation for the postcolonial theory offered by Gayatri Spivak in 1988 that the subaltern cannot speak, to which we'll be returning in §2.2.2.3. Spivak's contention that the subaltern cannot speak *as* the subaltern, cannot be heard in the voice of the subaltern, must always assimilate herself to the dominant colonialist discourse in order to be heard and thus to be understood as speak-ing, is aptly summed up (though with a predictable gender shift) in Fanon's pithy notion that the black man "must be black in relation to the white man." What Fanon gives us that Spivak does not, however, is the subaltern's phe-nomenology: the experience of that "flaw," somatic trace of that "betrayal," the sense of not being able to get around the counterregulatory and in some sense paralyzing introject of the colonizer–colonized relation, which forces the subaltern not only to *be* subaltern in relation to the colonizer (that much is implicit in the differentiality of Gramsci's definition of subalternity, which forms the core of Spivak's argument), but also to *feel* subaltern in relation to the colonizer even as s/he begins to "speak" (and be heard), even as s/he masters the colonizer's language and enters into the xenonormativity of the counterregulatory regime. Not only that; because he approaches subalternity at least partly phenomenologically, Fanon recognizes that the subaltern can speak with other subalterns: "As long as the black man is among his own, he will have no occasion, except in minor internal conflicts, to experience his being through others," which is to say, in Spivak's terms, to experience her speaking as a being-heard by others. As we've seen, Fanon himself realizes that this is not quite true: not only are there those "minor internal conflicts" that open up a gap or rupture in the "pure" experience of equality among the colonized, but the colonial "flaw" or the colonizer–colonized relational introject through and by which the colonized structures his or her reality and identity circulates colonial power differentials through the community of subaltern "equals" as well. Still, the fact that no perfect or pure equals exist to validate the subaltern's speaking or being only invalidates Fanon's insight in the abstract (anti)binary world of poststructuralist thought, where the subaltern is not a person or a group but a "space of difference" (Spivak, "Subaltern Talk" 293).

2.1.3.2 DECOLONIZATION AS FAILED DISALIENATION

In Chapter 5 of *Black Skin, White Masks,* "The Fact of Blackness," Fanon outlines for us a four-step Hegelian dialectic of decolonization as what he calls the "disalienation of the black man":

1. *Black self-loathing:* "The black man among his own in the twentieth century does not know at what moment his inferiority complex comes into being through the other" (110).
2. *Negritude or black pride:* "So here we have the Negro rehabilitated, 'standing before the bar,' ruling the world with his intuition, the Negro recognized, set on his feet again, sought after, taken up, and he is a Negro—no, he is not a Negro but the Negro, exciting the fecund antennae of the world, placed in the foreground of the world, raining his poetic power on the world, 'open to all the breaths of the world.' I embrace the world! I am the world!" (127).
3. *Confoundation:* Sartre's insistence in *Black Orpheus* that white supremacy is the thesis, negritude is the antithesis: "But this negative moment is insufficient by itself, and the Negroes who employ it know this very well; they know that it is intended to prepare the synthesis or realization of the human in a society without races. Thus negritude is the root of its own destruction, it is a transition and not a conclusion, a means and not an ultimate end" (quoted in Fanon, *Black Skin* 133).
4. *Violent revolution:* "The Negro is a toy in the white man's hands; so, in order to shatter the hellish cycle, he explodes" (140).[13]

The "hellish cycle" of the Hegelian dialectic traps the "black man" in thetic recurrences, repetitions, replications: everything always comes back to the other-generated inferiority complex. "The elements that I used," Fanon writes of the construction of his own corporeal schema, "had been provided for me not by 'residual sensations and perceptions primarily of a tactile, vestibular, kinesthetic, and visual character,' but by the other, the white man, who had woven me out of a thousand details, anecdotes, stories" (111)—and this weaving continues even in the romantic mythologies of negritude, certainly in Sartre's snapping shut of the dialectic on the "black man's" neck. And while in his later books, *A Dying Colonialism* and *The Wretched of the Earth,* Fanon romanticized revolution as a truly liberating purgation of that inferiorizing otherness,[14] the history that Albert Memmi traces in *Decolonization and the Decolonized* would suggest that the white colonizer continues to weave the body of the black (former) colonized even in nationalist revolution, even in decolonization, even in independence.

We have important deconstructions of the Hegelian dialectic as colonialist prison, notably Hélène Cixous's in *The Newly Born Woman:*

> With the dreadful simplicity that orders the movement Hegel erected as a system, society trots along before my eyes reproducing to perfection the mechanism of the death struggle: the reduction of a "person" to a "nobody" to the position of "other"—the inexorable plot of racism. There has to be some "other"—no master without a slave, no economico-political power without exploitation, no dominant class without cattle under the yoke, no "Frenchmen" without wogs, no Nazis without Jews, no property without exclusion—an exclusion that has its limits and is part of the dialectic. (71)

"But why," Robert Young asks in his commentary on this passage in the introductory chapter of *White Mythologies,* "this emphasis on Hegel?" His answer has to do with "the dominance of Hegelian Marxism from the thirties to the fifties" as "the particular context for the French poststructuralist assault"—the sense French intellectuals had in the 1960s and 1970s that "the dominant force of opposition to capitalism, Marxism, as a body of knowledge remains complicit with, and even extends, the system to which it is opposed. Hegel articulates a philosophical structure of the appropriation of the other as a form of knowledge which uncannily simulates the project of nineteenth-century imperialism . . ." (3).

But then, to continue Young's why-questioning, why "simulates"? Why "uncannily"? What is the specific relationship between Hegel's philosophical articulation and nineteenth-century imperialism that makes it seem to Young a simulation, and what is the relationship between this simulation and our poststructuralist response to it that makes it seem uncanny? In "On the Psychology of the Uncanny" (1906), the study with which Freud begins his 1925 essay on the uncanny, Ernst Jentsch situates the uncanny in ontological judgments suspended aporetically between the living and the lifeless, or between the real and the artificial: "doubt as to whether an apparently living being is animate and, conversely, doubt as to whether an apparently lifeless object may not be in fact be animate" (11). If we take Young to be referring to something like this ontological aporia in our response to Hegel, then "uncannily simulates" would suggest that Hegel's dialectic is a mimetic iteration of the imperialism and racism of his day whose mimesis is aporetically *constitutive* of "reality" as we understand it, so enmeshed with the group construction of reality that it becomes impossible for us to distinguish between "history" and "Hegel," or, by extension for Fanon, between "history" and "Sartre," between one white Frenchman's opinion and historical inevitability. But note that Jentsch specifically describes the aporetic effect of the uncanny as a group *affective* phenomenon: he wants to study "how the affective excitement of the uncanny arises in psychological terms" (8) and then explores those "psychological terms" along lines that seem predictive of object-relations psychology, where "objects" are not merely inert things but people and things as exosomata that seem to play an active role in the circulation of ideosomatic constructions of the familiar and the strange. Our "mistrust, unease, and even hostility" toward unfamiliar things, Jentsch writes, "can be explained to a great extent by the difficulty of establishing quickly and completely the conceptual connections that the object *strives* to make with the previous ideational sphere of the individual" (8, emphasis added).[15] And so if what makes Hegel's simulation uncanny is that it *feels* both real and strange—if "society" doesn't just "*trot along before my eyes* reproducing to perfection the mechanism of the death struggle" but reproduces that mechanism in and through my own felt response to the world, my emotional and behavioral orientation to other people and to the "historical" events I read about in books—then the uncanny simulation is precisely a regulatory somatic exchange among Hegel-reading intellectuals, a circulation of somatic mimeses that blur the lines between Hegel and history because that somatomimetic circulation of Hegel is so thoroughly constitutive of history as we "know" it.[16]

This somatic exchange is much closer to the rhetorical surface in Fanon's map of failed disalienation, which is explicitly grounded in a regulatory somatic exchange not just between Fanon and Jean-Paul Sartre but also between black and white intellectuals in Fanon and Sartre's day and after— between Fanon and Sartre, to put that differently, not just as individuals but as exemplary exosomatizations[17] of the decolonizing stage of the Manichean colonizer-colonized encounter. Actually, Fanon explicitly identifies his reaction to Sartre's book as part of a larger response among black intellectuals, specifically the black zealots of negritude—"Jean-Paul Sartre, in this work, has destroyed black zeal" (135)—and leaves Sartre's uncanny simulation or circulation of the ideosomatics of colonial racism in and through white intellectuals implicit. But how else but through such a white-(anti)colonizing-intellectual ideosomatic exchange do we explain the powerful effect that Sartre's book had on Fanon, or on "black zeal"? Reading Sartre, Fanon feels discouraged, and "black zeal" in the world outside his head is thereby destroyed? "In all truth," he writes, "in all truth I tell you, my shoulders slipped out of the framework of the world, my feet could no longer feel the touch of the ground. Without a Negro past, without a Negro future, it was impossible for me to live my Negrohood. Not yet white, no longer wholly black, I was damned. Jean-Paul Sartre had forgotten that the Negro suffers in his body quite differently from the white man. Between the white man and me the connection was irrevocably one of transcendence" (138). What gives Jean-Paul Sartre this power over Fanon's feeling of "the touch of the ground"? What makes that feeling-loss so viral that it spreads instantly and/or constantly to all "black men," all former possessors of "black zeal"? Surely it is not a *transcendent* connection, unless by transcendent Fanon means simply transpersonal: it is a *felt* connection, a somatic exchange. Sartre has this power over Fanon because he is the (anti) colonialist, the colonizer who refuses, the French Marxist intellectual who makes a powerful ally and role model because he hates colonialism and racism but who remains nevertheless a colonizer, a regulatory channel of the ideosomatics of colonial inferiorization. But this also means that Fanon can assume, by the virality of somatic mimeticism, that Sartre's de/recolonizing impact on him is circulated also through other black intellectuals—and, pushing Fanon's reading to the next level, I can assume that this re/decolonizing somatic exchange is circulated through other white anticolonial intellectuals as well, me at least, perhaps (depending on your background and inclinations) you too. "And so it is not I who make a meaning for myself," Fanon writes, "but it is the meaning that was already there, pre-existing, waiting for me" (134): somatic theory suggests that the "meaning that was already there" is the inferiorizing/imprisoning colonial dialectic, and the "there" is the somatic exchange, which constantly circulates that meaning through the group, rendering it always tangibly and pressingly *there,* near, under the skin.

2.1.3.3 CINEMATIC REPRESENTATION: *BINTA AND THE GREAT IDEA*

For a recent cinematic representation of that dialectic, let's watch the 2004 film about a small rural village in southern Senegal, *Binta and the Great Idea.*

The film opens on a lake scene, with a Senegalese fisherman paddling toward shore in a dugout canoe. Binta (Zeynavou Diallo à Bignona), the six-year-old narrator, introduces him in a voiceover as her father Sabu Diatta (Agnile Sambou à Mampalago). As Sabu's canoe approaches the shore another man, Souleyman (Ismaila Hercule Diédhoiu à Bignona), rides up on his bike and helps him beach his canoe, and asks him how the fishing was. Sabu says (I will cite the English subtitles provided by Amparo Benedicto of La Luna Titra, a Madrid-based film-subtitling firm), "Can't complain, good fishing," but Souleyman looks in the catch basket and sees only seven or eight tiny fish, and makes a little speech: "I don't know if I can handle so much weight. That's a lot of basket for so few fish. In Europe they can catch tons of fish with a lot less effort. In one day a single *tubab* [European] can catch more fish than you could eat in your whole life. God gave them the brains and technique to build great inventions. Those people know what they're doing. We should learn from them." Then his watch alarm goes off, signaling noon, and he starts bragging about it, saying it's Swiss. As they walk back to the village, he tells Sabu about how Europeans fish with cranes, gigantic nets, and fish-finders.

On their way they pass a group of women working in a ricefield; in her voiceover Binta points out her mother Aminata Kamara (Fatua Drámé à Mampalago) and says she works in the ricefields "with the other mothers. Each one has a piece of land but they work together because they like to help each other and they like being together."

Then we cut to the School Teacher (Alphousseyni Gassama à Bignona) teaching the kids tolerance in groups, saying that they have to mix the black with the white, the big with the small, the girls with the boys, because "we respect each other, we accept our differences": "That's how we'll make our school. And when you grow up, that's how you'll make the world of tomorrow."

Next, as a girl rings the recess bell and the kids run outside, Binta introduces us to her cousin Soda (Aminata Sané à Oulampane), who isn't allowed to go to school. Soda walks up to the outside of the school fence with a load of firewood on her head and looks sad. And now the staging becomes complicated: we cut to a woman identified as Soda's mother Fatu (Diariétou Sané à Ziguinchor) and her little brother out on a mat in the yard, the mother sorting through some grains in a basket, the little brother sitting cross-legged reading something; but when Soda arrives, fake-crying, she is now played by a different actress (Annette Tida Sambou à Ziguinchor), and is wearing different clothes. We only gradually realize that some villagers (mostly children) have been organized to stage a key generational conflict in Soda's family for the whole village, Soda begging to go to school, her father refusing to let her; this is a rehearsal, but all through the film we cut back and forth between rehearsals and the "real thing." Soda's mother-in-the-play says to Soda-in-the-play in a loud monotone: "Soda! Soda! Why did you take so long to bring the wood?" Soda throws down the wood and declaims: "Mother! I'm very tired! Very, very tired! Let me go to school like my little brother! I want to learn what is written in books," and starts fake-crying again. The mother-in-the-play says, in the same loud monotone: "Soda! You know your father will never agree!"

And now the metacinematic intervention is escalated, the irruption of European postmodernity in the "primitive" world of the Senegalese village expanded: saying "All right, all right," a man identified in the cast credits as "el Profesor del Teatro," the Theater Teacher (Moustapha Coly à Ziguinchor), comes onscreen and tells them how to play the scene. "Acting means putting yourself in someone else's skin," he says, "to understand them better. You are in mother's skin. You must understand how all mothers . . . how all mothers understand their children. She suffers. You must understand her. When you talk to her, you must speak with love and affection. Love and affection, you understand?" Mother: "Yes." Theater teacher: "Okay? This works." He walks off-screen. Mother to Soda: "We'll wait till he comes." An adolescent boy (Mohamed Sagna à Diabir) comes on bent over with a walking stick, made up as Soda's father, saying: "Knock knock knock." Mother to Soda: "It's your father." Father: "Knock knock knock." Mother: "Yes, come in." Father: "What's going on here?" Cut to the Theater Teacher, who is wearing a brown shirt with a Caterpillar corporate logo on it and looking decidedly skeptical.

Cut to Binta's mother Aminata nursing her baby, sitting next to Binta's father Sabu on an outdoor bench. Aminata: "That's not a good idea." Sabu: "I can't think of any other." Aminata: "You're crazy." Sabu: "For thinking of the future?" Sabu sees Binta, picks her up, hugs her: "Binta, will you help me with my idea?" Binta's voiceover: "My mommy says my daddy has birds in his head. I think that's why he is so nice." Cut to Sabu dictating to Binta: "Write: Thanks to my friend Souleyman, I heard about the amazing events happening in the world of the *tubabs*. Period. I am referring to, for example, the great geniuses that permit us to extract the maximum that the land has to offer. Period."

Cut to Soda's "real" mother (Awa Kéhé à Mampalago) first picking some fruit, then sitting with her basket of fruit by the side of the road. A truck-driver stops and blatantly cheats her, confusing her with simple multiplication and then giving her much less than he promises. Binta's voiceover: "My aunt never went to school."

Cut back to the rehearsal scene in the yard that we left earlier. Soda's mother-in-the-play tells her Soda's father-in-the-play that she got cheated because she doesn't know math, begs him to let Soda go to school. Father: "This is Africa. Women must stay at home. When she grows up she will marry.

No school." Another girl comes in, moving her fist as if knocking, saying hesitantly: "Knock knock knock." Theater Teacher: "Stop. Stop. Open the door before you enter." Girl: "There is no door." Theater Teacher: "It's true there is no door, but it's unnecessary. With a little imagination, everything is possible." Father: "Not everything. Fireworks, for example. Tell us how to make them without rockets." Theater Teacher: "Of course you can make fireworks without rockets. What matters is having something to celebrate."

Cut to some children dancing, first Binta, then a little girl with a metal peg for her left leg.

Cut to Sabu sealing the envelope of the letter Binta has been writing for him. Binta's voiceover: "My daddy also heard from his friend Souleyman that apparently the *tubabs,* thanks to the incredible quantities of fish that they are able to catch, make so much profit that they don't need to worry about each other." Sabu gets in a donkey cart and rides away.

Cut to a sick old woman coughing in bed; "real" Soda is sweeping in the room when she sees a woman's silhouette setting something down just outside the door-curtain; she goes out to find a basket of grain. The implication is that while Europeans don't care for each other, Africans do.

After a montage of Sabu riding in the donkey cart and arriving at the Lieutenant Governor's office, we see the Lieutenant Governor (Idrissa Diandy à Niaguls) laughing at the letter, but sending Sabu to the Civil Governor anyway.

Cut to Soda-in-the-play sweeping in the yard; she finds two colorful books, picks them up, looks at them; her mother sees her, asks her whether she's done sweeping, Soda says she wants to go to school, Fatu says I'll go tell your father. Cut to Soda's "real" mother talking to Soda's "real" father (Fanding Diandy à Niaguis). As they argue, "real" Soda edges up to the door to listen to them, and starts crying.

Cut to Sabu catching a bus. Binta's voiceover: "There was a third thing that Souleyman told my father about the progress in the world of the *tubabs.*" Cut to Souleyman and Sabu sitting on a bench under a tree. Souleyman: "And all that wealth permits them to have the guns to fight against fear and losing their wealth. Take France, for example. They have the atomic bomb! More progress is impossible." Sabu: "I think we should do something similar." Binta says she thinks this was the precise moment when her father got his great idea.

After a montage of the bus driving along with its door open, with Binta's voiceover telling us that Sabu is taking his letter to the Prefecture of Bignona, the capital of their province, we see the Civil Governor (Abdoulaye Coly à Bignona) reading aloud from his letter: "Therefore, and keeping in mind that if we follow the path shown to us by the First World, we risk that the children of our children will have no fish, no trees, no air . . . that the desire to acquire wealth will make us lose from [*sic*] our sense of solidarity and our fear of losing our wealth . . ." Sabu finishes: ". . . will lead us to destroy each other." Binta tells us in a voiceover that the Civil Governor sends Sabu to the Governor in Ziguinchor, the capital of the region.

Cut to the whole village gathered around a makeshift stage, where the girl and boy playing Soda and her father now finally perform the scene they have been rehearsing throughout, where she begs him to let her go to school and he refuses. Three more child actors playing Binta's family arrive and talk to them. Binta and Soda are in the audience watching. Soda's "real" parents are also watching, and laughing at the funny moments. As the other actors come up with reason after reason why Soda's father should let her go to school, Soda's "real" father in the audience begins to look troubled, and "real" Soda looks resentful.

After a montage of Sabu arriving in Ziguinchor, waiting and waiting to see the governor, we cut back to the makeshift stage and see a boy come out in Western clothes, with a backpack, looking like a university student: "A few years later. Let's see what has become of the children." Soda's little brother is a French teacher; Binta is a doctor. Nobody has seen Soda in ages. We keep cutting to close-ups "real" Soda's face, which shows more and more anger. Her "real" father cuts his eyes uneasily at her. Then Soda-in-the-play says she was married at 15 and has three children; she cries at this, and "real" Soda in the audience wipes her eyes: her surrogate's tears on stage are contagious. The actors all line up to face the audience. Binta's mother-in-the-play says to Soda's father-in-the-play, look, my daughter's a doctor, if you get sick she can cure you. Soda's father-in-the-play comes out with his back to the audience, faces Soda on stage, and mumbles: "I'm very sorry. I didn't understand." A boy carrying a backpack steps forward and says: "Dear parents. Let your children go to school." Soda-in-the-play steps forward and, while the others hum behind her, addresses the audience as "mother and father," asking them why they didn't let her go to school. As she goes on, "real" Soda stands angrily, trying to control herself. Finally she walks over in front of her "real" father, covering her teary eyes with her arm: "Father, I want to go to school. I don't want to be ignorant like you." Soda's "real" father by now is very uneasy, almost frantic, but he says and does nothing, only half-shakes his head. "I want to go to school. You have no right to deny me my future. I want to be someone." She walks away, and the audience explodes: "Let her go to school!" The boy playing Soda's father walks up to Soda's "real" father and shouts, pointing angrily: "Let her go to school! Who ever told you that in Africa women have to stay at home? Where is it written? This isn't the Africa we want for ourselves. Let her go to school!" The whole audience is yelling at him, pointing at him, gesticu-

lating angrily—the movie's most overwhelmingly obvious instance of ideosomatic counterregulation.

Cut to a secretary (Virginie Manga) coming out of the Governor's office
and asking if she can help Sabu. She lets him in, and the Governor (Yaya Mané
à Ziguinchor) reads the letter while Binta's voiceover reads the letter aloud:
"This is why I'd like to request permission to adopt a *tubab* child. Already
weaned, if possible, so that here he may develop as a person and acquire the
knowledge necessary to be happy in our humble community." Sabu chimes in,
finishing his letter: "That way this boy, when he becomes a man, will be able
to contribute to the development of humanity, which is of concern to us all."
The governor agrees, and we cut to a man pretending to throw fireworks up
into the sky; the camera pans up the palm trees rapidly, suggesting imagined
rockets shooting up into the sky, and as we see their fronds we hear explosions. The kids dance and laugh. Binta's voiceover: "My daddy says that all
the children in the world have the right to educate themselves in the spirit of
friendship, tolerance, peace, and fraternity. All the children. Even *tubab* children. My daddy says we must learn from the behavior of birds. Birds are so
intelligent that they take the best of the north and the best of the south."

The credits roll, telling us in Spanish that the film was written and directed
by Javier Fesser and produced by Luis Manso, and was "basada en una inqui-
etud personal de Javier Fesser y Luis Manso"—based in a personal inquietude
of its Spanish screenwriter/director and Spanish producer. We are also told
that the film was made in collaboration with UNICEF Spain and UNICEF Senegal, the Senegalese Ministry of the Interior, and the Senegalese Ministry of
Information and Pan-African Cooperation, and that its corporate sponsors
include Panasonic, ICO Global Communications, Renfe (Spanish rail), TVE
(Televisión Española), Comité Trust (a Madrid-based advertising agency),
Madrid Film (the distributor), and others.

So the question is this: who is trying to do what to whom in and with this
film? It seems clear that the film is a counterregulatory cluster: the School
Teacher trying to infect his charges with a counterregulatory regime that
sounds remarkably like Euro-American multiculturalist tolerance for diversity; the Theater Teacher trying to teach his actors a theatrical regime that
will incite the village ideosomatically to counterregulate Soda's father's "African conservatism," the rigid paternalism that would keep girls and women
at home; Sabu and Souleyman developing between them an ad hoc Euro-
African eclecticism that would "take the best of the north and the best of the
south." Unsurprisingly, given the film's Spanish makers and corporate sponsors, the counterregulatory impulses that drive its message are by and large
the best of the north: the multiculturalism, the feminism, the postmodern

metadrama, the veneration of European technology. The best of the south in Fesser's imagination is a romanticized "moral authority of the primitive"—the image of a rural Senegalese village as more communally caring and supportive than the wealthy and technologically advanced Europeans. Even this romanticism is couched in explicitly developmental terms, albeit at once personalized and universalized: Sabu wants the European child he adopts to be "already weaned, if possible, so that here he may develop as a person and acquire the knowledge necessary to be happy in our humble community. . . . That way this boy, when he becomes a man, will be able to contribute to the development of humanity, which is of concern to us all."

But who exactly is the target of this counterregulation? Almost certainly not African villages like Oulampane in southern Senegal, where the film was set and shot; among the "genius" gadgetry the villagers would need to watch it would be a DVD player and a TV set, not to mention electricity. The film stages a counterregulatory intervention in rural village life in Africa, but for whom? The "relevant constituencies" of the Senegalese Ministry of the Interior—i.e., the Senegalese elite? Spaniards, who watched the film on TVE, one of its sponsors? Americans, whose Academy of Motion Picture Arts and Sciences nominated the film for its Best Live-Action Short Film Oscar in 2007? These all seem like far likelier target audiences for the film than "the former colonized," or "the subaltern"—but what do they get out of it?

The only plausible answer, it seems to me, is that they get the satisfaction of a *sham* counterregulation: the illusion of a decolonization that will bring Africans and other former colonized subjects out of postcolonial poverty and into conformity with First World norms—but *idealized* First World norms, romanticized First World norms, which is to say not capitalist rapacity but "the spirit of friendship, tolerance, peace, and fraternity" (that last a telling reminder of a bloody French Revolution). Counterregulated Africans will also have access to European technology, but will not use it to fight bloody civil wars; the technology will somehow have been rendered benign, technology that "will be able to contribute to the development of humanity, which is of concern to us all."

Another way of saying this is that the sham counterregulation staged in the film is intended to reassure its First World audiences, to "show" them that "development" is working, is truly developing the Third World: that the "primitivism" that remains in Africa is an unfortunate legacy of precolonial cultures, not of colonialism, of African tribal patriarchy rather than French Revolutionary *liberté, égalité, fraternité* (which continues to be presented as the counterregulatory solution); that this primitivism is now being successfully rooted out, and the former colonies are moving up the ladder toward the

First World ideal; and that this geopolitical upward mobility is transpiring in an ideally cooperative rather than competitive spirit, so as not to challenge First World economic and cultural hegemony in any way. It is, after all, only an idealized development, one that creates an illusory amelioration, the *impression* of amelioration in the First World viewer's eye. The illusion, we might say, is of a Noble Savage First World: romanticized primitives with Swiss watches on their wrists and contentment in their hearts, celebrating the fulfillment of their developmental dreams with imaginary fireworks. Presumably they then go home and watch this film on imaginary TVs and DVD players, and feel good about the interactive balance between the north and the south.

If we were to generalize from the *Binta and the Great Idea* model to all decolonizing pressures, we would want to say that the counterregulatory impact of colonization on both the colonizer and the colonized has been ideosomatically stabilized in both populations and in their relationships, and continues to generate such ideosomatic stabilizations long after the political end of colonial rule—and that such stabilizations entail both pressures not to change and reassuring exosomatic images of change in which the former colonized seem to become more like the former colonizer's idealized self-image while nothing substantive actually changes. In this light, decolonization might be defined as the ideosomatic manipulation of counterregulatory exosomata as part of a continuing need to stabilize the old colonial regulatory regimes— or, with a French colonial sigh: *plus ça change, plus c'est la même chose.*

2.2 THEORETICAL SPINS: POSTCOLONIAL AFFECT IN BHABHA AND SPIVAK

> Contemporary postcolonial criticism, whatever its virtues, is also an elite affair, an expression of cultural conflict and contention within a global elite; former colonials who are integrated into the system no longer have any interest in criticism of the system of which they are part, but rather assert their new-found power through varieties of cultural nationalism. On the other hand, there is also an embarrassment or even pain in keeping alive memories of colonialism, or awareness of its legacies, as memories are likely to create cultural and psychological obstacles to assimilation into the system, while forgetting makes for easier assimilation—and acceptance.
>
> —Arif Dirlik, "Rethinking Colonialism" (439–40)

In a note positioned at the end of the first sentence of that epigraph, Dirlik says he is thinking of critics like Leo Ou-fan Lee, whose 1999 book *Shanghai*

Modern to Dirlik's mind embodies the "cultural nationalism" and the "forgetting" he describes. He does not mention in his essay either Homi K. Bhabha or Gayatri Chakravorty Spivak, the two most famous and influential poststructuralists among the global elite that contend for the production of postcolonial knowledge;[18] and indeed, elitist as both theorists unquestionably are, persistently as both have been attacked as "forgetters" of the painful legacies of colonialism, I want to argue in this final section of the Second Essay that both ultimately escape Dirlik's critique. Bhabha and Spivak may be abstract poststructuralist theorists, but they are also the two postcolonial theorists who are most determined to open up a space within the (anti)binary abstractions of their own poststructuralist thought for a phenomenological economy of affect; as such they are perhaps the most somatic of living postcolonial theorists, and thus the significant ground-breakers for my interventions in this book. To a large extent their tentative passing theorizations of affective economies are influenced by Deleuze and Guattari on the social machine as a body-without-organs, and by the Foucault of *The History of Sexuality* Volume One, both powerfully Nietzschean theoretical orientations that inform somatic theory as well, and that chart a radically different course for postcolonial theory from that abstract poststructuralist differentiality that would, say, thematize the subaltern as a "space of difference" (see §2.2.2.3).

While I will show in this section that the phenomenology of affective "economies" or "value-coding" is almost entirely buried in Bhabha and Spivak, however—almost crushed under the immaterial burden of poststructuralist abstraction—I do want to present my careful reading of their fairly rudimentary stabs at a somatics of postcoloniality as a *contribution* to somatic theory. Under no circumstances should my discussion of their thoughts be read as in any way dismissive.

2.2.1 Homi K. Bhabha

Homi K. Bhabha was born in 1949 to a Parsi family in Mumbai (formerly Bombay), India, and took his B.A. at the University of Mumbai before moving to the United Kingdom to take his M.A., M.Phil., and D.Phil. at Christ Church, Oxford. After working as a lecturer in the English department at Sussex University for ten years, he accepted a fellowship at Princeton and remained in the United States, doing visiting professorships at Princeton and the University of Pennsylvania, then accepting the Chester D. Tripp Professorship in the Humanities at the University of Chicago in 1997 and the Anne F. Rothenberg Professorship of English and American Literature at Harvard in 2001.

Bhabha's two essay collections of the 1990s, *Nation and Narration* (1990) and especially *The Location of Culture* (1994), secured his reputation in the top tier of postcolonial intellectuals worldwide; his densely brilliant poststructuralist rhetoric has helped establish *hybridity* as the critical slippage or leakage across key postcolonial binaries like the colonizer and the colonized, as indeed across any other cultural or linguistic barriers that previous postcolonial critics had tended to stabilize as well. In my discussion of Bhabha's explorations of postcolonial affect below, I'll be looking primarily at two essays from *The Location of Culture*, "The Postcolonial and the Postmodern" and "Sly Civility."

2.2.1.1 AFFECT ON THE MARGINS

In his 1994 essay "The Postcolonial and the Postmodern: The Question of Agency," Bhabha famously sets up postcolonial cultures, especially what he calls "the transnational dimension of cultural transformation—migration, diaspora, displacement, relocation" (172)—as a hybrid marginal check on universalizing and naturalizing myths of cultural unity. "In this salutary sense," he argues, "a range of contemporary critical theories suggest that it is from those who have suffered the sentence of history—subjugation, domination, diaspora, displacement—that we learn our most enduring lessons for living and thinking. . . . The natural(ized), unifying discourse of 'nation,' 'peoples,' or authentic 'folk' tradition, those embedded myths of culture's particularity, cannot be readily referenced. The great, though unsettling, advantage of this position is that it makes you increasingly aware of the construction of culture and the invention of tradition" (172).

This is, of course, the same kind of utopian spin on cultural displacement that we saw Deleuze and Guattari and others placing on nomadism and migrancy in the First Essay (§1.3.1): yes, it's "unsettling" to be torn from home and community, to lose almost every communal and locational prop for identity and reality, to be physically and emotionally brutalized, or, in the colonial context, to suffer occupation and enslavement, marginalization and privation—but there's an upside to all that too, an "advantage." It makes you aware that what seemed so natural was only naturalized, that what seemed universal was only universalized. Bhabha does not elaborate on why and for whom this awareness is an advantage—whether it is only advantageous for the postcolonial intellectual ("It is from this hybrid location of cultural value—the transnational or the translational—that the postcolonial intellectual attempts to elaborate a historical and literary project" [173]) or whether there are also advantages for the displaced themselves, the refugees, the colonized, the traumatized. A case could be made for the cognitive advantages to be gained by non-intellectuals from the denaturalizing of their loconormativities, advantages stemming from increased versatility or metanormativity in their allostatic responses to cultural displacement; one of the reasons Bhabha's utopian theory has been so heavily criticized is that he doesn't seem to be particularly interested in making that case, and so seems to be reveling in the intellectual advantages to *him* of other people's suffering, in the object lesson to be derived from postcolonial marginality against hegemonic Western constructions of sociopolitical reality.[19]

What I am suggesting, however, is that there is more going on in Bhabha's approach to postcolonial marginality than just this elitist theorizing—that nearly hidden in his abstract poststructuralist discourse is an extremely cautious, even *nervous,* move toward something vaguely approximating somatic theory. He hints at this move briefly in the opening lines of "The Postcolonial and the Postmodern," the passage I quoted as an epigraph to my Preface: "There is even a growing conviction that the affective experience of social marginality—as it emerges in non-canonical cultural forms—transforms our cultural strategies" (172). There is, in other words, a circulatory or economic effect to affect: feelings, felt experience, can be socially, politically, and culturally transformative; what the marginalized feel and experience in being marginalized can be felt transformatively by "us" as well. Bhabha does not theorize any of this in his essay (or elsewhere), and so does not explore just how "the affective experience of social marginality" is transferred to "us," leaving it entirely possible that the "transfer" is purely intellectual, of the object-lesson sort: we *study* "this hybrid location of cultural value" and draw the analytical implications from it for our "historical and literary project." It is this "catachrestic" reading-between-the-lines of Bhabha's vague hints at a transfer of affective experience, obviously, that leads to the accusation that he is using other people's suffering as fodder for high-flown poststructuralist theory. The other reading, the somatic reading, that "we" feel "their" affect, that the somaticity of marginalization is not so much *studied* as *circulated,* would obviate the accusation of coldly intellectual opportunism; but it would presumably also leave Bhabha open to another kind of accusation, of imposing a universalizing and consensualizing "liberal vision of togetherness" (190) on the marginalized, of naively assuming that we're somehow "all in this together," that "we" feel "their" pain because we're all one. That is the accusation I'm courting in this book, obviously—and Bhabha's reluctance to leave himself open to that accusation surely has something to do with his gigantic stature in the field.

Poststructuralist "differential" or "disjunctive" theories are much hipper than potentially liberal somatic ones.

It should be clear by this stage of my argument, however, that actually theorizing (rather than merely hinting at) the somatics of postcolonial culture opens up a counterhegemonic critique of liberal affective universalism; and perhaps I am projecting here, but it seems to me that Bhabha senses the same, at least as an inchoate theoretical directionality. He constructs his argument in "The Postcolonial and the Postmodern" negatively, of course, first theorizing discursive approaches to postcoloniality as a differential/disjunctive negation of unified myths of nation, culture, and identity,[20] and then arguing that this "language metaphor" itself "opens up a space where a theoretical disclosure is used to move beyond theory," used to construct a "liminal form of signification that creates a space for the contingent, indeterminate articulation of social 'experience' that is particularly important for envisaging emergent cultural identities" (179). The scare-quoted word "experience" there is a back-reference to the "affective experience" broached in the opening lines of the essay; now that he is contingently and indeterminately attempting to articulate or theorize that experience, Bhabha has air-brushed affect out of the formulation and set articulations of experience up as a double negation of hegemonic unities, discursive theorizations arising on the negative margins of unity myths and liminal articulations of experience arising on the negative margins of poststructuralist discursivity. Because poststructuralist theory has rigged a thousand alarm bells around pre- or post-discursive concepts like "experience," Bhabha instantly hedges—"But it is a representation of 'experience' without the transparent reality of empiricism and outside the intentional mastery of the 'author'" (179)—and yet insists, finally dropping the scare quotes around "experience," that "it is a representation of social experience as the contingency of history—the indeterminacy that makes subversion and revision possible—that is profoundly concerned with questions of cultural 'authorization'" (179).

Bhabha's examples of this "beyond theory" are taken from protosomatic thinkers like Roland Barthes and Mikhail Bakhtin, Barthes writing in *The Pleasure of the Text* of "the pulsional incidents [in a text], the language lined with flesh, a text where we can hear the grain of the throat, the patina of consonants, the voluptuousness of vowels, a whole carnal stereophony: the articulation of the body, of the tongue, not that of meaning, of language" (66–67, quoted in Bhabha, "Postcolonial" 180[21]), Bakhtin noting that "the utterance appears to be furrowed with distant and barely audible echoes of changes of speech subjects and dialogic overtones, greatly weakened utterance boundaries that are completely permeable to the author's expression" (quoted in Bhabha, 189). Tellingly, however, Bhabha almost exclusively cordons these hints at shared evaluative affect off into the quotations themselves, takes from Barthes and Bakhtin only the abstract binaries that will feed his post-structuralist habit and ignores the rest—ignores (and indeed tacitly affirms) Barthes's exoticization or orientalization of the "eternal East,"[22] for example, and neglects to mention that for Bakhtin those "barely audible echoes" are barely audible because mostly *felt*, that the "dialogic overtones" are affective (re)tonalizations and (re)attitudinalizations of *voice* that carry complexly col-lectivized saturations of evaluative accent. What remains of the Barthesian and Bakhtinian somatics of language are the "liminal forms of signification" that point binarily/negatively "beyond theory" and "outside the sentence," with no special inclination to explore that beyond and that outside:

> To evoke this "beyond theory," I turn to Roland Barthes's exploration of the cultural space "outside the sentence." In *The Pleasure of the Text* I find a subtle suggestion that beyond theory you do not simply encounter its opposition, theory/practice, but an "outside" that places the articulation of the two—theory and practice, language and politics—in a productive rela-tion similar to Derrida's notion of supplementarity. (179)

> Barthes's daydream is supplementary, not alternative, to acting in the real world, Freud reminds us; the structure of fantasy narrates the subject of daydream as the articulation of incommensurable temporalities, dis-avowed wishes, and discontinuous scenarios. The meaning of fantasy does not emerge in the predicative or propositional value we might attach to being outside the sentence. Rather, the performative structure of the text reveals a temporality of discourse that I believe is significant. It opens up a narrative strategy for the emergence and negotiation of those agencies of the marginal, minority, subaltern, or diasporic that incite us to think through—and beyond—theory. (181)

Because "social experience" or "affective experience" is (figured as) a plea-surable daydream on the supplementary margins of symbolically structured sententiality, it functions in Bhabha's theory as a rupture in hegemonic struc-turing through which "those agencies of the marginal, minority, subaltern, or diasporic" can be made to seem—retroactively—to emerge. It is not a positiv-ity that might be explored in its own right—that would smack of essential-ization, perhaps—but a space of negativity that Bhabha labors to thematize as a site of liberating retheorization. The "moment of displacement" that for Bhabha effects this emergence is not overtly affective or otherwise corporeal, but discursive, and so abstract:

> The individuation of the agent occurs in a moment of displacement. It is a pulsional incident, the split-second movement when the process of the subject's designation—its fixity—opens up beside it, uncannily *abseits*, a supplementary space of contingency. In this "return" of the subject, thrown back across the distance of the signified, outside the sentence, the agent emerges as a form of retroactivity, *Nachträglichkeit*. It is not agency as itself (transcendent, transparent) or in itself (unitary, organic, autonomous). As a result of its own splitting in the time-lag of signification, the moment of the subject's individuation emerges as an effect of the intersubjective—as the return of the subject as agent. (185)

Note there that the *pulses* in Barthes's "pulsional incidents," which he associated with "language lined with flesh, where we can hear the grain of the throat"—the meaty metabolic pulses of the body, of partially verbalized body language, of blood circulation and respiration, of chewing and swallowing and digesting, "their materiality, their sensuality, the breath, the gutturals, the fleshiness of the lips, a whole presence of the human muzzle" (Barthes 67)—have now become "the split-second movement when the process of the subject's designation—its fixity—opens up beside it," "splitting in the time-lag of signification." The pulsionality of signification is not, obviously, a materiality or a sensuality that can be corporeally felt; it can only be discursively theorized.

In his one attempt to work out the operation of his Lacanian theory of the time-lagged and therefore retroactive emergence of agency in a specific historical situation, however—his discussion of Ranajit Guha's analysis of Sunil Sen's remarks on the Tebhaga movement in Dinajpur—Bhabha tips his discursive hand more overtly toward a somatics of postcolonial agency, or what he calls "ambivalence at the point of 'individuation' as an intersubjective affect" (187). I take intersubjective affect there to mean shared feeling, but specifically the regulatory regime(s) of the somatomimetic exchange, the circulation of normative pressures and resistant counterpressures through a group; as we've been seeing, somatic theory does conceive individual identity and agency as group constructs, collective attributions circulated intersubjectively not only through each individual so constituted but also through the constitutive (initiating/ratifying) somatic economy of the group. And as we saw in §2.1, in (post)colonial contexts of radical ideosomatic counterregulation we are obviously going to find "ambivalence" and "hybridity" in the collective somatization of identities, agencies, and realities: "In the face of hostile propaganda of the Muslim League and the provocation of the newly-formed Muslim National Guard, the Muslim peasants came to the Kisan Sabha, sometimes inscribing a hammer and a sickle on the Muslim League flag. Young maulavis addressed village meetings. Reciting melodious verse from the Koran they condemned the jotedari system and the practice of charging high interest rates'" (Sen 49, quoted by Guha, 39, quoted by Bhabha, "Postcolonial" 187). Jostling here for leverage in the regulation of rebel behavior are several overlapping ideosomatic regimes, including at least traditional Muslim piety (the Koranic chanting), Islamic political activism (the Muslim League and its militant splinter group the Muslim National Guard), and Marxist agit-prop (the hammer and sickle, the economic protests).[23] Ranajit Guha thematizes this confluential competition among ideosomatic regimes as the "contradictions which are indeed the stuff history is made of" and rebel consciousness as therefore "self-alienated" (39), suggesting that overlapping ideosomatic regimes jostle for leverage in his theoretical imagination as well, postcolonial idealizations of indeterminacy not quite counterregulating an older nostalgic idealization of the pre-contradictory (foundational) truth and the pre-alienated (integrated) self. (Why else thematize polynormativity as "contradiction" and "alienation"?) Bhabha reads Guha's thematization of the scene as very close to his own, indeed as "an emblem of my notion of agency in the apparatus of contingency—its hybrid figuring of space and time" (187), by which he means contingency as both "contiguity, metonymy, the touching of spatial boundaries at a tangent, and, at the same time, [as] the temporality of the indeterminate and the undecidable" (186). Bhabha insists that "representing social contradiction or antagonism in this doubling discourse of contingency . . . cannot be dismissed as the arcane practice of the undecidable or aporetic"—a weak protest against those who accuse him of celebrating the postmodern fractalization of the self and so militating against identity-political activism—because, he says, his model "enables us to conceive of strategic closure and control for the agent" (186). The only problem there is that by "closure and control for the agent" he means no agentive phenomenology, no practical organizational orientation to the world and to self shaped in individuals by groups, but the *philosophical* constitution of the "historically or contextually specific subject" (186), and thus once again a discursive formulation concluded and controlled not by the subject but by the theorist.

2.2.1.2 Sly Civility

Bhabha takes up the topic of "affective ambivalence and discursive disturbance" (97) in an earlier chapter in *The Location of Culture* as well, "Sly Civility," a 1985 essay devoted to a deconstruction of the rhetoric of liberal universalism in John Stuart Mill and other nineteenth-century British imperialists who preach liberty and democracy for all times and places—except, of course, the colonies, where "a vigorous despotism is in itself the best mode of government for training the people in what is specifically wanting to render them capable of a higher civilization" (Mill, quoted in Bhabha, "Sly" 96). The resulting "affective ambivalence and discursive disturbance" is obviously an example of the polynormative somatics of counterregulatory "colonizerization."

The moment in Bhabha's essay that I want to focus on, however, appears in his title and late in his argument, the concept of "sly civility," which Bhabha borrows from an 1818 sermon by Archdeacon Potts: "If you urge them with their gross and unworthy misconceptions of the nature and the will of God, or the monstrous follies of their fabulous theology, they will turn it off with a *sly civility* perhaps, or with a popular and careless proverb" (quoted in Bhabha 99, emphasis in original). Bhabha thematizes this "off-turning" response as "the native refusal to satisfy the colonizer's narrative demand," noting that "the natives' resistance represents a frustration of that nineteenth-century strategy of surveillance, the *confession,* which seems to dominate the 'calculable' individual by positing the truth that the subject *has* but does not *know*" (99, emphasis in original). But "sly civility" (or what African-Americans call "tomming") is patently not just a "refusal to satisfy the colonizer's narrative demand": it is a refusal in the outward (kinesic) form of compliance, both "civility" (submission to the colonizer's kinesic regime) and "slyness" (resistance to the colonizer's narrative regime). Somatically speaking, Archdeacon Potts attempts to counterregulate the pagan colonized as/into Christians not just by "positing the truth that the subject *has* but does not *know*" but by "*urging* them with their gross and unworthy misconceptions," etc., putting ideosomatic pressure on them to reject their own religion and convert to Christianity—and the colonized exert a surreptitious counterpressure, kinesically performing their indirect speech act of evasion or passive resistance under the cover of a direct speech act of acquiescence.

Indeed, the passage from Freud's "Some Neurotic Mechanisms in Jealousy, Paranoia and Homosexuality" that Bhabha takes as his epigraph and uses to interrogate native sly civility is equally saturated with somaticity, with obsessive paranoid readings of the somatic exchange:

They [the paranoid], too, cannot regard anything in other people as indifferent, and they, too, take up minute indications with which these other, unknown, people present them, and use them in their "delusions of reference." The meaning of their delusions of reference is that they expect from all strangers something like love. But these people show them nothing of the kind; they laugh to themselves, flourish their sticks, even spit on the ground as they go by—and one really does not do such things while a person in whom one takes a friendly interest is near. One does them only when one feels quite indifferent to the passer-by, when one can treat him like air; and, considering, too, the fundamental kinship of the concepts of "stranger" and "enemy," the paranoiac is not so far wrong in regarding this indifference as hate, in contrast to his claim for love. (quoted in Bhabha 93)

Those "minute indications" are, of course, body language—laughter, gestures (flourishing their sticks), spitting—read and felt (correctly, Freud says) as signs of inner body states, as emotional indifference and thus as the opposite of the love the paranoiac needs and expects. Similarly, Bhabha argues, the native "urged" by the "paranoid" colonizing missionary indifferently refuses "to unify the authoritarian, colonialist address within the terms of civil engagement[, which] gives the subject of colonial authority—father *and* oppressor—another turn" (100). As I've been suggesting, the native in this encounter both agrees *and* refuses "to unify the authoritarian, colonialist address within the terms of civil engagement," which gives the subject of colonization—child and victim—yet another turn. Bhabha writes:

The authoritarian demand can now only be justified if it is contained in the language of paranoia. The refusal to return and restore the image of authority to the eye of power has to be reinscribed as implacable aggression, assertively coming from without: *He hates me.* Such justification follows the familiar conjugation of persecutory paranoia. The frustrated wish "I want him to love me," turns into its opposite "I hate him" and thence through projection and the exclusion of the first person, "He hates me."

Projection is never a self-fulfilling prophecy; never a simple "scapegoat" fantasy. The other's aggressivity from without, that justifies the subject of authority, makes that very subject a frontier station of joint occupation, as the psychoanalyst Robert Waelder has written. Projection may compel the native to address the master, but it can never produce those effects of "love" or "truth" that would center the confessional demand. If, through projection, the native is partially aligned or reformed in discourse, the fixed hate

which refuses to circulate or reconjugate, produces the repeated fantasy of
the native as in-between legality and illegality, endangering the boundaries
of truth itself. (100)

Obviously, yes, in diagnosing what he takes to be the "sly civility" of the
natives Archdeacon Potts is reading their body language; and it may well be
that Bhabha's mapping of Freud on paranoia onto the cleric's construction of
that body language is, if not accurate (for how would we ever know?), at least
useful. On the surface, all the Archdeacon wants to do is to convert the native
to Christianity; how do we then go about constructing what he wants below
that surface? We read *his* body language—and because he is physically absent
to us, long dead, in fact, that means reconstructing his kinesic body somatomimetically, and reading our reconstruction. We see him urging the natives,
pressing them, seeking to overwhelm their resistance with a swarm of partially
verbalized somatic aggression; and we see his frustration when they do not
respond as he expects, when they respond with incomplete conformity to his
counterregulatory pressures. Bhabha wants to push past this level of somatomimetic reconstruction, into the realm marked off by Freud in his remarks
on paranoia—wants to feel in the Archdeacon's initial body state a paranoid
desire for love that, thwarted, is converted to hatred and projected outward
onto the "refusenik" native. This seems extreme to me—surely what the Archdeacon wants from the natives is more submission than love?—but there's
really no arguing here, as Bhabha and I both base our readings of the Archdeacon's body states on our own competing somatomimetic reconstructions.

Where I think there is ground for argument, however, is Bhabha's reading of the "frontier station of joint occupation." If that frontier station is the
somatic exchange, the circulation of somatomimeses, then it is not so much
projection that compels the native to address the master as it is the circulation
of ideosomatic power, sociopolitical power channeled somatically through
the Archdeacon's body language into the native, who feels the power and
responds accordingly, civilly: reproduces the Archdeacon's English Christian
civility-pressures in his or her own body and displays them outwardly in the
body language of submissive politeness. This is a partial alignment or refor-
mation of the native not only in discourse, but in outward kinesic behavior as
well.

What bothers me about Bhabha's reconstruction of this encounter, however, is that the native doesn't participate in it, except to refuse. Bhabha's native
is a mere picture of "refusal," not a subject or an agent at all. Bhabha maps out
a similar reading, in fact, in "Articulating the Archaic": "In these instances of
social and discursive alienation there is no recognition of master and slave,

there is only the matter of the enslaved master, the unmastered slave" (131). Here too Bhabha presents the enslavement of the master as a positivity that can be theorized and the slave's subjectivity as a simple blank negativity: *un*mastered. Ironically enough, what Bhabha is doing in denying the postcolonial applicability of the Hegelian master–slave dialectic is *recuperating* that dialectic for the master, for the master's need for recognition from the slave, in tacit rejection of Fanon's insistence in *Black Skin, White Masks* that Hegel was wrong: "I hope I have shown that here the master differs basically from the master described by Hegel. For Hegel there is reciprocity; here the master laughs at the consciousness of the slave. What he wants from the slave is not recognition but work" (220n8). And, of course, he is completely ignoring Hegel's master–slave dialectic for the slave, the topic of Fanon's seventh chapter.[24]

It seems to me a relatively uncontroversial assumption that the colonized's partial kinesic alignment with the colonizer's ideosomatic pressures displaces him, counterregulates her—that in fact it is *impossible* to remain as blank and somatically unavailable as Bhabha seems to want to make these natives. The frontier station of joint occupation transforms not just the colonizer, as Bhabha seems to want to see it, but what Abdul JanMohamed calls the Manichean *relationship* between the colonizer and the colonized, and thus the identities, agencies, realities of both. And for any kind of discussion of the counterregulatory pressures channeled into decolonization, it would seem indispensable to me to theorize that key word "sly": the telling deregulatory pressures with which the native idiosomatizes his or her civility, the strategic contamination of submissive civility not just with refusal but with a counter-ideosomatic response aimed at minutely but significantly decolonizing (counterregulating) the frontier station of joint occupation.

As Bhabha reads the encounter, both the "slyness" and the "civility" are the colonizer's paranoid projections, love-and-hatred fantasies that situate the native "in-between legality and illegality, endangering the boundaries of truth itself." And while it's certainly true that we have no direct access to the native's body states—that any reconstruction of the encounter we undertake will be based on the Archdeacon Potts's verbal report—so what? We never have direct access to *anyone's* body states, even our own; all we ever have is somatomimetic reconstructions. Bhabha's strategy of restricting his analysis to the "paranoia" of the Archdeacon Potts and denying the reconstructed native even a vestige of somatomimetic agency is a *choice,* and in fact a choice that seems punitive to me, motivated less by a desire to open up a utopian decolonizing moment in the encounter than by an unrecognized somatic mimesis of what he takes to be the Archdeacon's paranoid construction of the native, a projection of Bhabha's own postcolonial love-thwarted-into-hatred onto this long-dead colonizer. But then, as Freud says, "the paranoiac is not so far wrong in regarding this indifference as hate, in contrast to his claim for love."

2.2.2 Gayatri Chakravorty Spivak

Born Gayatri Chakravorty in 1942 to middle-class parents in Kolkata (Calcutta), capital of West Bengal, India, Spivak took an undergraduate degree at the University of Kolkata in 1959 and then moved to the United States for graduate work, taking an M.A. in English at Cornell and then working on her Ph.D. (writing a dissertation on Yeats, directed by Paul de Man) while teaching at the University of Iowa. Her 1976 English translation of Jacques Derrida's *Of Grammatology*—and especially her brilliant 100-page introduction to that translation, which taught many English speakers, including me, how to read Derrida—brought her to national and international prominence; but it was her work with the Subaltern Studies group in the 1980s, especially her provocative 1985/1988 essay "Can the Subaltern Speak?" (see §2.2.2.3), that made her one of the most respected postcolonial intellectuals in the world. Her books include *In Other Worlds* (1987), *Outside in the Teaching Machine* (1993), *A Critique of Postcolonial Reason* (1999), *Death of a Discipline* (2005), *Other Asias* (2007), and the compilations *The Post-Colonial Critic* (1990) and *The Spivak Reader* (1995). She has continued to work as a translator in recent years as well, translating the contemporary Bengali writer Mahasweta Devi (*Imaginary Maps* [1994], *Breast Stories* [1997], *Old Women*, [1999], and *Chotti Munda and His Arrow* [2002] and the eighteenth-century Bengali poet-saint Ramproshad or Ramprasad Sen (*Song for Kali* [2000]); one of Mahasweta's novellas will serve as this essay's literary representation in §2.2.2.4.

Spivak describes herself as a Marxist, feminist, and deconstructionist, and in many ways each of those three methodologies corrects and complicates the other two, her Marxism leading her to ground discussions of "woman" and "discursive formations" in economic and class contexts, her feminism problematizing the male-oriented narratives of Marxism and playful antinarratives of deconstruction, and her poststructuralism making her profoundly suspicious of the (strategic) essentializing impulse that drives her identity politics as a Marxist and a feminist. Perhaps as a result, she is also always profoundly self-conscious about her own subject position as an elite postcolonial intellectual, ensconced at a prestigious university (Columbia) in the most powerful and predatory neocolonial country on the planet, and repeatedly undercuts her own positionings by laying bare her own interpretive strategies.

Spivak's interest in postcolonial affect seems to come out of something like this confluence of ideological and methodological orientations as well: out of her poststructuralist/Marxist interest in (but also profound skepticism toward) Deleuze and Guattari's retheorization of Marx on value in terms of desire, on the one hand, and her feminist interest in the female subaltern's body on the other. Like Bhabha, however, Spivak remains deconstructively wary of affect and extradiscursive "experience" in general, and her caution stunts her theoretical forays into affective value-coding, lets them languish in unexamined forms borrowed from liberal-humanist individualism, Cartesian mind-body dualism, and patriarchally hierarchized male–female divisions of psychosocial labor. I'll be looking at her tentative explorations of postcolonial affect in four subsections: her discussions of affective value-coding in several key essays from the 1990s, her discussion of Kant's "raw man" in his theorization of the sublime in *Critique of Judgment* in her own 1999 book *A Critique of Postcolonial Reason,* the controversial essay "Can the Subaltern Speak?," and her reading of Mahasweta Devi's novella "Douloti the Bountiful" in "Woman in Difference."

2.2.2.1 AFFECTIVE VALUE-CODING

In her 1992 autobiographical piece "Asked to Talk about Myself . . . ," Spivak writes:

> Experience is a staging of experience. One can only offer scrupulous and plausible accounts of the agencies or mechanics of staging. Chance and randomness are not to be ignored, yet cannot be accounted for. "What is it to stage?" "what is it to be staged?" are questions prior to, so to speak, broader, as it were, than "what is it to perform (being performed)?," "what is it to act (acting out)?" Most thinking about action allows room for some thought of staging. Deconstruction radicalizes it, repeatedly failing to account for it in a place where success is hard to tell from failure.
>
> One of the most tenacious names as well as strongest accounts of the agency or mechanics of staging is 'origin.' I perform my life this way because my origin stages me so: national origin, ethnic origin. And, more pernicious, you act this way because your origin stages you so. The notion of origin is as broad and robust and full of affect as it is imprecise. History lurks in it somewhere. And, even when we have gone around the claim to identity or essence, the question of origin does not disappear, as witness ideas of class origin, where class is clearly seen as a social inscription rather

than a human essence. My remarks here will also suggest that the question of origin is merely displaced when we answer it to ascribe available ways of instantiation for the performance of our sexual staging. To feel one is from an origin is not a pathology. It belongs to the group of groundings, mistakes that enable us to make sense of our lives. But the only way to argue for origins is to look for institutions, inscriptions and then to surmise the mechanics by which such institutions and inscriptions can stage such a particular style of performance. (9)

In the repeated phrase "the agency or mechanics of staging," I imagine that I understand what Spivak mean by the agency of staging, but wonder about the mechanics. Are we talking wires and pulleys? How do we get to those mechanics from the embodied staging of experience, sexuality, and feelings/affects about origins? Is Spivak suggesting a machine-metaphorics of embodied staging, along the lines of Deleuze and Guattari's social machine as a body-without-organs? Or is she differentiating between two orders or regimes of staging, one embodied, with agency, the other institutionalized, with mechanics? "The agencies *or* the mechanics of staging"?

In any case her insistence on "staging" here seems to adumbrate something like an ideosomatic perspective on performativity, on action as embodied performativity: when we act, when we perform our sexuality or our feeling that we are "from an origin," our performance is staged by someone or something else, some extrapersonal force that we do not understand, that may be partly "chance or randomness" but feels organized, directed, feels like a director's guiding hand, and seems to flow dispositionally out of our past ("origins") through our present into an organized future. Unlike Bhabha, Spivak approaches these questions phenomenologically, from the point of view of one caught up in these flows, these apparent organizations or stagings of our performances, and from that point of view is unwilling to theorize the "institutions and inscriptions [that] can stage such a particular style of performance"—indeed is eager to categorize our sense that our lives are being staged as grounding "mistakes," mistakes presumably because she assumes there is no such staging force, but *useful* mistakes that are "not a pathology" because they "enable us to make sense of our lives." That this sense-making is apparently individualistic, trapped in an isolated perspective from which collective groundings or stagings look like "mistakes," suggests that Spivak is not inclined to theorize embodiment, performativity, agency, affect, and staging ideosomatically—but clearly, here, she has an intimation of ideosomaticity.

Later in that autobiographical essay, in fact, she restages a pivotal event in her life when, in 1981, a ten-year close friendship with a Roman Catholic man came to an end and she went to a psychoanalyst to deal with her "deep sense of loss, not the least of which was a sense of myself as a violent person" (13). Spivak and her analyst spent a good deal of time talking about the Hindu goddess Kali, "who punished with a violence that she enjoyed"; the analyst ended by asking her "how can a man brought up with the blessed virgin be able to understand that there can be this model of female violence that is loved and honoured?" (14). At the time, Spivak found this staging of her Hindu origins "helpful," consoling; later she began to chafe against it, "as if I too were a monotheist who had organized my self image" (15). In her attempts to work through the complexities that begin to emerge for her out of these conflicted stagings of her origins, Spivak repeatedly invokes group constructions, cultural organizations of reality, sidles up to the shaping impact they may or may not have had on her orientations to the world, and then shies away—as in fact she does in presenting the analyst's invocation of Kali and the Virgin. The apparent double-voicing of "there can be this model of female violence that is loved and honoured" is problematic in several ways, one of which is that by reporting the analyst's words through free-indirect narration Spivak seems to collectivize the utterance, to make it emerge from what Julia Kristeva calls intersubjectivity or intertextuality and I would call the somatic exchange, but without theorizing (or apparently even noticing) the crucial Bakhtinian blurring of the lines between collective and individual agency. Another is that her polyphony grammatically elides or evades the question of the ontology and disseminatory channel of the model of Kali and the love and the honor attached to that model, in both the depersonalized existential construct "there can be" and the depersonalized passive construct "that is loved and honoured": there can be *where?* Loved and honored *by whom?* Are the model and the love and the honor in her head and violent body only, or in her parents' and siblings' heads and bodies as well, or "in" "the culture" of Calcutta Hinduism? And what does it mean to be both "in" that culture and "in" the heads and embodied performative orientations of Calcutta Hindus? The notion of the somatic exchange offers one explanation of the circulation of ideosomatic approval responses like "love" and "honor" for a punishing goddess image through the group of Calcutta Hindus, including Spivak's family; Spivak's "there can be" would appear to reflect an unwillingness to push her theorization in that direction. Her subsequent resistance to the analyst's formulation, "as if I too were a monotheist who had organized my self image," seems on the face of it to be an attempt to problematize the "I" and the "my" and the "self" of "I . . . had organized my self image"—an attempt to explore the group organization of self-image—but as it turns out Spivak is really only interested in the problematics of the "monotheist moment" which "is never far away, it does not supervene" (15).

Spivak returns to the problematic of affect in several essays in *Outside in the Teaching Machine* (1993), but, with the exception of a single essay that I want to read more carefully in §2.2.2.4—"Woman in Difference"—she does not really develop it there either. In "Marginality in the Teaching Machine," for example, she cites the extension of Marx's argument from value to affect that Deleuze and Guattari made in *Anti-Oedipus:* "they called it 'desire,' a word fully as misleading as 'value'" (62), misleading, as she tells us in *A Critique of Postcolonial Reason* (1999), "because of its paleonymic burden of an originary phenomenal passion" (105). "Their suggestion was that," she explains in *Outside in the Teaching Machine*, "since capital decoded and deterritorialized the socius by releasing the abstract as such, capitalism must manage this crisis via many reterritorializations, among which the generalized, *psychoanalytic* mode of production of affective value operates by way of a generalized systemic institution of equivalence spectacular in its complexity and discontinuity" (62). By the *Critique,* the problem has become that Deleuzean desiring-production is too diffuse to be of much analytical use: "By the time one gets to call the effects of all the desiring-machines everywhere *anything*—capital, or nature, or despot—a good deal of inaccessible coding has already taken place. To quote Derrida, this inaccessible is the undecidable through which all decisions must cut. For there is of course a tremendous political difference between the name being capital, or despot, or yet nature" (106). Because desire as "originary phenomenal passion" can be produced and channeled and organized (value-coded) in a wide variety of ways, or rather because desiring-production can be *named* in terms of a wide variety of paraphenomenal effects, ultimately as anything anywhere, its coding is inaccessible to us, undecidable, and nothing else needs to be said about it. But—really? This seems rather hastily dismissive. If desiring-production is value-coded as capital, it produces the capitalist body-without-organs; if it is value-coded as nature, as the environment, it produces the Earth or Gaia as body-without-organs. How is this coding inaccessible or undecidable? Spivak's deflection of Deleuzean desiring-production into the analytical abyss seems like an avoidance reaction to what I take to be the key question: what *is* affective value? How is it produced and disseminated, deterritorialized and reterritorialized? My own theorization of the somatic exchange is heavily influenced by *Anti-Oedipus,* which I read some time in the early 1980s, a few years before I began to theorize somatic response, so I know how *I* would read the production and dissemination of affective value—the somatomimetic circulation of evaluative (approval/disapproval) body language and body states within the group for purposes of the normative regulation of social behavior, identity, and reality—but is this how Spivak understands it as well? It is impossible to tell, as she never comments on the term, never even uses it in a context specific enough to enable her reader to guess at how she's using it. Later in "Marginality" she characterizes patriarchy as "traffic in affective value-coding," and opposes that to neocolonialism, which unpacks as "traffic in epistemic-cognitive-political-institutional value-coding" (76)—but does this imply that affective value-coding does not circulate through epistemic-cognitive-political-institutional value-coding? Is patriarchy for Spivak all affect and neocolonialism all the cognitive coding of political and institutional epistemes? Does the affective value-coding of patriarchy not also create and alter conditions of economic exploitation? Does a neocolonial power like the United States not attempt to saturate epistemic-cognitive-political-institutional value-coding with positive affective value-coding? And do the opponents of neocolonialism not attempt to recode negatively the affective value of U.S. "interests" and the policies and activities designed to protect those interests? I'm assuming Spivak would agree that the middle ground between the two poles of her casual binary is awash with overflows from each side; but she doesn't notice that there is a theoretical problem with her binary formulation, so she does not explore it further.

2.2.2.2 THE RAW MAN

The other significant discussion of postcolonial affect in *A Critique of Postcolonial Reason* comes at the other end of her first chapter, "Philosophy," the beginning, where Spivak walks us through a close reading of specific telling passages in Kant, Hegel, and Marx that invoke the figure of the colonized in passing as an early stage in a strategic teleologization. In Kant the first such passage is this one from the *Critique of Judgment*:

> That the mind be attuned to feel the sublime [*Die Stimmung des Gemüts zum Gefühl des Erhabenen*] postulates a susceptibility of the mind for ideas. For in the very inadequacy of nature to these latter, and thus only by presupposing them and by straining the imagination to use nature as a schema for them, is to be found that which is terrible to sensibility and yet is attractive. [It is attractive] because reason exerts a dominion over sensibility [*Sinnlichkeit* "sensuality, carnality, animality"] in order to extend it in conformity with its proper realm (the practical) and to make it look out into

the infinite, which is for it an abyss. In fact, without development of moral ideas, that which we, prepared by culture [*Kultur*], call sublime presents itself to the uneducated man [*dem rohen Menschen*] merely as terrible. In the indications of the dominion of nature in destruction, and in the great scale of its might, in comparison with his own is a vanishing quantity, he will only see the misery, danger, and distress which surround the man who is exposed to it. (§29; *Judgment* 104–5, *Urteilskraft* 111)

Der rohe Mensch is literally "the raw man," "raw" as in "rude" or "rough" or "uncouth," "man" in the old patriarchal sense, "man" as a normatively male and in German grammatically masculine "human being." Spivak's critique pushes Kant into the realm of subalternity by posing three questions: whether the raw man can ever be female, whether the raw man can ever be educated or cultured or "cooked," and how the European conception of the raw man is shaped by colonialism. She writes:

Those who are cooked by culture can "denominate" nature sublime [*erha-ben nennen*], although necessarily through a metalepsis ["that substitutes respect for the object for respect for humanity (in the subject)"]. To the raw man the abyss comes forth [*erhaben vorkommen*] as merely terrible. The raw man has not yet achieved or does not possess a subject whose *Anlage* or programming includes the structure of feeling for the moral. He is not yet the subject divided and perspectivized among the three critiques. In other words, he is *not yet* or *simply not* the subject as such [emphasis added], the hero of the *Critiques*, the only example of the concept of a natural yet rational being. This gap between the subject as such and the not-yet-subject can be bridged under propitious circumstances by culture. As Freud noted, the transformation of the abyss (of nature's infinity) from fearful to sublime through the supplementing mediation of reason—a violent shuttling from *Abgrund* to *Grund*—bears more than a resemblance to the Oedipal scene. (*Critique* 14–15)

Spivak notes that the raw man for Kant includes "specifically the child and the poor [and] can accommodate the savage and the primitive" (13), and constitutes in his normative maleness a *not-yet*-subjectivity that "under propitious circumstances" can be brought to full *as-such*-subjectification by culture—an ameliorative ("bring them up to our level") or counterregulatory regime that is associated historically with liberalism in Europe and paternalism in the colonies. To the extent that the raw man is a woman, however, she is, Spivak says, foreclosed in Kant as "naturally uneducable," irredeemably *roh* or raw—

uncookable, as it were, or unculturable no matter how much you cook her. The raw man, therefore, is *not yet* the subject as such; the raw woman, and especially the female subaltern, is *simply not* the subject as such. That last, the *female subaltern simply not,* is the *terminus ad quem* of Spivak's argument not just because she is a postcolonial feminist, but because she is a poststructuralist postcolonial feminist—because she needs the binary negation *simply not* in order to open up an aporetic break or rupture within Kant's idealized subject of judgment through the exclusion of the colonial other: "The aporia between the discontinuous texts of the raw man and the subject as such should make Kant's critique of judgment unreadable in the strictest sense. Its readability is bought by ignoring the aporia, passing through it by way of the axiomatics of imperialism" (34). It becomes possible to define (European male) culture as judgment only through the exclusion or abjection of the (non-European and ideally also non-male) subaltern—which, as Spivak suggests out of Derrida's deconstruction of Kant in "Economimesis" (21), is to the body politic of reason and transcendental idealism as vomit is to its body organic. Vomit is never "not yet" the subject as such; it is always "simply not" the subject as such.

The significant thing about Spivak's argument from the standpoint of somatic theory is that the differential "simply not" that she denominates as subalternity is ideally abstracted out of the realm of affect, while Kant's "not yet," his notion that the raw man may one day be subjectified to judgment by culture, is saturated in affect. Kant insists that we will not be able to *feel* the sublime ("zum *Gefühl* des Erhabenen") until our minds are "attuned" to it: he writes in German of "die Stimmung des Gemüts," from *die Stimme* "voice," in the sense of adjusting a musical instrument till it emits the right "voice" or sound. When he insists that the mind must be attuned to be susceptible or receptive to "ideas," therefore, he means susceptibility not to *der reine Vernunft* or pure reason but to imagistic mappings or schematizings of those feelings. Nature, he says, is inadequate to these mappings: we only find our way to those specific blendings of pain and pleasure that we call the sublime by "straining the imagination to use nature as a schema for them." Indeed he tells us in the previous section that subliminity "does not reside in anything of nature, but only in our mind, in so far as we can become conscious that we are superior to nature within, and therefore also to nature without us (so far as it influences us)" (104). This consciousness of "our" superiority to "nature within" is specifically not the "dominion" that reason exerts over "sensibility"—*die Sinnlichkeit* or sensuous experience, the world of feeling and sensation—but the *feeling* of reason's dominion over feeling, a *felt* superiority, and in that sense, as we saw in connection with Ngũgĩ on racism in the Preface, not necessarily (all that) conscious. Another way of putting this is that the feeling Kant is theorizing as the productive mental power that generates sublimity is a feeling of mind emerging out of body, a feeling of mental images and ideas struggling to be free of feelings—a movement in the body-becoming-mind to which "we" must be counterregulatorily attuned by "culture" (*Kultur*), which is to say, by the iterosomatizing pressures of the group. The raw man is regulated by his or her own group to experience "the indications of the dominion of nature in destruction, and in the great scale of its might," as danger, and thus to feel terror; the raw man becomes the cultured man or woman through a process of being iterosomatically "cooked," gradually counterregulated to experience that terror metanormatively as attractive, as thrilling in her or his imagistic mastery of its somatic power, and therefore as sublime.

What Kant offers us here, in other words, is a protosomatic theory of "reality" as regulated (constructed and maintained) collectively by "culture," by the ideosomatics of the group. His insistence that the "reality" of the sublime "does not reside in anything of nature, but only in our mind," and specifically in the somatic body-becoming-mind, is one founding principle of social-constructivist somatic theory, that reality is an ideosomatically regulated group construct; his insistence that individuals must be "attuned" to this group reality-construct is another, the philosophical basis of the notion that we are not subject(ifi)ed to regulatory group norms instantly but must undergo a long iterative somatization to them. In this context, the raw man is simply an outgrouper, someone who has not yet been iterosomatized as a member of the dominant ("cultured" or "cooked") group.

2.2.2.3 SPEAKING (OF) SUBALTERNITY

One way of reading Spivak's recurring insistence on the abstract differential binary as the key to subalternity, in fact, is that she is attempting to protect the subaltern out-grouper *against* affect, against a certain specific patronizing (power-laden) affect, the shared evaluative affect of (neo-/de)colonizing Western ameliorative liberalism, which sets a high affective price for group membership: allow yourself to be ideosomatically counterregulated by us or be invisible and inaudible to us. Certainly Kant's remark on the raw man is saturated with a regulatory contempt that is redolent of the missionary school or the teacher's college. Perhaps binary logic, given a poststructuralist spin, will provide a safe haven? If we reduce the argument between "not yet" and "simply not" to an affect/logic binary, so that the "yet" has evaluative/regulatory affect as its entelechy and the "simply" signals logical simplification as the exclusion of affect, then the "not yet" becomes a form of group directional (counterregu-latory) pressure, while the "simply not" marks out a reassuringly stable and indeed almost mathematical absence or lack—though of course (this is the poststructuralist spin) it is also an absence of absence, a lack of lack, an abyssal negation of the very binarizing instance that negates, and therefore ultimately not stable at all. Still, the desomatized subaltern would seem to be ideally pro-tected from the counterregulatory designs of the neocolonizing First World, the colonizing Second World, and the decolonizing Third World.

And indeed Spivak's most famous essay, the 1983 lecture that was first published in 1985 as "Can the Subaltern Speak? Speculations on Widow Sac-rifice," reprinted in a longer and more complexly argued form in Cary Nel-son and Lawrence Grossberg's *Marxism and the Interpretation of Culture,* and finally revised and reprinted in *A Critique of Postcolonial Reason,* does seem to emerge out of something like this protective gesture: Spivak was tired of postcolonial intellectuals pretending to speak for the subaltern and wanted somehow to situate the subaltern in a space ideally shielded from such appro-priations. Such a protected space is of course the "space of difference" (*Cri-tique* 271n118) that defines subalternity as the shifting negated opposite of whatever Western intellectuals want it to be, and specifically as an idealized instance of (post)colonial disenfranchisement that *cannot* be heard by power elites: "if the subaltern can speak," Spivak writes in "The New Historicism," "then, thank God, the subaltern is not the subaltern any more" (283); or, as she tells Howard Winant in a 1990 interview, "the subaltern is the name of the place which is so displaced . . . that to have it speak is like Godot arriv-ing on a bus" ("On the Politics" 91). Being heard by the power elite instantly desubalternizes the subaltern—but so presumably does being heard by other members of the erstwhile "subaltern" group, who also cease to be subaltern the instant no member of a power group is around to not-hear them.

To the extent that subaltern differentiality is intended or taken to work as a kind of epistemological guerilla theater, in which Laozi's "the dao that can be spoken is not the dao" becomes a playful cloaking device or shell game designed to mislead and distract the hegemonic reader, Spivak is arguably engaged in a Derridean or Deleuzean project that privileges intellectual play over (say) the economics of oppression. But this is precisely the project against which Spivak warns us in her article (in its 1988 incarnation):

> It is impossible for contemporary French intellectuals to imagine the kind
> of Power and Desire that would inhabit the unnamed subject of the Other
> of Europe. It is not only that everything they read, critical or uncritical, is
> caught within the debate of the production of that Other, supporting or

critiquing the constitution of the Subject as Europe. It is also that, in the constitution of that Other of Europe, great care was taken to obliterate the textual ingredients with which such a subject could cathect, could occupy (invest?) its itinerary—not only by ideological and scientific production, but also by institution of the law. However reductionistic an economic analysis might seem, the French intellectuals forget at their peril that this entire overdetermined enterprise was in the interest of a dynamic economic situation requiring that interests, motives (desires), and power (of knowledge) be ruthlessly dislocated. To invoke that dislocation now as a radical discovery ["nomad thought"] that should make us diagnose the economic (conditions of existence that separate our "classes" descriptively) as a piece of dated analytic machinery may well be to continue the work of that dislocation and unwittingly help in securing "a new balance of hegemonic relations." (280)

She cannot, therefore, protect subalternity from Western counterregulation simply by *hiding* it discursively, by dislocating it trickily; she has to *locate* it, say something positive about it, essentialize it. But of course that essentialization is in turn precisely the appropriative project against which she reacted in the first place, so that she seems aporetically trapped between two polarized interpretive strategies that are both complicit in the neocolonial/decolonizing counterregulation—and aporetically trapped not in the "good" or "playful" sense valorized by Derrida's North American followers, either, since that construction of the aporia too would remain complicit with empire in its dislocatory (Deleuzean) mode. All she can do, then, as Walter Montag remarks of the piece, is display "a dazzling array of tactical devices designed to ward off or pre-emptively neutralize the attacks of critics. We might say of Spivak what Althusser said of Lacan—that the legendary difficulty of the essay is less a consequence of the profundity of its subject matter than its tactical objectives: 'to forestall the blows of critics . . . to feign a response to them before they are delivered' and, above all, to resort to philosophies apparently foreign to the endeavor 'as so many intimidating witnesses thrown in the faces of the audience to retain the respect'" (par. 2).

Still, Spivak has clung to her original thesis with remarkable tenacity over the three decades since she first articulated it, revising her arguments substantially but in her revisions and interviews only rarely and equivocally deviating from her central claim that the subaltern cannot speak, which suggests that even in its radical deconstructive negativity it is a positive or essentializing claim, something that she believes is *true* of the heterogeneous class of the poorest and most radically disempowered people on earth.

The problem is, of course, that thematizing the deconstructive negativity of the "space of difference" as an essentializing positivity exposes it to both the affective protests coming out of identity politics and decolonizing social work (Spivak's claim would paralyze efforts to improve the subaltern's socioeconomic lot—the central accusation hurled at her in the late 1980s and early 1990s, beginning with Benita Parry's "Problems") and the counteraffective response of syllogistic logic.[25] Spivak's response to the former has been to express warm sympathy and political solidarity but not to budge on the default differential speechlessness of the subaltern, and her response to the latter has been to engage in more deconstructive dodging—which is to say that she has done the only thing that she can do in her situation, short of recanting the theory entirely: kept fine-tuning her original arguments in brilliantly evasive and never less problematic ways.

For example, at the end of the *Critique* version of the essay she responds in some detail to two early challenges, "Can the Subaltern Vote?" by Medovoi, Raman, and Robinson, and Abena Busia's "Silencing Sycorax," saying, for example, in response to Busia, that "I am not laying the blame for the muting [of the subaltern] on the *colonial* authorities" (308–9):

> As I have been saying all along, I think it is important to acknowledge our complicity in the muting, in order precisely to be more effective in the long run. Our work cannot succeed if we always have a scapegoat. The postcolonial migrant investigator is touched by the colonial social formations. Busia strikes a positive note for further work when she points out that, after all, I am able to read Bhubaneswari's case, and therefore she *has* spoken in some way. Busia is right, of course. All speaking, even seemingly the most immediate, entails a distanced decipherment by another, which is, at best, an interception. That is what speaking is.
>
> I acknowledge this theoretical point, and also acknowledge the practical importance, for oneself and others, of being upbeat about future work. Yet the moot decipherment by another in an academic institution (willy-nilly a knowledge-production factory) many years later must not be too quickly identified with the "speaking" of the subaltern. It is not a mere tautology to say that the colonial or postcolonial subaltern is defined as the being on the other side of difference, or an epistemic fracture, even from other groupings among the colonized. What is at stake when we insist that the subaltern speaks? (309)

I would submit, however, that Spivak does not in fact "acknowledge this theoretical point," here—that when it comes right down to it she cannot bring herself to accept the full implications of the notion that "all speaking . . . entails a distanced decipherment by another." After all, if that is "what speaking is," and that "distanced decipherment" that constructs speech as speech cannot construct Bhubaneswari Bhaduri's posthumous text as speech because as the subaltern she is "on the other side of difference," then no one can speak. If the subaltern cannot speak, this is Spivak's true conclusion: when run through the filter of deconstructive discourse analysis, all speech becomes impossible, because as would-be speakers we are all on the other side of difference to someone. It is obviously true that in "even seemingly the most immediate" speaking, with my friends and loved ones, I am always imposing a distanced decipherment on their words, which come to me across the gap of difference, and that decipherment invariably distorts what they are saying, so that all I am left with is my interpretive or "interceptive" construct of what they are saying, so that they can never *speak* as themselves, but must be assigned a mental category of speaking and meaning in my head; if all this is to be thematized as "not being able to speak," then no one can speak.

Walter Montag makes something like this point as well:

Even more curious than this transcendental turn itself is the argumentation Spivak musters to support her declaration, against all appearances, that the subaltern cannot speak. And she has called forth some very intimidating witnesses on her behalf, the primary one, of course, being Derrida. Who better than the translator of *Of Grammatology* to remind us of the relevance of Derrida's critique of Western logocentrism and phonocentrism to political life and to show the utter folly, if not the disingenuousness, of Foucault's call to publish the writings of prisoners as an integral part of the movement against the prisons, or the attempt to set up and archive for the workers' voices as part of the project of proletarian self-emancipation (a project which Spivak has already criticized in categorical terms)? It appears, however, that no one has thought to ask whether Derrida's arguments (especially in *Grammatology*, the work in which such questions are most extensively examined) lead to such conclusions. Is there anything in Derrida's critique of logocentrism that would allow us to say the subaltern cannot speak but must be spoken for, that is, represented both discursively and politically by those who can speak, those who are real subjects of speech? In fact, it would appear that Derrida's argument leads in precisely the opposite direction. For if we accept Derrida's arguments against the speaking subject as ideal origin of speech, present to its utterances as a guarantee of their truth and authenticity, that is, that speech is always already a kind of writing, material and irreducible, we are left only with the fact that there is no pure, original working class or subaltern (or ruling class), possessing a consciousness expressed in its speech or for that matter its acts. There is speech and writing (although these are only modalities of action which are in no way privileged) always and everywhere. It is precisely in and through the struggles that traverse these fields of practice that collectivities are constituted. (par. 8)

In this light, Spivak's repeated insistence that the subaltern cannot speak as him/her/itself to the power elites begins to seem fueled by an objectivist nostalgia for a *true* speaking, a speaking from the heart, a speaking full of the transcendental presence of intentionality, a speaking that is not merely a Kantian construct, not merely someone's "interception." In the context of subalternity, of course, this nostalgia is further charged with the liberal guilt of the postcolonial power elite, the longing for a "true understanding of those poor people," and an uncomfortable recognition that no such "true" understanding is possible—precisely the stance that Spivak first invented the theory to combat, but one that, this analysis would suggest, is recuperated in her theory in negated form.

What Montag calls the "struggles that traverse these fields of practice" and are constitutive of collectivities are in somatic terms the regulatory turbulence of the somatic exchange. In somatic theory speaking is not so much a private act that is "deciphered" or "intercepted" at a "distance" by "another" as it is saturated with group evaluative affect from the start; speech is invented as possible and regulated as meaningful by the somatic exchange, which *circulates* meaning through the group, in the sense of circulating the ideosomatized interpretive orientations that make meaningful communication a pragmatic possibility. It seems to Spivak that the subaltern cannot speak, at the simplest level, because the subaltern is not a member of her group, and therefore does not circulate the same interpretive orientations to speech. By the same token, anyone who does not speak one of her languages will similarly seem not to be able to speak—or, more radically still, anyone who speaks her language but speaks it in disturbingly out-group ways, like a white supremacist or a pathological misogynist, will likewise seem not to be able to speak. We often say about our undergraduate students that they can't talk, can't think, can't read—can't "speak"—because they can't conform their speech to the ideosomatic norms we circulate in our professorial groups. What Spivak was reacting against in writing "Can the Subaltern Speak?" was the liberal (Western modern) project that impels us to try to overcome these in-group/out-group barriers and "truly communicate"—to speak and be heard by others, to hear the speaking of others—with out-groupers that have historically been excluded from our middle-class groups, especially the socially, politically, and economically disenfranchised, and then—if we admit failure, perhaps even recognize the inevitability of failure—somehow to justify that failure intellectually. Spivak's essay is at the very least a radical insistence on the inevitability of this project's failure; but as many critics have argued, it functions also as an intellectual justification that essentializes subalternity as *restricted* by that failure, that indeed projects the failure of a complex but historically situated in-group/out-group dynamic onto the default "speechlessness" of subalternity as such.

In fact, the one alternative model that Spivak broaches to the cannot-speak negativity of the subaltern space of difference comes very close to this somatic conception. In "Subaltern Studies: Deconstructing Historiography," she reads the subaltern not as a (dis)unified (non-)subject at all but as a heterogeneous group that speaks collectively and anonymously through *rumor,* which she assimilates to Derrida's notion of writing from "Signature Event Context":

> If, then, 'rumour is spoken utterance *par excellence*' (*EAP* 256), it must be seen that its 'functional immediacy' is its non-belonging to any *one* voice-consciousness. This is supposed to be the signal characteristic of writing. Any reader can 'fill' it with her 'consciousness.' Rumour evokes comradeship because it belongs to every 'reader' or 'transmitter.' No one is its origin or source. Thus rumour is not error but primordially (originarily) errant, always in circulation with no assignable source. This illegitimacy makes it accessible to insurgency. (23)

"Supposed to be the signal characteristic of writing" is evasive there, of course: she means supposed by Derrida, and by poststructuralists like herself. But this is an interesting deflective strategy: the theorist who has been arguing that the subaltern cannot speak now admits that there is a kind of subaltern speaking that is actually more like writing, or more like writing as theorized by Jacques Derrida, as if her strongest reservation about the notion that the subaltern could speak had been all along that this claim would implicitly construct the subaltern as self-present and self-expressive subject. The subaltern can "speak," Spivak now seems to be saying, as long as her/his/its "speaking" is an oral form of "writing," "always in circulation with no assignable source." Most important for Spivak in this admission, it seems, is the reader-response constructivism of speaking-as-writing: "Any reader can 'fill' it with her 'consciousness.'" It's not the source of speech in individual intention that lends this speech authority; it's simply the being-heard and the being-circulated: "Let us also remember that the mind-set of the peasants is as much affected by the phonocentrism of a tradition where *śruti*—that which is heard—has the greatest authority, as is the mind-set of the historian by the phonocentrism of Western linguistics" (23). (Note there too Spivak's willingness to essentialize "the mind-set of the peasants," which is to say, to speak for the subaltern. As I'll be suggesting in a moment, this is inevitable. Speaking for others is a condition of being able to speak at all. But there is a strain of postcolonial guilt that would purify discourse of all such retrograde impulses.)

Interestingly, Margaret Mills has an article taking Spivak to task for refusing to hear the voices of the subaltern—Spivak's infamous question "seems more indicative of high theory's hearing problem than of any subaltern Philomena syndrome" (174)—in which she offers something very like this same model for the study of subaltern folklore: "If you buy (as I do) Marta Weigle's idea that gossip-anecdote can speak (constitute *and* articulate) cosmic order(s) just as much as cosmotactic *myths* do, then our data—anecdotes, gossip, incidents where we were present—are *always already* speaking 'theory'—somebody's theory, theory in the everyday—and it's our job to sort out *whose* theory" (174, emphasis in original). The difference, of course, is that Spivak is only able to entertain the possibility of the subaltern speaking if the speaking is done anonymously, by a heterogeneous group—and Mills's insistence that we "sort out *whose* theory" vitiates this.

Still, from the standpoint of somatic theory, it seems extreme to binarize the group's anonymous voice in rumor and gossip and the individual's named/bodied voice, given that the latter is conditioned by and saturated with the former. Rumor and gossip are precisely the regulatory speaking of the somatic exchange, the verbalized circulation of group evaluative affect—a much more effective hedge against hegemonic appropriations of the subaltern's voice, to my mind, than the twists and turns of deconstructive negativity—and any attempt anyone makes, from inside or outside the group, to identify the "original source" of a rumor or piece of gossip will continue to be conditioned by group-circulatory attributions of identity and meaning. Indeed it is only possible to spread rumors and gossip if one enters into that circulation, becomes a conduit for identity- and meaning-attributions, and in that capacity helps the group both to "sort out *whose* theory" and to diffuse gossiper identities through the group. I can only "start a rumor" if I am willing simultaneously to surrender my personal authorship of the rumor to the group *and* to take the blame for starting the rumor if the group should decide that it is essential to "sort out *whose* theory." A "rumor" that is not instantly collectivized, instantly disseminated through the somatic exchange as its group-speech (group-opinion, group-speculation), is by definition no rumor at all: it is mere deregulatory grumbling. On a higher level of generality this means that it only becomes possible to speak at all, to say things that others can hear and understand, insofar as one is willing to channel the group mind, to circulate meanings and identities through the somatic exchange. But this individual surrender to the group mind also entails a surrender to being spoken for, to having someone else explain what you mean, what you're trying to say, what your "mind-set" was in saying what you said, and in fact in some cases a surrender to having someone identify you as the speaker of what was spoken, the originator of a rumor or other verbal epidemic, the performer of the speech act that set the insurgency in motion, the *one* to be lionized in group history or handed over to the cops. In this sense Spivak has it exactly backwards when she insists that the subaltern cannot speak, but can only be spoken for: the capacity to be spoken for is the group condition of all speech. Speaking and being spoken for circulate the same communicative impulse through the somatic exchange. As for the puritanical stricture that the subaltern *should not* be spoken for—well, then no one should, and no one should spread rumors, and no one should belong to groups that regulate their behavior, and no one should ever say anything, etc.

Spivak's thinking throughout the "can the subaltern speak?" debate is hobbled, I suggest, by a certain binarizing orientation that she picks up from Derrida: either the subaltern is a fully self-present subject who speaks as the externalization of personal inward intention, or the subaltern cannot speak; either "speech is the immediate expression of the self" (23), or it is ideally cut adrift from self-expression, and therefore a form of "writing"; the subaltern either speaks or is spoken for by postcolonial elites. The somatic retheorization of speech and writing as ideosomatically conditioned, spoken/written/heard/read, and often individualized (attributed to individual speakers or writers as self-expression) by the group is itself steeped in Derridean thought, especially perhaps "Signature Event Context"; but it brings to the stark (anti)metaphysics of Derridean (anti)binaries the as-if correctives of Kantian, Nietzschean, and Burkean constructivism, according to which it's possible to recognize and analyze the ideosomatic constructedness of a speaking subject while still continuing to respond to the speaking of that subject *as if* it were fully ontologized. *Of course* the subaltern is a group construct. Of course the spoken-for construction of the subaltern by Western postcolonial intellectual groups will be complicit in neocolonialism. Of course I will never know what any given member of a subaltern group "really means." But nor will I ever know what Spivak "really means," or what I myself "really mean." And yet, iterosomatically guided by the various groups I belong to, I continue to live as if I could, continue to circulate (and act on) group attributions of meaning and identity to Spivak, myself, and the subaltern, flawed and incomplete and indeed propagandistic as they no doubt are. And in fact I respond with a good deal of discomfort to that totalizing fetish of epistemic purity that would require my knowledge to be perfect before I can legitimately allow myself to act on it, because it is only my epistemic uncertainties that allow me to act at all—even though, I suspect, my pragmatic impatience conceals and enables complicity in neocolonialism and other power-ideologies. The rampant contradictions in Spivak's theorization of the default speechlessness of the subaltern suggest to me that she is impatient also with that fetish—but, at least to date, perhaps because she is more determined than I am *not* to seem complicitous in power-ideologies, she remains as much affected by it as she says Indian peasants are by *śruti*.

2.2.2.4 LITERARY REPRESENTATIONS: "DOULOTI THE BOUNTIFUL"

It may well be that the specific examples Spivak has chosen in order to inter-rogate the concept of the subaltern have made it especially difficult for her to find her way out of abstract differentialities: the subaltern as *sati* and the sub-altern as the Third World female other of Kant's raw man, both in a sense the other of the colonizer's other, seem to trap affect as a black hole traps light, so densely desomatized that it seems impossible to discuss them in terms of their affective response to communal pressures. Her one piece where this is not the case is "Woman in Difference," the 1989/1990 essay originally published in *Cultural Critique* and reprinted in *Outside in the Teaching Machine* that reads Spivak's own English translation of Mahasweta Devi's Bengali novella "Douloti the Bountiful." Because Mahasweta specifically subjectifies Douloti as a tribal girl sold into bonded prostitution, in reading this story Spivak is in a sense beginning at the other end, the self or subject or affect end of "subal-ternity"; as a result the essay is Spivak's most extensive analytical mobilization of affect in her work to date, and her most determined attempt to thematize the subaltern woman not just as a binary effect of discourse but as an affective subjectivity.

I say "in a sense," though, because Spivak does still begin with the space of difference: Mahasweta, she says, "lingers in postcoloniality in the space of difference, *in decolonized terrain*" (105, emphasis in original).[26] The space of difference, not surprisingly, is the subaltern:

> Especially in a critique of metropolitan culture, the event of political inde-pendence can be automatically assumed to stand between colony and decolonization as an unexamined good that operates a reversal. But the

political goals of the new nation are supposedly determined by a regulative logic derived from the old colony, with its interest reversed: secularism, democracy, socialism, national identity, and capitalist development. Whatever the fate of this supposition, it must be admitted that there is always a space in the new nation that cannot share in the energy of this reversal. This space had no established agency of traffic with the culture of imperialism. Paradoxically, this space is also outside of organized labor, below the attempted reversals of capital logic. Conventionally, this space is described as the habitat of the *subproletariat* or the *subaltern*. Mahasweta's fiction focuses on it as the space of the displacement of the colonization-decolonization reversal. This is the space that can become, for her, a representation of decolonization *as such*. (77–78)

The idea here is that the decolonizing reversal should by rights reverse the exclusion of the subaltern into an inclusion, reverse the lack of "established agency of traffic with the culture of imperialism" into an established agency of traffic with the decolonizing culture of organized labor and capital logic, but, paradoxically, it doesn't: the exclusion remains an exclusion, the lack remains a lack, suggesting to Spivak that there is something in that subaltern "space" that by its very differential nature displaces or repels the reversal. This would make subalternity the negative or abyssal image of decolonization as positive ideal, and thus the perfect deconstructive "representation of decolonization *as such*." Noting that the positive ideal of decolonization reverses "empire" as "nation," Spivak asks: "(1) How does Mahasweta inscribe this space of displacement, if not with the lineaments of the nation? (2) What does it mean to say 'socially invested cartography of bonded labor?' and (3) How does Mahasweta suggest, even within this space, that the woman's body is the last instance, that it is elsewhere?" (78–79).

Her answer to that first question is that Mahasweta *names* subaltern communities, names and so "releases" them, allowing the reader "to grasp that the word 'India'—signifier of 'nation'—is sometimes a lid on an immense and equally unacknowledged subaltern heterogeneity" (79). Her answer to the second is that the novella's bond-slaves—all the central characters—are transcoded in the story into a "broad collectivity" or *shomaj*, the customary Bengali word for "society." These two answers clear the ground for her sticking point, the third:

There is no avoiding this, even if the story is read by way of the broadest possible grid: in modern "India," there *is* a "society" of bonded labor, where the only means of repaying a loan at extortionate rates of interest is hereditary bond-slavery. Family life is still possible here, the affects taking the entire burden of survival. Below this is bonded prostitution, where the girls and women abducted from bonded labor or *kamiya* households [as the eponymous Douloti is] are thrust together as bodies for absolute sexual and economic exploitation. These bodies are connected to bond slavery but are yet apart. . . . Woman's body is thus the last instance in a system whose general regulator is still the loan: usurer's capital, imbricated, level by level, in national industrial and transnational global capital. This, if you like, is the connection. But it is also the last instance on the chain of affective responsibility, and no third world-Gramscian rewriting of class as subaltern-in-culture has taken this into account in any but the most sentimental way: . . . (82)

Here, finally, are affects as the sole carriers of the "burden of survival," in the family life that is still possible in the next-to-last instance of bond-slavery, the life of Douloti's mother and father, the life Douloti too leads until at fourteen she is bought into *kamiya* prostitution. It is interesting that what does the heavy lifting here is "the affects," a fairly nonspecific catch-all category that presumably includes familial love and support; and that on the previous page Spivak describes "the precariously manipulative *function* called 'the nation-state'" as "coded and reterritorialized with the heavy paleonymic (historically stuffed) baggage of reason and affect" (81), an even more nonspecific catch-all category that lumps emotional states in with mental mappings of those states as rationality. There is a metaleptic shift in these two tropes, the rational-affective burden carrying the burden of survival; how should we understand that shift? What makes affect heavy, and what equips it to carry the heavy burden of survival? By the paleonymic baggage of reason and affect Spivak apparently means that reason and affect are historically overcoded or over-determined ("stuffed"); but what are they stuffed with? The paleonymic baggage of reason and affect is heavy, because it is historically stuffed; survival is another heavy burden, but this time *carried* by affect. And what kind of survival? Does Spivak mean specifically affective survival—that affective survival is made possible by the familial circulation of supportive affect? Or would she include economic and physical survival as well, the *entire* burden of survival being taken by the affects?

In any case, in "the last instance," the extreme case of bond-slavery, *kamiya*-prostitution, the affective value-coding of life as family life is almost completely blocked: not only are daughters taken from parents and wives from husbands, but the children with whom the *kamiya*-prostitutes are impregnated by clients are taken from their mothers and sent into the streets to beg as well. This does not prevent the prostitute-mothers from *feeling* a maternal belonging to their children, but their feeling is not value-coded as "maternal" by the social machine, as the children do not legally belong to them—because they do not belong to themselves. They belong to the "god," the master, the bond-holder. This affective value-decoding of their own bodies and their own intentionalities is reflected in Douloti's depersonalization, her desomatizing withdrawal of all affect: "The social system that makes [her father] Crook Nagesia a kamiya is made by men. Therefore do Douloti, Somni, Reoti [the bond-prostitutes] have to quench the hunger of male flesh. Otherwise Paramananda [the bond-holder] does not get money. Why should Douloti be afraid? She has understood now that this is natural. Now she has no fear, no sorrow, no desire" (61).

But it is here, I suggest, in her discussion of the affective value-(de)coding of mothering, that Spivak's vagueness about affect begins to hurt her:

> The affective coding of mothering extends from sociobiology all the way to reproductive rights. Before the mobilization of the reproductive rights debate began in the West, demanding the full coding of the woman's body in constitutional abstractions, Simone de Beauvoir had suggested that, in the continuum of gestation, birthing, and child-rearing, the woman passes through and crosses over her inscription as an example of her species-body to the task of producing an intending subject. . . .
>
> Among the women of this fiction ["Douloti the Bountiful"], pregnancy as the result of copulation with clients allows the working out of the inscription of the female body in gestation to be economically rather than affectively coded. (89)

What she means by "economically rather than affectively coded" is reasonably clear in the terms given us by Mahasweta: what happens to the prostitute-mother's newborn infant is determined not by social ideals of maternity but by the bond-holder's economic interests. Caring for an infant would take the mother away from servicing twenty to thirty clients a day and so cut into his profits; the infant must go, must be sent away.

> Somni put her hand to her cheek and said, "See what a strange thing. I was married in childhood, and I stayed with my man for so long. I had only one son. And Latia made me the mother of three sons in a row."
> —Those sons?

—They lie around the marketplace. They beg. They don't let you live with your child, and clients come up to one month before birth. Then I can't for three months.

—Then?

—The god lends money.

—Doesn't he let you keep them?

—No no, would he? When I am burnt up, I go see them. Reoti's son too is Latia's son. And it was Latia's *truck* that hit him and crippled him. As a cripple he gets more begging. He got a shirt too. (63)

Paramananda hasn't given food and upkeep, Latia has impregnated her time after time. Still was it correct of Somni to let her body get so chewed up? (67)

Douloti shook her head. Said, "Uncle Bono, if a kamiya woman becomes a whore the boss makes a lot of profit. No clothing, no cosmetics, no medicine. You have to borrow for everything and the boss adds all the loans to the first loan. No whore can repay that debt in her lifetime." (73)

So, okay: economics, not affect. But what conditions the economics? What makes not just the beneficiaries of this economic system but its victims as well cling tight to it, even desperately to it, like dying men to a float? The answer that Mahasweta has her characters give is tradition, religion:

It's best to go by set rules [Munabar, Douloti's father's Rajput bond-holder, says to his son]. Rule breaking is not good. (43)

Paramananda [the brahman master or "god" who is trying to convince Crook to let him "marry" Douloti in return for paying off his bond to Munabar] gripped Crook hard. Crook filled the sky with his screams. "Truth is being destroyed, the Law is being destroyed! This brahman, this god, is holding me [Crook is an untouchable], please! He must be plumb crazy." (46)

What word, what he should listen to, he didn't think at all. He said "yes" to whatever he heard. Because if the Master says something the machine in Crook's head stops working out of fear. He hears the Master's bellows, but grasps nothing. To say "Yes Sir" to the proprietor is a very long-standing habit. (49)

Rampiyari said, "How will it end? Paramanandaji told me that it is written in the great epics Ramayana and Mahabharata that ending bonded labor is against religion." (81)

—The boss can do what he likes with the person who becomes a bondslave [Paramananda's son Baijnath says to the nationalist radicals who want to end bond-slavery, upon taking over the whorehouse after his father's sudden death]. Yes or no?

—The government will end bondslavery.

—The big government *officers* in Palamu keep kamiyas and seokias. Who will stop bondslavery?

—I'll tell you, the big government. Delhi government.

—It can't be. Bondslavery is an ancient law. That is written in religious books.

—What book?

—I've heard. (84)

Is this pure economic value-coding? At the very least, even if we take Rampiyari and Baijnath to be using religion cynically to justify their manipulation of the bond-labor system to enhance their profits, by invoking religious books to defend a traditional injustice they value-code economics as divine law—something far greater and more powerful than sheer numbers. And Mahasweta gives us no indication that they are speaking cynically: they do seem to believe that the ancient religious books not only tolerate but *demand* bond-slavery. (Mahasweta tells us in the interview with Spivak that introduces the volume that "the bonded labor system was introduced by the British. They created a new class, which took away tribal land and converted the tribals into debt-bonded slaves. The present government of India had to introduce, in 1976, the Bonded Labor Abolition Act" [xii]. But the bond-holders in the novella don't know this. For them the system is traditional, therefore affectively crucial.) Munabar value-codes bond-labor economics as the rule of law, the law of rules, regulation as a guarantor of stability, protection against the insecurities of social change, which he tropes as the West Wind: is this simple cynical greed? Hasn't Munabar been *conditioned* to believe in bond-slavery, conditioned to believe that it is the natural way of the world, conditioned further to believe that bad things would happen not just to him but to everyone, to life itself, if it were abolished? In other words, isn't there an affective/evaluative (ideosomatic) conditioning that disposes these power-holders to hold onto their power? The fear that grips Crook Nagesia when the Master bellows or Paramananda grips him is obviously an affective/evaluative body state that tells him how to behave, what to believe and what to say and what to do in the presence of his social superiors; the Rajput and Brahmin bond-holders defend their economic system with considerably more poise and self-possession—the calm somatics of authority—but they too are clearly "organized" by tradition and religion through affective channels.

Of course it's true that the Master's ability to overlay his own nervous or anxious affect with the outward somatic display of authoritative "reason" would support Spivak's claim that what is at work here is economic *rather than* affective value-coding[27]: value-coding is no ontology but a social semiotizing process that makes things *be* what the authorities want them to *seem* to be, and in capitalist patriarchy the authority of the wealthy male is normatively value-coded as "rational" rather than "emotional," which is to say as the mind's dominion over the body. In this sense Spivak's insistence that "pregnancy as the result of copulation with clients allows the working out of the inscription of the female body in gestation to be economically rather than affectively coded" supports capitalist patriarchy's protective (re)ideosomatization of the authorities' feelings as numbers, the Master's body as thoroughly and calmly mastered by numeric mind. In this ideosomatic regime, only the lower orders are "value-coded" in terms of affect, the tears of powerless women and children, the fears of powerless men.

Indeed throughout her reading of the novella, Spivak repeatedly thematizes affect as Douloti's sentimental conservatism:

> Her relationship to her mother, who is still in the village, is filled with affect. In terms of the critical implications of our argument, it has to be admitted that this affective production, fully sympathetic, is yet represented *within* rather than prior to an accepted code. . . . Like the affection between mother and daughter, Douloti's affect for her village, again gently and beautifully written, is *within* a recognizable coding of sentiment. And indeed, as we see in the following passage, this unresisting nostalgia, dismissing planned resistance as futile, seems to rely on a conservative precapitalist coding of the sexual division of labor. . . . Douloti's affect for her home is thus staged carefully by Mahasweta as the "residual" bonding that works against social change and, ultimately, against the achievement of national social justice, a project in which the author is deeply involved as an activist. Mahasweta dismisses neither side, but presents Douloti's affect and, ultimately, Douloti herself, as the site of a real aporia. You cannot give assent to both on the same register. (92–93, emphasis in original)

This is all true; Spivak's aporetic reading of the ending is powerful and persuasive. But by thematizing affect in the story as Douloti's affect, and by implicit extension as the sanctioned body state of subaltern women, she also misses the more pervasive and more complex operation of affect in the men as well, not merely the tribals who have broken free of bond-slavery and joined the party of decolonizing nationalists—"Prasad roared out, 'That's enough, get out of here'" (84), "It is only Uncle Bono's breast that's bursting with an equal pain" (87)—but the stubbornly exploitative bond-holders as well, who are trapped by traditionalizing (iterosomatic) affect in the moils of their own destructive economic power. That this authoritarian male affect is another form of "'residual' [or, in the original article (126), 'regressive'] bonding that works against social change and, ultimately, against the achievement of national social justice" should be obvious but isn't, to Spivak, because she recuperates in her reading the patriarchal affective value-coding that assigns affect to women and reason to men.[28]

Restricting her thematization of affect to Douloti's nostalgic sentimentalism also numbs Spivak to the affective impact on the reader of the ending's aporetic speech act: "You cannot give assent to both on the same register. I am also arguing that, in terms of the general rhetorical conduct of the story, you also cannot give assent, in the same register, to the evocation of a space prior to value-coding, on the one hand, and the sympathetic representation of Douloti as a character, recognizable within an earlier discursive formation, on the other" (93). I think this falls apart, in fact. You *can* give "assent" to these cognitive structures, evocations of spaces and sympathetic representations, even in the "same register," since registers are just more cognitive structures that can quite easily tolerate this kind of dissonance. What Mahasweta does to us in portraying Douloti is not just to "evoke a space prior to value-coding" or to "represent" her sympathetically: rather, she gets us to identify with her, to simulate her body-becoming-mind states somatomimetically, and thus to feel with her as her body is progressively ravaged by venereal disease and finally she dies—but dies not angrily, not bitterly, not rebelliously, but gently, kindly, naively, acceptingly, infecting us not just with her death but with her sentimental acceptance of her death and of the system that caused it. The affective aporia Mahasweta is inflicting on us is nothing so statically representational as the evocation of a space, a space of difference or displacement or decolonization or anything so abstract; it makes us feel the ponderous polynormativity of the decolonizing counterregulation, the slow inertial grinding of the nationalists' decolonizing rage at injustice against everyone else's conditioned acquiescence to that injustice. What Mahasweta infects us with, in fact, is not just an aporia, an "undecidable in the face of which decisions must be risked" (Spivak 93), but radically opposed regulatory affects, social evaluative feelings that incline us to move in opposite directions, toward activism and toward quietism, toward the bringing about of a utopian world where Douloti would not have needed to die horribly at the age of thirty and toward a surrender to the status quo as not so bad after all. In this sense Spivak is quite right to say that for Mahasweta subalternity is "a representation of decolonization *as such*": in Douloti she feels, and tries to get her reader to feel, the clash of decolonizing normativities.

Displacement of Time/ Intergenerational Trauma/ Paleosomatic Regulation

WE HAVE EXPLORED the dysregulatory effects of refugee trauma and the counterregulatory effects of colonization; it remains now to examine the paleoregulatory effects of *both* refugee trauma and various severely traumatizing colonial practices (genocide, enslavement, cultural subjugation) on later generations. Let's begin by looking back at the passage from Nietzsche's *Genealogy of Morals* that I quoted in §2.1.1:

"How does one create a memory for the human animal? How does one go about to impress anything on that partly dull, partly flighty human intelligence—that incarnation of forgetfulness—so as to make it stick?" As we might well imagine, the means used in solving this age-old problem have been far from delicate: in fact, there is perhaps nothing more terrible in man's earliest history than his mnemotechnics. "A thing is branded on the memory to make it stay there; only what goes on hurting will stick"—this is one of the oldest and, unfortunately, one of the most enduring psychological axioms. In fact, one might say that wherever on earth one still finds solemnity, gravity, secrecy, somber hues in the life of an individual or a nation, one also senses a residuum of that terror with which men must formerly have promised, pledged, vouched. It is the past—the longest, deepest, hardest of pasts—that seems to surge up whenever we turn serious.

> Whenever man has thought it necessary to create a memory for himself, his effort has been attended with torture, blood sacrifice. The ghastliest sacrifices and pledges, including the sacrifice of the first-born; the most repulsive mutilations, such as castration; the cruelest rituals in every religious cult (and all religions are at bottom systems of cruelty)—all these have their origin in that instinct which divined pain to be the strongest aid to mnemonics. (II:3, 192–93)

"The residuum of that terror," "the past . . . that seems to surge up": these are among the first theorizations we have of what has come to be called the multigenerational transmission of trauma, historical trauma, or intergenerational trauma. Nietzsche's idea is that trauma is stored and repeatedly retrieved for what I am going to be calling the paleosomatic regulation not only of individuals but of whole civilizations: "only what goes on hurting" *generation after generation* "will stick" to a nation, to a civilization, or to "man." We saw in the Second Essay that this is a powerfully ideosomatic formulation—the mnemotechnics of pain involve the circulation of regulatory responses to pain through the somatic economy of the group—but Nietzsche does not theorize the somatics of the intergenerational transmission itself, the way in which traumatic pain conditions the memory not just of living people but of future generations as well. He just assumes it.

It is crucial for Nietzsche's later influence on Sigmund Freud that his explanatory strategy here is grounded in the medical metaphorics of disease and its symptomatologies, epidemiologies, and cures: he calls "the constantly spreading ethics of pity . . . the most sinister symptom of our sinister European civilization" (Preface:5, 154); he writes of the "cures" developed by "priestly aristocracies" for various disease-like evils and insists that "humanity is still suffering from the after-effects of those priestly cures" (I:6, 165–66); he calls the "descendants of every European and extra-European slavedom" the "carriers of the leveling and retributive instincts" (I:11, 176). His most complex exfoliations of this medical metaphor tend to be brief but suggestive lists of interpretive categories that he does not then pursue: "We need a critique of all moral values; the intrinsic worth of these values must, first of all, be called in question. To this end we need to know the conditions from which those values have sprung and how they have developed and changed: morality as consequence, symptom, mask, *tartufferie*, sickness, misunderstanding; but, also, morality as cause, remedy, stimulant, inhibition, poison" (Preface:6, 155).

When Freud picks up this idea of the multigenerational transmission of trauma, in his revisiting of his "historical" theory of the primal scene from *Totem and Taboo* in *Moses and Monotheism*, he takes over not only the medi-

cal metaphor but one telltale trope ("residuum of terror" > "mental residue");
but Freud is as unable to explain the transmission of trauma as Nietzsche is:[1]

> After the combination of brother clans, matriarchy, exogamy, and totemism
> had been established there began a development which may be described
> as a slow "return of the repressed." The term "repressed" is here used not in
> its technical sense. Here I mean something past, vanished, and overcome in
> the life of a people, which I venture to treat as equivalent to repressed mate-
> rial in the mental life of the individual. In what psychological form the past
> existed during its period of darkness we cannot as yet tell. It is not easy to
> translate the concepts of individual psychology into mass psychology, and I
> do not think that much is to be gained by introducing the concept of a "col-
> lective" unconscious—the content of the unconscious is collective anyhow,
> a general possession of mankind. So in the meantime the use of analogies
> must help us out. The processes we study here in the life of a people are
> very similar to those we know from psychopathology, but still they are not
> quite the same. We must conclude that the mental residue of those prime-
> val times has become a heritage which, with each new generation, needs
> only to be awakened, not to be reacquired. (*Moses* 169–70)

The "repressed" here is guilt over the murder of the father by the brothers, from
Totem and Taboo—repressed, as Freud suggests, in a displaced or analogical
sense, so that "something past, vanished, and overcome in the life of a people"
returns, slowly, as the *collective* equivalent of the return of the repressed in
"the mental life of the individual." What the repressed and ever slowly returning "mental residue" is in a civilization, how it was stored through its "period
of darkness," or how it is "awakened" in each new generation, he has no idea;
these are the questions that Heinz Kohut and other protosomatic attachment
theorists have attempted to answer. He can only trope the processes in question in terms of the reemergence into the light of something that has been
long relegated to the dark, the reawakening of something that has been put to
sleep, or the rediscovery of the residue of some long-past chemical reaction.

How then does the multigenerational transmission of trauma work?
This is a question that began to be asked again in the 1970s, first by Holocaust scholars, specifically in the context of the lingering effects of Holocaust
trauma on the children of Holocaust survivors, and then by scholars of other
traumatic histories as well, especially the genocide and various forced relocations and reeducations of Native Americans and the genocide and subjugation of Africans in the slave trade. And indeed after focusing for most of this
book on refugee and (de)colonized populations in other countries, in this last

essay I turn to intergenerational trauma in two groups in my own country: the paleoregulatory effects of genocide and cultural subjugation on Native Americans, and of genocide, slavery, and cultural subjugation on African Americans. As in the two previous essays, I will be following these empirical studies with a look at literary representations—James Welch's *The Death of Jim Loney* (1979), Toni Morrison's *Beloved* (1987), and Percival Everett's "The Appropriation of Cultures" (1996). Since there have not exactly been "theoretical spins" on intergenerational trauma, I will not provide a separate section for the postcolonial theory of historical trauma; but I will, in §3.2.4, build my conclusion around Dominic LaCapra's poststructuralist theorization of what he calls "historical trauma" in *Writing History, Writing Trauma* (1999).

3.1 EMPIRICAL STUDIES

The empirical study of what is variously called intergenerational trauma, historical trauma, and the trans- or multigenerational transmission of trauma—especially as massively anthologized in Yael Danieli's 1998 book *International Handbook of Multigenerational Legacies of Trauma*—typically encompasses the following:

1. studies of the original traumatizing experience(s), such as the American or Nazi Holocaust or other genocides, the dropping of the atomic bomb on Nagasaki and Hiroshima, war and the POW experience, enslavement, forced relocation, repressive regimes, and domestic violence;

2. studies of the effects of trauma on its survivors;

3. studies of the effects of parenting by trauma survivors on their children (the "mechanism" of intergenerational transmission, and thus the primary problem that Nietzsche and Freud failed to address); and

4. studies of post-traumatic stress disorder (PTSD) symptomatologies in populations who have not undergone trauma themselves and so can be assumed to have inherited some form of allostatic overload from some traumatized previous generation(s).

Some psychobiological studies of intergenerational trauma in humans and animals (Suomi and Levine, Yehuda et al., Krystal et al.) focus on (3) and (4), with background looks at (2); but the bulk of the work being done in the field seems prescriptively to require all four stages of the argument, for the perhaps obvious reason that it is impossible to establish with any empirical certainty that, say, disproportionately high rates of alcoholism, suicide, domestic violence, heart disease, and diabetes in Native American populations are the direct paleoregulatory endosomatic after-effects of the American Holocaust. By showing that trauma does radically counterregulate not only individuals but also the somatic economies that give their lives meaning and structure, that this counterregulation is demonstrably transferred virally from parents to children, and that populations who have not undergone severe trauma demonstrably suffer disproportionately high incidences of PTSD symptomatologies, intergenerational trauma scholars build a strong circumstantial case for the transgenerational transmission of trauma.

In the first chapter of Danieli's *Handbook*, "Intergenerational Memory of the Holocaust," Nanette C. Auerhahn and Dori Laub begin with what they call "forms of traumatic memory" in trauma survivors [(2) in the previous paragraph's list], ten in number, from the least to the most "memorious":

2a. not knowing, caused by "massive psychic trauma [that] breaks through the stimulus barrier and defies the individual's ability to formulate experience" (23);

2b. screen memories, "the creation of an alternative, possibly false, self that screens over the absence of memory" (25);

2c. fugue states, "the intrusive *appearance* of split off, fragmented behaviors, cognitions, and affect, which are pieces of the traumatic memory or experience" (28, emphasis in original);

2d. the retention of decontextualized fragments of the trauma, in which "the individual has an image, sensation, or isolated thought, but does not know with what it is connected, what it means, or what to do with it" (29);

2e. transference phenomena, involving "the grafting of isolated fragments of the past on to current relationships and life situations that become colored by these 'memories'" (30);

2f. overpowering narratives, in which some scene from the traumatizing experience is atemporally relived, so that "He or she is in the experience once again; he or she is the same age again" (31);

2g. life themes, in which the overpowering narratives are used to organize personality and behavior ("identity and striving") thematically, which requires the establishment of "a degree of distance from the traumatic event" (32);

2h. witnessed narratives, "in which the observing ego remains present as a witness," so that "knowing takes the form of true memory" (33);

2i. trauma as "metaphor and vehicle for developmental conflict" (33); and

2j. "action knowledge, in which knowing becomes consciously conse-
quential and thus determines subsequent action" (35).

Like most psychoanalytically oriented scholars of intergenerational
trauma, Auerhahn and Laub tend to study these forms of traumatic memory
in individuals: "although none of the various forms of traumatic memory
are mutually exclusive," they write, "and several may, to a greater or lesser
degree, coexist in any particular individual at any given point in time, it is
generally true that victims know mostly through retention of unintegrated
memories or by reliving such memories in transfererence phenomena" (36).
Somatic theory would situate these individual remembering and knowings in a larger circulatory economy of such knowings, which in fact—the
somatic economy—would be the collective structuring context in which it
becomes possible to distinguish between, say, decontextualized fragments
(2d) and transference phenomena (2e). How, after all, is the individual to
determine what is a false memory and what is a true one, what is a present
affect and what is a transferential affect grafted onto present relationships
from the past? This sort of determination can only be made by the group—
at a bare minimum by the analyst–patient dyad. Again like most psychoanalytically oriented scholars, Auerhahn and Laub tend to thematize these
group determinations not as collective constructs but as empirical truths,
objective facts—an epistemologically indefensible position that would seem
to have more to do with the group fetishization (ideosomatic idealization) of
scientism in the psychoanalytical community than it does with what can be
reasonably established empirically.

If we take the list of (2a–j) ten forms of traumatic memory Auerhahn
and Laub list not as a stable taxonomy of isolated memory *types* in individuals, then, but as a tentative formulation of group *constructions* of traumatic
dysregulations of knowing and remembering—as circulatory organizations of
deviations from ideosomatic regulations of reality and identity—then we can
retheorize their list as a collective portrait of the paleosomatic regulation that
will be retroactively constituted as the etiological ground zero of intergenerational trauma, the (dys)regulatory allostatic regime that will be thematized as
handed down from generation to generation.

Auerhahn and Laub next turn to a discussion of the "modes" of the intergenerational transmission of trauma, the problem that Nietzsche and Freud
left us, which they solve with Kohutian attachment theory:

We would like to briefly address the question of modes of transmission of memory from one generation to the next. No doubt the pathways are multiple, complex, and mediated by numerous variables. Using a population of women who were sexually abused as children, Armsworth, Mouton, De Witt, Cooley, and Hodwerks (1993) and Stronck and Armsworth (1994) have researched the indirect effects of parents' childhood trauma on the second generation, specifically the manner in which parents' own traumatic past induces insecure attachment to their own mothers and disconnected, intrusive, and flawed parenting styles that result in insecure attachments in their own children. We have focused in much of our work (see especially Auerhahn & Laub (1994); Auerhahn & Prelinger (1983); Laub & Auerhahn (1984, 1993); and Peskin et al. (1997) on a second pathway of intergenerational effects, that of direct effects, or what is sometimes called *vicarious traumatization*—the fact that children both pick up on the defensive structures of traumatized parents and intuit the repressed, dissociated, and warded off trauma that lurks behind the aggressive and traumatic overtones that are found in adults' parenting styles. It is an irony of the PTSD literature that it is widely accepted that therapists working with victims of trauma will suffer vicarious traumatization (see such recent publications as Pearlman [1995]), yet the fact that a young child who cannot readily differentiate his or her boundaries from those of the parent on whom his or her life depends should pick up on the parent's warded off, dissociated, and traumatized self and be seriously impacted by identification is still in dispute (see Solkoff 1992). (37–38)

What the authors seem to mean by their direct/indirect binary there is that insecure dyadic mother–child attachments transfer traumatoregulatory orientations that only indirectly "transmit trauma to" (actually *reconstruct trauma in*) the child, while weak ego boundaries in infancy and early childhood directly facilitate the transfer (or perhaps leakage) of the "parent's warded off, dissociated, and traumatized self." In somatic theory, however, this is a difference without a difference. There simply is no "self" that can be transferred without the regulatory orientations of the group: the dissociated and traumatized parental self is only available for somatomimetic reconstruction in the child because ideosomatic regulation circulates through both parent and child.

Like Nietzsche, Freud, and Kohut before them,[2] however, Auerhahn and Laub construct a model that is powerfully *proto*somatic; as Allan Schore (also relying heavily on Kohutian attachment theory) theorizes the somatic mimesis that makes the intergenerational transmission of trauma possible:

As episodes of relational trauma commence, the infant is processing information from the external and internal environment. The mother's face is the most patent visual stimulus in the child's world, and it is well known that direct gaze can mediate not only loving but powerful aggressive messages. In coding the mother's frightening behavior, Hesse and Main described "in non-play contexts, stiff-legged 'stalking' of infant on all fours in a hunting posture; exposure of canine tooth accompanied by hissing; deep growls directed at infant" (1999, p. 511). The image of the mother's aggressive face, as well as the chaotic alterations in the infant's bodily state that are associated with it, are indelibly imprinted into the infant's developing limbic circuits as a "flashbulb memory" and thereby stored in imagistic implicit-procedural memory in the visuospatial right hemisphere.

But within the traumatic interaction the infant is presented with another affectively overwhelming facial expression, a maternal expression of fear-terror. Main and Solomon (1986) noted that this occurs when the mother withdraws from the infant as though the infant were the source of the alarm, and they reported that dissociated, trancelike, and fearful behavior is observed in parents of type D infants. Studies show a specific link between frightening, intrusive maternal behavior and disorganized infant attachment (Schuengel, Bakersmanns-Kranenburg, and van IJzendoorn, 1999).

During these episodes, the infant is matching the rhythmic structures of these states, and this synchronization is registered in the firing patterns of the right corticolimbic brain regions that are in a critical period of growth. And thus not just the trauma but the infant's defensive response to the trauma, the regulatory strategy of dissociation, is inscribed into the infant's right-brain implicit-procedural memory system. In light of the fact that many of these mothers have suffered from unresolved trauma themselves (Famularo, Kinscherff, and Fenton 1992), this spatiotemporal imprinting of terror and dissociation is a primary mechanism for the intergenerational transmission of trauma. (125–26)

There, in "not just the trauma but the infant's defensive response to the trauma, the regulatory strategy of dissociation," is the somatic corrective that collapses the direct/indirect binary: the infant somatomimetically reconstructs not only the trauma (directly) but the parent's "defensive response to the trauma" (indirectly), builds both into an integrated paleoregulatory regime that is then passed down from generation to generation.

3.2 LITERARY REPRESENTATIONS: WELCH, MORRISON, EVERETT

I will, as I say, be taking a slightly different approach in this final essay: rather than moving more or less systematically through a series of empirical approaches and one or two literary representations to a series of postcolonial theoretical spins, I want to focus almost all of my attention this time on three different literary representations: James Welch's *The Death of Jim Loney* (1979), Toni Morrison's *Beloved* (1987), and Percival Everett's "The Appropriation of Cultures" (1996). My sense, in fact, is that novelists have explored the somatics of intergenerational trauma far more powerfully and insightfully than either the empirical scholars or the two poststructuralist theorists, Cathy Caruth and Dominic LaCapra, who have most systematically addressed it. In the remainder of this essay, then, I'll be looking first at Welch's attempt to pose the problem of intergenerational trauma without naming it or having the slightest idea what to do about it; then at Morrison's full-out exploration of the survival of the traumatic past into a repeatedly retraumatized present, in the return of the greedy revenant Beloved, with only the vaguest suggestion at a resomatizing solution to it; and finally at Everett's moral fable that explicitly offers resomatization as a utopian solution.

3.2.1 James Welch, *The Death of Jim Loney*

James Welch (1940–2003), son of a Blackfeet father and Gros Ventre mother, was one of the leading figures in the Native American Renaissance of the 1970s. He grew up and attended schools on the Blackfeet and joint Gros Ventre-Assiniboine Fort Belknap reservations in northern Montana, studied at the University of Montana under Richard Hugo, and in addition to teaching at the University of Washington and Cornell, served on the Parole Board of the Montana Prisons System in Missoula, where he lived until his death in 2003.

Welch wrote poetry (*Riding the Earthboy 40* [1990]) and history (*Killing Custer: The Battle of Little Bighorn and the Fate of the Plains Indians* [1994]), but he is best-known for his novels: *Winter in the Blood* (1974), *The Death of Jim Loney* (1979), *Fools Crow* (1986), *The Indian Lawyer* (1990), and *The Heartsong of Charging Elk* (2000). Two of those novels, *Fools Crow* and *Charging Elk*, are set in the Indian Wars era of the late nineteenth century, the former ending with the infamous Marias River massacre in 1870, in which

173 women, children, and a few old men of the Blackfoot Confederacy were slaughtered by Major Eugene Baker's men in retaliation for the Indian murder of a white trader, the latter stranding Charging Elk, taken to London in 1887 as a part of Buffalo Bill's Wild West show, in Marseilles, France, where he cannot speak more than a couple of words of English or French. The other three are set in contemporary times and places, especially the reservation towns in Montana where Welch grew up.

The novel I want to read in this section, *The Death of Jim Loney*, is in one critical sense an anomaly in Welch's literary production; as Ernest Stromberg writes:

> One of the most powerful explorations of the challenges to contemporary Native American identity takes place in James Welch's *The Death of Jim Loney*. In his second novel, Welch casts a grim shadow across the representational space of contemporary American Indian fiction. Unlike his other three novels—*Winter in the Blood, Fools Crow,* and *The Indian Lawyer*—*The Death of Jim Loney* refuses to provide the ultimately affirmative vision of Native American cultural survival that many readers have come to associate with contemporary American Indian fiction. For instance, in his first novel, *Winter in the Blood,* the critical consensus is that by the story's end the nameless narrator finally achieves access to a place in a larger Blackfeet cultural history, an access which will help him to develop a more meaningful, less alienated life. With his third novel, *Fools Crow,* Welch spins a historical fiction of the Blackfeet people before subjugation to white authority. Densely layered with ethnographic detail, *Fools Crow* portrays a rich and dynamic culture. Although this work ends with a chilling account of the brutal Marias River massacre, the novel's overall narrative celebrates Blackfeet history and tradition in what critic Owens calls a "full act of cultural recovery" (156). And in his most recent novel, *The Indian Lawyer,* Welch provides a protagonist, Sylvester Yellow Calf, who, after nearly succumbing to the Faustian temptation of power in the inauthentic white world, is "found" at the end of the story dedicatedly working to protect Indian water rights. (32–33)

The eponymous Charging Elk, too, in the novel published after Stromberg wrote, manages to build out of destructive circumstance a mode of survival that offers collective hope. That leaves only *Jim Loney* as a narrative emblem of the complete collapse of cultural meaning and direction, and thus of failure and despair: half-Indian, half-white, Jim Loney had "never felt Indian" (102) but certainly never identified with white culture either (his white girlfriend

Rhea "had said he was lucky to have two sets of ancestors. In truth he had none" [102]), and after spending the entire novel trying to create a collective past for himself, to think an ancestry and a history into being, fails, and commits a complex kind of suicide.

3.2.1.1 THE CRITICS

There have been roughly two kinds of critical response to this failure. One, represented by Kathleen Sands and John Purdy, reads the imagery of the novel as grounding Loney's death in Gros Ventre spirituality, and thus in what Stromberg calls a redemptive "authentic Indianness." The other, represented by Jennifer Lemberg, reads Loney's failure to construct a usable Indian past in terms of intergenerational trauma: in her reading, Loney does truly fail, and his suicide truly is cause for despair, but his failure becomes an indictment of the U.S. policies that decimated Indian populations and severely traumatized the survivors. What I want to suggest is that these readings are not mutually exclusive—that failure/success and authentic Indian/non-Indian are false dichotomies in the novel, and perhaps more broadly in and for the ideosomatic realities and identities that circulate through the novel and its readers as well.

As John Purdy lays out the former reading, it revolves around the "dark bird" Loney begins seeing early in the novel: "And he saw the smoke ring go out away from his face and he saw the bird in flight. Like the trembling, the bird was not new. It came every night now. It was a large bird and dark. It was neither graceful nor clumsy, and yet it was both. Sometimes the powerful wings beat the air with the monotony of grace; at other times, it seemed that the strokes were out of tune, as though the bird had lost its one natural ability and was destined to eventually lose the air" (Welch 20). Purdy explains:

> Loney later states that he has never seen a bird like his before in the surrounding country. The dark bird, however, bears a number of similarities to Bha'a, one of the most powerful beings in the world of the Gros Ventre. Like Coyote, or Sinchlep of the Salish and Na'pi of the Blackfeet, he is the most powerful agent of the "Supreme Being," and as such his influence is far-reaching. He is most commonly associated with summer thunderstorms, and in this connection a ceremony and a story have evolved around him. The Feather Pipe—one of the two most powerful pipes in Gros Ventre ceremonialism—is said to have been given by Bha'a to a boy who was unlike any of the other children in his village. Although there are

different versions of the story, they can be seen to relate to Loney. The boy who receives the pipe does not play with the other children but instead stays to himself; he is told in a dream that he is going to be given something so he moves his lodge away from the others in the village, and he is visited by Bha'a, who takes the boy's lodge and everything he owns but leaves him with the pipe (Flannery 446). Isolation, alienation, and vision are directly connected in the story to the power gift of Bha'a; the loss of material possessions and human companionship results in the gift of something immensely more valuable for individual and community alike: knowledge of new ceremonial actions and power derived from a relationship with a supernatural being. (69–70)

Loney, as his name suggests, is a loner. He has a girlfriend, Rhea, whom he loves, but as soon as he begins seeing the dark bird in visions, he begins to alienate himself from her as well ("they were lovers and he was blowing it. And he didn't know why" [22]); soon they are more or less broken up, and she is packing to move home to Dallas. He knows people in town, he grew up there, played high school basketball there, but has no friends, and often goes days without talking to anyone but his old dog, who early in the novel wanders off to die alone. "Isolation, alienation, and vision" are all defining attributes of Jim Loney. He receives nothing vaguely resembling a Feather Pipe in the novel, unless we count the shotgun his father gives him; but Purdy adds, following Sands, that Bha'a can give a man the power to become a great warrior and to stir up storms:

> As Sands demonstrates, Loney becomes a warrior after he is given the shotgun—as he foresees in his vision—but he also becomes a maker of storms. When Loney walks to Rhea's later, she comments about the severity of the wind. Loney replies, "I think I might have something to do with it" (28). The possibility that he might be affecting the weather is never explored, at least overtly, but this slight and seemingly inconsequential statement says a great deal about Loney's vision of the bird, the image of which remains with him. As he stares into Rhea's fireplace, he sees it again, and either it, or his memory of it, arises to direct his actions throughout the remainder of the novel. The novel ends, as does Loney's life, with a reference to his vision; the sense of complicity lingers, as does the sense that any distinction between Loney's vision of the bird and Loney himself has disappeared: "And he fell, and as he was falling he felt a harsh wind where there was none and the last thing he saw were the beating wings of a dark bird as it climbed to a distant place." (70)

Loney dies, in other words, not miserably, cold, alone, gunned down by a tribal cop; he dies a warrior's death, a death of great spiritual power that gathers him to his ancestors, whom he has been seeking throughout the novel in vain. As Welch told an interviewer, "He does orchestrate his own death. . . . He creates it, he creates a lot of events to put himself on top of that ledge in the end . . . he knows how his death will occur. And to me, that is a creative act and I think all creative acts are basically positive" (Bevis 176).

I think it would be difficult to deny that some such spiritual undercurrent is at work in the novel's imagery. The question, though, is what Welch is doing with it. If, as Purdy says, "the loss of material possessions and human companionship results in the gift of something immensely more valuable for individual and community alike: knowledge of new ceremonial actions and power derived from a relationship with a supernatural being," where do we see this power? Where is the knowledge of the new ceremonial actions? Loney dies, and the novel ends.[3] If he is indeed gathered to his ancestors, that is something we have to infer from the vaguely adumbrated Gros Ventre imagery; certainly there is no indication that his death will change anything, improve anything, bring the Gros Ventres in the novel or any of its readers new hope or new knowledge or new direction.

In *The Sacred Hoop*, Paula Gunn Allen offers a mitigated version of this "authentic Indian" reading, based only on the perception that Jim Loney chooses his death, and so dies like a warrior:

Loney dies like a warrior, out of choice, not out of defeat. Though he could not plan or control his life, he could, finally, determine his death. Perhaps the most destructive aspect of alienation is that: the loss of power, of control over one's destiny, over one's memories, thoughts, relationships, past, and future. For in a world where no normative understandings apply, where one is perceived as futile and unwanted, where one's perceptions are denied by acquaintance and stranger alike, where pain is the single most familiar sensation, the loss of self is experienced continually and, finally, desperately. (145–46)

While still grounded in the notion that *The Death of Jim Loney* is definitively shaped by Indian ritual and myth, Allen's 1992 reading pushes us hard in the direction of the intergenerational trauma reading offered in 2006 by Jennifer Lemberg: Loney lives in "a world where no normative understandings apply" not because he *just is* alienated, where he alone "is perceived as futile and unwanted, where [only his] perceptions are denied by acquaintance and stranger alike, where pain is the single most familiar sensation" for this random man in the world—and certainly not because alienation is any kind of general human condition—but because the historical traumas inflicted on Native Americans by expansionist white Americans over three and a half centuries have *depleted* the Indian world of normative understandings.

"The possibility that Loney has inherited a legacy of trauma," Lemberg writes, "is difficult to dispute" (70)—meaning that, based on the work done by Eduardo and Bonnie Duran, Maria Yellow Horse Brave Heart, and Lemyra M. DeBruyn applying intergenerational trauma theory to the American Holocaust, *as an Indian* Loney has indisputably inherited that legacy:

> As the Durans and Brave Heart write, "European contact decimated the indigenous populations of this hemisphere," through disease, alcohol, violence, and "policies systematically attacking the core of identity—language and the family system," including the creation of the boarding schools and the outlawing of religious practices ("Trauma of History" 62–64). The latter half of the nineteenth century brought the reservation system, the destruction of the buffalo herds, and the forced cession of land under the Allotment Act (Flanner 22–23; Brave Heart and DeBruyn 64). Like that of other Plains tribes, the history of the Gros Ventres was shaped by these events, the population decreasing sharply around the turn of the century following the settling of the boundaries of the Fort Belknap Reservation (Flannery 24). A period of "revitalization" followed, though after the Indian Reorganization Act the "reservation entered a period of steady decline" (Fowler 98–102). Loretta Fowler notes that the middle of the century, when Loney would have been growing up, was a time of "outright despair," for the Gros Ventres, as Termination Era policies led to economic hardship, a decrease in traditional practices, and an increase in migration away from the reservation. (99–102) (70–71)

Citing Loretta Fowler's account of the return of many Gros Ventres to the reservation in the 1960s, and the revivification of both ritual practices and economic opportunities (1), and Robert M. Nelson's argument to the effect that there were Gros Ventres Loney's age and older who were active on the reservation (101), Lemberg notes that "in portraying Loney's grief and isolation, Welch denies him access to these" (72). Loney has a family, but they are no help: his white father Ike lives locally but until late in the novel the two have not spoken in twenty-five years; his big sister Kate has moved to Washington, D.C., to work for the Bureau of Indian Affairs, and dismisses the past as nonexistent and not worth thinking about (91); his mother left the family when Loney was an infant and never made an attempt to contact her children again. The story his father put out was that his Gros Ventre wife Eletra had gone crazy and was probably dead, or in an insane asylum somewhere; in high school Loney discovers that his mother had gone to live with his schoolmate Yellow Eyes' father, on the reservation (118–19), but never tells anyone of his discovery, and never (until the end of the novel) asks anyone about her or attempts to look her up. Lemberg writes:

> His mother's absence is the sharpest reminder of Loney's personal dev-astation. As Owens writes, she "exists in some undefined place—maybe a madhouse, maybe death—just outside the picture," and her haunting presence appears in Loney's dreams and visions (149). What Loney even-tually learns of her story hints at larger meanings in her disappearance, as it is after marrying a white man that she goes from participating in traditional dances and training as a nurse to dissolution and death. Loney fantasizes about their reunion, consistent with the "compensatory fanta-sies" described by the clinicians, and his unresolved grief for her is an important part of the emotional crisis that leaves him immobilized at his kitchen table. (73)

"Loney's separation from his mother," Lemberg adds, "contributes to his feel-ing that he lacks an Indian identity" (73). He does not feel like an Indian, and is surprised to discover that others regard him as one, because he has an ideal-ized image of Indians as a functional community where "the old ones [passed] down the wisdom of their years, of their family's years, of their tribe's years, and the young ones [soaked] up their history, their places in history, with a wisdom that went beyond age" (Welch 102). "Focused as he is on memory and the past," Lemberg writes, "Loney understands Indian identity to be based on precisely those things he lacks. Rhea remarks that Loney 'is lucky to have two sets of ancestors' so that he 'can be Indian one day and white the next,' but he does not experience his background as an opportunity to create a multiple or hybrid self (14). Instead, he struggles with it as a heavy burden of loss" (73–74).

Lemberg's explanation of Loney's quasisuicidal death is that "he suffers from what Fine calls 'the guilt of nonparticipation,' worsened by his lack of a connection to a living, thriving community" (74), a reading that draws on Ellen S. Fine's discussion of the crushing effects of trauma on the next genera-tion, the children of the survivors:

> They are haunted by the world that has vanished; a large gap exists in their history, and they desire to bridge this gap, to be informed about what

occurred, to know something about members of their family who per-
ished. However, they feel frustrated by the impotence of incomprehen-
sion; the past eludes and excludes them. Repeatedly met with the silence of
their parents and relatives—who transmit the wounds of genocide, and not
the memory—they grow up in the "compact voice of the unspeakable," as
Nadine Fresco affirms. (Fine 43–44, quoted in Lemberg 72)

When Loney finally confronts and exculpates his father, then, he assigns all
guilt for his empty life to himself, the guilty nonparticipant: "Loney knew
who the guilty party was. It was he who was guilty, and in a way that made his
father's past sins seem childish, as though original sin were something akin to
stealing candy bars" (Welch 146). Lemberg comments: "His guilt contributes
to his desire to participate in an incident similar to those that he imagines
have preceded his birth: seeing himself as 'marked' by his wrongdoing, he
leaves his father's trailer prepared to be hunted down and killed" (74), prepared to reenact "a painful scene from American cultural narratives of Indians
being destined to perish" (75). As Louis Owens puts it, "Loney enacts the fate
of the epic Vanishing American" (155, quoted in Lemberg 78n2). He "recreates what seems to be an originary trauma. He engages in what historian and
trauma theorist Dominic LaCapra calls 'acting out,' a mode of dealing with
trauma in which 'the past is performatively regenerated or relived as if it were
fully present,'[4] rather than working through it, by engaging in the only kind
of 'cultural performance' he sees himself as being capable of, his death" (75).

3.2.1.2 THE DARK CONSTRUCTIVIST BIRD

Lemberg's discussion of the dark bird that Loney sees all through the novel,
and that seems to lead him upward out of death at the very end, opens a fruit-
ful interpretive avenue beyond the impasse at which the polarized readings of
the novel leave us:

> Earlier, when Loney is incapable of telling Rhea what troubles him, he
> instead tells her of the dark bird that appears in his visions. His description
> of the bird subtly replaces a description of his past. While the bird may
> indeed be a vision sent by his mother's people, as he suspects, unskilled as
> Loney is in tribal modes of understanding, its meaning always eludes him.
> It becomes a signifier that reveals nothing, an emblem of a past he cannot
> remember, both his own personal history and that of the Indian tribe to
> which he belongs. In this reading, the dark bird is the symbol of Loney's

absent memory, the loss that is always present to him: his missing mother and his inability to consider himself an Indian, which has rendered his existence meaningless. The absent memory that has haunted him throughout his life drives him to his own death, and the last things he sees before he dies are "the beating wings of a dark bird as it climbed up to a distant place" (179). The dark bird leads Loney onward, but, like his memory, it seems forever out of his reach. (75–76)

For Sands and Purdy, the dark bird is Bha'a, a powerful spirit unquestionably "sent by his mother's people" to lead him back to them, to reincorporate him into the tribe in death; for Lemberg, this may be true, but even in death Loney does not know how to surrender to that reincorporation, does not know how to let the vision circulate the ideosomatics of belonging through him, and so remains an outsider.

The telltale phrase in that quotation from Lemberg that I want to focus on is "as he suspects": Lemberg constructs the temporal sequence from Loney talking about his childhood to Loney talking about the dark bird as a conscious connection Loney draws not only between his *childhood* and the dark bird but specifically between the Gros Ventres and the dark bird. I suggest that this is problematic in useful ways. Here is what Welch gives us:

"But what is it that really troubles you? For pity's sake, don't you know I want to help you?"

"It's not something . . . I don't even know myself. It has to do with the past." But Loney realized this wasn't good enough. He had thought and said it too often to believe it anymore. "It has to do with certain things. I know it has to do with my mother and father, but there are other things. It has to do with an aunt I lived with when I was a kid. I loved her and she died. That's okay. It was enough to love her. But I would like to know who she really was and how she died and why. I don't know."

Rhea felt her hands loosen on the steering wheel. She hadn't realized how tense she had been. But Loney was talking finally and she held her breath, in her mind urging him on.

"I know this is kind of strange, but I see a bird—I don't know what kind of bird it is—but I see it every night. Sometimes it flies slowly enough so that I can almost study it, but even then . . . it is a bird I've never seen in real life. I don't know. It comes and I look at it and then it fades away." (104)

That's it. That is Lemberg's evidence for her suspicion that Loney suspects that the dark bird was sent to him by "his mother's people." The motherly "she" of which he is speaking before he breaks off and tells Rhea of the dark bird is not even his mother, whom he doesn't remember, but his father's girlfriend Sharon, a white woman he lived with for a few years after his father decamped. He does *mention* his mother, in the collocation "my mother and father," but he does not speak of her as having a "people." It would seem that "as he suspects" is actually Lemberg's way of incorporating the Sands/Purdy reading of the dark bird as Bha'a into her own, as something that Loney "suspects" but cannot grasp.

But Lemberg's interpretive overreach here points us, I suggest, to a telling failure in both readings: namely that nobody, not even Ernest Stromberg in his intelligent critique of the Sands/Purdy/Allen "authentic Indian" reading of the novel,[5] problematizes the novel's narrative structure, the Bakhtinian rather than Russian Formalist narrative structure, author-narrator-character rather than *fabula* and *syuzhet*. All the critics seem to be focused on what *Loney* knows or doesn't know; no one asks what the narrator or the author knows. At the very simplest level, it seems reasonable to agree with Lemberg that Loney is completely at sea with the Gros Ventre Bha'a mythology—and to argue that case even more strongly than she does, that he doesn't even *suspect* that the dark bird might be sent by his mother's people—and still at the same time consider the possibility that the close-third-person narrator knows and drops bread crumbs throughout the novel that will lead us to the "spiritual" meaning of the dark bird; or that the narrator doesn't know either but the author does.

Think for example of Martin Amis's complex novelistic exploration of perpetrator trauma in *Time's Arrow,* where the character lives time in a forward direction, as we do, but the narrator lives time backwards, starting with the character's death and moving "forward" to his birth. This allows Amis to give us a narrator who has no idea of the concentration camp traumata that might have caused the endosomatic symptomatologies he experiences inside the character's "revivified" and then (de)aging body, because from his narrative point of view they haven't happened yet: they're in the character's past but his future. As the narrator brings us closer to the concentration camp experience, where the character was a doctor performing medical experiments on internees, he begins to suspect that something bad is coming; but once he's there, he still fails to understand, because all he sees is the character taking in sick or tortured people or dead bodies and healing them, magically restoring them to relative health. From his sequentially backwards point of view, traumatizing torture becomes healing, leaving him essentially puzzled as to the origins of the character's endosomata from the period *after* the concentration camp in the character's life but *before* the concentration camp in the narration.

Amis, of course, clearly signals to his readers what he is doing by manipulating the clash between the unreliable narrator's backwards point of view and the traumatized character's forwards point of view—the narrator's puzzlement is ours too, until he brings us sequentially to the concentration camp and it all makes sense. We realize that the traumatic experience of inflicting grievous harm on fellow human beings destroyed the character's life ever after—even though he managed to escape Europe and hide out in the United States under an assumed name, and even to practice medicine. We reconstruct the reversed temporal sequence, restore cause and effect as an explanatory "fiction" to which the narrator does not have access, but to which the author deftly points us. The author and the reader communicate across the heads, as it were, of the unreliable narrator and the monstrous (but himself also traumatized) character.

If we assume that something like this is going on in *The Death of Jim Loney* as well, that Welch wants us to do the research Kathleen Sands did and discover that the dark bird is Bha'a, then the question becomes not only what does he allow the narrator and the character to know but *why* does he make it so difficult for everyone involved—character, narrator, and reader—to figure out what's going on. He could have tipped his hand much more clearly, as Amis does. He could have dropped hints of the Feather Pipe or other arcane narrative elements of the Gros Ventre myth; he could have had the narrator tell us outright that Loney had no idea what these images meant, because he was out of touch with the tribe and its stories, its ritual practices. He could have made the narrator patently unreliable, had the narrator offer patently and revealingly inadequate explanations of the dark bird imagery ("the dark bird that Loney kept seeing was not Bha'a, the powerful Gros Ventre spirit, it could not have been, because Loney knew nothing of his mother's people's ancient stories"), in order to signal to the reader that there is a hidden meaning to be worked out.

The fact that Welch doesn't do this is significant, I think. If in fact he does want us to identify the dark bird as Bha'a, he gives us no help in making the identification; he throws us entirely back on our own interpretive resources. In this sense he is doing to us the exact same thing he is doing to his character, Jim Loney, and, obviously, doing it to us *through* his doing it to Loney: asking a question that seems to have no answer; posing a problem that seems insoluble. The question is, of course, how to construct a usable past, a collective tradition, a temporal community that will structure our realities and identities meaningfully.[6] That is the question Welch asks and answers in his first novel, *Winter in the Blood*, whose unnamed narrator and protagonist spends the first three parts of the novel searching for the past that his (unsuspected) grandfather Yellow Calf gives him in the beginning of the fourth part. As Paul Eisenstein suggests, Welch uses a Hemingwayesque strategy of narrative omission to build suspense around this quest for meaning, withholding from the narrator and the character—and thus the reader as well—all sense of his tribe's spiritual tradition:

> As his interview with Bill Bevis reveals, lean sentences—when crafted poetically—enable Welch *to imply* the spiritual world that is so much a part of a Native American worldview. But more than that, Welch wants to imply the historical/ancestral cause of the narrator's malaise, that is to say, how this thirty-two-year-old man's inability to connect is, at least in part, determined by the voice which characterizes his and other Native Americans's [*sic*] (and the dominant culture's) historical consciousness. What exactly this consciousness ought to consist of—*the kind of life* blueprint that might be formulated therein—is omitted for the first three-fourths of *Winter in the Blood,* paralleling an omission that, for Welch, has characterized the transmission of history for over a century. The dominant culture's writing of history may record events (i.e., land surrendered, treaties signed), it may even extol a handful of minority individuals for their achievements, but its discourse cannot include the recounting of events that threaten the image of itself it must maintain. That image, the product of power relations that construct it, at every step determines what does and does not get told; stories of cruelty committed in its name are either concealed or rewritten for absorption into America's monocultural narrative. Beholden to the self-image that narrative is bent on reproducing, such telling only continues the cruelty. The history produced may protect the interests of its writers, but to do so, those writers must distort or leave out altogether certain occurrences, thus burying (and doing violence to) the larger body of communication that conveys the way of life and way of seeing of those they have subjugated. For minority cultures like those of Native Americans to resist absorption, for them to maintain identity, this body of communication—heretofore lacking, heretofore omitted—must be articulated. (5)

What the movement from *Winter in the Blood* to *The Death of Jim Loney* suggests, then, is that Welch grew dissatisfied with the solution he offered to the problem in the earlier novel—that it was too easy, too pat: that putting a character in the novel who possesses the omitted knowledge and can impart it to the questing protagonist makes the quest seem like a simple matter of opening the right door and possessing the treasure hidden behind it.

More than that, I would argue, the movement from Welch's first to second novel suggests a paradigm shift in Welch's conception or construction of the *nature* of the quest. If the answer exists and must simply be found, as it seems in *Winter in the Blood,* the quest is essentially objectivist; if not only the answer but the right question must be painstakingly (and in fact unsuccessfully) *sought,* then the quest is constructivist, based not on our ability to discover and embrace the truth about the past but on our willingness to build a working past, and our recognition that this is not just a facile matter of fantasizing one but of actually *feeling* the redemptive power of the newly created past tradition or "truth."

In fact the striking thing about all the conflicting readings of *The Death of Jim Loney* is that they are uncritically predicated on the objectivist assumption that the answer to Loney's questions *exists* and must simply be sought out, uncovered. Sands and Purdy assume that the answer lies in Gros Ventre mythology, and once they have provided the key, the mystery is solved. Lemberg assumes that the answer lies in the traumatic destruction of an Indian past, and once she has provided the key to that, the mystery is solved. What all of the novel's critics inchoately recognize, however, it seems to me, is that the keys they provide do not solve the novel's mystery at all—that if the dark bird is Bha'a, as Lemberg says of Sands's and Purdy's reading, Loney can't read it; and that if Loney's problem is intergenerational trauma, as Lemberg insists, *we* can't read it. It still makes no sense to us—precisely because that is the historical *effect* of intergenerational trauma, to suck collective meaning out of the world, to deobjectify our realities and identities. If objectivity is a communal construct, a collective exosomatization of the world, then the systematic decimation and dysregulation of the community in the American Holocaust disables objectification. The quest for the objective truth about the collective past is a phantom pain in the amputated communal limb, an illusory turbulence in the proprioception of the body politic. The trick, then, would be to create a new community that might circulate a new exosomatization of the world, might reobjectify what it needs to know in order to construct a coherent meaning, structure, identity, and reality.

And this, I suggest, is something like Welch's project in *The Death of Jim Loney.* It is certainly the project he and his narrator assign Loney himself. The patent failure of that project, however, signals not the objective impossibility of ever completing it but rather the expansion of the project to encompass the novel's readers, who take over from Loney and the narrator the quest for an interpretive construct of the past that will allow them—us—to impart both hope and collective meaning to the ending. In that sense Lemberg might be read as not so much overturning Sands and Purdy as collaborating with them in the construction of a collective reideosomatization of time's arrow from the pre-European past, through centuries of genocide and subjugation at the hands of white Americans, through the current confusion and alienation, into a transformed future. That this arrow's trajectory, indeed the arrow itself, is "only a fiction" is a failure in an objectivist purview, which requires the truth or nothing at all; in the post-Kantian constructivist purview of somatic theory, it is the only kind of realistic hope of success we have.

The methodological implication of this constructivist perspective is that the "diagnosis" of intergenerational trauma must by default be imposed on the primary endosomatic signs and symptoms as a kind of etiological myth: we begin with the disproportionately high prevalence of suicide, alcoholism, domestic violence, obesity, diabetes, and other disorders in a population whose ancestors are known to have suffered severe trauma, and *organize* those disorders narratively by reading them as transferentially caused by a history of trauma.

3.2.1.3 CATHARSIS

What makes this etiological diagnosis more than hypothetical or phantasmatic is its ideosomatization as fact by the group. A good example of this is the group therapy led by Maria Brave Heart-Jordan with her own tribe, the Lakota, grounded in collective mourning, social support for the painful affects arising out of the working-through of historical traumata, "codifications in self- and object representations as well as world representations, . . . validation and normalization of the trauma response and techniques such as visualization and pseudohypnotic suggestibility" (Duran et al., "Healing" 351). The "codifications in self- and object representations as well as world representations" there constitute a cognitive response aimed at reorganizing the group construction of reality and identity; the rest of those therapeutic strategies are counterregulatory interventions aimed at restructuring the circulatory group affects that undergird the cognitive response, make it feel real. In other words, what Brave Heart-Jordan is attempting to engineer is an ideosomatic counterregulation of Lakota culture through the recognition and healing of an allostatic "soul wound" that is collectively constructed as paleosomatically regulating the body politic. In this therapeutic process the intergenerational trauma model is both the definiens and the definiendum, both the channel by which reality is reobjectified and reregulated and the objective reality that is thus reconstituted, so that constitutive group belief in the narrative of intergenerational trauma facilitates healing, which in turn confirms the objective truth of the narrative.

In fact, in summarizing the results of Brave Heart-Jordan's therapeutic experiment, Duran et al. invoke a contested Aristotelian term: having noted that "education about the historical trauma leads to increased awareness about trauma, its impact, and the grief-related affects," they report that "the process of sharing these affects with others of similar background and within a traditional Lakota context leads to a *cathartic* sense of relief" ("Healing" 351, emphasis added). It is no accident, perhaps, that a psychotherapeutic model should refer back to catharsis theory—the chain of influence from Jacob Bernays on catharsis through Nietzsche to Freud is well known—but note that Aristotle's theory is itself arguably protosomatic, in his insistence that tragedy strategically *awakens* in the audience the emotions of pity and terror precisely in order to effect a therapeutic purgation or purification of those emotions. As Charles Segal writes, this theory is grounded in the ancient Greek belief that "the sharing of tears and suffering creates a bond of common humanity between mortals" (149); what Aristotle adds to that tradition is a model for analyzing the ways in which tragic drama *instigates* and structures this sort of shared emotional healing process:

> The ritual and emotional aspects of catharsis come together closely in the formal lament that ends many plays, for these lamentations in themselves, with their release in tears, constitute the cleansing discharge of emotion, and they are also part of a ritual act. Aristotle here, as often, is firmly within Greek cultural practice, in this case the free expression of emotion in weeping. . . .
>
> Viewing Aristotle's catharsis theory in the light of such passages suggests that the emotions of pity and fear are 'cleansed,' that is, purified, made cleaner, in the sense that we feel them vicariously for others. Such emotional participation—that is, the arousal and catharsis of pity and fear and similar emotions—enlarges our sympathies and so our humanity. . . .
>
> This expansion of our sensibilities in compassion for others, I would suggest, is also part of the tragic catharsis. (Segal 164–65)

In somatic terms what is happening here is that a dramatic construct, an invented story, acted out on stage, elicits an empathetic somatomimesis in the audience: they shudder at horror, physically shrink away from fearsome things, shed tears of pity for the sufferers on stage. The fact that these feelings circulate not only between actors and audience members but among the audience as well works iterosomatically to constitute the actions being performed as "real," and in particular the blood guilt and pollution that almost invariably forms the core of ancient Greek tragedy therefore also as a "real" threat to the community. The outpouring of shared emotion in the climax effects a group ritual-becoming-dramatic-becoming-therapeutic purification of the blood guilt—which is, Segal argues, the origin of drama out of ancient religious ritual—or a somatic dysregulation/reregulation cycle that ideosomatizes a threat to group stability only in order to effect an ideosomatic restabilization:

> The ancient audience too, we should recall, is accustomed to group emotional participation in both public and private rituals, and so would also be accustomed to the resolution of intense emotion through the performance of ritual-like actions within the play. To this aspect of tragedy, as we shall see, the ritual meaning of Aristotle's catharsis as 'purification' would be especially relevant. The presence of death, particularly physical contact with a corpse, as anthropologists like Mary Douglas point out, is a source of disorder and pollution. The rites of lament and burial that frequently end Greek tragedies effect closure by literally putting an end to this disorder. In epic and drama, from the *Iliad* on, such rituals help the audience to achieve a sense of 'purification' from the strong and dangerous emotions through ritual participation and to experience the restoration of order and communal solidarity that rituals produce. (150)

The American Holocaust, obviously, was not exactly a "source of disorder and pollution," but if we read "disorder" broadly enough, to encompass the dysregulatory effects on the American Indian survivor groups of "total environmental and 'lifeworld shock' [and] genocidal military actions" (Duran et al., "Healing" 343), of forced removal from traditional homelands, and of the "systematic assault on Native cultures" (344), the cathartic effects of historical-trauma therapy undertaken by Maria Yellow Horse Brave Heart-Jordan with the Lakota is remarkably similar to the cathartic effects of ancient Greek tragedy as theorized by Aristotle. In both cases the telling or performance of a powerfully mythic/historical story elicits and circulates an empathetic affective response that collectively constitutes the story as true, as real, as historical, and then transforms therapeutically ("purifies" cathartically) the feelings of pity, fear, and grief through collective mourning, the collective working-through of traumatosomatic affect, the "codifications in self- and object representations as well as world representations, . . . validation and normalization of the trauma response and techniques such as visualization and collective mourning pseudohypnotic suggestibility." That the dramatic spectacle (Aristotle's *opsis*) is obviously visual, and that stage plays have long been understood as wielding a kind of "pseudohypnotic suggestibility" in and for their audiences, further underscore the parallels here.

What I'm suggesting, then, is that *The Death of Jim Loney* offers not so much a static *image* of the protagonist's inclusion in or exclusion from the Indian community as rather an *invitation* to the kind of collective cathartic dramatization of the past that we've been seeing at work in the plays Aristotle theorized. The collective involved in that dramatization and that potentially cathartic transformation of the audience includes Kathleen Sands and John Purdy in their persuasive insistence that Jim Loney is rescued in death by the dark spirit bird Bha'a, and Jennifer Lemberg in her equally persuasive insistence that Jim Loney is not and cannot be rescued by Bha'a because the community that might wield Bha'a as its redemptive spirit has been destroyed by white America, and Maria Yellow Horse Brave Heart in her cathartic work with the Lakota—and it includes me as well, perhaps, in my attempts to theorize all these scholars *as* the community that might wield Bha'a or any other symbol or vision or story as a redemptive spirit.

For Aristotle catharsis is, after all, an audience effect. It is found neither in the text nor in the criticism of the text, nor in the actors' bodies, but in the circulation of shared affect through the bodies of the audience. In a sense it is a construct of the somatics of literature, imagined as drama: the reader of Welch's novel projects a theatrical performance in which exosomatic actor-images body forth the confusions, the failures, and perhaps the mythical hopes that Welch circulates through his narrator and characters, and is aided in this projection by other readers like Sands, Purdy, and Lemberg. If the projection works, the novel can be experienced as cathartic.

Even more, however, it is a construct of the somatics of culture, for which the literary text is merely an occasion, a channel. What it channels to and through us is at least a paleoregulatory Indian culture of unnamed hopelessness and despair, based on our sympathetic endosomatization of Jim Loney's destructive isolation from the community and confusion about the sources of his identity. What it channels through us, in other words, is not just isolation but a *culture* of isolation, a paleosomatic economy of isolation that circulates shared depersonalization or desomatization through us. This would be the somatics of intergenerational trauma, which Jennifer Lemberg theorizes as Jim Loney's problem, but through the circulatory effects of the somatic economy of literary response becomes ours as well. In a sense it "becomes ours" only symbolically, by imaginative projection; unlike Jim Loney, we can put the book down and walk away from his isolation, confusion, despair, and death. Somatically speaking, however, this "symbolic" projection is far more powerful than we have thought, far more communally inclusive: as Lev Tolstoy would say, Welch *infects* us with Jim Loney's despair, which is what we mean when we say that the novel is "depressing" or "bleak." (As Mick McAllister writes: "If you thought *Winter in the Blood* was depressing! *The Death of Jim Loney,* also set on a contemporary Montana reservation, is a kind of *Leaving Las Vegas* with a young Indian protagonist, Jim Loney. You can probably guess how it ends?") The paleosomatics of post-traumatic despair is a cultural prison that can trap those who only experience it "vicariously," by having it circulated through them by the community.

If we are persuaded by Kathleen Sands and John Purdy, however, and come to project a cathartic ending onto the novel, what happens then is not simply that we *think* about the novel differently, nor even that we *feel* about it differently, but that the novel becomes the occasion or channel for the circulation of a cathartic or therapeutic *culture,* a shared resomatization of paleoregulatory post-traumatic despair, confusion, and isolation.

3.2.2 Toni Morrison, *Beloved*

> Morrison's use of apocalypse to figure trauma is a method for engaging politics and history, not avoiding them. Trauma—the apocalypse of the psychoanalytic narrative, a formative and revelatory catastrophe—obliterates (removes from memory) old modes of life and understanding at the same time that it generates new ones. After the trauma, everything is changed, even as the trauma itself has been forgotten. And yet, the impact of the trauma is continually felt in the form of compulsive repetitions and somatic symptoms. The attempt to work through these effects and remember the traumatic event gives shape to a new narrative, a new history. And, as Morrison recognizes, trauma and symptom, remembering and forgetting, are not merely personal but also social and historical phenomena. Her representation of the familial and political forms taken by the forgetting and remembering of infanticide recalls Cathy Caruth's observations on the role of trauma in the construction of historical narratives. "History can be grasped," Caruth writes, "only in the very inaccessibility of its occurrence." And yet, "history, like trauma, is never simply one's own. . . . [H]istory is precisely the way we are implicated in each other's traumas" ("Unclaimed Experience" 187, 192).
>
> —James Berger, "Ghosts of Liberalism:
> Morrison's *Beloved* and the Moynihan Report" (410–11)

In almost every way the intergenerational transmission of trauma is less of a mystery in Toni Morrison's *Beloved* than it is in *The Death of Jim Loney:* not only are the intergenerationally traumatizing effects of slavery everywhere explicitly foregrounded in the novel, but the novel itself is named after a revenant who physically embodies the paleoregulatory effects of slave trauma, the survival of trauma beyond the death of its own generation. In fact Beloved's first (unpunctuated) monologue in Part II (248–52) begins with a paragraph about her undifferentiated longing for her mother ("I am not separate from her there is no place where I stop" [248]) but then is saturated with horrific images of the Middle Passage ("those able to die are in a pile I cannot find my man the one whose teeth I have loved a hot thing the little hill of dead people a hot thing the men without skin push them through with poles the woman is there with the face I want the face that is mine they fall into the sea which is the color of the bread" [249]), suggesting that she is "more" (314) than Denver's sister, as Denver herself later guesses. Some critics, such as Deborah Horvitz (162–63), read this monologue as voiced by Sethe's mother, who did come over on the Middle Passage; but while the speaker of this monologue dies (but says "I am not dead" [252]) and Sethe's mother survives, the implication seems to be that Beloved is the revenant or paleoregulatory reincarnation not just of the daughter Sethe killed but of *all* slave trauma, the "*Sixty Million and more*" who died on the Middle Passage, to whom the novel is dedicated, and the untold millions who died in slavery as well.

Despite Morrison's willingness to give intergenerational trauma a demanding human body in her novel, however, her treatment of it still remains a mystery. Who is Beloved, exactly? Why does she haunt 124 Bluestone Road, first as a "baby ghost," then as a flesh-and-blood revenant? What does the haunting mean for the cognizing and possible healing of intergenerational trauma? What does her double exorcism mean, first (as the vindictive baby ghost) by Paul D, then (as the revenant Beloved) by the community women led by Ella? Beloved's apparition and disapparition have something to do with hearing the voices and feeling the bodies of the ancestors, obviously, but Beloved is also violent, capricious, tyrannical, narcissistic, an infant in a 19-year-old body, and Paul D and Ella seem to be quite right to want to be rid of her. It seems, in other words, to be equally healing for her to return and to be driven out. What do we do with that?

Nearly every critic who has published on *Beloved* has addressed these questions; all have slightly but often significantly different answers.[7] James Berger, whose introductory remarks I gave above in the epigraph to this section, engages the phenomenon of intergenerational trauma (or in his terms "historical trauma") most explicitly, but he is interested specifically in the novel as a whole read as Morrison's response to parallel denials of historical trauma on the right and the left in the 1980s:

The discourse of race on the 1980s, then, was constrained by a double denial: Reaganist conservatives denied American racism, and descendants of the New Left denied any dysfunction within African American communities.

Toni Morrison's novels oppose both forms of denials. *Beloved* is a challenge to all American racial discourse of the 1980s—to Reaganist conservatism and to the New Left and black nationalism. The novel revives the liberal position of Frazier, Myrdal, and Moynihan, placing historical trauma—the continuing apocalypse within history—at the center of American race relations. (414)

Berger's reading of the novel is largely social-historical, an attempt to situate it in this debate on race and racism in the 1980s; he interprets the incidents in the novel briefly (415–16), mainly in order to show the urgency with which Morrison's critics read both the infanticide and the final exorcism as a healing process, part, he argues, of that idealizing denial of dysfunction in African-American communities, a dysfunction that Morrison in fact stresses, places center-stage, and seeks to understand as the product of historical trauma.

Most critical studies of the novel examine the dysfunctional familial dynamic more closely, almost invariably recognizing the ongoing power of historical or intergenerational trauma—it would be difficult to ignore completely in this novel—but without quite knowing what to do with it. One of the best readings of this dynamic, in my opinion, is Caroline Rody's "Toni Morrison's *Beloved*: History, 'Rememory,' and 'A Clamor for a Kiss,'" and I'd like to explore her reading in some detail for a few pages here.

While Rody does not cite Cathy Caruth's 1991 article in her 1995 reading, her approach is based on something like Caruth's notion, cited by Berger in the epigraph, above, that "history is precisely the way we are implicated in each other's traumas" ("Unclaimed" 192, *Unclaimed* 24):[8] in a way her project is to retheorize the historical novel based on the model of *Beloved,* more generally perhaps on the model of magic realism as a generic channel of postcolonial resistance favored mostly by South American novelists (85). The problem as Rody presents it is not only that historical trauma leaves what Morrison's Ella calls "holes" in stories—"Ella wrapped a cloth strip around the baby's navel as she listened for the holes—the things the fugitives did not say; the questions they did not ask. Listened too for the unnamed, unmentioned people left behind" (Morrison 108)—or, as Rody puts it, that "*Beloved* is manifestly about the filling of historical gaps" (84). It is also that the collective forgetting and remembering of traumatic events send turbulences through the impulse to *write* history, or what Rody calls "historiographic desire":

For an African-American writer, slavery is a story known in the bones and yet not at all. "How could she bear witness to what she never lived?" asks Gayl Jones's *Corregiadora* (103), crystallizing the paradox of contemporary black rewritings of slavery. Writing that bears witness to an inherited tragedy approaches the past with an interest much more urgent than historical curiosity or even political revisionism. Inserting authorial consciousness into the very processes of history that accomplished the racial "othering" of the self, novels of slavery make their claims to knowledge and power face-to-face with destruction. We might think of such fictions as structures of historiographic desire, attempts to span a vast gap of time, loss, and ignorance to achieve an intimate bond, a bridge of restitution or healing, between the authorial present and the ancestral past. (88)

I would add only that the present consciousness that is linked up with "the very processes of history that accomplished the racial 'othering' of the self" is not only authorial but lectorial as well, and that the "intimate bond" or "bridge of restitution or healing" is a *circulation* of traumatic and therapeutic images through the somatic economy in which the novel includes its author and readers. And indeed Rody seems to want to go somewhere like a somatic economy as a model for this knowing "in the bones and yet not at all": "When first conceiving her rewriting of Margaret Garner's life, Morrison has said, 'It was an era I didn't want to get into—going back into and through grief'" (45). This 'grief' seems almost a palpable atmosphere; in the personal psychological return required to write *Beloved*, it was not history Morrison had to go 'back into and through' but an intensity of hovering emotion attributed neither to the ancestors nor to herself but filling the space between them" (90). "Palpable atmosphere," "hovering emotion": these are manifestly somatic experiences, and the notion that the emotion "fills the space" between the ancestors and Morrison herself seems like Rody groping toward a formulation of the somatic exchange. Without somatic theory, though, we are left with a series of tropes: "known in the bones," "palpable atmosphere," "hovering emotion," "filling the space between them." Known where? Palpable how? Hovering where? Filling what space? Reading *Beloved* as sensitively and complexly as she does, Rody has a powerful intuition about the interpersonal phenomena she is attempting to trope in Morrison's novel, but the tropes mostly work in her reading like the blind men's descriptions of the elephant in the Mullah Nasrudin parable— "like a tree trunk," "like a saber," "like a leather fan," "like a snake," "like a wall": they don't add up to an explanation.

This infinite intuitive approach to a vision of the somatic exchange is even more obviously at work in Rody's discussion of Sethe's notion of "rememory": "'Rememory' as trope postulates the interconnectedness of minds, past and present, and thus neatly conjoins the novel's supernatural vision with its aspiration to communal epic, realizing the 'collective memory' of which Morrison speaks. For while the prefix 're' (normally used for the act, not the property of consciousness) suggests that 'rememory' is an active, creative mental function, Sethe's explanation describes a natural—or a supernatural—phenomenon. For Sethe as for her author, then, to 'rememory' is to use one's imaginative power to realize a latent, abiding connection to the past" (93). "The interconnectedness of minds," yes: but what are the connections? And what does she mean by "minds"? Are the minds in this characterization just another trope in a string of tropes: bones, atmospheres, emotions, spaces, and minds? Or should we assume that Rody is now describing the actual seat of the interconnectedness? And what about Rody's suggestion that "Sethe's explanation describes a natural—or a supernatural—phenomenon"? Obviously the traumatic revenant Beloved is the supernatural phenomenon, but the self-correction of "a natural—or a supernatural" suggests that Rody sees the supernatural events in the novel as a screen of some sort for a natural phenomenon—but what?

My greatest qualm about Rody's formulation there, though, comes in her last sentence there: "For Sethe as for her author, then, to 'rememory' is to use one's imaginative power to realize a latent, abiding connection to the past." The words that bother me in that sentence are "imaginative," "realize," "latent," "abiding," and "connection." Working backwards: again, what kind of connection? How and where does it abide? "Latent" is another vague trope for "in the bones": what kind of latency? Does "realize" mean "make real" or "become aware of"? Since it's an imaginative power that is used to "realize" that latent connection, I'm assuming Rody means "make real"; but since the connection is abiding, I'm also assuming that it isn't *un*real before the imaginative power is used to make it real, only latent. But what is the real/unreal/made-real phenomenon Rody is trying to describe through this semantic fog?

What bothers me even more than these individual words, though, is the suggestion that Morrison and Sethe are somehow doing the same thing in the novel, in "rememorying" slave traumata. For most of the novel, the "latent, abiding connection to the past" is a nightmare for Sethe that she uses her imaginative power *not* to realize. Sethe's connection with her past is born not out of her rememorying but out of the natural—or supernatural—phenomenon of Beloved's haunting, first as an angry ghost, then as a greedy 19-year-old revenant infant; and as she is terrorized by her rememories of Sweet Home, so too is she terrorized and nearly consumed by Beloved's greed for her substance, her life, the milk of her stories. Beloved returns not because Sethe imagines her; she returns and then *demands* that Sethe rememory her. And while there is undoubtedly an emotional overlap between Sethe's terror of rememories and Morrison's reluctance to enter into the grief she mentions, it seems unnecessarily reductive to me to equate the two "rememoryings," by author and character, as the rather bland process of imaginatively realizing a "latent, abiding connection to the past."

Look, for example, at the actual passage from *Beloved* that Rody is commenting on here:

"I was talking about time. It's so hard for me to believe in it. Some things go. Pass on. Some things just stay. I used to think it was my rememory. You know. Some things you forget. Other things you never do. But it's not. Places, places are still there. If a house burns down, it's gone, but the place—the picture of it—stays, and not just in my rememory, but out there, in the world. What I remember is a picture floating around out there outside my head. I mean, even if I don't think it, even if I die, the picture of what I did, or knew, or saw is still out there. Right in the place where it happened."

"Can other people see it?" asked Denver.

"Oh, yes. Oh, yes, yes, yes. Someday you be walking down the road and you hear something or see something going on. So clear. And you think it's you thinking it up. A thought picture. But no. It's when you bump into a rememory that belongs to somebody else. Where I was before I came here, that place is real. It's never going away. Even if the whole farm—every tree and grass blade of it dies. The picture is still there and what's more, if you go there—you who never was there—if you go there and stand in the place where it was, it will happen again; it will be there for you, waiting for you. So, Denver, you can't never go there. Never. Because even though it's all over—over and done with—it's going to always be there waiting for you. That's how come I had to get all my children out. No matter what."

Denver picked at her fingernails. "If it's still there, waiting, that must mean that nothing ever dies."

Sethe looked right in Denver's face. "Nothing ever does," she said. (43–44)

This is a bogeyman story: "it's going to always be there waiting for you." The terror that feeds Sethe's attempts to block out the past also feeds her determination that no child of hers ever have to confront that past as a present, as "a rememory that belongs to somebody else." Denver, she says, is never to go to Sweet Home, because the traumata that Sethe and Paul D and Grandma Baby and the other slaves experienced there are real, and will traumatize her too. It is the same terror that causes her to murder her unnamed two-year-old daughter to "keep her safe," to protect her from Sweet Home and the traumatizing experience of slavery. How exactly, then, are the dangerously real shared rememories Sethe theorizes the same as the imaginative "realization" of a "latent, abiding connection to the past" undertaken in the novel by Morrison?

In somatic terms, it should be clear, rememories are paleoregulatory exosomata, traumatic memory images circulated so intensely through the group of (ex-)slaves that they seem to take on an independent reality of their own, and so seem to keep the traumatizing degradations and dehumanizations of slavery alive and frighteningly potent more than a decade after emancipation. For Sethe, clearly, the serial hauntings of 124 by the baby ghost and then the beloved revenant are the literal fulfillments of her dire warning to Denver: Beloved *is* the rememory of her murdered daughter, the flesh-and-blood rememory that cannot die because nothing ever does. She is not a memory *image* of the murdered child somehow "realized" by Sethe's "imaginative power"; she is *real.* She is, to Denver, "a rememory that belongs to somebody else," a living and breathing and ferociously hungry and seductive rememory that belongs to her mother Sethe. The latent but abiding memory image realized through imaginative power of which Rody writes is the Beloved not of Sethe but of Morrison—and, through participation in the viral somatic economy fleshed forth by the novel, of Morrison's reader as well. That's the difference: Sethe believes that exosomata are real, and (in consequence?) her exosomatized revenant daughter *is* real; Morrison knows the power of *belief* in the reality of exosomata, and so creates a fictional world in which that belief seems fully justified. In that sense *Beloved* is for Morrison a representation of the reality not of ghosts or revenants but of the belief in ghosts or revenants as real—a representation, to put that differently, not of the ontology of occult beings but rather of the ontologization of exosomata *as* occult beings.

This distinction between Sethe's traumatized/traumatizing rememories of the past and Morrison's fictionalization of those rememories would also seem to be the obvious answer to the charge leveled by James Berger that Morrison's critics are trying to whitewash the dysfunctionality in African-American culture by reading the exorcism of Beloved as a healing: "Events in the United States today make it difficult to agree with readers who claim that the exorcism of Beloved represents a successful working through of America's racial traumas. Indeed, in my view, such optimistic interpretations of *Beloved* participate in the repressions and denials of trauma that the novel opposes. For instance, Ashraf Rushdy holds as exemplary Sethe's friend Ella's repressive attitude toward the past, arguing that by 'exorcising Beloved, by not allowing the past to consume the present, [Ella] offers Sethe the opportunity to reclaim herself' (584)" (415). Surely there is an important epistemological distinction to be made here between "not allowing the past to *consume* the present" and repressing or forgetting the past? It seems to me that the two can intelligently be equated only if Beloved *is* the past, if Beloved is the *whole* traumatizing paleosomatic past of slavery, and if there is only one way to experience her/it, as a real flesh-and-blood "rememory that belongs to somebody else." By failing to distinguish between the two, Berger is able to assimilate Ella's group's exorcism of Beloved and the community's subsequent forgetting of Beloved—along with the critical celebration of that ending as a healing process—to the dual denials he is examining, of white racism on the right and of intergenerational trauma and its endosomatic dysfunctionality in the African-American community on the left. As soon as we recognize that there is a key difference between ontologizing an exosomatized past and putting the exosomata into a story as *fiction,* Berger's whole argument collapses. "What these and similar interpretations miss, in my view," he writes, "is that Beloved's story is not over, that the child will return—indeed, has returned" (416): yes, but to whom, and in what form? If the revenant has only one form (real flesh-and-blood) and only one allegorical referent (the repressed past), then her exorcism can only mean the (temporary) re-repression of the past, which is bound to fail because the repressed will continue to return, for example in the endosomatic symptomatologies of paleoregulatory cultural dysfunction. But note Berger's endnote to that last passage: "I agree entirely with Deborah Horvitz that 'the paradox of how to live in the present without canceling out an excruciatingly painful past remains unresolved at the end of the novel. At the same time, something healing has happened' (166). See also Caroline Rody, who describes how *Beloved* brings 'history to an unclosed closure and the haunt to our own houses' (113)" (419n15). *Beloved* brings "the haunt to our own houses" *as a fiction.* "The child will return—indeed, has returned"—*as a fiction.* This is how Morrison engages (without resolving) "the paradox of how to live in the present without canceling out an excruciatingly painful past": she cancels out the traumatized/traumatizing ontologization of an exosomatized past without canceling out the past or any of the pain it continues to inflict, indeed by *exacerbating* the pain it inflicts in order to free us from the paleosomatic regulation that is sustained by repression. By reworking a traumatic past as fiction, a fiction in which a traumatizing exosoma comes to flesh-and-blood life and then is "exploded" through a communal exorcism, Morrison makes us relive *and resomatize* that past. By reading the novel we become able to experience the "haunt" as a painful fiction: painful because so powerfully grounded in the traumatizing past that we have repressed, traumatizing both for the African Americans descended from the victims of slavery and for the European Americans descended from its perpetrators; but a painful *fiction* that serves to reminds us that the exosomatic images (bogeymen, the walking dead) that terrorize us in its pages—as well as, perhaps, the paleoregulatory endosomatic symptomatologies (poverty, crime, drug abuse) that plague many African-American communities—are *constructs*, somatic regimes that can with great communal effort be banished, exorcised.

3.2.3 Percival Everett, "The Appropriation of Cultures"

Let's now look quickly at one recent fictional representation of this sort of communal resomatization of paleoregulatory trauma, Percival Everett's 1996 story "The Appropriation of Cultures." In the story Daniel Barkley is an independently wealthy black man who spends his evenings playing jazz with some older musicians near the University of South Carolina campus in Columbia:

> Daniel played standards with the old guys, but what he loved to play was old-time slide tunes. One night, some white boys from a fraternity yelled forward to the stage at the black man holding the acoustic guitar and began to shout, "Play *Dixie* for us! Play *Dixie* for us!"
>
> Daniel gave them a long look, studied their big-toothed grins and the beer-shiny eyes stuck into puffy, pale faces, hovering over golf shirts and chinos. He looked from them to the uncomfortable expressions on the faces of the old guys with whom he was playing and then to the embarrassed faces of the other college kids in the club.
>
> And then he started to play. He felt his way slowly through the chords of the song once and listened to the deadened hush as it fell over the room. He used the slide to squeeze out the melody of the song he had grown up hating, the song the whites had always pulled out to remind themselves and those other people just where they were. Daniel sang the song. He sang it slowly. He sang it, feeling the lyrics, deciding that the lyrics were his, deciding that the song was his. *Old times there are not forgotten* . . . He sang the song and listened to the silence around him. He resisted the urge to let satire ring through his voice. He meant what he sang. *Look away, look away, look away, Dixieland.*
>
> When he was finished, he looked up to see the roomful of eyes on him. One person clapped. Then another. And soon the tavern was filled with applause and hoots. He found the frat boys in the back and watched as they

stormed out, a couple of people near the door chuckling at them as they passed. (24)

The "uncomfortable expressions on the faces of the old guys" and "the embarrassed faces of the other college kids in the club" are Everett's rather milder versions of Morrison's Beloved, endosomatizations of paleoregulatory trauma, the lingering somatic effects of slave trauma and perpetrator trauma, respectively. Daniel has grown up hating *Dixie* specifically, Everett tells us, because it was "the song the whites had always pulled out to remind themselves and those other people just where they were," a personal response to events occurring in his own lifetime; but the song has that somatic power to remind and to place and to hierarchize because it evokes paleoregulatory endosomata, because it continues to channel ancient wounds into the present. There is nothing overtly racist about the song itself, its melody or lyrics; it is the circulation of racist response to the song through the somatic economy in the American South that continues to charge it with the paleosomatic history of the enslavement and cultural subjugation of African Americans over several centuries. In a sense that history is over—the history of slavery in the American South ended in 1863, the history of the systematic legal oppression of African Americans ended in the 1960s and 1970s—but the singing of this song makes it clear that the history only really ended in the history-book sense, in terms of laws and dates. In the somatic economy of the South, in the paleoregulatory circulation of somatic responses to slavery and Jim Crow, it is an ongoing phenomenon.

Hence the significance of Daniel's subversive appropriation of this one cultural channel of paleosomatic regulation: by playing *Dixie* in such a way as to make it his own, "feeling the lyrics, deciding that the lyrics were his, deciding that the song was his," he launches a counterregulatory impulse out into the audience, an attempt to resomatize the song as an inclusive Southern anthem, white *and* black. In that sense, in fact, he is only mediately and strategically making the song *his*: he makes it his in order to make it ours; he circulates the revisionary exosoma of one black jazz musician "owning" the quintessential hymn of Southern plantation nostalgia through the crowd in order to infect the whites and the blacks in the club—including those up on stage with him—with this resomatized ownership, so that it becomes collective. That he is successful in this attempt is clear both from the applause—which also "circulates" slowly—and the disgusted exit of the racist frat boys. Daniel's exosomatic transracial ownership of the song does infect the crowd, does transform their ideosomatic response to the history of whites subjugating blacks, so that, when the small portion of the crowd that is not ideosomatically transformed by this new impulse "storms out," the newly inclusive group chuckles at them. They are no longer an ideosomatic threat to the collective; their barely suppressed racism no longer causes embarrassment.

As the crowd congratulates Daniel, he tries to process what just happened:

> Daniel didn't much care for the slaps on the back, but he didn't focus too much energy on that. He was busy trying to sort out his feelings about what he had just played. The irony of his playing the song straight and from the heart was made more ironic by the fact that as he played it, it came straight and from his heart, as he was claiming southern soil, or at least recognizing his blood in it. His was the land of cotton and hell no, it was not forgotten. At twenty-three his anger was fresh and typical, and so was his ease with it, the way it could be forgotten for chunks of time, until something like that night with the white frat boys or simply a flashing blue light in the rearview mirror brought it all back. He liked the song, wanted to play it again, knew that he would. (25)

The paleoregulatory anger is there, in other words, and his singing of the song is fueled by it; but by refusing to satirize it, by "playing the song straight and from the heart," he finds in himself a *love* for the song, and through that love a love for the South, the land of cotton—despite the fact that he will not forget the traumatic past that the song has for so long helped channel into the present. Again, this is not about forgetting the past or canceling the past; it's about resomatizing the past, rechanneling the paleosomatics of past trauma so that it no longer traumatizes. Another way of putting this is that the anger remains, but it no longer paleoregulates behavior, or no longer paleoregulates behavior quite so rigidly or binarily—it no longer makes it impossible for Daniel to love things ideosomatically associated with the targets of his anger.

In the next few weeks, Daniel begins to extend his new resomatizing approach to the South's past to other areas as well: after a dream in which he "stopped Pickett's men on the Emmitsburg Road on their way to the field and said, 'Give me back my flag'" (25), he buys a 1968 three-quarter-ton truck with "a full rear cab window decal of the Confederate flag" (26), and, when his friend Sarah asks what he needs a truck for, he replies, "I'm not buying the truck. Well, I am buying a truck, but only because I need the truck for the decal. I'm buying the decal" (27). Sara thinks he has flipped: "You need a job so you can be around people you don't care about, doing stuff you don't care about. You need a job to occupy that part of your brain. I suppose it's too late now, though." Daniel replies: "You should have seen those redneck boys when

I took *Dixie* from them. They didn't know what to do. So, the goddamn flag is flying over the State Capitol. Don't take it down, just take it. That's what I say" (28). And when the racist couple delivers the truck to Daniel's place, and they are disturbed by the ideosomatic dissonance of a middle-class black man living in a nice house buying a redneck truck, he explains, "I was just lucky enough to find a truck with the black power flag already on it" (28), and points to the Confederate flag. "You mean," he says, when they look blankly at him, "you didn't know?" (28). When whites later aggressively ask him what he's doing with that flag, he tells them that he's "flying it proudly. . . . Just like you, brothers" (29). One guy seems inclined to fight him over that word, "brothers," but then a car full of young black men drive up and ask what's going on, and the white man backs off. Daniel sends his new resomatizing impulse into this new group as well, saying to the black teenagers, "'We fly the flag proudly, don't we, young brothers?' Daniel gave a bent arm, black power, closed-fist salute. 'Don't we?' he repeated. 'Don't we?'" (29). Daniel keeps playing *Dixie* at white bars, fast enough to dance to, slow enough to cry to, keeps driving his truck around town and resomatizing the Southern-pride symbols, and gradually the community begins to circulate the new resomatizations as well:

> Soon, there were several, then many cars and trucks in Columbia, South Carolina, sporting Confederate flags and being driven by black people. Black businessmen and ministers wore rebel flag buttons on their lapels and clips on their ties. The marching band of South Carolina State College, a predominantly black land grant institution in Orangeburg, paraded with the flag during homecoming. Black people all over the state flew the Confederate flag. The symbol began to disappear from the fronts of big rigs and the back windows of jacked-up four-wheelers. And after the emblem was used to dress the yards and mark picnic sites of black family reunions the following Fourth of July, the piece of cloth was quietly dismissed from its station with the U.S. and state flags atop the State Capitol. There was no ceremony, no notice. One day, it was not there. (30)

And Everett concludes his story: "*Look away, look away, look away . . .*" (30).

"The Appropriation of Culture" is, of course, a utopian parable; it's easy enough to dismiss Everett's moral lesson as unrealistic, impractical, a mere wish-fulfillment fantasy. But it should be clear that his moral lesson *is* grounded in something like the somatic model I've been developing in this book, according to which a phenomenon like racism is both *social* (a "mere" interpersonal fiction) and *real* (a deeply felt orientation that seems so stable as to be virtually impossible to change). What makes Everett's fable seem unrealistic, I suggest, is bad theory: the impulse to treat racism as innate and there-fore impossible to change, and the binarizing corollary according to which if racism *is* this malleable, it must be—or we must thematize Everett as assuming that it is—a mere performative mask, a role we can put on or take off at will.

Much the same critique was leveled, in fact, at Judith Butler's *Gender Trou-ble:* if identity is performative, then being gay or straight or masculine or femi-nine isn't "real"; it's a mere role or game or fiction that can be donned or doffed from one moment to the next. It didn't help Butler in combating that false binary that she didn't have somatic theory to draw on to explain her sense that performative identities are "deep-seated play," a performative presentation of something you feel deeply: for where does that deep feeling come from?

> When and where does my being a lesbian come into play, when and where does this playing a lesbian constitute something like what I am? To say that I "play" at being one is not to say that I am not one "really"; rather, how and where I play at being one is the way in which that "being" gets established, instituted, circulated, and confirmed. This is not a perfor-mance from which I can take radical distance, for this is deep-seated play, psychically entrenched play, *and this "I" does not play its lesbianism as a role.* Rather, it is through the repeated play of this sexuality that the "I" is insistently reconstituted as a lesbian "I"; paradoxically, it is precisely the *repetition* of that play that establishes as well the *instability* of the very category that it constitutes. For if the "I" is a site of repetition, that is, if the "I" only achieves the semblance of identity through a certain repetition of itself, then the I is always displaced by the very repetition that sustains it. ("Imitation" 18)

And so on: Butler goes on for another twelve lines, and in some sense for the rest of her essay, deconstructively worrying this notion of "repetition," a con-cept that can indeed be deconstructed forever because it is only an abstract concept, yanked out of the social and (I would argue) somatic context implied by Butler's word "circulated" there, or more generally that whole list of parti-ciples. Obviously, it seems to me, "being" can only be "established, instituted, circulated, and confirmed" by the group; and the group circulation of identity images only has the power to constitute identity as "reality" to the extent that what the group is circulating is *somatized* images.

By the same token, place, race, and trauma too are "established, insti-tuted, circulated, and confirmed" ideosomatically and paleosomatically by the group. They are, to put that differently, "deep-seated play," in Butler's term, not in the sense that play is *fun* but in her specific insistence that "it is precisely the *repetition* of that play that establishes as well the *instability* of the very category that it constitutes." The somatic economy that circulates stabilizing images of home and place and is so disturbingly disrupted in the refugee experience, or that circulates counterregulatory colonizing impulses that remain unstable but astonishingly persistent in a decolonizing context, or that continues to circulate allostatic adjustments to long-past trauma and thus to keep the trauma present and alive and active, is "deep-seated play, psychically entrenched play," ideosomatized play that *can* be replayed, reiterated, resomatized—but only through the kind of therapeutic *group* recirculation that Everett explores in "The Appropriation of Culture," or that Morrison explores in the epilogue (unnamed final section) of *Beloved.* It is only as Daniel is able to infect other members of the community with his resomatizations of racist symbols, and they begin to circulate them too, rather than simply responding to them with bafflement, that Everett's moral fable begins to nudge us toward a post-racist utopia.

3.2.4 Conclusion: Acting Out and Working Through

In *Writing History, Writing Trauma,* Dominic LaCapra adapts the Freudian distinction between "acting out" and "working through" to the historical analysis of trauma:

> I would make a correlation that will be significant in my later argument—a correlation that indicates the desirability of relating deconstructive and psychoanalytic concepts. I would argue, or at least suggest, that undecidability and unregulated *difference,* threatening to disarticulate relations, confuse self and other, and collapse all distinctions, including that between present and past, are related to transference and prevail in trauma and in post-traumatic acting out in which one is haunted or possessed by the past and performatively caught up in the compulsive repetition of traumatic scenes—scenes in which the past returns and the future is blocked or fatalistically caught up in a melancholic feedback loop. In acting out, tenses implode, and it is as if one were back there in the past reliving the traumatic scene. Any duality (or double inscription) of time (past and present or future) is experientially collapsed or productive only of aporia and double binds. In this sense, the aporia and the double bind might be seen as marking a trauma that has not been worked through. Working through is an articulatory practice: to the extent one works through the trauma (as well as transferential relations in general), one is able to distinguish

between past and present and to recall in memory that something happened to one (or one's people) back then while realizing that one is living here and now with openings to the future. This does not imply that there is a pure opposition between past and present or that acting out—whether for the traumatized or for those empathetically relating to them—can be fully transcended toward a state of closure or full ego identity. But it does mean that processes of working through may counteract the force of acting out and the repetition compulsion. These processes of working through, including mourning and modes of critical thought and practice, involve the possibility of making distinctions or developing articulations that are recognized as problematic but still function as limits and as possibly desirable resistances to undecidability, particularly when the latter is tantamount to confusion and the obliteration or blurring of all distinctions (states that may indeed occur in trauma or in acting out post-traumatic conditions). (21–22)

Working through, of course, is the ideal model for the talking cure, here extended to historical and critical processes in general; what is striking about the literary representations of intergenerational trauma that we've been considering here is that the fictional works themselves set up a working-through for their readers but not for their characters, or even their narrators, all of whom continue to act out. What is most interesting about Toni Morrison's *Beloved* and Percival Everett's "Appropriation of Cultures" in this sense is that the central characters in those works act out trauma *therapeutically,* and thus chart an interesting middle ground between the two binary poles LaCapra theorizes.[9] Because Morrison and Everett give their characters "objective" (exosomatic) correlatives of intergenerational trauma to work or play with, to "act out" with—the revenant Beloved in Morrison's novel, the song *Dixie* and the Confederate flag in Everett's story—their acting out has something like the same therapeutic effect as a more conscious, analytical, "articulatory" working through would have had (perhaps an even more powerfully therapeutic effect, in fact). In *The Death of Jim Loney,* Jim is given no such exosomatic correlative and so cannot act out therapeutically—and fails in his self-appointed task of working through—leaving him the sole option of acting out endosomatically until he dies. The process of working through his intergenerational trauma is thus left to his critics.

From the standpoint of somatic theory, the weakness in LaCapra's approach to trauma is its individualism: just as the unattainable ideal product of working through is for him "full ego identity," so too are both acting out and working through processes definitively undergone by the individual. Even empathy, which LaCapra precariously maneuvers into his model, remains an individualistic phenomenon: there are those who are traumatized, and those who empathize with trauma victims, and each person experiences the trauma individually. He recognizes that empathetic identification with trauma victims is itself traumatizing, suggesting something like the somatic economy that I've been theorizing here, in which shared affect is circulated regulatorily through the group; he even insists that what others might call "illusions" are in fact "regulative ideals" (4), suggesting that he is in fact very close to somatic theory; but he continues to binarize the individual and the group and to associate the former with health and the latter with trauma:

> Unchecked identification implies a confusion of self and other which may bring an incorporation of the experience and voice of the victim and its reenactment or acting out. As in acting out in general, one possessed, however vicariously, by the past and reliving its traumatic scenes may be tragically incapable of acting responsibly or behaving in an ethical manner involving consideration for others as others. One need not blame the victim possessed by the past and unable to get beyond it to any viable extent in order to question the idea that it is desirable to identify with this victim, or to become a surrogate victim, and to write (or perform) in that incorporated voice. (28)

The important question here, I suggest—and I'm guessing that LaCapra would agree—is not whether the individual should merge with the group or remain ideally isolated from group experience, but where the working through comes from and how it is channeled: what is the locus of the therapeutic sorting out of pasts and presents, selves and others, that may make it possible for the traumatized to begin to "act responsibly or behave in an ethical manner." Another way of asking that question is to note that "unchecked identification" is not simply one of two binary poles—that there is an entire sorites series of "identification," several positions in which might be characterized as "unchecked"—and then to wonder who or what does the "checking": the individual, the group, or some complex configuration of the two. To put it in psychoanalytical terms, the critical question is whether the working through is an individualistic process undergone in and by the analysand and only guided and observed by the analyst, as Freud would have it, or a collective—(counter)transferential—process undergone by the analyst–analysand dyad, or any other group, as in Lacan's revisionary reading. It does seem to me that LaCapra leans toward the Freudian approach, while somatic theory draws from the Lacanian notion that the movement toward health involves not a rationalist (analytic) splitting of self from other and past from present but a collective *(re)organization* of selves and others, pasts and presents, through the transferential and countertransferential circulation of shared affect.

To reframe this notion more generally, we might say that "identification" is the circulatory effect of the somatic exchange and "checking" is the regulatory impulse imposed on identification by the group. In this sense there would be no such thing as "unchecked identification": only dysregulation of group controls (checking) or group empathy (identification), the former leading to the form of allostatic overload known as post-traumatic stress disorder, the latter leading to the form of allostatic overload that I discussed in *Estrangement and the Somatics of Literature* as depersonalization or desomatization.

In that sense the three postcolonial experiences we've been exploring in this book, the refugee encounter, (de)colonization, and intergenerational trauma, might be seen as three different dysregulations of group "checking": the first imposed on a culture more or less randomly, as a byproduct of natural or societal violence; the second imposed on a culture systematically, "civilizingly," by an occupying foreign power; and the third imposed on a culture from within, endosomatically, as a result of the "dynastic" reproduction of long-past dysregulations.

But in fact the three dysregulations overlap. In the First Essay, for example, we saw the emergence of mythological nation-building among the Hutu refugees as a paleoregulatory recirculation not only of their collective traumatizations through internecine violence and forced relocation but also of their colonial counterregulation at the hands of the British. The counterregulations imposed on colonized cultures in the Second Essay were designed to disrupt or dysregulate the existing local somatic economies, and the cultures' allostatic adjustment to those counterregulations became paleoregulatory as well, continuing to shape "decolonization" in the colonial image in generations born into political (but not cultural) independence. The forced relocations of Indians in the Americas and Africans to the Americas, and their cultural subjugation and genocide at the hands of the "civilizing" white colonizers, continue to dysregulate the present paleosomatically.

At the broadest level, this book is about the persistence of ideosomatic regulation *as* reality—as what members of groups are conditioned by the somatic exchange to experience as reality. When an existing ideosomatic regulation is disrupted, whether accidentally (as by a natural disaster) or through deliberate destructive violence or the concerted counterregulatory pressures of a colonization process, the resulting dysregulation itself tends to become the new ideosomatic regulation that is circulated paleosomatically through the group, so that the group's allosomatic adjustment to dysregulation persists as "reality" for generations, often for hundreds of years.

At issue here methodologically, I suggest, is not simply the fact that we need something like somatic theory to explain these phenomena—the persistence of cultural regimes long past the era of their situational relevance, often "regimes" that are stored unconsciously or even physiologically, indeed often allostatic regimes born out of a collective response to trauma and chronic stress, and the power of these regimes to naturalize group constructs as realities and identities. It is also, and more important, that without somatic theory it would be difficult even to construct them as related phenomena in need of explanation—difficult to ask the questions that might problematize the many local and topical remedies that have been offered, like "refugees need to be integrated into the community," "postcolonial cultures need to break free of the legacy of colonialism," and "the descendants of trauma victims need to work through their ancestors' trauma therapeutically." What do these panaceas, and the postcolonial phenomena to which they are offered as solutions, have in common? Somatic theory is one way of rendering such questions askable. Whether the answers I have offered to those questions are viable, or even a useful step on the road to viable explanations, is up to you.

allostasis: **homeostatic** adaptation to changed conditions; raises the baseline set-point at which homeostatic stability is achieved, causing **allostatic load.**

allostatic load: the destabilizing effects on the group or individual organism of chronic **allostatic** adaptation; caused by the incomplete activation or inactivation of stress hormones, or repeated abrupt on/off fluctuations, leaving the organism exposed to too much stress or too many stress hormones, or both by turns.

allostatic overload: an **allostatic load** of traumatizing intensity or duration.

body-becoming-mind: a Deleuzean construction for the operation of the **homeostatic** emergence of feelings as mental mappings of emotions and other body states, and of thoughts as mental mappings of feelings.

counterideosomatic: referring to any specifically rebellious or **deregulatory** impulse against **ideosomatic** regulation; a subset of **idiosomaticity,** which includes both *failures* and *refusals* to conform; to be distinguished from **ideosomatic counterregulation,** which is organized around an oppositional group norm.

counterregulation: see **ideosomatic counterregulation.**

depersonalization: the chronic **desomatization** of the self, others, or familiar things; usually a defense against **allostatic overload.**

deregulation: see **idiosomatic deregulation.**

desomatize: to withdraw (usually defensively or self-protectively) **somatic response** from an individual's interaction with a person or thing; similar to Freud's concept of "withdrawal of cathexis" or Lacan's of "foreclosure," except that what is being withdrawn or foreclosed is not libido but evaluative behavioral memory; chronic desomatization is usually called **depersonalization.** See also **endosomatize, exosomatize, ideosomatize, idiosomatize, iterosomatize, resomatize, somatize.**

displacement: in postcolonial studies, the relocation of persons from their homelands or the **counterregulation** of their culture; in psychoanalysis, the rechanneling of affect from feared to safe objects; in poststructuralist language theory, the deferral of meaning along the syntagmatic chain of signifiers.

dysregulation: see ideosomatic dysregulation.

endosoma: a physiological symptom(atology) (pain, illness, addiction, etc.) read as a physical manifestation of a relational (ideosomatic) injury or trauma.

endosomatic: referring to "inside the body" symptomatologies read etiologically as manifestations of a relational (ideosomatic) injury or trauma. Roughly synonymous with the clinical term "psychosomatic."

endosomatize: to manifest an outward (relational, group-circulated) injury inwardly, in physical pain, illness, addiction, or other physiological dysregulation; a "primary" process that is imagined secondarily as an etiological interpretation of an empirically experienced physical symptomatology. Close to what clinicians refer to as "somatization," except that the mental pain "somatized" as physical pain is traditionally thought of individualistically, as something the individual subject suffers, rather than, as in somatic theory, a form of ideosomatic turbulence. See also desomatize, exosomatize, ideosomatize, idiosomatize, iterosomatize, resomatize, somatize.

exosoma: a somatized image of an object, including skin and its pigmentation, circulated regulatorily through the somatic exchange.

exosomatic: in anthropology, referring to tools and other "outside the body" technologies, or more broadly to material culture; in somatic theory, referring to the somatization of objects, places, skin colors, and so on, the circulation through the somatic exchange of a somatized image or exosoma of the object.

exosomatize: to circulate iteratively through the somatic exchange a somatized image or exosoma of a place or a thing. See also desomatize, endosomatize, ideosomatize, idiosomatize, iterosomatize, resomatize, somatize.

homeostasis: the self-regulation of a group or individual organism, aimed at stabilization of the inner and outer environment; somatic markers are homeostatic or self-regulatory mappings of potentially destabilizing body states; ideosomatic regulation is group homeostasis. See also allostasis.

ideosomatic counterregulation: the attempt to circulate a new "corrective" set of regulatory/normative pressures through the somatic exchange; found in both colonization and decolonization; typically leads to polynormativity. See ideosomatic regulation.

ideosomatic dysregulation: a breakdown in the circulation of regulatory/normative pressures through the somatic exchange, generating allostatic load. See ideosomatic regulation.

ideosomatic regulation: the homeostatic conformation of the somatic states of all involved by means of normative pressures circulated through the somatic exchange.

ideosomatic reregulation: an attempt to repair or restore the dysregulated circulation of regulatory/normative pressures through the somatic exchange. See ideosomatic regulation.

ideosomatics: the regulatory group-normative circulation of somatic response through group members' perceptions, attitudes, understandings.

ideosomatize: to somatize collectively; to circulate regulatory group-normative (dis)approval pressures through the somatic exchange, and thus to install regulatory somatic markers in the autonomic nervous system of each group member. See also desomatize, exosomatize, idiosomatize, iterosomatize, resomatize, somatize.

idiosomatic deregulation: the attempt to decrease the regulatory power of the group over individual actions; as it becomes a new group regime, it becomes ideosomatic reregulation or counterregulation.

idiosomatics: somatic response perceived by the group as deviant, divergent, insufficiently regulated by ideosomatic norms.

idiosomatize: to **somatize** group-deviantly, un- or **counterideosomatically;** to circulate failed, incomplete, or dissident conformity-response through the **somatic exchange,** and thus (intentionally or unintentionally) to set up **somatic** dissonance with established **ideosomatic markers.** See also **desomatize, exosomatize, ideosomatize, iterosomatize, resomatize, somatize.**

iterosomatics: the iterative circulation of normative **somatic response** through a group over a period of time, creating a feeling of "natural" or "organic" grouping; the absence of iterosomatic circulation in a group creates "granfalloons" (Vonnegut); derived from the protosomatic "genealogy" of Nietzsche ("A thing is branded on the memory to make it stay there; only what goes on hurting will stick") and the "archeology" of Foucault, as well as Deleuze's and Guattari's insistence that "the social machine fashions a memory."

iterosomatize: to circulate normative **somatic response** through a group over a period of time; the process is phenomenologically "naturalizing," making group constructions feel like reality. See also **desomatize, exosomatize, ideosomatize, idiosomatize, resomatize, somatize.**

loconormativity: **ideosomatic** norms constructed and maintained (circulated **iterosomatically**) by the hegemonic group in the current location. See also **panicked loconormativity, metanormativity, polynormativity, xenonormativity.**

metanormativity: the ability to perform the multiple shifting normativities of different groups.

mimesis, somatic: see **somatic mimesis.**

paleoregulatory: referring to **paleosomatic regulation.**

paleosomatic regulation: the continuing circulation through a group of long-outdated **ideosomatic** norms formed around **allostatic overloads;** temporal **xenonormativity.** Typically an etiological interpretation placed on **endosomatic** symptoms. May be referred to adjectivally as **paleoregulatory.**

panicked loconormativity: a desperate attempt to protect and police the ideal naturalization of **loconormative ideosomatics** through the analytical containment of the refugee (or anyone else whose deviance from loconormativity seems to threaten that ideal); derived from Judith Butler's "panicked heterosexuality."

polynormativity: the simultaneous regulation of a group by two or more **ideosomatic** regimes, typically stratified either temporally (older and newer) or spatially (**loconormative** and **xenonormative**), or both.

proprioception of the body politic: the collectivized body of **ideosomatic regulation,** which identifies the parts and sets the limits of the group **body-becoming-mind.** Defined in Robinson, *Estrangement* (106–12).

regulation: see **ideosomatic regulation.**

reregulation: see **ideosomatic reregulation.**

resomatize: to circulate **counterregulatory** or **reregulatory** (therapeutic or "corrective") **somatic responses** through the **somatic exchange.** See also **desomatize, exosomatize, ideosomatize, idiosomatize, iterosomatize, somatize.**

somatic: referring to an affective body state that is felt as evaluatively oriented (toward approval or disapproval).

somatic exchange: the circulation of group norms, values, orientations, and inclinations through the **somatic** economy of those involved, in the form of somatic approval and disapproval responses that are viewed as outward body language and mimetically simulated as inward body states; the result is a rough conformation of **somatic states** in all involved, or **ideosomatic regulation.**

somatic marker: a tiny subliminal quantum of emotional pleasure or pain emitted by the ventral-tegmental area of the autonomic nervous system to signal what the organism has learned from experience; offers "gut-level" guidance for decision-making (Damasio's hypothesis).

somatic mimesis: the almost instantaneous mimicking of other people's body language and concomitant simulation of their **somatic states;** the transfer mechanism of the **somatic exchange;** also called "somatomimesis" (adjectival form "somatomimetic," noun form for the process "somatic mimeticism").

somatic response: the felt phenomenology of **somatic marking;** referred to colloquially in terms of the "gut" ("gut reaction," "gut feeling," "gut instinct," "gut check," "go with your gut," "know something in your gut"), a synecdochic use of the enteric nervous system to represent the entire autonomic nervous system.

somatic state: an emotional body state that is felt as evaluatively oriented (toward approval or disapproval), displayed as body language, and **somatomimetically** simulated by others involved as part of the **somatic exchange.**

somatic transfer: the transmission of **somatic response** from one person/body to another, through **somatomimetic** simulation.

somatize: to mark a thing somatically (see **somatic marker**); similar to Freud's "to invest/cathect" (*besetzen*), with the difference that somatization invests not libido but evaluative behavioral memory. See also **desomatize, exosomatize, ideosomatize, idiosomatize, iterosomatize, resomatize.**

virality: the self-replicativity of **somatic mimesis,** leading to the contagion of **somatic response** from body to body within a group and from group to group.

xenonormativity: ideosomatic norms constructed and maintained (circulated **iterosomatically**) by the hegemonic group(s) in refugees' culture of origin; hegemonic xenonormativity is typically successfully imported (**loconormativized**) **counterregulatorily** by colonizers in colonies and by Western aid organizations in refugee camps (often leading to **polynormativity**); subaltern xenonormativity is typically unsuccessfully imported by refugees and other migrants (but partial success may lead to **metanormativity**).

NOTES

PREFACE

1. For studies of the genealogy of racism, see Jordan, Gossett, Montagu, and West.

2. For this critique, see especially Ahmad, but also JanMohamed, Slemon and Tiffin, and Dirlik "Grinch," "Aura," "Response." For discussion, see Moore-Gilbert 17–22.

3. For discussion of the proprioception of the body politic, see my *Estrangement* 106–12.

4. For discussion of Williams's "structures of feeling," see my *Estrangement* 221–23.

FIRST ESSAY

1. For a contrasting view, see Brennan's *Transmission of Affect,* which rejects mimetic theories of affect transmission in order to argue that affect is transmitted chemically, mainly by smell (pheromones). Ironically enough, Brennan agrees with me that shared affect is the basis of all ethics, all societal regulation of behavior, a claim utterly vitiated by her insistence that affect is transmitted physically rather than imaginatively: if I am considering a course of action that will harm someone not physically present, the only channel of shared affect that can have any significant ethical impact on my decision is not smell but my imaginative reconstruction and imitation of the absent person's body state. There is also a time problem with her claim: the hormonal transfers she discusses take minutes to transform the target organism; the Carpenter Effect has been measured to transform the imitating organism within several hundred milliseconds. The apparent instantaneity of shared affect could not possibly be created chemically.

2. The direction in which I take somatic theory is heavily influenced by Foucault:

> Imbedded in bodies, becoming deeply characteristic of individuals, the oddities of sex relied on a technology of health and pathology. . . . The power which

thus took charge of sexuality set about contacting bodies, caressing them with its eyes, intensifying areas, electrifying surfaces, dramatizing troubled moments. . . . There are equal grounds for saying that it [modern society] has, if not created, at least outfitted and made to proliferate, groups with multiple elements and a circulating sexuality: a distribution of points of power, hierarchized and placed opposite to one another; 'pursued' pleasures, that is, both sought after and searched out; compartmental sexualities that are tolerated or encouraged; proximities that serve as surveillance procedures, and function as mechanisms of intensification; contacts that operate as inductors. . . . [A]ll this made the family, even when brought down to its smallest dimensions, a complicated network, saturated with multiple, fragmentary, and mobile sexualities. (*History of Sexuality* 1:44–46)

Where I deviate from Foucault is in his conception of "power" as a force with agency; my understanding of how normative pressures get circulated through groups is far less centralized, based more on Heidegger's notion of *das Man*, Wittgenstein's notion of social practices, and Elias's and Bourdieu's notions of *habitus*. Another Nietzschean book that has significantly shaped my conception of ideosomatic regulation is the *Anti-Oedipus* of Deleuze and Guattari; see §1.3.1 for discussion.

3. Both the placebo effect and its opposite, the nocebo effect, in which a patient who does not trust the doctor gets worse, are ideosomatic effects, based on guided response to group norms governing the doctor's effective authority, the patient's expected obedience, the contextual significance of the doctor-patient relationship, and the instrumental significance of treatments. Some scholars (see Jospe and Thompson) estimate that as much as 50 percent of the efficacy of modern medicine relies on ideosomatized belief structures: as unconscious collective support for the purely mechanical activities of cutting tissue, setting bones, and intervening chemically in various physiological processes we are trained to expect to get better under a doctor's care, expect to get better when we like our doctor, expect to get better when we swallow a pill, and *want* to get better to please the doctor—and often do get better when those expectations are met.

4. For an extended discussion of this sort of cultural misunderstanding, and what small recourse we have when confronted with it, in terms of metalocutionary implicature (adapting H. Paul Grice) and reimmediatization (adapting Charles Saunders Peirce), see chapter 14 of my *Performative Linguistics*.

5. For a problematic excluded-middle argument about groups and territories that is clearly in need of somatic theory, see Warner "Voluntary." Warner devotes the first pages of his article to an attack on what he calls the "liberal mathematics" that equates the individual with the group with the territory with home with the government with the state with democracy: "Questions of identity are resolved through associations and attachments that can be described by first-degree equalities. Individual/group identity is solved by homogeneous grouping. Home/place identity is solved by attaching the individual/group to a specific place that comes to be called home. Individual/group/homogeneous grouping is inseparable from home/place; the identity of one is equal to the other" (164). "For [William E.] Connolly," Warner adds, "these associations and alignments, or rather the desire for alignments that are part of the search for a 'singular hegemony of any set of identities' (Connolly, *Identity* 1991a:158), are elements of a politics of homesickness and place" (164). This seems reasonable—except, perhaps, to the extent that this characterization seems to carry with it the implicit suggestion that, because a politics of homesickness is typically

dolled up as something else, something nobler, like "liberal political philosophy," it is itself necessarily cheap and tawdry, something to be ashamed of: I see no need to sneer at people who get homesick.

But Warner is hunting bigger game: he wants, ultimately, to demolish the notion that group identity may be definitively connected with place *at all*. He cites Cuny et al.'s introduction to their edited collection *Repatriation:* "One of the more interesting common denominators found in the case studies is the formation of politically organized, cohesive communities by uprooted peoples. Rounded up by the host government and relocated to refugee camps, refugees are placed in unaccustomed communal situations that may change their way of life and crowd them in among strangers. In these circumstances refugees show an impressive ability to organize and cohere as a new community with its own mores and values" (quoted in Warner, "Voluntary" 165). This empirical observation seems unexceptionable to me: groups may be disrupted by the scattering of members and the destruction of place, but human beings are adaptable. They can regroup. And Warner's first gloss of this passage, "The relation between individual and group does not have to be physically grounded" (165), suggests that Warner wants to carve out a middle ground between "has to be" and "can't be," between "groups are always physically grounded" and "groups are never physically grounded." But then he draws his binary conclusion: "It is the relations with other people that ground man in his existence, and not the physical grounding of the individual and group with a given space" (165). Based on this principle, he argues his main case that refugees (and generally humans) can never go home in the simple nostalgic sense, because by the time they get there both they and what they have idealized (narrativized) as "home" have changed.

Somatic theory would be most interested there in the middle that Warner so assiduously excludes: the ways in which it is the relations with other people that ground us in our social *and* physical existence, that iterosomatize a random collection of people as "our group," as a "homogeneous group," and a specific place as "home," as "ours," as the "true" setting of community. For example, Warner summarizes Emanuel Marx's article "The Social World of Refugees": "In Marx's analysis, the social world is based on relationships that are not related to physical space. Social networks are not tied to a particular place since the dynamics of interpersonal relationships are not territorial in nature" (164). Viewed somatically, these absolute negations ("not related," "not tied," "not territorial") are a bit simplistic. It should be quite obvious that it matters enormously to a congregation whether their services are held in their usual church, a high school gym, or a slaughterhouse—the dynamics of a church congregation are in that sense powerfully territorial. That territoriality is not absolute—it can be changed—but it has a felt tenacity that may make it seem, phenomenologically, to many members of the congregation, absolute. A face-to-face university class is not absolutely bound to the classroom—the specific classroom they are assigned to is only gradually, over the first few weeks of the semester, ideosomatized as "their own"—but it does substantially change the intellectual and socioemotional dynamic of the class's "social network" when the professor gives in to the students' pleading and they all go out and sit on the lawn, or meet in a coffee house. And while it is almost certainly true that refugees (and the rest of us, having moved away) can never go home again, that is not because social relationships "are not related to physical space"; on the contrary, it is precisely because social groups somatize specific spaces and places as "their own," as "home," as "familiar," even as "sacred," that the disruption and reconfiguration of social relationships makes homecoming problematic. In order to *feel* as if one were returning home, one would have to return not only to the same place but to the same group that somatized that place as home and to the same time frame in which that somatization was ongoing.

For a more flexible discussion of the "performance of terrains of belonging," drawing on Judith Butler's theories of performative identity, see Fortier; see also Probyn.

6. For a review of the research on refugee children's assimilation, see Huyck and Fields (who in fact suggest that traumatized children may be even more at risk than their parents and grandparents); for a study of elderly Chinese migrants to New Zealand, see Abbott et al.

7. Significantly, though, Pfister-Ammende gives examples of communists and other "politically oriented unions of those electing to fight" who "proved equally strong" (10), and Zionists, from Vonnegut's point of view almost certainly to be considered another granfalloon, who were typically also able to maintain stable ideosomatic regulation in refugee camps. Presumably this divergence stems from Vonnegut's membership in the "karass" (a team of people that "do God's Will without ever discovering what they are doing" [14]) of what Pfister-Ammende calls *Problematiker:* "They are as little rooted in their social environment as they are dedicated to a clear-cut spiritual idea. Rootless individuals of this type also need the world, but in a different way. Their vitality does not spring from an inner relatedness to the world, since they do not give themselves away to it; instead they take what the world offers them. They are not deeply attached to the world as a whole or to any of its individual manifestations. They are not object-related, nor do they have a binding commitment and unshakable superpersonal hold" (13). Vonnegut's membership in this karass makes it seem as if many functioning ideosomatic groups are in fact sham groups.

8. Pfister-Ammende writes:

> Four situational reactions were found common to persons uprooted from their social milieu and compelled to flee:
>
> 1. Fear of the persecutor with subsequent tendency to develop anxiety when the real danger is over, coupled with projection on to neutral persons of the new environment.
> 2. Hypertrophy of the instinct of self-preservation with deterioration of moral values. The main sphere affected appears to be that of moral behavior based on super-ego control of the drives. The ego-ideal, the "personal ethos" (Binder 1951) tends to remain unaffected.
> 3. Clinging to values that have remained intact or to the lost homeland amounting in some cases to fixation.
> 4. Overvaluation of the country of asylum or of persons in authority, a projection of savior phantasies which have remained in a mental vacuum without object-cathexis owing to the frustration inherent in expulsion from their own country. (7)

9. En route to their discussion of the stressors of exile proper [(3)–(4)], for example, Miller et al. deal with preflight (1) and flight (2) stressors among Bosnian refugees—especially the violence brought by the war (345–46). In her study of mental illness among Somali refugees, Carroll similarly quotes stories told by the refugees of the disruption of their happy lives by the outbreak of civil war in 1991 (121–22). For rare studies focused on dysregulation in the preflight context, see Zolberg, Suhrke, and Aguayo, and Gorden-

ker; for studies focused on the dynamics of refugee flight, see Kunz and Prins; for a study focused on refugees just arriving at a refugee camp, see Drumm, Pittmann, and Perry. For useful summaries of refugee research, most of which, as I say, is focused on problems of assimilation [(3)–(4)], see Cohon, and Dewind and Kasintz.

10. For a discussion of the virality of literature, see my *Estrangement*: Lev Tolstoy argues in *What Is Art?* that literary texts both emulate and themselves participate in this performative power to "infect" readers with the author's feelings and sensation, Viktor Shklovsky theorizes the estrangement device, and Bertolt Brecht theorizes the estrangement effect as infection with a defamiliarizing twist, an estrangement designed to infect the reader or the theatergoer with deestrangement.

11. Papa Doc reigned from 1957 to 1971, Baby Doc from 1971 to 1986, having become president for life at age 19 upon his father's death. The first wave of Haitian "boat people" left the island in 1972; the second wave, consisting of some 40,000 people, occurred in the winter of 1991–92, during the Tonton Macoute coup that overthrew President Jean-Bertrande Aristide and installed General Raoul Cédras in the presidency. Danticat, implicitly setting her story in the context of that second wave, has her girl write: "they've closed the schools since the army took over. no one is mentioning the old president's name. papa burnt all his campaign posters and old buttons. manman buried her buttons in a hole behind the house. she thinks he might come back. she says she will unearth them when he does" (*Krik? Krak!* 4).

Part of Danticat's anger and frustration in the writing of the story no doubt stems from the decision first of President George H. W. Bush not to grant *any* Haitian boat people asylum in the United States—to instruct the Coast Guard to interdict the boats and return them to Haiti. This move was widely criticized, among others by presidential hopeful Bill Clinton, as a violation of the Geneva Convention on Refugees, of which the United States was a signatory; but upon assuming office in January of 1993, Clinton continued the Bush policy, arguing that he was actually saving Haitian lives by preventing refugees from drowning in the treacherous ocean crossing. On June 21, 1993, the U.S. Supreme Court decided (by a vote of 8–1) in favor of the Clinton administration that the interdiction of Haitian refugee boats did not violate the Geneva Convention on Refugees (*Sale v. Haitian Centers Council*).

12. It is important to note that Danticat does not *frame* these wishful invocations of magic as performatives, direct or indirect; the reader is coached to construct them that way not by anything Danticat does explicitly or even implicitly in writing the story but by the ideosomatized conventionality of *you*-address, a group structuring of emotional response to which the reader has been somatically conditioned by his or her own groups. All Danticat has to do to bring the reader into the transformative somaticity of these indirect performatives is to have her storytellers address their wishes and longings to *you*.

13. For discussion, see also Butler, *Gender Trouble* 141–43, and Bell, "Mimesis" 135–36.

14. For an extended discussion of "doubling," or what Friedrich Schleiermacher calls *das Doppeltgehen* "doubled-going"—"daß der wenigstens nicht doppelt geht wie ein Gespenst" ("Ueber" 64), "that he at least does not go doubled like a ghost" ("On" 236)—see the "Magical Doubles" chapter of my *Translation and Taboo*, especially 176–89.

15. In light of Freud's famous association of sadism with the death drive, it is significant to note that Danticat explicitly invokes doubling and mimetic violence in order to explain the dysregulated/dysregulatory violence channeled through the Tonton Macoutes: "There

were many cases in our history where our ancestors had *doubled*. Following in the *vaudou* tradition, most of our presidents were actually one body split in two: part flesh and part shadow. That was the only way they could murder and rape so many people and still go home to play with their children and make love to their wives" (156). This suggests, in fact, that the dynastic trauma is passed on not only from mothers to daughters but from fathers to sons, perhaps mothers to sons as well—and that the sexual violence unleashed on female bodies in this novel is thus the product of doubling in a double sense, the effect of doubling both on women (causing them to turn their violent impulses both inward, against their own bodies, and outward, against their daughters' bodies, in "testing") and on men (causing them to rape, beat, murder, and otherwise brutalize other bodies). Her 2005 novel *The Dew Breaker* is a powerful exploration of a man like this, a former Tonton Macoute now living in the U.S., through his relationships with his wife and daughter.

16. For discussion of the notion that we are all deterritorialized, see Warner, "We Are All Refugees," which draws on Connolly's reading of Nietzsche on homesickness in the last chapter of *Political Theory and Modernity* in order to argue that "we all have a certain homesickness that cannot be fulfilled," that, "no matter where we are, even in our countries of origin, we are all strangers to ourselves," so that "the protected home that distinguishes us from refugees is only an illusion" (371). Or, as Warner sums up his argument:

> To categorize certain people as refugees suggests that we deny the refugeeness inside us all, or deny the "normalcy" that is part of all refugees. Categorizing people as refugees serves an important legal function. It allows millions of people the right to international protection which they may otherwise not enjoy. On the other hand, the categorization delimits one group from another, creating insiders and outsiders. This brief essay has argued that the bridge between the two groups is shorter than one may imagine, and that the solution to the "refugee experience" may be more complex, as, indeed, is the solution to our own existence. (372)

Even at home, in other words, surrounded by familiar people and things, we do not feel at home; we still (always) miss some inchoate idealized "home" or "community" to which we have no access, and in that sense are forever phenomenologically "in flight" from or toward home. Equally indebted to Nietzsche on this point, of course, are Heidegger and Freud in their theorizations of *das Unheimliche*, the uncanny or the unhomely. See Homi Bhabha's postcolonial theorization of the unhomely in *The Location of Culture* (9–18); on Freud, see Cixous and Kristeva (182–92); on Heidegger, see McNeill; and on both, see Krell. (See also Ziarek on Kristeva's discussion of strangers, foreigners, and the uncanny.)

I will be returning to Nietzsche's argument in the *Genealogy* about the "civilizing" transmission of "slave morality" from generation to generation—one of the topics usefully illuminated by Connolly, *Identity/Difference* 151–54—in my theorizations first of colonization as counterregulation in §2.1, and then of intergenerational trauma as paleosomatic regulation in the introductory paragraphs of the Third Essay.

17. See also Kaplan's *Questions of Travel* (85–91) on Deleuze and Guattari, and especially 91–96 on the spread of Deleuzean romanticizations of the nomad through Euro-American cultural studies in the 1980s and 1990s; and see 96–98 for a reading of Spivak's "Can the Subaltern Speak?" as a critique of this development. For a discussion of that essay in this book, see §2.2.2.3.

18. For an extended reading of Nietzsche's "ecology" of somatic coding in the *Genealogy*, see §4.3 of my "Ecologies of Translation."

SECOND ESSAY

1. I'm thinking specifically here of Judith Butler's reading of Foucault in *Gender Trouble*:

> In a sense, for Foucault, as for Nietzsche, cultural values emerge as the result of an inscription on the body, understood as a medium, indeed, a blank page; in order for this inscription to signify, however, that medium must itself be destroyed—that is, fully transvaluated into a sublimated domain of values. Within the metaphorics of this notion of cultural values is the figure of history as a relentless writing instrument, and the body as the medium which must be destroyed and transfigured in order for "culture" to emerge. (166)

2. The entire island of Hispaniola was originally named Santo Domingo by the Spanish and Saint-Domingue by the French. In 1697, the western portion of the island was officially recognized by Spain as a territory of France, whereupon it kept the French name Saint-Domingue and the larger Spanish territory on the eastern part of the island continued to be called Santo Domingo. When Saint-Domingue won its independence from France in 1804, it was renamed Haiti; when Santo Domingo won its independence from Spain in 1844, it was renamed la Republica Dominicana or Dominican Republic. Like many American and British authors of the nineteenth and early twentieth centuries, James rather confusingly refers to the French colony that became Haiti as "San Domingo."

3. For a useful overview and critique of scholarly readings of Nietzsche on physiology, see Brown, who notes that *On the Genealogy of Morals* has the most references—33 in all—to physiological phenomena of all Nietzsche's works (64). Emden's piece on Nietzsche's neurophysiological conception of rhetoric in that same collection is less germane, as it does not deal with *On the Genealogy of Morals* and is more concerned with what contemporary research Nietzsche had read before writing his early lectures on classical rhetoric.

4. For Nietzsche's stomach disorders, see Moore 77–78.

5. For a passing postcolonial discussion of Nietzsche on slave morality, see Beverley: "In both Gramsci's and Guha's construction of the subaltern one can detect a residual trace of Nietzsche's characterization of slave morality as founded on resentment of the low for the high. It is true that the characterization is itself turned on its head to constitute now a theory of the epistemological privilege and agency of the subaltern, in the way Marx claimed that he had turned the Hegelian dialectic upside down. But the subaltern would be well within its rights to reply: Fuck you" (38).

The only other study I have found that comes close to addressing the postcolonial implications of Nietzsche's theory of slave morality is an article by Mark Migotti with the promising title of "Slave Morality, Socrates, and the Bushmen: A Reading of the First Essay of *On the Genealogy of Morals*"; but Migotti is not interested in the emergence of a slave morality in a colonial or postcolonial context. The San or Bushmen work in his argument not as the victims of (de)colonization but as an egalitarian "ur-community" that offers a potential counterexample to Nietzsche's empirical claims about slave morality and slave revolts: "By examining and rejecting the idea that the egalitarian culture of the San might pose a knock-down counter-example to the slave revolt hypothesis, we have, it seems to me, been brought to recognize a deeper and more precise sense in which the history of GM I is a history of *western* morality" (778). That Western moralists were still involved in the enslavement of black Africans throughout most of Nietzsche's lifetime—indeed slavery was abolished in Brazil in the exact same year in which he wrote *On the Genealogy of*

Morals, 1888—and that Nietzsche's pronouncements on slave morality and slave revolts might therefore tell us something about the European colonization of other cultures, never seems to occur to Migotti.

One more: in a 1995 interview, Albert Memmi says, "I love reading Nietzsche, for example, but he always places himself outside circumstances. This is the shortcoming of philosophers" (Wilder, "Irreconcilable" 177). It seems to me that in taking issue with the relative tolerance to pain in "Negroes" and "bluestockings," not to mention in theorizing the genealogy of "slave morality," Nietzsche places himself far more radically and controversially inside circumstances than many of his critics.

6. Does Memmi mean that European Americans are decolonized but African Americans are not? Or that no one in the former English colony that became the United States is decolonized, because—what, they aren't *recently* decolonized?

7. See also Dirlik's "American," "Empire?," "Spectres," and "Globalization."

8. See, e.g., the articles by Nietschmann, Ryser, and Connor; for an overview of Fourth World theorizing, see Seton.

9. See, e.g., Caren Kaplan's strictures against the "theoretical tourism" of Deleuze and Guattari's minoritarianism:

> "Becoming minor" is a strategy that only makes sense to the central, major, or powerful, yet it is presented as an imperative for "us all." Constructing binaries between major and minor, between developed and undeveloped, or center and periphery, in Deleuze and Guattari's collaborative texts modernity provides borders and zones of alterity to tempt the subversive bourgeois/intellectual. Becoming minor, a utopian process of letting go of privileged identities and practices, requires emulating the ways and modes of modernity's "others." (*Questions* 88)

10. Indeed there is a rhetorical excitement to his third chapter that Fanon himself seems hard put to quell:

> During the time when I was slowly being jolted alive into puberty, I had the honor of being able to look in wonder on one of my older friends who had just come back from France and who had held a Parisian girl in his arms. I shall try to analyze this problem in a special chapter.
>
> Talking recently with several Antilleans, I found that the dominant concern among those arriving in France was to go to bed with a white woman. As soon as their ships docked in Le Havre, they were off to the houses. Once this ritual of initiation into "authentic" manhood had been fulfilled, they took the train for Paris.
>
> But what is important here is to example Jean Veneuse. (72)

The stories about the Martinican blacks sleeping with white prostitutes in Paris are digressions from his discussion of the René Maran novel, but thrilling ones that he is only with great difficulty able to defer to a later chapter.

11. For further feminist discussions of this moment in Fanon, see Wright 124–33; Fuss; and McClintock 360–63.

12. The classic study of the colonizer–colonized relation in Memmi as "Manichean" is JanMohamed; see also Alschuler for a Jungian "psychopolitical" study of that relation in terms of narcissism, under the rubric of "duo." Tony Judt situates the tendency to understand the colonizer–colonized relation in Manichean terms in the context of French intel-

lectual thought in the years immediately following the Second World War: "Everything was classified in Manichean terms. Communists/capitalists, Soviet Union/United States, right/wrong, good/evil, them/us. . . . It was once again Sartre who gave this idea its more rarified expression. Hell being other people" (54, quoted in Gibson 210n1). Note that Fanon too writes of a colonized/racialized "Manichean conception of the world . . . white or black, that is the question" (*Black Skin* 44–45)—but attributes it to Mayotte Capécia.

13. For a detailed and useful reading of this chapter in the sociohistorical context of both Césaire on Negritude (and the sociohistorical context that Fanon saw as undermining the effectiveness of Negritude) and Dominic La Capra on intergenerational trauma, see Wilder, "Race."

14. Cf. the conclusion to *A Dying Colonialism:*

> The originality and the impatient richness of the Revolution are now and forever the great victories of the Algerian people. This community in action, renovated and free of any psychological, emotional, or legal subjection, is prepared today to assume modern and democratic responsibilities of exceptional moment.
>
> . . . It is true that independence produces the spiritual and material conditions for the reconversion of man. But it is also the inner mutation, the renewal of the social and family structures that impose with the rigor of a law the emergence of the Nation and the growth of its sovereignty.
>
> We may say firmly that Algerian man and Algerian society have stripped themselves of the mental sedimentation and of the emotional and intellectual handicaps which resulted from 130 years of oppression. . . .
>
> The Revolution in depth, the true one, precisely because it changes man and renews society, has reached an advanced stage. This oxygen which creates and shapes a new humanity—this, too, is the Algerian Revolution. (179–81)

In *The Wretched of the Earth* he is less sanguine: "But if we want humanity to advance a step further, if we want to bring it up to a different level than that which Europe has shown it, then we must invent and we must make discoveries. . . . For Europe, for ourselves, and for humanity, comrades, we must turn over a new leaf, we must work out new concepts, and try to set afoot a new man" (315–16). He envisions here the same utopian decolonized future, but envisions it now as the product of hard work rather than as a magical transformation brought about in the twinkling of an eye by the revolution.

For discussions of Fanon's revolutionary thought, see Bulhan (esp. Part III) and Perinbaum.

15. Note that Jentsch's primary examples of the uncanny effect of psycho-ontological uncertainty are children, "hysterics" (i.e., women), and "primitive man, . . . [whose] ignorance is therefore hidden from him to a great extent by the everyday" (9): "The affective position of the mentally undeveloped, mentally delicate, or mentally damaged individual towards many ordinary incidents of daily life is similar to the affective shading that the perception of the unusual or inexplicable generally produces in the ordinary primitive man" (10). What is required for the experience of the uncanny is significant dysregulation of the group's ideosomatic construction of reality, and the ideosomatics of reality-construction seem to Jentsch to be on a considerably firmer footing (and therefore the phenomenon of the uncanny far less common) among groups of educated European men than among these "other" groups—suggesting that one of the ways groups of educated European males regulate the ideosomatic construction of reality is by repressing their own uncertainties and

confusions and projecting them onto their childish, womanish, lower-class, "primitive," and mentally deranged others. Indeed Jentsch's conception seems to be definitively shaped by the circulatory exosomatization of Western colonialist images of the "primitive" or the "native":

> Conversely, the same emotion occurs when, as has been described, a wild man has his first sight of a locomotive or of a steamboat, for example, perhaps at night. The feeling of trepidation will here be very great, for as a consequence of the enigmatic autonomous movement and the regular noises of the machine, reminding him of human breath, the giant apparatus can easily impress the completely ignorant person as a living mass. There is something quite related to this, by the way, when striking or remarkable noises are ascribed by fearful or childish souls—as can be observed quite often—to the vocal performance of a mysterious being. The episode in *Robinson Crusoe* where Friday, not yet familiar with the boiling of water, reaches into simmering water in order to pull out the animal that seems to be in it, is also based on an inspiration of the writer that is psychologically very apposite. (11)

Women and children, for Jentsch, are the "primitives" or "fearful or childish souls" in "our" (male European) midst; when "we" white educated males have our rare experiences of the uncanny, it is like the surfacing of something long since outgrown in us, or what Freud will call the return of the repressed.

16. Note that Fanon is not really interested in this postcolonial assault on the Hegelian dialectic; in Chapter 5 of *Black Skin, White Masks* he just happens to experience Sartre's invocation of the dialectic as paralyzing. Cf. his discussion in *A Dying Colonialism* of the decolonizing transformation of the colonized's use of the colonizer's language: "What is involved here is not the emergence of an ambivalence, but rather a mutation, a radical change of valence, not a back-and-forth movement but a dialectical progression" (90n8).

17. For a useful discussion of Fanon in terms of the impact on French intellectual circles of Alexandre Kojève's lectures on Hegel's master–slave dialectic in the late 1930s (among those in attendance were Lacan, who is cited in *Black Skin* [152n15], and Merleau-Ponty, whose lectures Fanon attended in Paris, and whose concept of embodied "lived experience" is implicitly interwoven with Fanon's analysis throughout), see Gibson, chapter 1 (on Sartre and Merleau-Ponty esp. 24–27).

18. Dirlik does deal with Bhabha and Spivak and generally postcolonial theory and criticism in "Past," "Response," and "How the Grinch."

19. For critiques of Bhabha, see Parry "Signs," Lazarus, Ahmad, Cedric Robinson, Loomba, Tiffin, the articles in Slemon and Tiffin, and Moore-Gilbert (chapter 4, esp. 132–40).

20. "However, the 'signs' that construct such histories and identities—gender, race, homophobia, postwar diaspora, refugees, the international division of labour, and so on— not only differ in content but often produce incompatible systems of signification and engage distinct forms of social subjectivity. To provide a social imaginary that is based on the articulation of differential, even disjunctive, moments of history and culture, contemporary critics resort to the peculiar temporality of the language metaphor" (Bhabha, "Postcolonial" 176). His examples are taken from Cornel West, Stuart Hall, Hortense Spillers, Deborah McDowell, Houston A. Baker, Jr., and Henry Louis Gates, Jr.

21. Bhabha apparently quotes this passage from memory: he adds "a text of" in front of

"pulsional incidents" and renders "the articulation of the body, of the tongue, not that of meaning, of language" as "the articulation of the tongue, not the meaning of language."

22. See, e.g., Moore-Gilbert:

> While it is surprising that Bhabha makes no comment on Barthes's exoticism, more problematic is the fact that he is in fact at times seduced by Barthes's rigid ontological distinction between the "sentence," and what is "outside the sentence"; consequently, despite himself, he reinscribes rather than displaces a whole series of binary oppositions between (neo)colonial and postcolonial culture. The West, for Barthes and Bhabha alike, is associated with writing, the symbol, pedagogy (all of which denote monological, fixed and authoritarian qualities), abstract forms of thought and a conception of culture as an epistemological object of the kind associated with the museum, in other words divorced from everyday experience. Meanwhile, the postcolonial is associated with the "text," the voice, the sign, performance (all of which denote dialogical, democratic and mobile properties), sensual modes of apprehension, and a conception of culture as active, present and enunciatory. The oppositions which Bhabha sets up between Casablanca (which he uses to figure the West, by virtue of the film of that name) and Tangiers are in fact schematic to the point of caricature, with the effect that the West itself then takes on all the qualities of fixity and repetition associated with the "eternal East" of Orientalist discourse. This is nothing other than the "reverse ethnocentrism" of which he (like Spivak) so often complains. (128–29)

23. In Elizabeth Jane Bellamy's reading of this moment in Bhabha's essay, "these disjunctive and only partial modes of opposition militate against a truly collective action. Thus the Muslim peasants are less the site of 'individuation' (in the bourgeois, Western sense of the word) than the site of 'ambivalence' as 'an intersubjective affect' induced by the incommensurability between the religious and the militant" (347). But what manner of unified truth would "a truly collective action" be, and why should we conceive of conflicting ideosomatic regimes as "militating" against it? To be "truly collective," must an action be instigated and regulated by the intersubjective affect of a single group? If one or more members of the group engage in the action for "the wrong reasons," does it thereby become a *false* collectivity? And why must "individuation" and "ambivalence" be binarized? Is individuation ever anything less than ambivalent? Bhabha himself does not binarize them; he writes of "ambivalence at the point of 'individuation' as an intersubjective affect" (187), suggesting that for him scare-quoted "individuation" *is* the intersubjective affect whose "point" or transformative verge is characterized by ambivalence. I would revise that formulation only by calling individuation the attributive *product* of the somatic exchange, which will always be characterized by "ambivalence" in the sense of being shot through with conflicting ideosomatic and idiosomatic pressures, but in the counterregulatory contexts of colonization and decolonization will in fact be not just "ambivalent" but actively polynormative.

24. I would also suggest, however, that Moore-Gilbert is wrong to conflate this passage from "Articulating the Archaic" with the passage from "The Other Question" that JanMohamed critiques: "What is denied the colonial subject, both as colonizer and colonized, is that form of negation which gives access to the recognition of difference" (Bhabha, "Articulating" 75). For one thing, I think that both Moore-Gilbert and JanMohamed take Bhabha out of context, reading him to be saying that there *is* no "form of negation which

gives access to the recognition of difference" between colonizer and colonized, that for Bhabha colonization mutually transforms both the colonizer and the colonized until there is no difference between them, until they become a single unified subject. (JanMohamed writes that "Bhabha asserts, without providing any explanation, the unity of the 'colonial subject (both colonizer and colonized)'" [59]; Moore-Gilbert seconds him in arguing that Bhabha's remark tends "to produce an unwarranted unification of colonizer and colonized as a (single) 'colonial subject' which discounts the deep objective differences in the political power and material conditions of these 'secret sharers'" [147].) What Bhabha is saying there specifically is that *both types* of colonial subject are denied that form of negation. He's not unifying them; he's comparing them on a single point of similarity. The other thing is that the passages from "Articulating the Archaic" and "Sly Civility" do differentiate clearly between colonizer and colonized, by assigning the former an enslaved/paranoid subjectivity and reducing the latter to the blank negativity of refusing mastery.

25. For a representative logical critique of Spivak's essay, see Moore-Gilbert 98–109: Spivak presents the subaltern as "wholly Other," a purely discursive/differential category, and "as a 'real' and concrete historical category, more particularly as a material effect of the export overseas of Western capitalism" (103); "this politically comforting reconstruction of motive . . . makes Bhaduri 'signify' (if not literally speak), in apparently blatant contradiction of the assertion that the subaltern 'as female cannot be heard or read'" (105); "Spivak at times seems to present [the subaltern] as a forever passive and helpless victim of forces beyond his/her control. This makes it rather difficult to understand, let alone accept, her complaint about the West's historic 'refusal to acknowledge the colonial peoples, postcolonial peoples, as agents'" (107).

One strategy for logical critique that I haven't seen, but that I adumbrate myself in §2.2.2.3 in connection with Kant, is fuzzy logic—for clearly the aporetic series of subaltern not-yet-subjectivities en route to the subject-as-such is a sorites series: is the subaltern a subject yet? Not yet. Fuzzy logic would make the differentiality that is subalternity aporetic and therefore "unreadable" in a perhaps less strict sense than the one Spivak charts out:

Imagine that "we" (a member of the Western or Indian English-speaking intellectual elite) are standing at one end of a long corridor, with an Indian tribal woman (TW1) and Spivak (GCS) standing together in the center and another Indian tribal woman (TW2) at the far end. GCS takes one step toward us, away from TW1 in the center, and TW2 takes one step toward TW1: is TW1 still subaltern, and is she still silenced by power? Almost certainly yes. Because TW1 is still in the company of a member of the elite, *not yet* among her own, she is still subaltern and cannot speak. GCS and TW2 take another step, both in the same direction, GCS away from TW1, TW2 toward her. Is TW1 still subaltern, and is she still silenced by power? Probably still yes. They take another step, and another, and another. At some point GCS will be standing with us, chatting easily in English, and TW1 and TW2 will be alone in the center of the corridor, and we will want to say that TW1 is no longer subaltern and now can speak. But at what point in the sorites series did the politico-ontological transformation from subaltern to not-subaltern occur?

It is, of course, demeaning to use logical puzzles to talk about the poorest and most disenfranchised people on the planet; but my point is not simply to use logic against logic, to cancel the effects of Spivak's binary logic with a slightly more complex logic. It is also to show that the "not yet" that Spivak would deny Kant, grounded as it is not merely in fuzzy logic but in *affective* fuzzy logic, in the liberal-progressivist evaluative affect of colonialist thought, is, in the end, less demeaning than Spivak's desomatized binary logic, which would make the subaltern's politico-ontological status depend on the on-off gates in the Western observer's head. And in fact I would guess that Spivak herself knows this, and feels uneasy about it; after all, she begins her famous essay, in its 1985, 1988, and 1999 forms, with a deconstruction of that binary logic in Ranajit Guha's formulation of subalternity in his introduction to the first volume of *Subaltern Studies:*

> In subaltern studies, because of the violence of imperialist epistemic, social, and disciplinary inscription, a project understood in essentialist terms must traffic in a radical textual practice of differences. The object of the group's investigation, in this case not even of the people as such but of the floating buffer zone of the regional elite—is a *deviation* from an *ideal*—the people or subaltern—which is itself defined as a difference from the elite. It is toward this structure that the research is oriented, a predicament rather different from the self-diagnosed transparency of the first-world radical intellectual. What taxonomy can fix such a space? (*Critique* 271–72)

Her insistence, despite this diagnosis, on retaining the Gramscian definition of subalternity as a "space of difference" suggests that she finds "the violence of imperialist epistemic, social, and disciplinary inscription" so inexorable that the radical intellectual can do nothing *but* continue to understand the project of subaltern studies essentializingly—or rather, perhaps, anti-essentializingly, but in Spivak's own Derridean purview, of course, that binary opposition remains complicit in the same essentializing stance.

26. I quote here from the original version of the article in *Cultural Critique,* because in this one case Spivak's editing for the reprinted version in *Outside* seems to me to have introduced unnecessary syntactic confusion: Mahasweta, she writes there, "lingers in post-coloniality and even there in the space of difference *on decolonized terrain* in the space of difference" (77). The remainder of the quotations from this essay are taken from *Outside,* and page citations reflect that pagination.

27. It may be that the most problematic term in Spivak's borrowings from Deleuze and Guattari is "code," a term they take from Saussurean linguistics to indicate the discursivity of laws and rules, the social organizations or codifications of experience and behavior. To the extent that she intends "affective value-coding" to mean the discursive organization of affective value, she is binarizing discourse and affect in ways that would appear to recuperate Cartesian mind-body or subject-object dualisms—or, for that matter, Western power discourse and the silenced body of the subaltern woman. A more interesting reading of "affective value-coding," however, would be that value is "coded" in and by and through affect—that Spivak is troping affect as the "discourse" by which value is "coded." This latter (protosomatic) construction of affective value-coding would have to depend heavily on the metaphoricity of affect = discourse and affective approval/disapproval=code, of course, but I think that is a useful metaphorical orientation—that is, until Spivak begins making distinctions like "economically rather than affectively coded," "represented *within* rather than prior to an accepted code," and "the figuration of the woman's body before the affective coding of sexuality" (93). Then the spatial (economic vs. affective) and temporal (prior to vs. within) binaries of coding render the metaphor problematic in ways that Spivak does not address, because she does not theorize her terms. In a protosomatic metaphorization of the normativizing circulation of approval/disapproval body language and body states as "affective value-coding," evaluative affective states would certainly saturate and normatively condition economic coding as well; indeed it's hard to imagine what economic coding would look or feel or act like without affective coding. Those evaluative affective states would also saturate and normatively condition representation and figuration, of course;

somatically speaking "representation," "figuration," and "code" are not so much cuts the group makes in the affective flows, as Deleuze and Guattari would say, as they are bodily-becoming-mental mappings of affective channels of social organization and circulation—homeostatic attempts to understand and regulate those flows whose relation to the flows is iterative rather than scissive.

If on the other hand the "code" of affective value-coding is thematized as a clearly bounded discursive structure, with spatial boundaries that separate it from economic value-coding and temporal boundaries that separate it from pre-affective/pre-coding regimes (or perhaps pre-regimes?) of representation or figuration, then affect = discourse is not a trope at all but a simple post-linguistic ontology.

For a reading of Nietzsche on the "somatic codes" developed for the comparative corporeal-becoming-affective calculations of guilt and debt, see my Ecologies of Translation (§4.3).

28. See also Shetty's passing remarks on Spivak's reading of "Douloti the Bountiful" (71) as a counterpoint to her discussion of motherhood as an "allegorical seme" in Mahasweta's "Stanadayini" 67–73, and Judith Butler's reading of Spivak on Devi in Undoing Gender 229–30. That book concludes with an essay whose title seems to promise a philosophical rethinking of Spivak's essay—"Can the 'Other' of Philosophy Speak?"—but it is an autobiographical reflection on Butler's own theoretical speaking from outside philosophy, and does not even mention Spivak.

THIRD ESSAY

1. And, strikingly, Cathy Caruth is as unable to theorize the intergenerational transmission of trauma as Freud is, despite the fact that Moses and Monotheism is the central text in Unclaimed Experience, a text to which she devotes fully two of her chapters, chapters 1 and 3. She does not seem to be aware of Freud's roots in this area (as in so many others) in Nietzsche. See also notes 21, 26, and especially 28.

2. For discussions of Nietzsche's protosomatic theory, see §4.3 in my Ecologies of Translation and §2.1 in the current volume; for Schore's protosomatic reading of Kohut, see my Estrangement 46.

3. Judith A. Antell seems to be arguing for some such ceremonial transformation in the novel, but her description remains vague:

> Like the writings of Momaday, Welch's novel is best understood in the context of the dream/vision ritual structure of plains tribal life. Welch, like Momaday, uses correct ritual sequencing of events rather than the chronological lines of organizational life. It is this structure of Welch's novel which holds the major clue to its function as a tribal document (Allen, 1986:9386). The Death of Jim Loney is ritualistic in approach, structure, theme, symbol, and significance, and in order for Jim to confront and resolve the bicultural and colonial problems to which he is exposed, he must participate in the ritual tradition—a tradition that affirms the power of the female. For Jim Loney, as for Abel and Tayo, the solution to male alienation is personal integration through insight and action, and the ritual for Jim, as for Abel, leads him to the decision to arrange his own death. (219)

What "personal integration"? What "insight"? The power of what female? Antell isn't saying. But perhaps she means something like "in order for Jim to confront and resolve the bicultural and colonial problems to which he is exposed, he *would have to* participate in the ritual tradition—a tradition that affirms the power of the female—*but he can't*"? Perhaps she's setting up this ritual tradition grounded in the power of the female as the impossible goal that Loney finds himself unable to reach? Not really: "So, while on the surface the novels of Momaday, Welch, and Silko appear to be stories of alienated Indian men, they are really much more the stories of female power as acknowledged through ritual and ceremony" (219–20). In the case of *The Death of Jim Loney,* at least, this strikes me as wishful thinking.

4. Lemberg here quotes from the *Critical Inquiry* article version of LaCapra's chapter in *Writing History, Writing Trauma,* "Trauma, Absence, Loss" 716. We will be returning to LaCapra's trauma theory in §3.2.4.

5. Stromberg, it seems to me, seriously overstates his case. He argues, for example, that the reading offered by Sands, Allen, and Purdy, to the effect that Loney dies a warrior's death of his own choosing, "reveals a critical paradox: Loney, who declares he does not feel Indian and who spends much of the novel seeking a state of authenticity, is read as the novel's representation of authentic Indian identity" (38). But of course they only argue that he *becomes* something like a "representation of authentic Indian identity" at the end—that that is the *goal* of his quest, and he reaches it—not that he represents "authentic Indian-ness" all the way through. He also insists on reading Loney's wish to belong to *some* community, white or Indian (Welch 14), as an "imperative of purity that is part of a process of 'othering' which has no room for overlap or admixture. Loney's desire to be wholly Indian or wholly white is not a natural response to a genetic condition but is an internalization of a powerful cultural logic" (39)—and in order to make this case utterly ignores Welch's recontextualization of this moment later in the novel when the narrator remarks that Rhea "had said he was lucky to have two sets of ancestors. In truth he had none" (102).

6. For example:

> He was restless. He had been thinking of his life for a month. He had tried to think of all the little things that added up to a man sitting at a table drinking wine. But he couldn't connect the different parts of his life, or the various people who had entered and left it. Sometimes he felt like an amnesiac searching for the one event, the one person or moment, that would bring everything back and he would see the order in his life. But without the amnesiac's clean slate, all the people and events were as hopelessly tangled as a bird's nest in his mind, and so for almost a month he had been sitting at his table, drinking wine, and saying to himself, "Okay, from this very moment I will start back—I will think of yesterday, last week, last year, until all my years are accounted for. Then I will look ahead and know where I'm going." But the days piled up faster than the years receded and he grew restless and despondent. But he would not concede that his life had added up to nothing more than the simple reality of a man sitting and drinking in a small house in the world (20–21).

> He thought of his earlier attempts to create a past, a background, an ancestry—something that would tell him who he was. Now he wondered if he had really tried. (88)

7. A very short list of Morrison's critics who have addressed these issues would include Boudreau, Caesar, Cooley, Coykendall, Davis, Ferguson, Finney, Fitzgerald, Fritz, Handley,

Henderson, Horvitz, House, Jablon, Kelly, Krumholz, Lawrence, Mathieson, Mohanty, Osagie, Phelan, Powell, Rody, Rushdy, Schapiro, Vickroy, and Wyatt.

8. "If PTSD must be understood as a pathological symptom," Caruth writes in her introduction to *Trauma*, "then it is not so much a symptom of the unconscious, as it is a symptom of history. The traumatized, we might say, carry an impossible history within them, or they become themselves the symptom of a history that they cannot entirely possess" (5). Without somatic theory, of course, Caruth is unable to bridge the binary between "the unconscious" and "history," but she is on the right track: if "history" is the ideosomatization of experience, the organization of collective experience via the circulation of shared affect through the group, then traumatic history does indeed endosomatize individuals as its symptoms. In *Unclaimed Experience,* the 1996 book-length study that incorporates her 1991 essay by that title as its first chapter (on Freud, her central theoretical interest, especially his theorization of individual trauma in *Beyond the Pleasure Principle* and historical trauma in *Moses and Monotheism*), her concern is primarily with history as the painful verbal repetitions of traumatic experience that was not understood when it was first encountered: "In trauma, that is, the outside has gone inside without any mediation" (59). This becomes a model not only for historiography but for the history of psychoanalysis as well:

> Freud suggests that psychoanalysis, if it lives on, will live on not as the straightforward life of a known and understood theory, but as the endless survival of what has not been fully understood. If psychoanalysis is to be continued in its tradition, it is paradoxically in what has not yet been fully grasped in its survival that its truest relation to its insight must be found. I would suggest that trauma theory is one of the areas today in which this survival is precisely taking place, not only in the assuredness of its transformation and appropriation by psychiatry but in the creative uncertainties of this theory that remain, for psychiatry *and* psychoanalysis, in the enigma of trauma as both destruction *and* survival, an enigma that lies at the very heart of the Freudian insight itself. (72)

In her theorization of "historical trauma" (67–72), based on a close reading of *Moses and Monotheism,* Caruth does not problematize the question of the *intergenerational transmission* of trauma; she writes about historical trauma as if the survival of a traumatized/traumatizing paleoregulatory regime from generation to generation in the life of a culture were no more mysterious (but also no less) than the survival of PTSD symptomatologies in the life of a traumatized individual: "The history of chosenness, as the history of survival, thus takes the form of an unending confrontation with the returning violence of the past" (69). Implicit in that rather sketchy formulation is the notion that "the history of chosenness" is an overt (verbalized) paleoregulatory regime that both expresses and carries (endosomatizes) the covert (nonverbalized, repressed, unconscious) "unending confrontation with the returning violence of the past."

9. LaCapra also mentions in passing that fiction seems to be much better suited to the study of historical trauma than history, because it can generate "a plausible 'feel' for experience and emotion which may be difficult to arrive at through restricted documentary methods. One might, for example, make such a case for Toni Morrison's *Beloved* with respect to the aftermath of slavery and the role of transgenerational, phantomlike forces that haunt later generations" (13–14). He does not notice the excluded middle that *Beloved* seems to insert into his acting-out/working-through binary.

Abbott, Max W., Sai Wong, Lynne C. Giles, Sue Wong, Wilson Young, and Ming Au. "Depression in Older Chinese Migrants to Auckland." *Australian and New Zealand Journal of Psychiatry* 37.4 (August 2003): 445–51.

Adolphs, Ralph. "Neural Mechanisms for Recognizing Emotion." *Current Opinion in Neurobiology* 12.2 (2002): 169–78.

Agamben, Giorgio. *Homo Sacer: Sovereign Power and Bare Life*. Translated by Daniel Heller-Roazen. Stanford: Stanford University Press, 1998.

Ahmad, Aijaz. *In Theory: Classes, Nations, Literatures*. London: Verso, 1992.

———. "The Politics of Literary Postcoloniality." *Race and Class* 36.3 (1995): 1–20.

Alarcón, Norma. "Anzaldua's Fronteras: Inscribing Gynetics." In *Displacement, Diaspora, and Geographies of Identity*, edited by Smadar Lavie and Ted Swedenburg. 41-53. Durham, NC: Duke University Press, 1996.

Allen, Paula Gunn. *The Sacred Hoop: Recovering the Feminine in American Indian Traditions*. Boston: Beacon Press, 1992.

Alschuler, Lawrence R. "Oppression, Liberation, and Narcissism: A Jungian Psychopolitical Analysis of the Ideas of Albert Memmi." *Alternatives* 21 (1996): 497–523.

Amis, Martin. *Time's Arrow*. New York: Vintage, 1992.

Anderson, Benedict. *Imagined Communities: Reflections on the Origin and Spread of Nationalism*. Revised and extended edition. London: Verso, 1991.

Anglesey, Zoe. "The Voice of the Storytellers: An Interview with Edwidge Danticat." *MultiCultural Review* 7.3 (September 1, 1998): 36–39.

Antell, Judith A. "Momaday, Welch, and Silko: Expressing the Feminine Principle through Male Alienation." *American Indian Quarterly* 12.3 (Summer 1988): 213–20.

Appadurai, Arjun. *The Social Life of Things*. Cambridge: Cambridge University Press, 1988.

Auerhahn, Nanette C., and Dori Laub. "Intergenerational Memory of the Holocaust." In Danieli, *International Handbook* 21–41.

Balint, Michael. "Trauma and Object Relationship." *International Journal of Psychoanalysis* 50 (1969): 429–36.

Barsamian, D. "Edwidge Danticat: The Haitian American Writer Explores How People Live with 'The Scars of Dictatorship.'" *The Progressive* 67.10 (2003): 29–33.

Barthes, Roland. *The Pleasure of the Text.* 1973. Translated by Richard Miller. New York: Hill and Wang, 1975.

Bateson, Gregory. "Toward a Theory of Schizophrenia." In *Steps to an Ecology of Mind,* 201–27. 1972. Reprint. New York: Ballantine Books, 1985.

Bell, Vikki. "Historical Memory, Global Movements and Violence: Paul Gilroy and Arjun Appadurai in Conversation." *Theory, Culture and Society* 16.2 (1999): 21–40.

———. "Mimesis as Cultural Survival: Judith Butler and Anti-Semitism." *Theory, Culture and Society* 16.2 (1999): 133–61.

Bellamy, Elizabeth Jane. "'Intimate Enemies': Psychoanalysis, Marxism, and Postcolonial Affect." *South Atlantic Quarterly* 97.2 (Spring 1998): 341–59.

Berger, James. "Ghosts of Liberalism: Morrison's *Beloved* and the Moynihan Report." *PMLA* 111 (May 1996): 409-20.

Beverley, John. "The Dilemma of Subaltern Studies at Duke." *Nepantla* 1.1 (2000): 33–44.

Bevis, Bill. "Dialogue with James Welch." *Northwest Review* 20.2-3 (1982): 163-85.

Bhabha, Homi K. "Articulating the Archaic: Cultural Difference and Colonial Nonsense." In Bhabha, *Location* 123–38.

———. *The Location of Culture.* London and New York: Routledge, 1994.

———. "The Postcolonial and the Postmodern: The Question of Agency." In Bhabha, *Location* 171–97.

———. "Sly Civility." In Bhabha, *Location* 93–101.

Boudreau, Kristin. "Pain and the Unmaking of Self in Toni Morrison's *Beloved.*" *Contemporary Literature* 36.3 (Fall 1995): 324–34.

Brady, Mary Pat. "The Fungibility of Borders." *Nepantla* 1.1 (2000): 171–90.

Braidotti, Rosi. *Nomadic Subjects: Embodiment and Sexual Difference in Contemporary Feminist Theory.* New York: Columbia University Press, 1994.

Brave Heart, Maria Yellow Horse. "The Return to Sacred Path: Healing the Historical Trauma and Historical Unresolved Grief Response among the Lakota through a Psychoeducational Group Intervention." *Smith College Studies in Social Work* 68.3 (1998): 288–305.

———, and Lemyra M. DeBruyn. "The American Indian Holocaust: Healing Historical Unresolved Grief." *American Indian and Alaska Native Mental Health Research* 8.2 (1998): 60–82.

Braziel, Jana Evans. "Daffodils, Rhizomes, Migrations: Narrative Coming of Age in the Diasporic Writings of Edwidge Danticat and Jamaica Kincaid." *Meridians: Feminism, Race, Transnationalism* 3.2 (2003): 110–31.

Brennan, Teresa. *The Transmission of Affect.* Ithaca, NY: Cornell University Press, 2004.

Brown, Richard S. G. "Nietzsche: 'That Profound Physiologist.'" In Moore and Brobjer 51–70.

Bulhan, Hussein Abdilahi. *Frantz Fanon and the Psychology of Oppression.* New York and London: Plenum Press, 1985.

Busia, Abena. "Silencing Sycorax: On African Colonial Discourse and the Unvoiced Female." *Cultural Critique* 14 (Winter 1989–90): 81–104.

Butler, Judith. "Can the 'Other' of Philosophy Speak?" In Butler, *Undoing* 232–50.

———. "Foucault and the Paradox of Bodily Inscriptions." *Journal of Philosophy* 86.11 (November 1989): 601–7.

———. *Gender Trouble: Feminism and the Subversion of Identity.* 1990. Reprint. London and New York: Routledge, 1999.

———. "Imitation and Gender Insubordination." In *Inside/Out: Lesbian Theories, Gay Theories*, edited by Diana Fuss. 13–31. London and New York: Routledge, 1991.

———. *Undoing Gender*. New York and London: Routledge, 2004.

Caesar, Terry Paul. "Slavery and Motherhood in Toni Morrison's *Beloved*." *Revista de Letras* 34 (1994): 111–20.

Carpenter, William B. *Principles of Mental Physiology, with Their Applications to the Training and Discipline of the Mind, and the Study of Its Morbid Conditions*. New York: Appleton, 1874.

Carroll, Jennifer K. "*Murug, Waali*, and *Gini*: Expression of Distress in Refugees from Somalia." *Journal of Clinical Psychiatry* 6.3 (2004): 119–25.

Caruth, Cathy. "Unclaimed Experience: Trauma and the Possibility of History." *Yale French Studies* 79 (1991): 181–92.

———. *Unclaimed Experience: Trauma, Narrative and History*. Baltimore: Johns Hopkins University Press, 1996.

———, ed. *Trauma: Explorations in Memory*. Baltimore: Johns Hopkins University Press, 1995.

Chambers, Iain. *Migrancy, Culture, Identity*. London and New York: Routledge, 1994.

Chatterjee, Partha. *Nationalist Thought and the Colonial World: A Derivative Discourse?* Minneapolis: University of Minnesota Press, 1986.

Cixous, Hélène. "Fiction and Its Phantoms: A Reading of Freud's *Das Unheimliche*." *New Literary History* 7.3 (1976): 525–48.

———, and Catherine Clément. *The Newly Born Woman*. 1975. Translated by Betsy Wing. Minneapolis: University of Minnesota Press, 1986.

Cohon, J. Donald. "Psychological Adaptation and Dysfunction among Refugees." *International Migration Review* 15.1/2 (Spring–Summer 1981): 255–75.

Connolly, William E. *Identity/Difference: Democratic Negotiations of Political Paradox*. Ithaca, NY: Cornell University Press, 1991.

———. *Political Theory and Modernity*. Oxford: Blackwell, 1989.

Connor, Walker. "A Nation is a Nation, is a State, is an Ethnic Group is a . . ." *Ethnic and Racial Studies* 1.4 (1978): 377–400.

Cooley, Elizabeth. "Remembering and Dis(Re)Membering: Memory, Community and the Individual in *Beloved*." *University of Mississippi Studies in English* 11–12 (1993–95): 351–60.

Corbett, Bob. Untitled review of Edwidge Danticat, *Krik? Krak!* http://www.webster.edu/~corbetre/haiti/bookreviews/danticat3.htm. November 25, 2006.

Coronil, Fernando. "Listening to the Subaltern: The Poetics of Neocolonial States." *Poetics Today* 15.4 (Winter 1994): 643–58.

Coykendall, Abby. "Resuscitating the Literal from the Spectral Figural: History and (Re)production in Toni Morrison's *Beloved*." *Theory Buffalo* (Fall 1996): 107–22.

Cuny, Frederick C., Barry N. Stein, and Pat Reed, eds. *Repatriation during Conflict in Africa and Asia*. Dallas: Center for the Study of Societies in Crisis, 1992.

Damasio, Antonio R. *Descartes' Error: Emotion, Reason, and the Human Brain*. New York: Putnam, 1994.

———. *The Feeling of What Happens: Body and Emotion in the Making of Consciousness*. New York: Harcourt, 1999.

———. *Looking for Spinoza: Joy, Sorrow, and the Feeling Brain*. New York: Harcourt, 2003.

Danieli, Yael, ed. *International Handbook of Multigenerational Legacies of Trauma*. New York: Plenum Press, 1998.

Danticat, Edwidge. *Breath, Eyes, Memory.* New York: Vintage/Random House, 1994.
———. *The Dew Breaker.* New York: Vintage/Random House, 2004.
———. *The Farming of Bones.* New York: Soho Press, 1998.
———. *Krik? Krak!* New York: Vintage/Random House, 1996.
Davies, Carole Boyce. *Black Women, Writing and Identity.* London and New York: Routledge, 1994.
Davis, Christina. "*Beloved:* A Question of Identity." *Présence Africaine: Revue Culturelle du Monde Noir/Cultural Review of the Negro World* 145 (1988): 151–56.
De Beauvoir, Simone. *The Second Sex.* 1949. Translated by H. M. Parshley. New York: Vintage, 1993.
De Voe, Dorsh Marie. "Framing Refugees as Clients." *International Migration Review* 15.1/2 (Spring–Summer 1981): 88–94.
Deleuze, Gilles, and Félix Guattari. *Anti-Oedipus.* Vol. 1 of *Capitalism and Schizophrenia.* 1972. Translated by Robert Hurley, Mark Seem, and Helen R. Lane. London: Athlone Press, 1983.
———. *A Thousand Plateaus.* Vol. 2 of *Capitalism and Schizophrenia.* 1980. Translated by Brian Massumi. Minneapolis: University of Minnesota Press, 1987.
Devi, Mahasweta. *Breast Stories.* Translated and introduced by Gayatri Chakravorty Spivak. Kolkata, India: Seagull Books, 1997.
———. *Chotta Mundi and His Arrow.* Translated and introduced by Gayatri Chakravorty Spivak. Oxford: Blackwell, 2002.
———. "Douloti the Bountiful." In Devi, *Imaginary Maps* 19–93.
———. *Imaginary Maps: Three Stories by Mahasweta Devi.* Translated and introduced by Gayatri Chakravorty Spivak. New York and London: Routledge, 1995.
———. *Old Women.* Translated and introduced by Gayatri Chakravorty Spivak. Kolkata, India: Seagull Books, 1999.
———, and Gayatri Chakravorty Spivak. "The Author in Conversation." In Devi, *Imaginary Maps* xi–xxii.
Dewind, Josh, and Philip Kasintz. "Everything Old Is New Again? Processes and Theories of Immigrant Incorporation." *International Migration Review* 31.4 (Winter 1997): 1096–111.
Dirlik, Arif. "American Studies in the Time of Empire." *Comparative American Studies* 2.3 (2004): 287–304.
———. "Empire? Some Thoughts on Colonialism, Culture, and Class in the Making of Global Crisis and War in Perpetuity." *Interventions* 5.2 (2003): 207–17.
———. "Globalization as the End and the Beginning of History: The Contradictory Implications of a New Paradigm." *Rethinking Marxism* 12.4 (Winter 2000): 4–22.
———. "How the Grinch Hijacked Radicalism: Further Thoughts on the Postcolonial." *Postcolonial Studies* 2.2 (1999): 149–63.
———. "The Past as Legacy and Project: Postcolonial Criticism in the Perspective of Indigenous Historicism." *American Indian Culture and Research Journal* 20.2 (1996): 1–31.
———. "The Postcolonial Aura: Third World Criticism in the Age of Global Capitalism." *Critical Inquiry* 20 (Winter 1994): 328–56.
———. "Response to the Responses: Thoughts on the Postcolonial." *Interventions* 1.2 (1999): 286–90.
———. "Rethinking Colonialism: Globalization, Postcolonialism, and the Nation." *Interventions* 4.3 (2002): 428–48.
———. "Spectres of the Third World: Global Modernity and the End of the Three Worlds." *Third World Quarterly* 25.1 (2004): 131–48.

Drumm, Rene, Sharon Pittman, and Shelly Perry. "Women of War: Emotional Needs of Ethnic Albanians in Refugee Camps." *AFFILIA* 16.4 (Winter 2001): 467–87.

Duran, Bonnie, Eduardo Duran, and Maria Yellow Horse Brave Heart. "Native Americans and the Trauma of History." In *Studying Native America: Problems and Prospects,* edited by Russell Thornton. 60–76. Madison: University of Wisconsin Press, 1998.

Duran, Eduardo, and Bonnie Duran. *Native American Postcolonial Psychology.* Albany: State University of New York Press, 1995.

Duran, Eduardo, Bonnie Duran, Maria Yellow Horse Brave Heart, and Susan Yellow Horse-Davis. "Healing the American Indian Soul Wound." In Danieli, *International Handbook* 341–54.

Eagleton, Terry. "In the Gaudy Supermarket." *London Review of Books* 21.10 (May 13, 1999): 3–6.

———. "Nationalism. Irony and Commitment." In *Nationalism, Colonialism, and Literature,* edited by Terry Eagleton, Fredric Jameson, and Edward Said. 23–39. Minneapolis: University of Minnesota Press, 1990.

Eisenstein, Paul. "Finding Lost Generations: Recovering Omitted History in *Winter in the Blood." MELUS* 19.3 (Fall 1994): 3–19.

Emden, Christian J. "Metaphor, Perception and Consciousness: Nietzsche on Rhetoric and Neurophysiology." In Moore and Brobjer 91–110.

Everett, Percival. "The Appropriation of Cultures." *Callaloo* 19.1 (1996): 24–30.

Fanon, Frantz. *Black Skins, White Masks.* 1952. Translated by Charles Lam Markmann. New York: Grove Press, 1967.

———. *A Dying Colonialism.* 1959. Translated by Haakon Chevalier. New York: Grove Press, 1965.

———. *The Wretched of the Earth.* 1961. Translated by Constance Farrington. New York: Grove Press, 1968.

Felman, Shoshana. *The Scandal of the Speaking Body: Don Juan with J. L. Austin, or Seduction in Two Languages.* 1980. Translated by Catherine Porter, 1984. Revised edition. Stanford: Stanford University Press, 2003.

Felson, Marcus, and R. V. G. Clarke. *Opportunity Makes the Thief: Practical Theory for Crime Prevention.* London: Home Office, 1998.

Ferguson, Rebecca. "History, Memory and Language in Toni Morrison's *Beloved.*" In *Feminist Criticism: Theory and Practice,* edited by Linda Hutcheon, Susan Seller, and Paul Perron. 109–27. Toronto: University of Toronto Press, 1991.

Fine, Ellen S. "The Absent Memory: The Act of Writing in Post-Holocaust French Literature." *Writing and the Holocaust,* edited by Berel Lang. 41–57. New York: Holmes and Meier, 1988.

Finney, Brian. "Temporal Defamiliarization in Toni Morrison's *Beloved.*" *Obsidian II: Black Literature in Review* 5.1 (Spring 1990): 20–36.

Fitzgerald, Jennifer. "Selfhood and Community: Psychoanalysis and Discourse in *Beloved.*" *Modern Fiction Studies* 39.3–4 (Fall/Winter 1993): 669–87.

Flannery, Regina. *The Gros Ventre of Montana, Part I: Social Life.* Washington, DC: Catholic University of America Press, 1953.

Flores-Borquez, Mia. "A Journey to Regain My Identity." *Journal of Refugee Studies* 8 (1995): 95–108.

Fortier, Anne-Marie. "Re-Membering Places and the Performance of Belonging(s)." *Theory, Culture and Society* 16.2 (1999): 41–64.

Foucault, Michel. *The History of Sexuality. Volume 1: An Introduction.* Translated by Robert Hurley. New York: Random House/Pantheon, 1978.

———. "Nietzsche, Genealogy, History." Translated by Donald F. Bouchard and Sherry Simon. In *Language, Counter-Memory, Practice: Selected Essays and Interviews*. By Foucault. Edited by Donald F. Bouchard. 139–64. Ithaca, NY: Cornell University Press, 1977.

———. *Surveiller et punir. Naissance de la prison*. Paris: Gallimard, 1975. Translated by Alan Sheridan as *Discipline and Punish: The Birth of the Prison*. New York: Pantheon, 1977.

Fowler, Loretta. *Shared Symbols, Contested Meanings: Gros Ventre Culture and History, 1778–1984*. Ithaca, NY: Cornell University Press, 1987.

Francis, Donette A. "'Silences Too Horrific to Disturb': Writing Sexual Histories in Edwidge Danticat's *Breath, Eyes, Memory*." *Research in African Literatures* 35.2 (Summer 2004): 75–90.

Fresco, Nadine. "Remembering the Unknown." *International Review of Psycho-Analysis* 11 (1984): 417–27.

Freud, Sigmund. "The Economic Problem of Masochism." 1924. In *The Ego and the Id and Other Works*, edited and translated by James Strachey. 155–70. Vol. 19 of *The Standard Edition of the Complete Psychological Works of Sigmund Freud*. London: Hogarth Press and the Institute of Psycho-analysis, 1961.

———. *The Interpretation of Dreams*. 1900. *The Standard Edition of the Complete Psychological Works of Sigmund Freud*, edited and translated by James Strachey. Vols. 2 and 3. London: Hogarth Press and the Institute of Psycho-analysis, 1953.

———. "The Uncanny." 1919. *An Infantile Neurosis and Other Works*, edited and translated by James Strachey. 219–52. Vol. 17 of *The Standard Edition of the Complete Psychological Works of Sigmund Freud*. London: Hogarth Press and the Institute of Psycho-analysis, 1955.

Friedman, Howard S. "The Interactive Effects of Facial Expressions of Emotion and Verbal Messages on Perceptions of Affective Meaning." *Journal of Experimental Social Psychology* 15.5 (September 1979): 453–69.

———, and Ronald E. Riggio. "Effect of Individual Differences in Nonverbal Expressiveness on Transmission of Emotion." *Journal of Nonverbal Behavior* 6.2 (Winter 1981): 96–104.

———, Louise M. Prince, Ronald E. Riggio, and M. Robin DiMatteo. "Understanding and Assessing Nonverbal Expressiveness: The Affective Communication Test." *Journal of Personality & Social Psychology* 39.2 (August 1980): 333–51.

Fritz, Angela DiPace. "Toni Morrison's *Beloved*: 'Unspeakable Things Unspoken, Spoken.'" *Sacred Heart University Review* 14.1–2 (Fall 1993–Spring 1994): 40–52.

Fuss, Diana. "Interior Colonies: Frantz Fanon and the Politics of Identification." In *Identification Papers: Readings on Psychoanalysis, Sexuality, and Culture*. London and New York: Routledge, 1995.

Gates, Henry Louis, Jr. "Editor's Introduction: Writing 'Race' and the Difference It Makes." *Critical Inquiry* 12.1 (Autumn 1985): 1–20.

Gibson, Nigel C. *Fanon: The Postcolonial Imagination*. Cambridge, UK: Polity Press, 2003.

Gillespie, R.D. *Psychological Effects of War on Citizen and Soldier*. New York: Norton, 1942.

Gilroy, Paul. "Nationalism, History, and Ethnic Absolutism." *History Workshop Journal* 30 (1990): 114–20.

Gordenker, Leon. "Early Warning of Disastrous Population Movement." *International Migration Review* 20.2 (Summer 1986): 170–89.

Gossett, Thomas. *Race: The History of an Idea in America*. Dallas: Southern Methodist University Press, 1965.

Handley, George B. "A New World Poetics of Oblivion." In *Look Away: The U.S. South in New World Studies,* edited by Jon Smith and Deborah Cohn. 25–51. Durham, NC, and London: Duke University Press, 2004.

Handley, William R. "The House a Ghost Built: Nommo, Allegory, and the Ethics of Reading in Toni Morrison's *Beloved." Contemporary Literature* 36.4 (Winter 1995): 676–701.

Hatfield, Elaine, John T. Cacioppo, and Richard L. Rapson. *Emotional Contagion.* Cambridge: Cambridge University Press, 1994.

Heidegger, Martin. *Being and Time.* 1927. Translated by John Macquarrie and Edward Robinson. London: SCM Press, 1962.

Henderson, Mae G. "Toni Morrison's *Beloved:* Re-Membering the Body as Historical Text." In *Comparative American Identities: Race, Sex, and Nationality in the Modern Text,* edited by Hortense J. Spillers. 62–86. London and New York: Routledge, 1991.

Horvitz, Deborah. "Nameless Ghosts: Possession and Dispossession in *Beloved." Studies in American Fiction* 17.2 (Autumn 1989): 157–67.

House, Elizabeth B. "Toni Morrison's Ghost: The Beloved Who Is Not Beloved." *Studies in American Fiction* 18.1 (Spring 1990): 17–26.

Huyck, Earl E., and Rona Fields. "Impact of Resettlement on Refugee Children." *International Migration Review* 15.1/2 (Spring–Summer 1981): 246–54.

Iyasere, Solomon O., and Marla W. Iyasere, eds. *Understanding Toni Morrison's* Beloved *and* Sula. Troy, NY: Whitston, 2000.

Jablon, Madelyn. "Rememory, Dream History, and Revision in Toni Morrison's *Beloved* and Alice Walker's *The Temple of My Familiar." College Language Association Journal* 37.2 (December 1993): 136–44.

James, C. L. R. *At the Rendezvous of Victory: Selected Writings.* London: Allison & Busby, 1984.

———. *Beyond a Boundary.* 1963. Reprint. Durham, NC: Duke University Press, 1993.

———. *The Black Jacobins: Toussaint L'Ouverture and the San Domingo Revolution.* 1938. 2nd revised edition. New York: Random House, 1963.

———. "Black Sansculottes." In James, *At the Rendezvous* 159–62.

———. "Rastafari at Home and Abroad." In James, *At the Rendezvous* 163–65.

Jameson, Fredric. *The Political Unconscious: Narrative as a Socially Symbolic Act.* Ithaca, NY: Cornell University Press, 1981.

JanMohamed, Abdul R. "The Economy of Manichean Allegory: The Function of Racial Difference in Colonialist Literature." *Critical Inquiry* 12.1 (Autumn 1985): 59–87.

Jensen, F.A.S. "Psychological Aspects of the Social Isolation of Refugees." *International Migration Digest* 3.1 (Spring 1966): 40–60.

Jentsch, Ernst. "On the Psychology of the Uncanny." Translated by Roy Sellars. *Angelaki* 2.1 (1995): 7–16.

Johnson, David. "Genocide: Rwanda." In *A Historical Companion to Postcolonial Thought in English,* edited by Prem Poddar and David Johnson. 159–61. New York: Columbia University Press, 2005.

Jordan, Winthrop. *White Over Black: American Attitudes Toward the Negro, 1550–1812.* New York: Norton, 1968.

Jospe, Michael. *The Placebo Effect in Healing.* Lexington, MA: Lexington Books, 1978.

Jurney, Florence Ramond. "Exile and Relation to the Mother/Land in Edwidge Danticat's *Breath Eyes Memory* and *The Farming of Bones." Revista/Review Interamericana* 31.1–4 (January–December 2001). http://www.sg.inter.edu/revista-ciscla/volume31/jurney.pdf. December 16, 2006.

Kant, Immanuel. *Kritik der Urteilskraft.* 6th edition. Edited by Karl Vorländer. Leipzig: Felix Meiner, 1924. Translated by J. H. Bernard as *Critique of Judgment.* New York: Hafner; London: Collier Macmillan, 1951.

Kaplan, Caren. "Deterritorializations: The Rewriting of Home and Exile in Western Feminist Discourse." *Cultural Critique* 6 (Spring 19878): 187–98.

———. *Questions of Travel: Postmodern Discourses of Displacement.* 1996. 3rd edition. Durham, NC, and London: Duke University Press, 2000.

Kelly, Robert W. "Toni Morrison's *Beloved:* Destructive Past Becoming Instructive Memory." *Griot: Official Journal of the Southern Conference on Afro-American Studies* 14.2 (Fall 1995): 20–23.

Krell, David Farrell. "*Das Unheimliche:* The Architectural Sections of Heidegger and Freud." *Research in Phenomenology* 22 (1992): 43–61.

Kristeva, Julia. *Strangers to Ourselves.* Translated by Leon S. Roudiez. New York: Columbia University Press, 1991.

Krumholz, Linda. "The Ghost of Slavery: Historical Recovery in Toni Morrison's *Beloved.*" *African American Review* 26.3 (Fall 1992): 395–408.

Krupnick, Mark, ed. *Displacement: Derrida and After.* Bloomington: Indiana University Press, 1983.

Krystal, John H., Linda M. Nagy, Ann Rasmusson, Andrew Morgan, Cheryl Cottrol, Steven M. Southwick, and Dennis S. Charney. "Initial Clinical Evidence of Genetic Contributions to Posttraumatic Stress Disorder." In Danieli 657-68.

Kunz, Egon F. "The Refugee in Flight: Kinetic Models and Forms of Displacement." *International Migration Review* 7.2 (Summer 1973): 125–46.

Lacan, Jacques. *Ècrits: A Selection.* 1966. Translated by Alan Sheridan. London: Tavistock, 1977.

LaCapra, Dominick. "Trauma, Absence, Loss." *Critical Inquiry* 25 (Summer 1999): 696–727.

———. *Writing History, Writing Trauma.* Baltimore: Johns Hopkins University Press, 2000.

Laozi. *Tao Te Ching.* Translated by Gia-Fu Feng and Jane English. 1972. New York: Random House/Vintage, 1989.

Lawrence, David. "Fleshly Ghosts and Ghostly Flesh: The Word and the Body in *Beloved.*" *Studies in American Fiction* 19.2 (1991): 189–201.

Lazarus, Neil. "Disavowing Decolonization: Fanon, Nationalism and the Problematic of Representation in Current Theories of Colonial Discourse." *Research in African Literatures* 24.2 (1993): 69–98.

Lemberg, Jennifer. "Transmitted Trauma and 'Absent Memory' in James Welch's *The Death of Jim Loney.*" *SAIL* 18.3 (Fall 2006): 67–81.

Leys, Ruth. *Trauma: A Genealogy.* Chicago: University of Chicago Press, 2000.

Loomba, Ania. *Colonialism/Postcolonialism.* London and New York: Routledge, 1998.

———. "Overworlding the 'Third World.'" *The Oxford Literary Review* 13 (1991): 164–92. Reprinted in Patrick Williams and Laura Chrisman, eds., *Colonial Discourse and Post-Colonial Theory.* 305–23. Hemel Hempstead: Harvester Wheatsheaf, 1993.

Malkki, Liisa H. *Purity and Exile: Violence, Memory, and National Cosmology among Hutu Refugees in Tanzania.* Chicago: University of Chicago Press, 1995.

Marx, Emanuel. "The Social World of Refugees: A Conceptual Framework." *Journal of Refugee Studies* 3.3 (1990): 189–203.

Mathieson, Barbara Offutt. "Memory and Mother Love in Morrison's *Beloved.*" *American Imago: Studies in Psychoanalysis and Culture* 47.1 (Spring 1990): 1–21.

McAllister, Mick. "James Welch: American Novelist, American Indian." http://www. dancingbadger.com/james_welch.htm. February 18, 2007.

McClintock, Anne. *Imperial Leather: Race, Gender, and Sexuality in the Colonial Context.* London and New York: Routledge, 1995.

McEwen, Bruce S. "Protective and Damaging Effects of Stress Mediators." *New England Journal of Medicine* 338.3 (January 15, 1998): 171–79.

McNeill, Will. "*Heimat*: Heidegger on the Threshold." *Heidegger Toward the Turn: Essays on the Work of the 1930s,* edited by James Risser. 319–49. Albany: State University of New York Press, 1999.

Medovoi, Leerom, Shankar Raman, and Benjamin Robinson. "Can the Subaltern Vote? Representation in the Nicaraguan Elections." *Socialist Review* 20.3 (July–September 1990): 133–49.

Memmi, Albert. *The Colonizer and the Colonized.* 1957. Translated by Howard Greenfeld. 1965. Reprint. Boston: Beacon Press, 1991.

———. *Decolonization and the Decolonized.* 2004. Translated by Robert Bononno. Minneapolis: University of Minnesota Press, 2006.

Michaelsen, Scott, and David E. Johnson, eds. *Border Theory: The Limits of Cultural Politics.* Minneapolis: University of Minnesota Press, 1997.

Migotti, Mark. "Slave Morality, Socrates, and the Bushmen: A Reading of the First Essay of *On the Genealogy of Morals.*" *Philosophy and Phenomenological Research* 58.4 (December 1998): 745–79.

Miller, Kenneth E., Gregory J. Worthington, Jasmina Muzurovic, Susannah Tipping, and Allison Goldman. "Bosnian Refugees and the Stressors of Exile: A Narrative Study." *American Journal of Orthopsychiatry* 72.3 (2002): 341–54.

Mills, Margaret. "Feminist Theory and the Study of Folklore: A Twenty-Year Trajectory toward Theory." *Western Folklore: Issued by the California Folklore Society* 52.2–4 (April–October 1993): 173–92.

Mohanty, Satya P. "The Epistemic Status of Cultural Identity: On *Beloved* and the Postcolonial Condition." *Cultural Critique* 24 (Spring 1993): 41–80.

Montag, Warren. "Can the Subaltern Speak and Other Transcendental Questions." *Cultural Logic: An Electronic Journal of Marxist Theory and Practice* 1.2 (Spring 1998): 9 paragraphs. http://clogic.eserver.org/1-2/montag.html. November 25, 2006.

Montagu, Ashley. *Man's Most Dangerous Myth.* Oxford and New York: Oxford University Press, 1974.

Moore, Gregory. "Nietzsche, Medicine, and Meteorology." In Moore and Brobjer 71–90.

———, and Thomas H. Brobjer. *Nietzsche and Science.* Aldershot, UK, and Burlington, VT: Ashgate, 2004.

Moore-Gilbert, Bart. *Postcolonial Theory: Contexts, Practices, Politics.* London: Verso, 1997.

Morrison, Toni. *Beloved.* 1987. New York: Vintage, 1994.

N'Zengou-Tayo, Marie-José. "Children in Haitian Popular Migration as Seen by Maryse Condé and Edwidge Danticat." In *Winds of Change: The Transforming Voices of Caribbean Women Writers and Scholars,* edited by Adele S. Newson and Linda Strong-Leek. 93–100. New York: Peter Lang, 1998.

Nelson, Robert M. *Place and Vision: The Function of Landscape in Native American Fiction.* American Indian Studies 1. New York: Peter Lang, 1992.

Ngũgĩ wa Thiong'o. *Moving the Centre: The Struggle for Cultural Freedoms.* London: James Currey; Nairobi: EAEP; and Portsmouth, NH: Heinemann, 1993.

Nietschmann, Bernard Q. "Economic Development by Invasion of Indigenous Nations." *Cultural Survival Quarterly* 10.2 (1986): 2–12.

———. "Fourth World Nations: Conflicts and Alternatives." 1985. *Fourth World Documentation Project reprint,* May 28, 1995. http://www.tamilnation.org/selfdetermination/fourthworld/bernard.htm. January 28, 2007.

———. "The Fourth World: Nations versus States." In *Reordering the World: Geopolitical Perspectives on the Twenty-First Century,* edited by G. J. Demko and W. B. Wood. 225–42. Boulder, CO: Westview Press, 1994.

Nietzsche, Friedrich. *Zur Genealogie der Moral.* 1887. *Werke in drei Bände,* edited by Karl Schlecta. Vol. 2. Munich: Carl Hanser, 1999. 761–900. Translated by Francis Golffing as *The Genealogy of Morals: An Attack. The Birth of Tragedy and The Genealogy of Morals.* New York: Anchor/Doubleday, 1956. 147–299. Translated by Walter Kaufmann as *On the Genealogy of Morals: A Polemic. Basic Writings of Nietzsche,* edited by Walter Kaufmann. New York: Random House, 1968. 439–599.

Ong, Aihwa. *Buddha Is Hiding: Refugees, Citizenship, the New America.* Berkeley and Los Angeles: University of California Press, 2003.

———. "Making the Biopolitical Subject: Cambodian Immigrants, Refugee Medicine and Cultural Citizenship in California." *Social Science and Medicine* 40.9 (1995): 1243–57.

Osagie, Iyunoiu. "Is Morrison Also among the Prophets? 'Psychoanalytical' Strategies in *Beloved.*" *African American Review* 28.3 (Fall 1994): 423–40.

Owens, Louis. *Other Destinies: Understanding the American Indian Novel. American Indian Literature and Critical Studies.* Norman: University of Oklahoma Press, 1992.

Parry, Benita. *Postcolonial Studies: A Materialist Critique.* London and New York: Routledge, 2004.

———. "Problems in Current Theories of Colonial Discourse." *Oxford Literary Review* 9.1–2 (1987): 27–58.

———. "Signs of Our Times: Discussion of Homi Bhabha's *Location of Culture.*" *Third Text* 28–29 (Autumn/Winter 1994): 1–24.

Pedersen, Stefi. "Psychopathological Reactions to Extreme Social Displacements (Refugee Neuroses)." *Psychoanalytic Review* 36 (1949): 344–54.

Perinbaum, B. Marie. *Holy Violence: The Revolutionary Thought of Frantz Fanon.* Washington, DC: Three Continents Press, 1982.

Pfister-Ammende, Maria. "The Problem of Uprooting." In *Uprooting and After . . . ,* edited by Charles Zwingmann and Maria Pfister-Ammende. 7–18. New York: Springer-Verlag, 1973.

Phelan, James. "Toward a Rhetorical Reader-Response Criticism: The Difficult, the Stubborn and the Ending of *Beloved.*" *Modern Fiction Studies* 39 (1993): 709–28.

Poon, Angelia. "Re-Writing the Male Text: Mapping Cultural Spaces in Edwidge Danticat's *Krik? Krak!* and Jamaica Kincaid's *A Small Place.*" *Jouvert: A Journal of Postcolonial Studies* 4.2 (Winter 2000): 30 paragraphs. http://152.1.96.5/jouvert/v4i2/anpoon.htm. November 22, 2006.

Powell, Betty Jane. "'will the parts hold?': The Journey Toward a Coherent Self in *Beloved.*" In Iyasere and Iyasere 143–54.

Prins, S. A. "The Individual in Flight." In *Flight and Resettlement,* edited by Henry Brian Megget Murphy. 25–32. Paris: UNESCO, 1955.

Probyn, Elspeth. *Outside Belongings.* London and New York: Routledge, 1996.

Purdy, John. "Bha'a and *The Death of Jim Loney.*" *SAIL* 5.2 (1993): 67–71.

Robinson, Cedric. "The Appropriation of Frantz Fanon." *Race and Class* 35.1 (1993): 79–91.

Robinson, Douglas. "Ecologies of Translation." Unpublished book manuscript.

———. *Estrangement and the Somatics of Literature.* Baltimore: Johns Hopkins University Press, 2008.

———. *Performative Linguistics: Speaking and Translating as Doing Things with Words.* London and New York: Routledge, 2003.

———. *Translation and Taboo.* DeKalb: Northern Illinois University Press, 1996.

Rody, Caroline. "Toni Morrison's *Beloved*: History, 'Rememory,' and a 'Clamor for a Kiss.'" In Iyasere and Iyasere 83–112.

Rohrkemper, John. "'The Site of Memory': Narrative and Meaning in Toni Morrison's *Beloved*." *Midwestern Miscellany* 24 (1996): 51–62.

Rushdy, Ashraf H. A. "Daughters Signifyin(g) History: The Example of Toni Morrison's *Beloved*." *American Literature* 64.3 (September 1992): 567–97.

Ryser, Rudolf C. "The Rules of War and Fourth World Nations." *Fourth World Journal* 1.1 (1985): 53–72.

———. "States, Indigenous Nations, and the Great Lie." 1986. http://www.cwis.org/fwdp/International/greatlie.txt. January 28, 2007.

———. "Toward the Coexistence of Nations and States: Remarks before the Moscow Conference on Indigenous Peoples' Rights, September 13–18, 1993." http://www.cwis.org/fwdp/International/moscow93.txt. January 28, 2007.

Said, Edward. *Culture and Imperialism.* New York: Random House/Vintage, 1994.

———. *Orientalism.* London: Penguin, 1977.

Saldívar, José David. *Border Matters: Remapping American Cultural Studies.* Berkeley: University of California Press, 1997.

Sale v. Haitian Centers Council. 113 S. Ct. 2549, 125 L. (92–344), 509 U.S. 155 (1993). http://www.law.cornell.edu/supct/html/92-344.ZS.html. December 16, 2006.

Sands, Kathleen Mullen. "*The Death of Jim Loney*: Indian or Not?" *SAIL* 7.1 (Spring 1980): 61–78.

Schapiro, Barbara. "The Bonds of Love and the Boundaries of Self in Toni Morrison's *Beloved*." In Iyasere and Iyasere 155–72.

Schleiermacher, Friedrich. "Ueber die verschiedenen Methoden des Uebersezens." 1813. In *Das Problem des Übersetzens,* edited by Hans Joachim Störig. 38–70. Darmstadt: Wissenschaftlicher Buchgesellschaft, 1963. Translated by Douglas Robinson as "On the Different Methods of Translating." In *Western Translation Theory from Herodotus to Nietzsche,* edited by Robinson. 1997. 2nd edition. 225–38. Manchester: St. Jerome Press, 2002.

Schopp, Andrew. "Narrative Control and Subjectivity: Dismantling Safety in Toni Morrison's *Beloved*." In Iyasere and Iyasere 204–30.

Schore, Allan N. *Affect Dysregulation and Disorders of the Self.* New York: Norton, 2003.

———. *Affect Regulation and the Origin of the Self: The Neurobiology of Emotional Development.* Mahwah, NJ: Erlbaum, 1994.

———. *Affect Regulation and the Repair of the Self.* New York: Norton, 2003.

Segal, Charles. "Catharsis, Audience, and Closure in Greek Tragedy." In *Tragedy and the Tragic: Greek Tragedy and Beyond,* edited by M.S. Silk. 149-72. Oxford: Clarendon, 1996.

Sen, Ramproshad. *Song for Kali: A Cycle.* Translated and introduced by Gayatri Chakravorty Spivak. Kolkata, India: Seagull Books, 2000.

Sen, Sunil Kumar. *Agrarian Struggle in Bengal, 1946–47.* New Delhi: People's Publishing House, 1972.

Seton, Kathy. "Fourth World Nations in the Era of Globalisation: An Introduction to Contemporary Theorizing Posed by Indigenous Nations." *CWIS: The Fourth World Journal.* http://www.cwis.org/fwj/41/fworld.html. January 28, 2007.

Shea, Renee H. "Traveling Worlds with Edwidge Danticat." *Poets & Writers* 25.1 (January 1, 1997): 42–51.

Shetty, Sandhya. "(Dis)figuring the Nation: Mother, Metaphor, Metonymy." *Differences* 7.3 (Fall 1995): 50–79.

Slemon, Stephen, and Helen Tiffin, eds. *After Europe: Critical Theory and Post-Colonial Writing.* Mundelstrup, Denmark: Dangaroo, 1989.

Soguk, Nevzat. *States and Strangers: Refugees and Displacements of Statecraft.* Minneapolis: University of Minnesota Press, 1999.

Spivak, Gayatri Chakravorty. "Asked to Talk about Myself . . ." *Third Text* 19 (Summer 1992): 9–18.

———. "Can the Subaltern Speak? Speculations on Widow Sacrifice." *Wedge* 7.8 edited by Cary Nelson and Lawrence Grossberg (Winter/Spring 1985): 120–30. Reprinted in *Marxism and the Interpretation of Culture.* Urbana: University of Illinois Press, 1988. 271–313. Reprinted in Spivak, *Critique* 269–311.

———. *A Critique of Postcolonial Reason: Toward a History of the Vanishing Present.* Cambridge, MA, and London: Harvard University Press, 1999.

———. "Displacement and the Discourse of Woman." In Krupnick 169–95.

———. "Marginality in the Teaching Machine." In Spivak, *Outside* 53–76.

———. "On the Politics of the Subaltern." Interview with Howard Winant. *Socialist Review* 90.3 (July–September 1990): 80–97.

———. "The New Historicism: Political Commitment and the Postmodern Critic." In *The New Historicism,* edited by H. Aram Veeser. 277–92. London and New York: Routledge, 1989.

———. *Outside in the Teaching Machine.* London and New York: Routledge, 1993.

———. "Subaltern Studies: Deconstructing Historiography." In *Selected Subaltern Studies,* edited by Ranajit Guha and Gayatri Chakravorty Spivak. 3–32. New York: Oxford University Press, 1988.

———. "Subaltern Talk: Interview with the Editors (29 October 1993)." In *The Spivak Reader: Selected Works of Gayatri Chakravorty Spivak,* edited by Donna Landry and Gerald MacLean. 287–308. London and New York: Routledge, 1996.

———. "Woman in Difference: Mahasweta Devi's 'Douloti the Bountiful.'" *Cultural* Critique 14 (Winter 1989–90): 105–28. Reprinted as "Woman in Difference" in Spivak, *Outside* 77–95.

Stein, Barry N. "The Refugee Experience: Defining the Parameters of a Field of Study." *International Migration Review* 15.1/2 (Spring–Summer 1981): 320–30.

Stromberg, Ernest. "The Only Real Indian Is a Dead Indian: The Desire for Authenticity in James Welch's *The Death of Jim Loney.*" *SAIL* 10.4 (1998): 33–53.

Suomi, Stephen J., and Seymour Levine. "Psychobiology of Intergenerational Effects of Trauma: Evidence from Animal Studies." In Danieli 623-38.

Taussig, Michael. *Mimesis and Alterity: A Particular History of the Senses.* London: Routledge, 1993.

Thompson, W. Grant. *The Placebo Effect and Health: Combining Science and Compassionate Care.* Amherst, NY: Prometheus Books, 2005.

Tiffin, Helen. "Transformative Imageries." In *From Commonwealth to Post-Colonial,* edited by Anna Rutherford. 428–35. Mundelstrup, Denmark: Dangaroo, 1992.

Turner, Victor W. "Magic, Faith, and Healing." In *An Ndembu Doctor in Practice*. New York: Collier Macmillan, 1964.

Vega, William A., Bohdan Kolody, and Juan Ramon Valle. "Migration and Mental Health: An Empirical Test of Depression Risk Factors among Immigrant Mexican Women." *International Migration Review* 21.3 (Autumn 1987): 512–30.

Vickroy, Laurie. "The Force Outside/The Force Inside: Mother-Love and Regenerative Spaces in *Sula* and *Beloved*." In Iyasere and Iyasere 297–314.

Vonnegut, Kurt, Jr. *Cat's Cradle*. New York: Dell, 1963.

Warner, Daniel. "Voluntary Repatriation and the Meaning of Returning Home: A Critique of Liberal Mathematics." *Journal of Refugee Studies* 7.2–3 (1994): 160–73.

———. "We Are All Refugees." *International Journal of Refugee Law* 4.3 (1992): 365–72.

Welch, James. *The Death of Jim Loney*. New York: Penguin, 1979.

———. *Winter in the Blood*. New York: Penguin, 1974.

West, Cornel. "A Genealogy of Modern Racism." In *Race Critical Theories: Text and Context*, edited by Philomena Essed and David Theo Goldberg. 90–112. Oxford: Blackwell, 2002.

Wilder, Gary. "Irreconcilable Differences: A Conversation with Albert Memmi." *Transitions* 71 (1996): 158–77.

———. "Race, Reason, Impasse: Césaire, Fanon, and the Legacy of Emancipation." *Radical History Review* 90 (Fall 2004): 31–61.

Wright, Michelle M. *Becoming Black: Creating Identity in the African Diaspora*. Durham, NC, and London: Duke University Press, 2004.

Wyatt, Jean. "Giving Body to the Word: The Maternal Symbolic in Toni Morrison's *Beloved*." Iyasere and Iyasere 231–57.

Yehuda, Rachel, Jim Schmeidler, Abbie Elkin, George Skye Wilson, Larry Siever, Karen Binder-Brynes, Milton Wainberg, and Dan Aferiot. "Phenomenology and Psychobiology of the Intergenerational Response to Trauma." In Danieli 639-56.

Young, Robert. *White Mythologies: Writing History and the West*. London and New York: Routledge, 1990.

———, ed. *Untying the Text: A Post-Structuralist Reader*. Boston, London, and Henley: Routledge & Kegan Paul, 1981.

Ziarek, Ewa Plonowska. "The Uncanny Style of Kristeva's Critique of Nationalism." *Postmodern Culture* 5.2 (1995). http://muse.jhu.edu/cgi-bin/access.cgi?uri=/journals/postmodern_culture/v005/5.2ziarek.html. February 20, 2007.

Zolberg, Aristide R., Astri Suhrke, and Sergio Aguayo. "International Factors in the Formation of Refugee Movements." *International Migration Review* 20.2 (Summer 1986): 151–69.